CHINESE STOCK MARKETS

股市

CHINESE STOCK MARKETS

A Research Handbook

Dongwei Su

Department of Finance
Ji Nan University, China

World Scientific
New Jersey • London • Singapore • Hong Kong

Published by

World Scientific Publishing Co. Pte. Ltd.

5 Toh Tuck Link, Singapore 596224

USA office: Suite 202, 1060 Main Street, River Edge, NJ 07661

UK office: 57 Shelton Street, Covent Garden, London WC2H 9HE

Library of Congress Cataloging-in-Publication Data

Su, Dongwei.

Chinese stock markets : a research handbook / Dongwei Su.

p. cm.

Includes bibliographical references and index.

ISBN 9810245122 (alk. paper)

1. Stock exchanges--China. 2. Stocks--China. 3. Securities--China. I. Title.

HG5782 .S8 2003

332.64'251--dc21 2002033184

British Library Cataloguing-in-Publication Data

A catalogue record for this book is available from the British Library.

Printed in Singapore by World Scientific Printers (S) Pte Ltd *to Jinyu Su, Yuande Lin and Dongyang Su*

Preface

The commercialization of state-owned enterprises and development of stock markets in China during the past decade have been impressive by any standards. As of the end of October 1999, stock markets in Shenzhen and Shanghai had 930 companies listed, with a market capitalization of US$340 billion or about 30% of GDP, approximately the same as that of Singapore, Thailand, Malaysia and Indonesia put together. There are now 38 million individual stockholders, second in number only to the US. A relatively complete securities legal framework has taken its initial shape. In addition, there are 43 H-shares and 42 Red Chips listed in the Hong Kong stock exchange, with a market capitalization exceeding US$86 billion, or 17% of the Hong Kong market capitalization. With the return of Hong Kong in 1997, the mainland inherited a world class financial centre, with deep and mature banking and securities markets. It is increasingly recognized that stock markets will play a positive role in China's emerging socialist market economy and create tremendous amount of investment opportunities for domestic and international investors.

The extraordinary expansion and rapid growth of Chinese stock markets have been accompanied by some difficulties. Problems include fuzzy property rights and legal protection for investors, large initial public offering (IPO) underpricing, high costs of capital, ineffective corporate governance, market segmentation and high stock-market return volatility. In particular, the following questions provide researchers with an interesting area of research:

(1) Are returns predictable in Chinese stock markets? How well do the stock markets in China function relative to other developed and

emerging markets?

(2) Are Chinese stock markets volatile? Does stock-market return volatility change over time? How frequent are "big surprises" in Chinese stock markets? What are the causes for these "big surprises"?
(3) What explains differences in prices and expected returns between the classes of shares that can be bought by Chinese citizens and foreign investors? Is the time-series variability in the spread between domestic and foreign share returns consistent with differences in risk exposures and expected risk premiums?
(4) Why are domestic shares more volatile than foreign shares? How are the variation in volatility-related expected intensity of information flows and the amount of informed trading related to information correlates, such as the number of investors, change in profits, and firm size?
(5) Was the extraordinarily large IPO underpricing caused by bribery and insider trading, high level of government policy uncertainty, or government's desire to encourage wide public participation in the equity markets? What explains the cross-sectional differences in underpricing? Why the degree of underpricing is much smaller for foreign-listed IPOs? Why do Chinese IPOs perform much worse in the long-run than those in other countries?
(6) What are the critical differences in firm characteristics (liquidity, leverage, and investment opportunities) between firms that issue new shares after their IPOs and those that do not? Among the firms that do issue new equities after their IPOs, do agency costs, political costs and information asymmetry affect their choices of different financing methods? How can we explain the variation in abnormal announcement day returns across different financing methods?
(7) Is accounting information value-relevant in the Chinese stock markets? Why do investors over-react to earnings release in domestic markets? To what extent have analysts' earnings forecasts affected the market valuation of stocks?
(8) What are some of the debates on privatization and reform of state enterprises? What was China's past experience? How can listed-companies deal with owner and manager relationships and organize efficient corporate governance structure? Will China jump into the

> sea of private enterprise or remain suspended in a trance-like state under the notion that market socialism will solve its problems?

Chinese Stock Markets: A Research Handbook is the first to provide a comprehensive study of the aforementioned issues in a technical manner drawing upon rigorous theoretical and quantitative analyses. A salient feature of this handbook is its breadth of coverage. While individual chapters may be narrow but deep in scope, the handbook as a whole encompasses diverse subjects and cuts across a number of fields in finance–investments, financial markets and institutions, international finance, risk management, corporate finance, and corporate governance. The handbook is intended as a specially compiled research monograph and a benchmark of reference which, I hope, will be of considerable use to academia, practitioners, and policy-makers interested in issues surrounding state enterprise reform and equity market development in China.

This handbook has nine chapters. Every one except the first two chapters brings together a set of rigorous academic research studies on issues that enhance the existing body of knowledge in emerging markets. These chapters typically begin with a discussion of the economics and finance theory underlying the application, outline issues in econometric implementation (including measurement issues), and then detail important empirical findings. Each chapter engages readers in a carefully designed topic involving replication and extension of cutting-edge research in a coherent framework.

This handbook has benefited from the comments and insights of a large number of people, particularly my dissertation advisors at Ohio State University. Numerous colleagues and friends have also provided constructive and challenging suggestions. I owe special thanks to Yuande Lin, who read each chapter with great care and offered many terrific suggestions. I take pleasure to thank the following people in numerous ways: Torben Andersen (Northwestern University), James Ang (Florida State University), Warren Bailey (Cornell University), Prasad Bidakota (Kansas State University), David Brasington (Tulane University), Zhiwu Chen (Yale University), Gregory Chow (Princeton University), Georgio DeSantis (University of Southern California), Xinghai Fang (Shanghai Stock Exchange), Yue Fang (University of Oregon), John Fernald (Board of Governors of the Federal Reserve System), Belton Fleisher (Ohio State University), Yan He (San Francisco State University), Gary Jefferson (Brandies University),

Pok-sang Lam (Ohio State University), David Li (Hong Kong University of Science & Technology), J. Houston McCulloch (Ohio State University), Barry Naughton (University of California at San Diego), Masao Ogaki (Ohio State University), Min Qi (Kent State University), Bruce Reynolds (Cornell University and Union College), Jay Ritter (University of Florida), Alan Viard (Federal Reserve Bank at Dallas), Xin Zhang (China Securities Regulatory Commission) and Zhenlong Zheng (Xiamen University and University of California at Los Angeles).

The experience of transforming a manuscript into final book form is due in large part to the dedication, thoroughness, and highest professional standards of the publishing team in World Scientific. In particular, it is a pleasure for me to thank my editor, Joy Quek, for her meticulous work and great professionalism.

DS

Contents

Chapter 1

Development of Chinese Stock Markets

1.1 Introduction

China has experienced unprecedented growth in Gross Domestic Product (GDP) from 1987 to the present, growing at an average rate of 9.5% per year (see Figure 1.1). Its economy today is more than four times as large when the reforms were first introduced in 1979. The reform has affected all sectors of the economy and has lifted a enormous number of people out of starvation and into the consumer middle class. The commercialization of the Chinese economy has also opened it up to foreign direct investment. The continuous market development has been impressive by any standards.

Prior to 1978, the entire financial system in China was controlled by state owned banks. Investments were channeled through direct grants from the state budgetary funds or from government allocated bank credits. Therefore, China's move towards market economy with modern financial market was a remarkable breakthrough in terms of ways of raising much needed capital for economic development.

In 1990, there were no stock markets. As of October 31, 1999, 930 companies were listed in the Shanghai Securities Exchange (SHSE) and Shenzhen Securities Exchange (SZSE), with a market capitalization of US$340 billion or about 30% of GDP, approximately the same as that of Singapore, Thailand, Malaysia and Indonesia put together. There were 38 million individual stockholders, second in number only to the U.S.. In addition, there are 43 H-shares and 42 Red Chips listed in the Hong Kong stock exchange, with a market capitalization exceeding US$86 billion, or 17% of the Hong Kong market capitalization. With the return of Hong Kong in

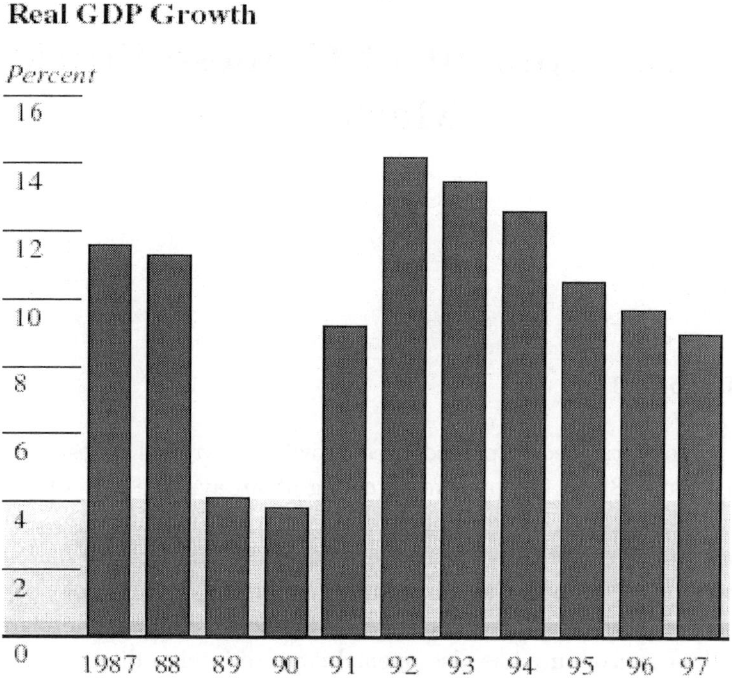

Fig. 1.1 Real GDP Growth

1997, the mainland inherited a world class financial center, with developed and mature banking and securities markets. Because China continues to have a high savings rate of 36% of GDP and a high current account surplus, much domestic savings have been pumped into domestic capital markets. Bank assets and securities market capitalization (including equity and bond markets) accounted for 139% and 41% of GDP in 1999, respectively.

Considerable achievements have also been made in the legal and regulatory framework for domestic capital markets. In addition to the enactment of the banking and central bank legislation, and the *PRC Company Law*, the latest piece of law is the *PRC Securities Law*. Furthermore, private enterprises are now permitted to go public in China, and more state-owned corporations are allowed to raise funds in international capital markets. Because these firms have to adhere to more stringent accounting standards and disclosure requirements, they usually have better corporate governance practices and are more responsive to market needs. Needlessly to say, such commercialization and corporatization better prepare Chinese firms to meet global challenge and competition. It is increasingly recognized that stock markets will play an important role in China's transition towards a market economy with modern financial system and create tremendous amount of investment opportunities for domestic and international investors.

1.2 Setting the Scene: Shanghai and Shenzhen in the Early Reform Period

The development of the stock markets is one of the most important elements of China's reform in the financial system. Before 1949, Shanghai was a major banking and financial center with a stock market similar in size to that of Tokyo and considerably larger than that of Hong Kong. Fluctuations in the Shanghai stock exchange over the period 1919-1949 had a lot of influence on other world-class financial markets. In fact, Shanghai was the world's third largest after New York and London.

For approximately three decades after the Communist Party took power in 1949, the government strictly controlled virtually all channels of investment. All investments made by enterprises were either from direct grants from the state budgetary funds or from government allocated bank credits. Shanghai's previous role as an international financial and commercial center was reduced to a domestic Chinese industrial center. During those three decades, the entire Chinese financial system was dominated by the state-owned banks, such as the People's Bank of China (PBOC), a few specialized banks and their local branches. The official process that allocated investments across regions and industrial sectors was often bureaucratic, and in many cases, caused inefficient use of resources.

Before the economic reform was embarked, Shenzhen was just a small remote town close to Hong Kong in southern China. When China began its open-door economic policy, Shenzhen became one of four Special Economic Zones (SEZs), receiving a lot of preferential policies from the central government and attracting a consistent flow of investment from Hong Kong and abroad. After many years of economic development, Shenzhen became one of the major metropolitan cities in China. Its population is close to 3 million and has one of the highest skilled work forces in China. Both Shanghai and Shenzhen has established themselves as sound investment places for domestic and international investors.

As the structural reform in China continued, the central government experienced a decline in fiscal revenues. This prompted the Ministry of Finance (MOF) to sell bonds to cover its budget deficit. The issuance of long-term treasury bonds in 1981 was the government's first experiment in raising capital and signified the official re-opening of China's securities markets. The distribution of treasury bond issues was through mandatory purchase quotas divided among local governments, enterprises and individuals.[1]

Since the early 1980s, China's financial sector experienced major institutional changes. The PBOC ceased its commercial banking functions and turned into China's central bank. Four major subsidiaries of PBOC, namely, the Industrial and Commercial Bank of China, the Agricultural Bank of China, the Peoples Construction Bank of China, and the Bank of China were turned into commercial state banks, and a number of urban and rural credit unions were established as subsidiaries of the four commercial state banks. As the central bank, the PBOC controls the money supply, determines interest rate, and handles foreign exchange reserves through its division, the State Administration of Exchange Control. Commercial state banks passed on PBOC's policy and replaced the government budget funds as the main financial channels for enterprise investments. In addition, China International Trust and Investment Corporation (CITIC) and its subsidiaries were established throughout the 1980s and became the major consulting firm and investment bank in China. CITIC invested and lent funds raised from international financial institutions, such as the World Bank and International Finance Corporation. The whole banking system was decentralized, and inter-bank competition was encouraged. However, interest rate remained under government's control. Monetary and credit policy continued to take the form of a credit plan that was implemented by PBOC through a set of credit quotas for each commercial state bank. All levels of government still constantly intervene the daily businesses of virtually all financial institutions.

During the early reform period, government saving has dropped sharply in response to deteriorating financial position of state-owned enterprises. However, household saving has increased very rapidly in response to the

[1] Although there was no secondary market to trade treasury bonds at that time, the issuance of bonds paved the way for further fund raising activities by state-owned and private enterprises, eventually leading to the first publicly issued stock for Beijing's Tianqiao Department Store in 1984.

new opportunities created by transition. Individual incomes were higher, but there was a lack of alternative financial instruments. Individuals were forced to either hold cash or deposit in the state banks where interests were controlled at levels lower than the market rate. Naughton (1987) found that total household saving, including both in-kind and financial saving, jumped rapidly from 7% of household income in 1978 to 17% in 1982, and have continued to increase steadily since. Even more crucially, financial saving tripled, increasing from 2.3% of household income in 1978, to an average of 6.8% in the years 1980-83. As of 1995, households were generating 70% of domestic saving, over 25% of GDP. There was 2194 billion *yuan* in deposits in banks, accounting for 38% of the GDP.

In response to the changes in savings pattern, China's financial reform deepened as more competition was introduced into the banking system. In 1981, the central government began to issue treasury bonds to finance deficits. Shortly thereafter, the authorities permitted the issuance of other types of bonds–including various provincial and local government bonds and enterprise bonds. Enterprise bonds were strictly controlled in order to avoid conflicts with the priorities set in the credit plan. As of the end of 1989, the total issue of securities amounted to 166 billion *yuan*, of which 99% were bonds.

In 1984, as China began to experiment further economic reform, the issuance of bonds paved the way for stock issues as alternative methods of raising capital. The first real step was taken in 1984, when 11 state-owned enterprises (SOEs) became shareholding corporations. This led to the first publicly issued stocks by Feile Acoustics in November 1984, with 10,000 shares at 50 *renminbi yuan* per share. Two months later, Yenchung Industrial Corporation and Beijing Tianqiao Department Store both issued shares to the public. However, there was no over-the-counter market in China and virtually no trading of stocks and bonds before 1986.

1.3 The Establishment of Secondary Markets

The secondary markets for securities started when over-the-counter (OTC) markets were set up in Shanghai, Beijing, Tianjin, Shenyang, Harbin and Guangzhou to trade corporate bonds and shares in 1986. At that time, the markets dealt exclusively with bond trading.[2] The turnover was thin and the liquidity was low because the public had very little knowledge of the concept of equity markets. Despite that, Shanghai quickly emerged as the major bond trading center in the nation. By the end of 1987, eight trading counters had been opened in Shanghai. Four professional brokerage houses, namely, the International Securities Corporations, the Haitung Securities Corporation, the Shenyin Securities Corporation, and the Chenshing Securities Corporation, were established in late 1980s. They helped government issue bonds and firms issue stocks.

On December 19, 1990, the first government-approved securities market, Shanghai Securities Exchange (SHSE), was established to allow investors and enterprises to participate in stock trading. It adopted a non-profit corporate membership system and dealt with spot transactions, not including derivative securities. It recruited members nationwide so that it might serve as a nationwide securities transaction center. Most of the listed companies on SHSE are based locally in the Shanghai area. The establishment of SHSE not only marked the beginning of organized securities sales, but also heralded the first use of computers in stock and bond trading in China, thereby putting an end to all paper transactions by offering investors the improved efficiency of computer-aided investing. Quickly after trading started, SHSE was doing so well that their was excess demand over supply of securities which led to dramatic increases in share prices. A few issues skyrocketed to more than 800 percent times their original issuing price. Public interest on stocks was, to say the least, piqued.[3]

In 1987, the Shenzhen Development bank began to issue shares to the public. In the next three years, five more issues were floated and actively traded in the OTC market in Shenzhen. The unique role of Shenzhen in the Chinese economy led to the formal establishment of the Shenzhen Securities Exchange (SZSE) in July 1991. Most of the companies listed on SZSE were based in industrial and commercial cities in inland China. SZSE was subject to identical regulation and trading procedures as the SHSE with respect to debt and equity issues. For example, both securities

[2]Because of a very small number of shares outstanding in a few corporations, stock transactions only represented 1%, 2%, and 1% of total securities transactions in 1986, 1987, and 1988, respectively.

[3]As early as the closing month of 1990, more than 400,000 residents in Shanghai had taken part in securities trading (Fang, 1991).

exchange operate under an auction market environment without specialists or market-makers. The highest authority of both securities exchanges is the general meeting of members and the board of directors, which consists of the chairman, vice-chairman, president and three managing directors. A supervisory committee oversees the day-to-day trading operation. The president is the legal representative who controls daily operation of the exchange.

In 1992, the SHSE and SZSE further standardized their transactions through a sophisticated over-the-counter computer network known as the Securities Trading Automated Quotation System (STAQS), based on the U.S. NASDAQ.[4] Under this network, brokerage houses located throughout the country could purchase and sell stocks and bonds on behalf of investors, just like how the NASDAQ market worked in the U.S.. Trading is continuously conducted by an order-driven computerized matching system. Buy or sell orders are put into the central computer either through the terminals on the floor or the remote terminals at the broker's office. The bid and offer prices and other transaction information are shown on every terminal and transmitted through a satellite system to all the member brokers nationwide.[5] In that year, "share fever" really took hold. The trading volume increased tenfold and the SHSE index quadrupled.

The business scope for SHSE and SZSE includes providing place and facilities for trading and managing the settlement and delivery for all listed stocks. The main duties of the exchanges include: (1) to formulate trading rules; (2) to publish the trading information; (3) to report business and management to relevant authorities; (4) to take technical and temporary measures to suspend or stop the trading; (5) to deal with supervision; and (6) to supervise listed companies and corporate members.

There are mainly two types of stocks traded in SHSE and SZSE: A-shares, which are bought and sold only by Chinese investors; and B-shares, which are restricted to foreign investors.[6] There is a complication in B-

[4]The system provided members with real-time price quotations, direct and indirect reading facilities, clearance and settlement, trading information, financial news and other related services.

[5]Real-time quotations from SHSE and SZSE can now be picked up anywhere on the mainland, even in Tibet. Some 800 listed companies, large and small, can be bought and sold by Chinese citizens in any of the offices of the 700 brokerage firms that dot China's towns and cities.

[6]While the domestic share market has attracted the interest of more than a few local

shares trading since foreign exchange is under strict control by the State Administration of Exchange Controls. Subscriptions, dividends, and cash distributions to foreign shareholders are paid in foreign currencies (in U.S. dollar at SHSE and in Hong Kong dollar at SZSE), based on the same-day official exchange rate. Besides A- and B-shares, a company can issue shares traded in foreign exchanges (subject to relevant authorities' approval, of course). The following is a list of China-related equity shares:

- A-Shares: They are shares solely available to domestic Chinese investors. A-shares are denominated in the Chinese currency, *renminbi* (RMB), subscribed for and traded in RMB by domestic investors. A-shares can be further classified into four categories according to the ownership: state shares (held by the government or its agencies), legal-person shares (held by other companies or institutions), employee shares, and individual shares (held by the public). Currently, shares held by the general public are the only shares that can be traded on the exchanges, although a few employee and legal-person shares are traded on STAQ. By the end of 1998, there were 842 listed A-shares in SHSE and SZSE with a total market capitalization of RMB 1,950.6 billion, equivalent to 24.43% of GDP;
- B-Shares: These securities have exactly the same ownership and dividend rights as do A-shares but can be purchased (and held) only by holders of foreign passports (including by those who hold a Hong Kong passport). The separation of A- and B-share markets reflects the central government's policy of restricting the foreign control of vital SOEs and its desire to prevent manipulation of China's fledgling stock markets from abroad. Maintaining a distinct stock market for foreign investors in which they participate using their own currency also helps prevent the devaluation of *renminbi* from excessive sales. As of December 1998, there were 103 Chinese companies selling B-shares worth U.S.$4.37 billion
- H-Shares: These are the stocks of SOEs incorporated in mainland but listed on the Hong Kong Stock Exchange (HKSE). H-share

speculators, state treasury bills represent the most viable investment alternative for the average risk-averse Chinese investor. As a result, China's bond markets have developed rapidly since SHSE and SZSE were established. The annual rate of issuance has risen dramatically from 19 billion yuan (US$2.3 billion) in 1991 to more than 190 billion yuan (US$22.9 billion) in 1996.

issuers are subject to more stringent disclosure rules than A-share issuers. H-shares are denominated in Hong Kong dollars and can be traded by any investor. By the end of 1998, 43 firms had issued H-shares.

- Red Chips: Similar to H-shares, red chips are listed on the HKSE. Red chip issuers are typically companies controlled by mainland government or SOEs but incorporated in Hong Kong. The Hong Kong entity is usually a shell corporation of the mainland counterpart and is capitalized through the public offering. It is usually able to purchase assets located on the mainland through what is known as an "asset injection". The managers of many red chip companies have excellent political connections with the mainland central administration.
- L-Shares and N-Shares: These are the stocks of Chinese enterprises that have chosen to list on either the London Stock Exchange (LSE) or New York Stock Exchange (NYSE), respectively[7]
  N-shares are shares in Chinese companies that trade in the form of American Depository Receipts (ADRs), especially those listed on the NYSE. These companies are the best managed and most profitable companies in China.[8]

Table 1.1 and Figure 1.2 present ownership structure based on different share types in Chinese stock markets.

As Tables 1.2, 1.3, and 1.4 and Figures 1.3 and 1.4 indicate, the amount of capital raised, trading volume, turnover ratio and the total market capitalization of the Chinese stock markets have increased significantly over time. By the end of 1998, there were 842 companies listed in the SHSE and SZSE with market capitalization of RMB1,950.6 billion, equivalent to 24.43% of GDP. There were 1,011 listed securities including equity shares (A- and B-shares), securities investment funds, government bonds (for both spot and repo trading), corporate bonds, and corporate convertible bonds. China's listed companies had issued a total of 74.61 billion shares in the

[7]The first N-share listed on the NYSE was Brilliance China Automotive Holdings, which went public in 1992. One L-share exists on the LSE, and is jointly listed in Hong Kong.

[8]Nine Chinese companies are listed on the NYSE: Beijing Yanhua Petrochemical Co.; China Eastern Airlines Corp.; China Southern Airlines; Guangshen Railway Co.; Huaneng Power International Co.; Jilin Chemical Industrial Co.; Shandong Huaneng Power Development; Yanahou Coal Mining Co.; and Shanghai Petrochemical Co.. Another 19 N-shares are traded over-the-counter.

Table 1.1 Ownership Structures in Chinese Stock Markets 1994-97

Types of Shareholding	Holders	% in total shares
State shares	Central government, local governments, or solely government-owned enterprises.	28% - 34%
Legal person shares	Business agencies, local governments who helped in starting up the company.	31%-33%
A-shares	Chinese citizens and domestic institutions. The Government requires that A-shares should account for no less than 25% of total outstanding shares when a company goes public.	17%-32%
B-shares	Foreign portfolio investors, people from Hong Kong, Macau and Taiwan. B-shares are quoted and traded in USD or HKD.	5% on average
Employee shares	Workers and managers of the company. Such shares are usually offered at a substantial discount.	5% on average
H-shares	Any investors. H-shares are listed on the Hong Kong Stock Exchange.	0.2%-1.1%

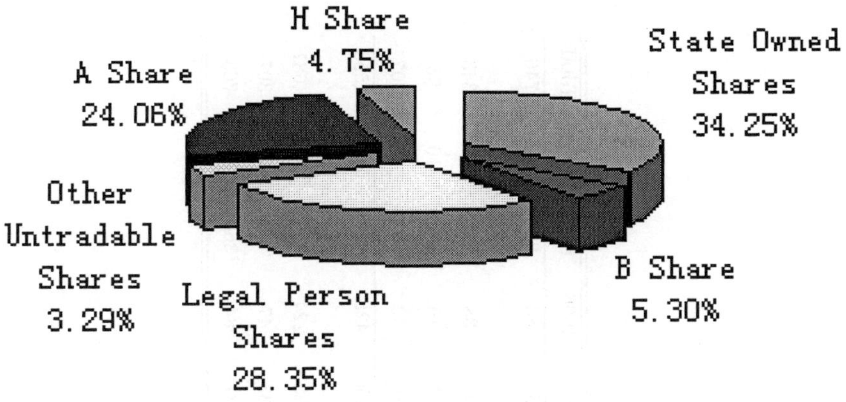

Fig. 1.2 Share Ownership Structure (Source: CSRC)

markets and had raised a total of RMB 355.31 billion. The total amount of shares can be broken down as follows: (1) A-share market: 34.302 billion shares and RMB 168.709 billion; (2) B-Share market: 9.598 billion and US$ 4.745 billion; and (3) H-share markets: 30.719 billion shares and US$ 10.02 billion. There were 662 corporate members, 39.11 million investors accounts, and more than 2,400 interconnected retail branches and trading centers. (See Tables 1.2, 1.3).

There are a number of differences between the SHSE and SZSE. Many companies listed in the SZSE are joint ventures with close relations with firms in Hong Kong, thus they have better international exposure. By contrast, the SHSE is dominated by state-owned enterprises and is more closely monitored by the central government. With regard to foreign investment, the SHSE requires that all foreign investors must subscribe for B-shares through a financial institution approved by the exchange while the SZSE allows foreign investors to subscribe for B-shares either directly or through a financial intermediary. Figure 1.5 plots the time-series of composite stock indices for Shanghai and Shenzhen exchanges.

1.4 The Participation of International Investors

A driving force in China's remarkable advances in securities markets has been the need to access foreign capital used to fuel the operations of SOEs.

Table 1.2 Shares Offering in China (1987–1997)

	1987	1988	1989	1990	1991	1992	1993	1994	1995	1996	1997	1998	Total
Shares issued (in 100 million)	10	25	7	4	5	21	96	91	32	86	268	102	746
A-share	10	25	7	4	5	10	43	11	5	38	106	79	343
B-share						11	13	10	11	16	25	10	96
H-share							40	70	15	32	137	13	307
Capital raised (RMB 100 million)	10	25	7	4		94	375	327	150	425	1,294	837	3,553
A-share	10	25	7	4		50	195	50	23	224	655	440	1,687
B-share						44	38	38	33	47	81	26	307
H-share							61	89	31	84	360	38	763

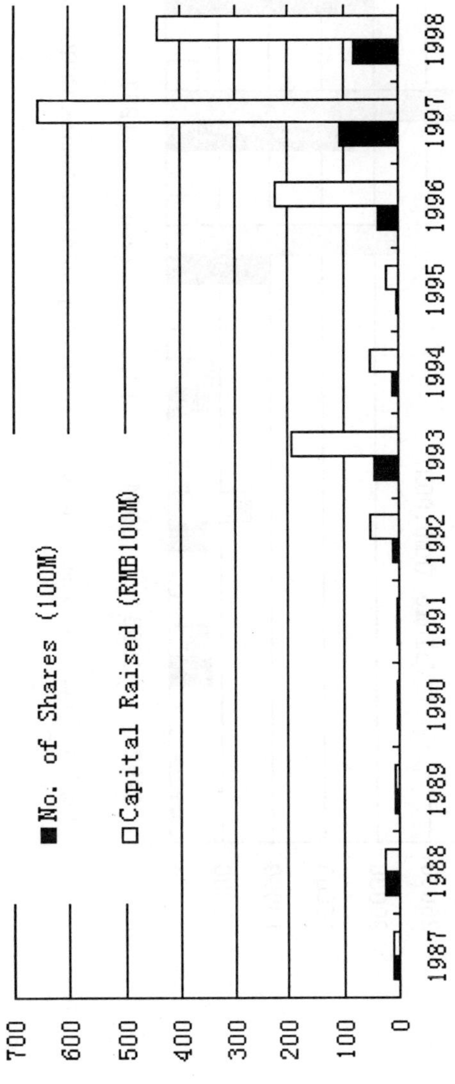

Fig. 1.3 Capital Raised from A-share Market (Source: CSRC)

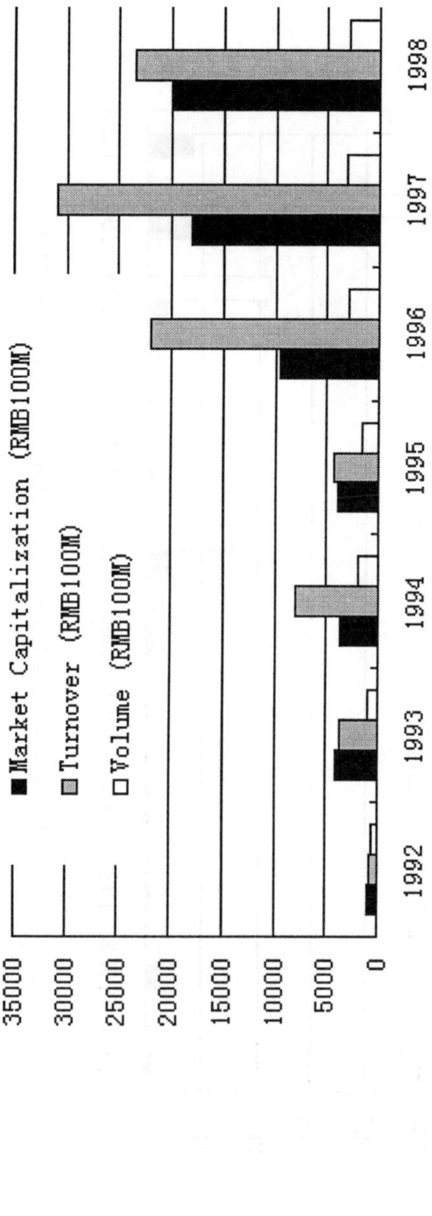

Fig. 1.4 Trading Volume, Turnover and Market Capitalization (Source: CSRC)

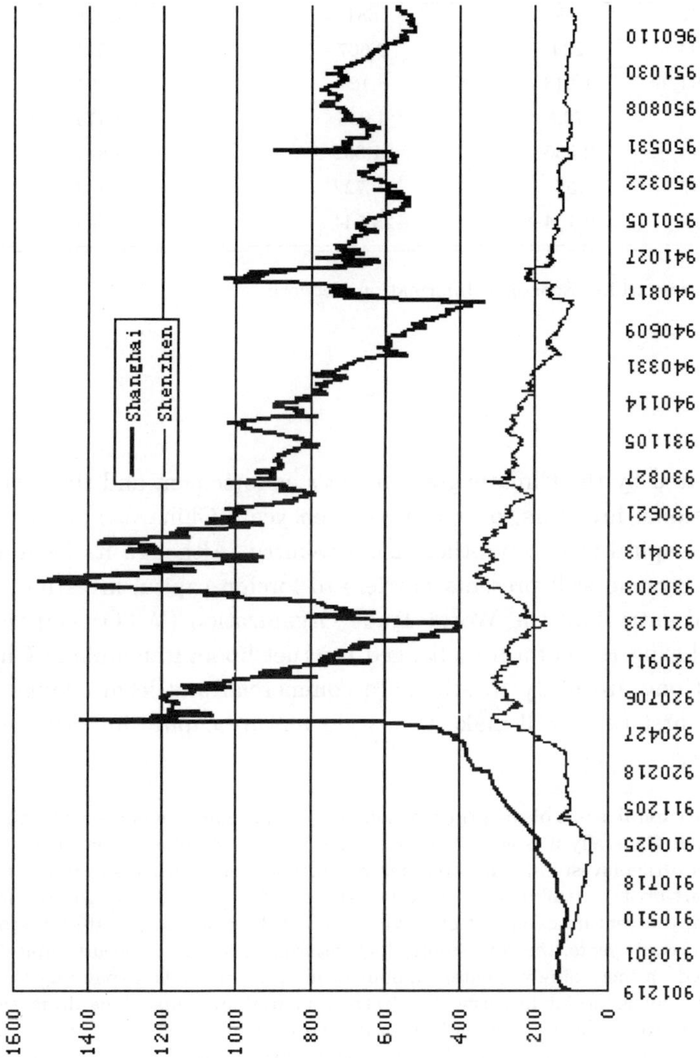

Fig. 1.5 Times-series of composite stock indices for Shanghai and Shenzhen

Table 1.3 Market Statistics

Shenzhen and Shanghai Stock Exchanges			
Year	Trading Volume (in 100 million)	Turnover (RMB 100 million)	Total Market Capitalization (RMB 100 million)
1992	38	681	1,048
1993	234	3,667	3,531
1994	1,013	8,127	3,691
1995	705	4,036	3,474
1996	2,533	21,332	9,842
1997	2,561	30,722	17,529
1998	2,154	23,544	19,505

Source: China Economic Information Network

Stimulated by the Chinese government's endorsement and the activities of institutional investors, over the past ten years China has attracted more foreign capital than any other Asian country. Although its legal and regulatory system still presents barriers to foreign capital investing, China's planned entry into the World Trade Organization (WTO) and the emergence during 1999 of a fully-fledged Internet boom in mainland China and Hong Kong are likely to stimulate commercial and legal changes which, for the first time, will make U.S.-style venture capital investing in China possible.[9]

[9]Venture capital is one of the principal sources of finance for companies with high growth potential. Generally it is not a long-term investment. Essentially, venture capital (held by capital-rich investors) is injected into an entrepreneur's business in return for equity. The start-up is nurtured for a period of time, and, once sufficient returns have been realized, the venture capitalist exits via a trade sale, a sale to private investors, or an IPO. In recent years, the consistently high returns achieved by venture capitalists have attracted an increasingly greater amount of investment funds, expanding the amount of money available for investment in entrepreneurial start-ups. The dramatic growth of venture capital investment in hi-tech industries, first in the United States and more recently in Europe, has spurred significant interest in venture capital investment in China and other parts of Asia. Many of the leading U.S. venture capital firms have opened offices outside the United States to take advantage of emerging foreign markets

Table 1.4 GDP and Stock Market Capitalization

Year	GDP (RMB 100 million)	Market Capitalization Amount	As a Percentage of GDP
1992	26,638	1,048	3.93
1993	34,634	3,531	10.2
1994	46,759	3,691	7.89
1995	58,478	3,474	5.94
1996	67,885	9,842	14.5
1997	74,772	17,529	23.44
1998	79,748	19,506	24.46

Source: China Securities Regulatory Committee

A major player in the markets for foreign shares is international investment banks, which trade and underwrite B-, H-, L-, N- and red-chip shares and arrange specific project finance or raise funds for mainland companies with global debt issues denominated in foreign currency. However, with the exception of a handful of international investors who possess significant sales and trading networks in mainland China, most investors have found the domestic B-share market to be too immature and thinly traded to warrant large scale participation. While a number of international investment banks maintain a presence in mainland China with a view towards future development, they prefer to focus their efforts on underwriting sizeable equity and bond offerings in markets like Hong Kong and New York which are dominated by sophisticated institutional investors and deep-pocketed individuals. The sheer market capitalization and liquidity such markets can boast are vital for selling large deals successfully. Only 14 international

and lower-priced opportunities. It comes as no surprise that China, recipient of the world's second highest amount of foreign direct investment, has attracted the attention of technology-oriented venture capitalists. The emergence of an Internet boom in Asia, and China's expected entry into the WTO are stimulating an additional inflow of venture capital to China's hi-tech sector.

investment banks currently participate in underwriting B-shares.[10]

For the most part, international investors have chosen to concentrate their efforts on bringing mainland corporations go public through H-share or red chip listings. The HKSE, in addition to attracting cash flows from a local population of sophisticated individual investors, boasts capital liquidity supplied by sizeable domestic and overseas institutions. As a result, buying shares in Chinese companies is not only a good investment, it's good insurance. Beijing Enterprises, for instance, is the investment arm of the Beijing municipal government. It also owns some McDonald's restaurants in Beijing. In 1997, its not-yet-issued H-shares were over-subscribed by a factor of 1200. In fact, the issue had attracted investment capital of about Hong Kong Dollar 200 billion, or about twice the money supply in Hong Kong. People had withdrawn so much cash as a consequence of the issue, that Hong Kong banks had asked Beijing Enterprises not to cash the checks it had received–at least not until the banks could deal with their shortage of vault cash.

Competition among investment banks to lead Hong Kong deals is fierce, as they battle among each other to gain market share and establish themselves as globally recognized leaders in China-related equity issuance. Nevertheless, share issues have been awarded fairly evenly among investment bankers, as the relevant Chinese authorities have tried to maintain a stable of investment banks with which to do business. This policy of encouraging balanced opportunities for as many international investors as possible has worked well to spread financial risk.

In the minds of the foreign creditors or investors acquiring equity stakes on mainland Chinese companies, there are a number of important concerns. One is the degree of institutionalization of the Chinese equity and bond

[10]In addition to underwriting, one of the areas of interest by international investment banks in recent years has been in advising multinationals on their investments within the mainland China. With increasing frequency, foreign corporations entering the Chinese market have been seeking to form joint ventures with local businesses rather than setting up their own operations. This activity has warranted the advisory services of investment banks with in-house expertise in providing investment analysis and corporate structuring. Given the operating inefficiencies of Chinese state enterprise sector and its need for significant restructuring and consolidation, international investors have been anticipating a wave of merger and acquisitions. A slice of this potentially lucrative pie could supply a needed revenue stream for investment banks with offices in the mainland, as well as introducing them to a stable of newly revamped corporate entities looking for help raising funds in the capital markets.

markets, which determines the range of investment banking services. Another is the extent of liquidity flows and the level of investor sophistication. The most vulnerable sector in this respect is domestic asset management, where foreign investors yet to capture the investing dollars of the Chinese population through vehicles similar to U.S. mutual funds. Mutual funds will likely bring stability to the market by introducing the philosophy of long-term investing to the public at large, thereby reducing the influence of short-term speculation that widely characterizes the market.

International investors also wish that Chinese government would open bond markets to further underwriting business, issuing debt for private enterprises in both the domestic and global arenas. The most obvious regulatory problem in this regard is the convertibility of the *renminbi*. As some economists have argued, making the *renminbi* fully convertible in the capital account will result in a merger of A- and B-shares, thereby leveling the playing field for participation by all local and overseas investors.

In addition to these equity and bond market openings, international investment professionals will love to develop businesses for the more sophisticated financial services such as currency hedging and financial derivatives. The demand for these capabilities within China also seems pinned to currency reform, as only when the *renminbi* is fully convertible and allowed to float freely will companies need to worry about hedging their foreign currency risk. Nonetheless, this promises to be a profitable sector of the investment industry for international investors, as only they have the risk management systems and expertise to manage these types of contracts on a large scale.

1.5 The Role of Mutual Funds and Other Institutional Investors

Institutional investors are financial institutions, such as pension funds, life and causality insurance companies, and mutual funds, that invest money on behalf of others.

The role of institutional investors in financial markets is likely to become more important in the coming decade. For this reason, institutional investors will increasingly exert an impact on the functioning of financial markets. The inter-relations between institutional investors and the functioning of financial markets are multi-dimensional and complex, encompassing a number of distinct policy issues.

The increasing importance of institutional investors means that their impact on the functioning of financial markets is steadily growing. Institutional investors have been growing in size dramatically over the past decade. In most OECD (Organization for Economic Cooperation and Development) countries, institutional saving institutions play a key role in domestic financial systems. For example, U.S. pension funds as a group control over $5 trillion in assets. Using a sample of OECD countries, Merton (1995) finds that institutional savings institutions represent, on average, 16% of total financial assets in those countries.

Three basic activities can be distinguished to define the growing role of institutional investors on financial markets. There are: (1) Institutional investors are collectors of savings from households. (2) Institutional investors are suppliers of funds in the market for securities and other financial assets. (3) Institutional investors are participants in primary and secondary markets for bonds, equities, foreign exchanges, and financial derivatives.

The involvement of institutional investors in capital market transactions is increasing in tandem with their growing financial clout. A strong community of institutional investors seems to be a recondition for the development of liquid securities markets with sophisticated financial vehicles. In view of the growing influence that institutional investors exert on the structure of capital markets, it is generally recognized that policy-makers need to take a closer look at both the functioning and the regulation of these institutions. The regulation includes the functioning of the fund management profession, the impact of changes in demography of pension schemes on the efficiency of the allocation of savings, and the influence of the international portfolio diversification.

The participation of institutional investors in the Chinese stock markets began in 1992 when the Zi Bo Township Enterprise Investment Fund was established as the first company-style close-end fund. In the same year, *Shenzhen Investment Fund Regulatory Provisions* was enacted as the symbol of standardization of China's mutual fund markets. The Shanghai government formulated *Managerial Methods of Investment Trust Fund in Shanghai.* In August 1993, the SHSE published the *Experimental Methods of Fund Stock Listing on the Shanghai Stock Exchange.* In 1994, Seng Yian and Nan Fang Securities Exchange centers were connected with the SHSE and SZSE. This led to the formation of two nation-wide mutual fund exchange markets in Shanghai and Shenzhen. At Shanghai's fund market, there were one listed fund (i.e., Zi Bo Fund) and eleven net listed funds, among which eight were Seng Yan's funds and three are Guangdong's funds, with a total market value of 662 million *renminbi yuan*. The total trading volume was 11,740 million *renminbi yuan* and 30,567 million *renminbi yuan* in 1994 and 1995, respectively. At Shenzhen's fund market, there were ten listed funds with a total market value of 2,050 million *renminbi yuan*. The total trading volume was 24,015 million *renminbi yuan* and 30,452 million *renminbi yuan* in 1994 and 1995, respectively. Looking at the trading volume and market performance, mutual fund markets in Shanghai and Shenzhen had become an important and integrated part of China's domestic equity markets.

To establish a mutual fund, an application needs to be filed with the PBOC, which is required to review the application within 90 days from the day it receives all required documents, and approve the application with the State Council's relevant division. The SZSE stipulates that fund managers and trustees shall obey the following rules:

- cannot take the business of securities underwriting;
- cannot take the business of trust loan or provide loan guarantee;
- cannot make investment with unlimited liability;
- cannot participate in trust trading;
- cannot trade securities with the funds from the same manager;
- cannot invest on beneficiary receipts of the other funds;
- cannot invest in company stocks which have relations to the fund managers or trustees;
- the investment in a listed stock shall be no more than 10% of net value of the fund;
- the investment in a listed stock shall be no more than 10% of the total shares of the company; and
- other investment limitation requirements ruled by government organs in charge.

Because mutual funds in China are listed and traded in the securities market, they have to meet the information disclosure requirements on securities. The requirements on listing documents and public announcement, the publication of the fund's net capital, and the semi-annual and annual reports are similar to that of a listed stock. The income of a fund mainly includes share dividend, interest, and capital appreciation. There is no tax imposed on fund investment in China. However, investors have to pay 1%

of managerial fee based on the market value of their investment. In the SHSE and SZSE, the service fee for trading one fund unit is one *renminbi yuan*, the commission fee is 0.4% of the trading value, and the settlement fee is 0.1% of the trading value.

1.6 After the Fifteenth National Congress: Increasing Reversal to Capitalism

National congresses are among the most important political events in China. The 15th National Congress of the Communist Party of China (CPC), held in September 1997, saw the Jiang Zemin administration take new steps in preparation for the coming 21st century. A number of historical events, especially the death of Deng Xiaoping and the transfer of sovereignty of Hong Kong from the Great Britain to China, kept the Chinese people focused on the a number of crucial issues. The 15th National Congress formally designated Deng Xiaoping Theory as the Communist Party's guiding thought and pushed the cause of building socialism with Chinese characteristics comprehensively to the 21st century.

In his report to the Party's 15th National Congress, President Jiang Zemin made a comprehensive and profound exposition on China's economic and political problems and set forth the task of deepening economic and political reforms, with emphasis on balancing reform, development and stability for China's economy.

During the 15th National Congress, Premier Li Peng proposed the following plan to restructure China's SOEs, nearly 70 percent of which are profit-losing ones:

- Taking reform of SOEs as the central point in economic restructuring, the government will take practical measures to change the way enterprises operate, with the establishment of a modern enterprise system as its orientation.
- Guiding enterprises according to their type and aiming at improving the state sector of the economy as a whole, the government will carry out a strategic reorganization of SOEs by learning to manage large enterprises well while relaxing control over small ones.
- The government will explore and developing various forms of public ownership of firms.

- The government will reform SOEs through internal reorganization and the establishment of more effective corporate governance structure.
- The government will encourage mergers, standardize bankruptcy procedures, retrain laid-off workers, and increase government efficiency by reducing staff employees.
- The government will promote a social security system.

Since September 1997, China has been busy carrying out strategic corporatization and reorganization of SOEs with full steam. This was manifested in the adoption of a major plan for reorganizing the State Council in March 1998 and the acceleration of SOE restructuring. Under Li Peng's program, all but 3,000 SOEs will be corporatized in an effort reduce the over-sized state sector. China will also focus on strengthening approximately 1000 strategic and key SOEs that are critical to the country's economic interests. Efforts have been made to support the development of hundreds of major enterprise groups that are pivotal to the national economy. This strategy will likely entail bankruptcies, mergers and acquisitions, and public stock offerings, an ownership diversification process known as privatization but usually termed corporatization in China.

The vast majority of China's 300,000 SOEs are small, inefficient, and severe threat to nation's economy. They are typically unprofitable and have been subsidized by the state banks for years. As a result, the banking system is crippled by a gridlock of non-performing loans to unprofitable state enterprises, resulting in capital starvation among more viable state and non-state firms. The strategic corporatization and reorganization of SOEs will not weaken the state sector, but rather concentrate limited state funds in the areas of real need. Reducing government control over thousands of enterprises in China will help to create a more efficient and modern financial system. This in turn will help to develop a more competitive economy, bolster fledgling capital markets and speed China's integration into the global economy.

In revamping the ownership structure of SOEs and achieving success in enterprise reform, the government has been developing a flexible and market-driven financial system to ensure that capital resources are channeled toward efficient uses, and away from hopeless causes backed by political clout. Liberalizing interest rates, establishing full currency convertibility, and opening the securities industry to private investors–both domestic and foreign–are among the strategies proposed to spur the development of more efficient capital markets for the 21st century. (See Figure 1.6.) A deregulated financial system would enable Chinese firms to compete according to their efficiency, and price and quality of their goods and services. Such a market-based environment would help ease trade friction between China and other countries and pave the way for its accession to the WTO.

Many experts have suggested that for those SOEs that play a controlling role in economic fields touching upon national security and social stability, they need to maintain a dominant role in infrastructure and vital basic industries. In the backbone industries, such as machinery, electronics and petrochemicals, a group of large conglomerates should be supported to promote the competitiveness of China's economy in the world economy. The re-shuffle of the state sector does not mean selling off all the SOEs because it could lead to the loss of state assets and encroachment of employees' interests.[11] This tendency has somewhat been curbed under the guidance of policies adopted by the central government. As long as a complete legal system and its effective enforcement are in place, the strategic re-shuffle proposed by the Fifteen National Congress will not weaken the state sector, but rather concentrate limited state funds in the areas of real need.

To step up the reform of the financial system to meet the needs of the establishment of a socialist market economic system, the core are to strengthen the currency regulation function of the central bank and the financial supervisory system, to promote the commercialization of state-owned banks, to improve the capital structure and quality of the commercial banks, to vigorously but steadily develop and regulate the financial market, to improve and enact financial laws and regulations, and to learn modem financial management expertise to improve corporate governance.

In the spirit of the Fifteenth National Congress, China launched a series of reform measures in order to further standardize and develop the securities market and to adapt to economic globalization and internationalization of the securities market.

- Reforming the stock-issuing system. Enterprises are free from the restriction of the form of ownership in the issuing and listing of

[11]Plant closures have begun throughout China. Wang Zhongyu, Minister of the State Economic and Trade Commission, said that only the strong would survive. China had some 100,000 jobs that will be lost as the result of closing all or most of the weak companies. Wang said that another worry was the corruption at the managerial level. Managers often failed to pay workers and absconded with a company's assets.

At present, we are facing a number of difficulties, especially irrationality in the economic structure, low efficiency in the economy, heavy loss by some State-owned enterprises, and rising unemployment. To address these problems, the Chinese government will further enhance the economic system reform and take effective measures to change the growth pattern. Particularly, we will speed up the reform of State-owned enterprises, focusing on invigorating the large ones while further relaxing the control over small ones. We will standardize bankruptcy procedures, encourage mergers and acquisition, and promote re-employment. We are fully confident that, within the next few years, the performance of State-owned enterprises will be improved fundamentally.

Statement by LIU ZHONGLI,
Governor of the Bank for the People's Republic of China

Fig. 1.6 Liu Zhongli's Speech

stocks. SOEs, collective enterprises and joint ventures can all apply for the issuance and listing of stocks.

- Encouraging online securities commission deals. The China Securities Regulatory Commission (CSRC) published *Temporary Management Method for Online Securities Commission Deals* and *Approval Procedures for Securities Companies Online Commission Deals* in the first half of this year, thus providing necessary conditions for the standardized development of online commission deals. As a result, over 40 securities companies have submitted their applications for online commission deals to the CSRC.
- Establishing the Growth Enterprise Market (GEM). This project helps to create a favorable environment for direct finance by hitech enterprises and growing medium and small enterprises as well as provide investment opportunities for venture capital. In the meanwhile, related preparatory work concerning the formulation of regulations and systematic development of GEM is being stepped up.
- Fostering institutional investors. China will carry out pilot activities of sino-foreign joint venture mutual funds. In addition, the CSRC and the China Insurance Regulatory Commission (CIRC) will cooperate in establishing insurance and pension funds by the pilot mutual fund companies. If successful, foreign mutual funds can have a chance to enter China's securities market.

In short, there has been increasing reversal to capitalism after the Fifteenth National Congress. Securities markets will play an important role in China's transformation into a market economy with modern capital markets.

1.7 Problems and Dilemmas

So far China's financial and economic reform has been successful, especially in comparison with Russia and other former Soviet Union countries. However, a number of problems are still outstanding:

First of all, The economic importance of SOEs is waning. Many SOEs cannot run in full capacity due to an over-supply of the products and repetitive construction, a result of government interference in the many years of the past. Moreover, many enterprises are overburdened by debts, as they blindly sought to develop big and comprehensive projects without adequate funding; the banks were forced to issue excessive amount of currency and grant loans. In addition, many enterprises are overstaffed under a big employment pressure. Local governments often pressed enterprises to recruit more people than they needed. As a consequence, SOEs now contribute just a third of the industrial output (against 75 percent in 1981). It is increasingly difficult for the central government to cover the loss of SOEs and maintain a bloated employment. In 1996 the number of people laid off by SOEs increased sharply to 10 million. In 1986, SOEs produced two-thirds of all manufacturing goods and accounted for four-fifths of export growth. In 1996, propped up with subsidies and hiding behind tariffs and other protection, SOEs can still account for half of all manufacturing goods, but barely a fifth of the growth in exports. Losses in the state sector now exceed profits. About 70 percent of the 100,000 state firms are money-losing enterprises. The state sector has imposed huge costs on the rest of the economy.

Second, Chinese stock market is overwhelmed with individual investors, most with limited understanding of financial risk and investment, but is lack of long-term institutional investors such as mutual funds, pension funds and insurance companies. In stark contrast with world-class financial markets, there are about 45 million individual investors but only 23 investment funds in China by the end of 1999. Two important decisions were made in August 1999. The first was to allow state-owned enterprises to invest in the stock markets and if they held stocks for a period of at least six months. The second was to allow life insurance companies to allocate up to 15 percent of their assets portfolio for investment in the stock market. However, it is yet to be seen whether the trend of encouraging the establishment of institutional investor will persist.

Third, although it is recognized that foreign capital is an important source of funds for domestic firms, foreign investors are not allowed to invest in domestic equity markets. Foreign investors in B- and H-share markets tend to be institutional investors, who constitute yet another set of long-term investors. It is crucial not to turn them away. H-shares are traded in Hong Kong and are subject to the fluctuation of international financial markets. They are regulated by the Hong Kong authorities who have a long track record that is up to international standards. But B-shares are regulated by mainland Chinese authorities who yet need to establish a track record. H-shares are reasonably liquid while B-shares are plagued with illiquidity problem. In addition, the pricing of H-shares still lags behind their counterpart A-shares. The pricing of B-shares is even wider apart from their counterpart A-shares. An appropriate difference between the prices of the stocks of the same quality in different markets is understandable, but a wide gap is obviously abnormal. Current A-stock prices are two to six times the price of equivalent H-shares. And the price of A-shares are around 2.5 to three times the price of equivalent B-shares. When the A-share stock prices are so much higher than the B- or H-share prices for the same company, the market price is obviously too high for A-shares.

Fourth, non-tradable shares (state and legal person shares) have become the rot at the heart of China's stock markets. They put the characteristic in that slogan "stock markets with Chinese characteristics". They enable the government to claim that share issuance is not akin to privatization. This strategy has been useful, but the problem is that the state is that legal person and state shares afflict the markets in different ways. Legal person shares are held by approved state institutions, usually firms under the control of the same local government. They typically hold about 30 percent of a company. They receive dividends and tend to be active shareholders. A World Bank study in 1997 found that legal person shareholders are often elected to their companies' board of directors. Through that, legal person shareholders gained voting power on major decisions, as well as inside information on the firm. To crown it all, legal person shareholders face little threat of a hostile takeover. That puts them in a powerful position. However, legal-person shareholders often abuse their powers. They frequently "borrow" assets, usually cash, from their listed companies, and it's rare for firms to be paid back. Whatever harm it may do the company, small shareholders can only watch and weep. Of the 841 companies listed at end of 1998, 467 of them had their funds used by their majority shareholder. State shareholders, in contrast, often don't have enough power. State shares are usually managed by the State Asset Management Bureau (SAMB), from its headquarters in Beijing or local offices. Their ultimate owner is the State Council. The SAMB passes dividends onto the Ministry of Finance, for inclusion in the national budget. It therefore lacks an important monetary incentive to supervise the firms it owns.

Fifth, Chinese stock market is much more volatile than matured markets. For example, the Shanghai composite index is about 800 times as volatile as the NYSE composite index, and 400 times more volatile than the Hong Kong Hang Seng index. There are two possible explanations for the high stock-market volatility in China. One is that the fundamentals for Chinese stocks are more volatile than industrialized countries. For instance, China's monetary policy is more unpredictable and subjective than that of the U.S. monetary authority. It is common to see the Chinese central bank loosens the money supply, the economy over-reacts to easy credit, and the central bank suddenly intervenes and tightens the credit. On the contrary, the U.S. Federal Reserve (as well as the monetary authorities in Germany and Japan) typically announces its monetary policy changes well in advance. In this sense, the macroeconomic policy is more volatile in China.

Another reason for high stock-market volatility is the strong presence of noise traders. When there is more news (including gossips) flows into the market, there is more extreme movements in stock prices. There is more suspicion of insider trading and other securities violations. People often fail to incorporate a company's fundamentals into stock prices. Their trading is more likely to be based on mood swings and things that they thought to be informative but are not information in reality.

Sixth, the development of financial instruments has been limited to the capital market. No nationally integrated money market has yet been developed, and most banks lack the skills to develop new products that could create competition in the financial sector. Although local inter-bank centers have been emerged since 1986 and have played a useful role in the local redistribution of surplus funds, they have not operated as inter-bank markets in the traditional sense. Since non-bank financial institutions and even some manufacturing enterprises can participate, these centers often serve as long-term financing channels for non-bank and non-financial institutions, thereby circumventing the credit plan.

The absence of nationally organized money markets–one of the salient features of China's financial sector in the early 1990s–is related to its slow start on interest rate liberalization, its lack of a modern payment and settlement system, and the state banks' inefficient administrative organization. The lack of nationally integrated inter-bank and money markets has, in turn, hampered efforts to achieve the transition to indirect instruments of monetary policy. In the absence of an inter-bank market where surplus funds could be redistributed, the existing indirect instruments have been used to channel liquidity from one region or entity to another. The authorities have regulated liquidity by adjusting reserve requirements and using the PBOC's lending facilities for banks while maintaining relatively stable interest rates.

The present economic and financial problems require, therefore, further active steps in reforming the entire banking system and the state-owned enterprises. There are more than 300,000 SOEs, a third of which are industrial. Most of SOEs employ urban workers. They also account for up to 90 percent of all loans granted by state banks. However, SOEs produce less than 40 percent of the nation's industrial output, and their share has been falling relative to firms of other types of ownership.[12]

Despite some progress in the development of property rights in China, it is still rather difficult to draw the line between the state as owner and as manager. The latter still has been delegated excessive control from the government and the party. The absence of clear definitions of ownership has also been an obstacle to foreign investment. The obscure separation of ownership and management has led to a process of "spontaneous privatization" which is taking place in many small state firms, a growing number of which are being stripped bare by managers and local government officials who seize assets and leave debts behind.

To reduce spontaneous privatization, the central government is determined to keep the 1,000 or so largest SOEs of vital national interest under its control. This is sensible for the time being, but will be costly in the long-run. The enormous increase in state bank lending (the so called "policy loans") to support the survival of these SOEs represents the price of delaying serious state enterprise reform.[13] Bad debts have amounted 22 percent of the total credit extended by the four major state banks and up to 80 percent of the portfolios of other commercial banks. In short, China's banking system is almost insolvent, i.e., its bad debts exceed its capital.[14]

[12]Section 2.3 provides more detailed analysis on ownership structure and firm's performance. Figure 2.1 presents shares of industrial output according to different types of ownership of firms.

[13]This is also referred to as "soft budget constraint". A firm is said to have soft budget constraint if it expects to be bailed out in case of financial trouble. Soft-budget constraint can lead to failure to abide financial principles by the management and is therefore a source of inefficiency.

[14]The truth is that state-owned industries owe the state banking system a great deal of money due to the soft budget constraint. About US$600 billion in bank loans are outstanding in China. (90 percent of the loans are given to SOEs.) These loans account for an unusually high proportion of all financing equivalent to about 70 percent of the GDP. China has only one private bank and its capital markets are immature, so the

Over the long-term, the costs of the financial system for the state sector will surely mount. Lending is growing faster than state output while bank profits shrink steadily as a proportion of assets.

In summary, after years of reform, no other emerging market economy faces greater challenges than the mainland Chinese economy. Ultimately, the future of China's capital markets does not rely on the success or failure of one specific reform. Rather, it depends on a host of policies yet to be implemented by the central government. With an economy that is increasingly linked to the globe (external trade has accounted for approximately 38% of GDP in 1999) and on the brink of joining the WTO, China must rapidly reform its state enterprises and banking sectors to enable these to compete with foreign firms on a global footing. State-owned enterprises still accounts for roughly one-third of GDP and employment. State-owned banks also account for 75% of total banking assets. What are urgent now are to set up a new investment mechanism in which the roles of the government and the enterprises are separated, to reform and improve the financial system to make the cost of capital small, and to establish and improve the social security system.

job of financing investment rests almost entirely on the shoulders of state banks. Those banks also have an unusually high proportion of bad loans (about 30 percent of the GDP) which they have small hope of ever having repaid. Bad loans in China would swallow up banks' capital several times over if banks had to account for them. By any conventional calculation the banking system is insolvent.

Chapter 2

Structural and Institutional Characteristics

2.1 Introduction

The most salient feature of China's securities market is the emphasis on state control of the financial markets. When stock exchanges were first established in Shanghai and Shenzhen, legislation on securities came under the jurisdiction of a number of ministries and commissions under the State Council such as the China Securities Regulatory Commission (CSRC), the Ministry of Finance (MOF), the People's Bank of China (PBOC) and the State Asset Management Bureau (SAMB). In addition, the Shanghai and Shenzhen municipal governments, the local branches of PBOC, and the local divisions of the various ministries and commissions were also involved in exercising the regulatory, supervisory and administrative functions for the securities markets in Shanghai and Shenzhen. During the early stage of development of securities markets, there was not only an overlapping of legislative power but also a lack of demarcation of the administrative and supervisory functions at different levels and in different departments.

Since 1992, the CSRC supervises and regulates securities markets in China. The PBOC acts as the approval authority for traders and securities firms while the State Council Securities Policy Commission determines the annual number of listing and volume of issues. The state planning commission sets quotas for stock and debt listings during a given year. These quotas are then divided among provinces. In the bond quota allocation, preference is given to infrastructure projects and 300 designated SOEs. Announced quotas appear to change according to market conditions. Additional regulatory constraints include outlawing share issues for financial and real estate companies and forbidding mutual holdings between securities institutions and non-securities financial institutions.

Enterprises requesting a foreign share listing are required to obtain approval from the Ministry of Foreign Trade and Economic Cooperation. Individuals are limited to a maximum of 25% of a firms B-Shares and total foreign ownership is limited to 49% of public shares. Foreign firms may establish representative offices but not local securities branches or subsidiaries. All transactions involving foreign investors require the partnership of a local broker.

Foreign banks are prohibited from selling mutual funds to Chinese citizens or institutions and must obtain government approval to participate in underwriting. Foreign securities firms are prohibited from introducing new domestic financial products, although they may offer off-shore derivatives. However, repatriation of profits requires government approval. Furthermore, Chinese residents may not invest overseas without government approval.

It is widely recognized that a well-functioning securities market can provide an opportunity to raise capital for investments, enhance the efficiency of state assets and social resources, reduce the debt-servicing burden, mobilize savings deposits through facilitating an increased availability of assets, and create a higher yield with a lower risk, hence a higher return on savings. In contrast, central planning does not provide the most efficient means to channel funds from savers to borrowers. Major structural problems of the emerging Chinese security markets include its artificial pricing mechanism, the limited number of listed securities and a lack of modern communication facilities and training.

- Arbitrary Pricing: Arbitrary government intervention can lead to mispricing of capital assets. China currently operates under a dual interest rate system, with an official rate and a market rate. When rates are high, state enterprises experience higher cost of capital. State-ownership can be somewhat of a bottleneck to stock market development because the use of funds raised through issuing stocks remains subject to government control. Furthermore, the government has self-imposed ill-liquidity through prohibiting employees to sell employee shares. Limited domestic mobility of capital also constricts market development.
- Limited Number of Listed Securities: The securities markets pro-

vide an opportunity to raise capital through both promoters subscription and public flotation. Without securities markets, firms have to rely on retained earnings. However, experimentation with stock issues in China has remained limited and the amount of funds raised has been small.

- Over Dependence on Household Savings: Although China benefits from a high savings rate, one of the highest in the world, the Chinese banking system have become overly dependent on household savings. (Household savings are estimated to account for 60% of deposits.)
- Lack of External Capital: The availability of external capital is an important element in creating a viable securities market. External capital is a means to supplement but not replace internal source of funding. Foreign exchange restrictions can inhibit market development. The current exchange controls have led to an over-valued *renminbi* and the a black market for foreign currency that further thwarts the ability of the government to effectively implement strict monetary policies.

These weaknesses in the current system lead to increases in cost of capital for Chinese firms which, in turn, makes it more difficult for them to compete with foreign firms. One could argue that Chinas has used its security market more as a means to shift funding of inefficient state enterprises from the government to the public than as a means to fairly value companies. Under the present heavy regulation and strict control of financial markets, China has the potential to benefit from a further opening of markets. China's financial reform needs to include a greater use of interest rates as an opportunity cost to determine cost of capital.

2.2 Regulatory Framework

2.2.1 *Organizations in Charge*

According to *Managerial Regulation of the People's Bank in P. R. China* announced in 1986 and other relevant regulations, the security organs in charge at Shanghai and Shenzhen during the period of the second half of 1980s to the beginning of 1990s are PBOC Shanghai Branch and Shenzhen Branch. Since the beginning of 1990s, because of the security regulation was increasingly complex, the State Planning Commission, the State Reconstruction Committee and the Department of Finance are involved in the security management.

In 1992, the State Council decided to establish the Chinese Security Exchange Commission (CSEC) and its enforcement agency, the CSRC. In April 1993, the State Council published *Provision of Security Issuing and Trading*, which stipulates that the CSEC is the organ in charge of the nation's security market and is entitled to manage the nation's security market according to the law; and that CSRC is CSEC's enforcement agency which exercises the power of management and supervision of security issuing and trading according to relevant laws and regulations. The chairman of the CSEC must be one of the vice premier and the chairman of the CSRC must be one of the vice chairmen of the CSEC. The CSRC has its routine working departments such as issuing department, law department and others. If necessary, the State's security organs in charge may establish branch organs at local administration, exercising the power of management and supervision. However, up to now, all the local security organs in charge are established by the local governments. Since then, China's security organs in charge have gone through a transitional period from being concurrently in charge to specialized in charge.

The CSRC, whose members are high-level government officials from various state ministries, exists to create policies and guidelines for regulating the exchanges. The CSRC exists to execute and enforce these policies through day-to-day direct market supervision by its staff of trained securities professionals. Though the recent passage of securities regulations has further empowered both CSRC and PBOC with the authority to oversee market development, the PBOC has retained the ability to license and supervise certain securities issues, thereby complicating the power structure. Before the enactment of the *P.R.C. Securities Law*, the effectiveness of the CSRC and PBOC has been limited due to unclear definition and delineation of the exact roles of the various supervisory authorities. They must rely upon a complex series of overlapping guidelines to do their job. When the *Securities Law* came into effect in July 1999, the power of the CSRC was enhanced.

According to China's *Company Law* and security regulations, the CSRC, whose functions are similar to that of the U.S. Securities Exchange Commission, has the following responsibilities:

- Formulating policies, plans, laws and regulations concerning securities and futures markets;
- Supervising securities and futures markets and regional/provincial supervisory institutions;
- Overseeing the issuance, trading, custody and settlement of equity shares, convertible bonds and securities investment funds; approving the listing of corporate bonds; supervising the trading activities of listed government and corporate bonds;
- Supervising the listing, trading and settlement of domestic futures contracts; overseeing domestic institutions involved in futures business abroad;
- Supervising the activities of listed firms and their shareholders who are liable for information disclosure in securities markets;
- Supervising securities and futures exchanges, their senior management and securities associations;
- Supervising securities and futures firms, securities investment fund managers, securities registration and settlement firms, futures settlement institutions and securities and futures investment consulting institutions; approving the qualification of fund custody institutions and supervising their business; drafting rules on the qualification of senior management for the above institutions; granting the qualification of those involved in securities- and futures-related business;
- Supervising direct or indirect issuance and listing of shares abroad by domestic firms; supervising the establishment of securities institutions abroad by domestic institutions; and supervising the establishment of domestic securities institutions by foreign organizations;
- Supervising information disclosure and proliferation related to securities and futures and overseeing statistics and information resources management for securities and futures markets;
- Helping grant the qualification of law firms, accounting firms, asset-appraisal firms (and their professional staff) engaged in securities and futures intermediary businesses, and supervising their activities.

In the beginning of 1996, The State's Planning Commission and the Ministry of Finance formulated *Rules of Collecting Fees for Management and Supervision on Security and Futures Market.* According to the Rules,

- CSRC may collect management and supervision fees in the amount of 0.25% and 0.04% of the annual trading value from the relevant stock exchanges and futures exchanges.
- CSRC may collect management and supervision fees in the amount of 0.1% and 5% of the registered capital from the relevant security corporations and companies which are concurrently undertaking security business.
- CSRC may charge 30,000 *renminbi yuan* application fee from companies which apply to issue stocks.

2.2.2 *Securities Laws and Regulations*

Because China's securities market was established in an economic environment that bears little resemblance to a typical market-oriented economy. There was not even a complete set of nationally applicable commercial laws for people to comply with. When the two stock exchanges in Shanghai and Shenzhen were established in China's most dynamic economic zones, in the wake of their birth with only 13 local companies listed, the two local governments started to supervise/regulate the exchanges according to local legislation. In the rocky course of the exchanges' evolution from local markets into national markets, the inconsistency of local legislation and inadequacy of supervision led to serious disorder and low efficiency of the markets. The infamous "August 10th" incident in Shenzhen in 1992, an ill-fated initial public offering (IPO) through a lottery distribution method going awry, was a harsh lesson which triggered the establishment of China's national securities regulatory agency and reform of securities-related legal system. The setting up of the CSRC in 1992 started a new era of securities legislation and enforcement in China.

With several years of painstaking efforts, a series of laws and regulations governing the securities market have been enacted. At a time, there were over 250 pieces of national securities-related laws, regulations and rules covering all aspects of the securities market, from public offering to listing and trading of shares, from information disclosure of listed companies to supervision of financial intermediary, from clearing and settlement to legal liabilities and securities fraud, and from corporate governance to overseas listing of Chinese companies. All existing market products including equity shares, securities investment funds, convertible corporate bonds and commodities futures contracts are also legislated. *Administration of Issuing and Trading of Shares Tentative Regulations* (1993), *P.R.C. Company Law* (1994) and *Overseas Listing of Chinese Companies Limited by Shares Special Rules* (1994) marked important legislative milestones before the *P.R.C. Securities Law* was eventually enacted in December 1998. The criminalization of securities fraud and insider trading in 1997's *P.R.C. Criminal Law Amendments* was also an important step to secure orderly operation of the market and combat securities-related crimes. Rules such as *Merger & Acquisition Rules* and *Corporate Governance Rules* have been put on top of the CSRC's rule-making agenda.

2.2.2.1 *P.R.C. Company Law*

On December 29, 1993, the Standing Committee of the Eighth National People's Congress adopted the *P.R.C. Company Law*, which came into effect on July 1, 1994 and was amended on December 25, 1999. In addition to state enterprises, collective enterprises, township and village enterprises, and private enterprises, the *Company Law* recognizes two additional kinds of corporate legal persons in China: limited liability companies and joint stock companies. The law restricts the number of shareholders for limited liability companies to no more than 50 or will be otherwise unsuitable for listing.

Under the *Company Law*, approval from the relevant State Council departments or from provincial government departments must be obtained before a company can be incorporated. The law provides two methods of incorporation for joint stock companies. Such entities may be incorporated by promotion or by public subscription. If a company is incorporated by promotion, the entire registered capital of the company must be subscribed for by at least five promoters. More than half of the promoters must reside within mainland China. According to the *Special Regulations on the Overseas Offering and Listing of Shares by Joint Stock Limited Companies*, SOEs or enterprises with the majority of their assets owned by the government can be restructured as joint stock limited companies, and under some special circumstance, they may issue shares to overseas investors. These companies, if incorporated by promotion, may have fewer than five promoters and can issue new shares once incorporated. If a company is incorporated by public subscription, at least 35 percent of its total shares must be subscribed for by the promoter and the remaining shares must be offered to the public.

The registered capital of a joint stock limited company is divided into shares of equal par value. According to the *Company Law*, the registered capital of a company is the amount of its total paid up capital as registered with the relevant Bureau for Industry and Commerce. The minimum registered capital of a joint stock company is *renminbi* 10 million. The total capital of a joint stock company which proposes to apply for its shares to be listed on a stock exchange must not be less than *renminbi* 50 million. The liability of shareholders of a joint stock company is limited to the extent of the shares held by them, and the liability of the company is limited to the full amount of all the assets owned by it.

Under the *Company Law*, joint stock companies are permitted to invest in other joint stock companies and limited liability companies. However, apart from investment companies and holding companies specified by the State Council, the amount of a joint stock company's aggregate investment in other companies may not exceed 50 per cent. of its net assets and a joint stock company's liabilities with respect to such holdings is limited to the amount invested.[1]

Among numerous tasks to develop and strengthen the securities market, the CSRC needs to tackle with several pressing legal and structural issues. The *P.R.C. Company Law* (1993), China's prime corporate legislation enacted when modern corporation system were just introduced to the country as a brand-new vehicle on the road of SOE reforms, has increasingly shown its many inadequacies and some innate problems. The current public offering system for equity and debt instruments needs to undergo further conceptual and procedural changes to facilitate the market-based pricing of securities and to make the corporate mechanism function in its real sense. Corporate governance can never be overemphasized to upgrade the accountability of listed companies and to enhance the roles played by their directors and management. The development of the B-share market and overseas listing of Chinese companies are calling for improvement of transparency and removal of policy and technical barriers for higher liquidity. Acknowledging these issues and many more, CSRC is doing everything

[1]The *Company Law* stipulates that companies which had been established previously under various laws and regulations prior to the implementation of the law would not be affected by the *Company Law*, but companies which had not wholly complied with the provisions of the *Company Law* would have to satisfy the relevant requirements within a specified period of time. The State Council has subsequently promulgated detailed implementing measures to bring the *Company Law* into force.

within its power to persuade the country's legislators to amend, or better yet, to overhaul the *P.R.C. Company Law*, to reform the IPO system, to gradually abolish the political approval system and to allow market force to come into play, and to introduce educational programs to train and examine senior management and directors of listed companies. All these efforts, hopefully, will pay off to make China's corporate legal framework and practice more conducive to the new environment and to the fast growth of the securities market.

2.2.2.2 *P.R.C. Securities Law*

Securities enforcement was developed along with the securities legislation and market development in China. When the CSRC was established in 1992, the government and the regulators were totally inexperienced in securities market enforcement due to the fact that China's securities market had emerged from a long-lasted planned economy. Without necessary power to fulfill its regulatory duties, CSRC's enforcement capability was very much limited. Chinese stock markets was described by many as a "gambling place" characterized by the unsophisticated, short-term speculators and the manipulation of institutions. Little was there for the long-term market growth and confidence of investors at home and abroad.

With rules and regulations coming gradually into place and regulators becoming more experienced in practice, the general securities enforcement capacity has been greatly enhanced. In 1998, over 100 cases of complaints were lodged and investigated by the CSRC. 56 of those were concluded with administrative sanctions imposed and three suspects were transferred to judicial authorities for criminal prosecution. The number of prosecutions in 1998 was more than the total number of cases handled by the CSRC between 1995 and 1997. These cases involved various malpractices such as market manipulation, false financial statement, fraudulent conducts, insider trading, and illegal IPO and overseas futures transactions. The treatment of serious cases such "Qiong Minyuan" fraudulent accounting statements and practice, "Hong Guang" false financial statements and "9703 Pollywood Contract" price manipulation have won extensive public acclaim and served to build up investors' confidence. In the course of building channels for foreign investment in China through overseas listing of Chinese companies and development of B-share markets, international cooperation in terms of enforcement, information exchange, and mutual assistance have become an important field for both the CSRC and its overseas counterparts. The CSRC has so far established bilateral Memorandum of Understandings (MoUs) and similar arrangements with 13 regulatory counterparts in the world.[2]

On December 29, 1998, the *P.R.C. Securities Law* was passed by the Standing Committee of the National People's Congress. The law took effect on July 1, 1999. This is the first national securities law in mainland China, and it is divided into 12 chapters and 214 articles regulating, among other things, the issue and trading of securities, takeovers by listed companies, securities exchanges, securities companies and the duties and responsibilities of the State Council's securities regulatory authorities.[3] The *Securities Law* is the fundamental law which comprehensively regulates activities in the Chinese securities market. Perhaps the most important accomplishment of the making of the law is to indicate a consensus view among the Chinese authorities that:

- The nature of the stock market and its role and function within the Chinese socialist market economy has now been firmly entrenched;
- any effective regulation of the stock market must have a strong legal foundation; and
- given the existing realities of the stock market against the background of the Asian financial crisis in 1998, the authorities believe that legal regulation of the stock market cannot be further delayed.

The Law thus arguably indicates that, since the stock market is now an integral part of the Chinese socialist economy, the use of securities as a tool of capital formation will be encouraged and the quality of the stock market will thereby improve with time. In other words, it provides a firm basis for the belief that greater business opportunities, both domestically and overseas, will be created in the Chinese capital market. For example, Article

[2]According to an article published by China Online on November 5, 1999, the CSRC has already signed MoUs on the supervision of securities markets with the regulatory agencies in Hong Kong, U. S., Singapore, Australia, U. K., Italy, Japan, Malaysia, Brazil, Ukraine, France, Luxemburg and Germany. Under the terms of the MoUs, China and the above countries and regions plan to share information, exchange and train staff, thus paving the way for Chinese companies to tap funds from international capital markets.

[3]See Appendix A, which excerpts from "The PRC Securities Law and the Development of the Mainland Securities Market" by Alexandra Lo, for a more detailed summary of the *P.R.C. Securities Law*.

29 of the *Securities Law* provides that Chinese enterprises which intend to directly or indirectly issue or list their securities outside the mainland China must first obtain approval from the State Council's regulatory authorities. Article 213 of the *Securities Law* provides that specific measures shall be formulated separately by the State Council if specific shares of Chinese companies are to be subscribed and traded in foreign currencies by person and organization outside mainland China.[4]

In addition, the law provides strong legislative support for the CSRC in the discharge of its enforcement functions, giving CSRC the power to investigate, to impose administrative sanctions, and to transfer cases to administrative and judicial authorities. To ensure all securities laws and regulations are effectively and consistently enforced, the securities regulatory system has been restructured to form a centralized and unified regulatory system, with CSRC as the prime regulator over the securities market and the local regulatory agencies transformed into regional offices of the CSRC. The enforcement capacity of CSRC will be further strengthened after additional enforcement branches of CSRC are established in the near future.[5]

As the securities markets in Shanghai and Shenzhen grow rapidly to have listed today about 1000 companies with a market capitalization of about 3 trillion *renminbi* accounting for 30% of the country's GDP, a complete securities legal framework has to be developed over time. The enacted *P.R.C. Securities Law* is only a foundation of an ambitious reform project. A great amount of work is still ahead to solve the inconsistencies and contradictions amongst laws and rules, and to clearly define the essential terms and gradually refine the legal framework. The current task of the CSRC is to make the legal system work more effectively through updating the *P.R.C. Securities Law* and make the law fully operational. No longer "a tiger without teeth", the Chinese regulator is sharpening its teeth to meet

[4]In the meanwhile, the issue and trading of foreign shares (including H shares and B shares) are still mainly governed by the rules and regulations promulgated by the State Council and the CSRC.

[5]An efficient operation of the present regulatory and enforcement system will, of course, rely on people who are running it. Proper regulation and enforcement is an "art" that all securities regulators must grasp. Therefore, in the process of consolidating China's regulatory system, it is of paramount importance to equip regulatory personnel with enforcement techniques, procedural rules and administrative skills. With the fast development of the markets, the regulator is still facing great challenges in its enforcement work.

the challenges of a rapidly growing market. To this end, the Chinese government and the regulators are committed to establishing a complete, fair and balanced legal system in the next few years.

At the turn of the new millennium, China is at the most critical moment of her economic development and reforms. To achieve her development goals in the next millenium, China needs to attach great importance to the role to be played by her securities market at this transitional stage. On the basis of the achievement in the securities legislation and enforcement, the regulators will have to work harder to regulate the market according the rules of the market itself. The CSRC will experience its own transition from regulating the market through administrative means to doing that through market-oriented means and self-regulatory mechanisms. Only in such a way can the CSRC become a true 'policeman' of the market instead of an administrator. It is encouraging that the regulator is already on such a track. A developed securities law and matured regulators will surely be needed to safeguard a fair, efficient, orderly and sustained development of China's securities markets.

2.3 Ownership Structure

The dilemma for designing any good corporate governance structure is how to make corporate executives accountable to the other contributors to the enterprise whose investments are at risk while still giving those executives the freedom, incentives, and control over resources for competitive purposes. Ownership structure reforms in China can be characterized, similar to other recent economic reforms, as gradual and pragmatic. Effectively separating ownership from management for SOEs is complicated by the fact that the State, or its agents, carry out shareholder functions otherwise performed by private owners in market economic systems. A further complication is that political reasons foster management's dependence upon, rather than its separation from, the ownership. For example, many industrial managers of the mid 1980s owed their jobs to the personal connections they held with bureaucratic superiors and depended on these connections for bail-out from serious economic problems that plagued their firms. Both commercialization and corporatization move the status of SOEs from political institutions more towards economic entities. In order for the commercialization and corporatization to be effective, a mechanism must be designed to ensure that state's ownership is one of limited liability so as to hold the management accountable for its losses. The Chinese government has been working on this important ownership aspect of SOE reform. Table 2.1 presents the time-line of measures and legislation undertaken by the State to enforce ownership structure reform. Figure 2.1 shows shares of industrial output by ownership between 1978 and 1996.

When enterprise reform was launched in 1984, the main barriers to Chinese economic development were seen as bureaucratic rigidity, inefficiency, and the irrationality of central planning. The ownership reform was not meant to change the fundamental rules of the game but merely to provide more incentives for enterprises to maximize their profits and increase their efficiency. It was not anticipated that when price liberalization would be undertaken, that fundamental structural changes would also take place, i.e. the allocation of resources would no longer be dominated by the state. The command and control system was fundamentally dismantled and the reform took on a life of its own; it was not foreseen by the original designers and that this would require further change in government policies to accommodate such an evolution. The wide gap between intentions and outcomes imposed pressures on the existing institutional structures and demanded further institutional adjustment.

Granting SOEs more autonomy without separating ownership and managerial rights seemed to improve productivity and economic growth but simultaneously triggered social and economic problems which devastated the reform and the economy as a whole. The undesirable outcomes, including corruption, increased predatory activities, inflation, and the near bankruptcy of the state, have become the main stimulus for further reform in China since the early 1990s. The commercialization and corporatization of existing SOEs were centered on the arbitrariness in distributional relations between the State and the enterprise and their related incentive problems. There were done by clarifying property rights and operational rights to achieve a higher degree of accountability and to form competitive and independently-managed industrial conglomerates integrating industry, business, scientific research, and finance into one entity. This entity would be able to utilize market forces to promote optimum use of existing resources and to rationalize internal organization and structure. By early 1993, more than 10,000 companies had been merged into such conglomerates.

Within the share holding restrictions imposed by the CSRC are specific rules ensuring that no individual Chinese or foreigner can purchase a ma-

Table 2.1 Time-line for Ownership Reform

Year	Legislation and Reform
1984	*Provisional Regulations on the Enlargement of Autonomy of State Industrial Enterprises* allowed SOEs to make price setting, output sales, and input purchases decisions when producing at above-quota levels
1985	Enterprise income tax replaced profit remittance as the form of SOE payments to the state government
1986	Contract (Management) Responsibility System created a contract-based relationship between medium-sized and large SOEs and the state government which defined output, profit remittance, and taxes Law permitting bankruptcy (became effective in 1988)
1988	Enterprise Law legalized the *Provincial Regulations* of 1984 Contract Responsibility System extended to all SOEs regardless of size
1990	Limited liability private companies and "shareholding" options for SOEs Stock exchanges established in Shanghai and Shenzhen
1991	Several large SOEs transformed into joint-stock companies and listed their shares on domestic and international stock exchanges
1992	*Enterprise Bill of Rights* guaranteed non-interference by the state in SOE operations (14 specific rights granted) Provincial regulations issued for limited liability companies and joint-stock companies
1993	Company Law established legal framework for the corporatization and commercialization of SOEs It also established the corporate governance structure of SOEs
1994	Company Law became effective

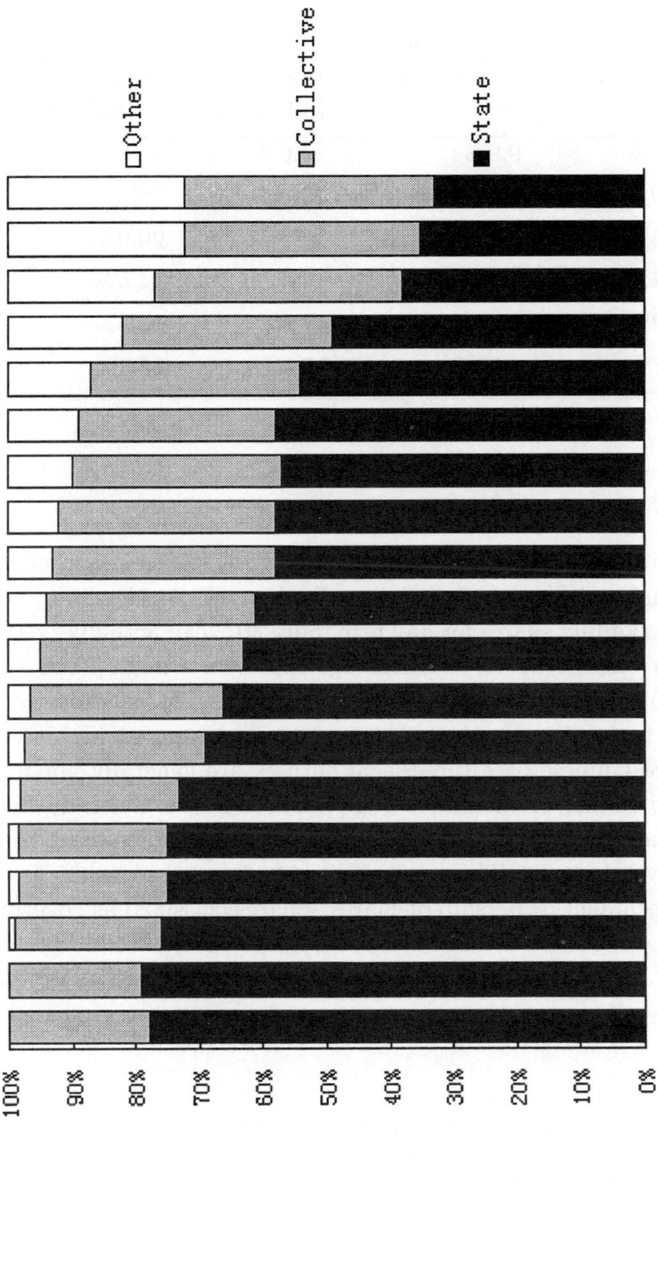

Fig. 2.1 Shares of Industrial Output by Ownership (1978-1996)

Table 2.2 Ownership of Shares on the Shanghai and Shenzhen Securities Exchanges

	Percentage of Shares Held by			
	Government	Legal Entities	Domestic Individuals	Overseas Funds & Individuals
1992	63.1%	9.9%	21.0%	5%
1993	59.9%	10.7%	22.4%	7%
1994	51.3%	18.0%	9.8%	20.9%
1995	56.7%	14.9%	14.0%	14.5%
1996	49.2%	17.5%	17.6%	15.8%
1997	45.7%	20.8%	17.0%	16.5%

jority stake in any listed company. Table 2.2 presents ownership of shares on the Shanghai and Shenzhen Securities Exchanges. As shown on the table, of the outstanding shares for any firm, only 30% can actually be traded in Shanghai or Shenzhen. Government agencies own a large proportion of total stock, 46% in 1997, down from 63% in 1992. The category of legal entities refers to legally constituted autonomous organizations. It is crucial that in the Chinese case these legal entities are generally not mutual funds, pension funds, or insurance companies, but are generally holding companies established by government agencies as a management tool for government-owned stocks. Thus, most Chinese observers consider them as secondary government ownership of shares. Shares classified as government of legal-entity owned are not allowed to circulate on the exchange. Thus, approximately two-thirds of total share value on the securities exchanges did not circulate.[6]

[6]It should be noted that after the Fifteenth National Congress, restructuring of SOEs involved a much more rapid rate of ownership conversion, increased privatization, and much greater use of joint stock corporations. Government limitations requiring that the state maintain majority or controlling interests were repealed.

2.4 Listing Standards and Procedures

2.4.1 *Requirements for Stock Listings*

Options available to a company for a stock exchange listing include:

- Domestic listing of A-shares;
- Domestic listing of B-shares;
- Overseas listing of Foreign Investment Shares;
- Red-chip listing which can take various forms.

A company could list its domestic investment shares (in the form of A-shares) or foreign investment shares (in the form of B-shares) in Shanghai or Shenzhen or its foreign investment shares on exchanges which have signed a Memorandum of Understanding with the CSRC or undertake a red-chip listing. The relevant laws and regulations governing stock listings are the *Administration of the Issuing and Trading of Shares Tentative Regulations*, *P.R.C. Company Law*, and *P.R.C. Securities Law.*

2.4.1.1 *A Shares*

A-shares are different from other categories of domestic investment shares such as state-owned shares. A-shares are domestic investment shares issued by Chinese companies which are listed on the SHSE and SZSE. A-shares may only be subscribed by and traded among Chinese citizens and/or entities.

Under the *Administration of the Issuing and Trading of Shares Tentative Regulations* promulgated on April 22, 1993, before listing on the SHSE or SZSE, a shareholding company (also referred to as a joint stock limited company) must first be established. The procedure and requirements for establishing a shareholding company are set out in the *Company Law.* Note that the minimum amount of registered capital is *renminbi* 10 million which has to be paid up in cash at the time of filing application and supported by capital verification certificates.

A shareholding company must comply with the following criteria in order to apply for listing:

- The shares must be issued to the public (as opposed to a private placement);

- The total share capital after a public offering must not be less than *renminbi* 50 million;
- The amount of share capital subscribed by sponsors must be at least *renminbi* 30 million and must represent at least 35% of the total share capital issued;
- At least 25% of the shares must be issued to the public and not more than 10% of this amount may be subscribed by the staff and workers. For Chinese companies with an issued share capital totaling a nominal value of more than *renminbi* 400 million, the percentage of shares issued to the public must account for not less than 10% of the total shares of the company;
- There must be more than 1,000 individual shareholders holding shares with a nominal value of over *renminbi* 1,000 and the total nominal value of shares held by those individuals must be at least *renminbi* 10 million;
- Except for a newly-formed company limited by shares, the Chinese company must have made profits in each of the last three years;
- If a shareholding is established by restructuring an existing enterprise, the existing enterprise must have a three-year track record of earning profits;
- Any other conditions imposed by the CSRC. (See the *P.R.C. Securities Law.*)

The *Securities Law* stipulates that Chinese companies proposing to issue and list their A-shares must first be approved by the CSRC. The CSRC must make a decision within three months from the date on which an application is received. The stock exchange from which a company is seeking a listing is required to verify applications and make a final decision within six months from the date on which an application is received. The company and the stock exchange should arrange for the procedure regarding the listing of the shares once an application is approved. The *Securities Law* also sets out general regulation on securities trading, continuing disclosure, insider dealing and other prohibited trading acts on A shares.

2.4.1.2 *B-Shares*

Foreign investment shares may be listed as B-shares on the SHSE or SZSE. The term "B-shares", "domestically listed foreign investment shares" and "special *renminbi*-denominated shares" all refer to the same thing–ordinary shares of Chinese shareholding companies that are denominated in *renminbi* but traded in foreign currencies, such as U.S. dollars, on a Chinese securities exchange. B-shares can only be subscribed by and traded among foreign legal and natural persons and other entities, legal and natural persons from Hong Kong, Macau and Taiwan, and Chinese citizens who are resident abroad.

The regulatory framework surrounding the issue of B-shares was simplified by the State Council in December 1995 by the introduction of *Provisions on Listing of Foreign Investment Shares Inside China by a Shareholding Company* on December 25, 1995 and the *Provisions on Listing of Foreign Investment Shares Inside China by a Shareholding Company: Implementing Rules* on May 3, 1996. These provisions clarified the procedures involved in applying for approval to issue B-shares. They also set out the application procedures and approval requirements for companies seeking to issue B-shares in order to increase their share capital. The provisions contain important matters such as information disclosure, and the trading of B-shares by stock brokers and agents.

The key contents of the provisions on B-Share listings include the following:

- The CSRC is responsible for the regulation and supervision of the issuing and trading of B-shares and related activities in relation to B-shares;
- In addition to the directors, supervisors and managers of a B-share company, other senior management personnel, including a shareholding company's chief financial officer, secretary and other executives specified in the company's articles of association, owe duties of good faith and diligence to the company;
- Chinese citizens residing outside mainland China may purchase B-shares;
- The derivative forms of B-shares, including warrants and depository receipts, may be circulated and traded outside China.

The B-Share listing implementing rules set out further detailed provisions governing the issue and trading of B-shares. They expand upon the application procedures set out in the B-share listing provisions to gain approval for the issuance of B-shares and list the documents to be submitted to the CSRC in support of an application. The key contents of the B-share listing implementing rules are as follows:

- An over-allotment option (commonly known as a "Greenshoe") may be granted by a Chinese shareholding company to the underwriters. With the approval of the CSRC, a company may set aside up to 15% of the total amount of the proposed B-share issue which constitutes the option. Such reserved shares will be considered as part of the issue;
- The distribution period for B-shares may not exceed 90 days;
- The governing law of the underwriting agreement must be Chinese laws;
- Within 15 days after the closing date of the initial share distribution, the lead underwriter must submit to the CSRC a distribution report and a list of the 10 largest holders of its B-shares, and details of their holdings. The distribution report must contain details of the distribution process;
- Domestic brokerage houses are required to report to the CSRC details of the number of B-shares held by them as a result of participating in the underwriting of a B-share issue;
- In addition to appointing Chinese accounting and auditing firms, B-share companies may also appoint foreign accounting and auditing firms that comply with the Chinese regulations to audit or review their financial statements;
- B-share companies must give prior notice to their auditors of dismissal or non-renewal of appointment and the auditors are entitled to present their views on any matter concerning the company's financial situation before the company's shareholders in the annual meeting. The *P.R.C. Securities Law* (Article 213) states that shares of Chinese companies designated for subscription and trading by foreign investors (B-shares an H-shares) are governed by measures separately formulated by the State Council.

B shares are subject to a strict annual quota system. Each year, the State Council decides the amount of B-share quota in U.S. dollars for that year. For example, the quota was US$1 billion in 1993. The B-share listing provisions did not stipulate listing venue. In practice, the Shanghai Securities Exchange attracted bigger and more reputable companies to list their shares.

2.4.1.3 *Overseas' Listing of Foreign Shares*

All foreign listings must be approved by the CSRC and the foreign stock exchange (and regulatory authority, such as the SEC in the case of a U.S. listing). Foreign shares (such as H-shares) must be issued in registered form and denominated in *renminbi* even though they are traded in foreign currencies. Depository receipts issued over H-shares are also treated as foreign shares.

Before a Chinese company can undertake an overseas listing at a desired overseas exchange by means of a direct listing, the overseas exchange has to sign a Memorandum of Understanding (MoU) with the CSRC. The MoU deals with cross-border regulatory issues such as supervision, disclosure requirements and securities enforcement.

In addition to complying with the requirements prescribed by the stock exchange on which the shares are listed, a company seeking to list overseas must also comply with the *Articles of Association of Companies Seeking a Listing Outside the P.R.C. Prerequisite Clauses* issued by the Securities Office of the Restructuring Commission and effective as of September 19, 1994, *P.R.C. Company Law*, and *P.R.C. Securities Law*. Key contents of the Prerequisite Clauses include the following:

- State enterprises to be restructured into shareholding companies may have fewer than five promoters;
- The period between an overseas listing and a subsequent issue may be less than 12 months;
- A 45-day written notice is required to convene shareholders' meetings;
- A quorum of 50% of voting shares is required to convene a general meeting and shareholders must give a 20-day notice of their intention to attend a general meeting;
- The articles of association are binding not only on a company and its shareholders, directors, supervisors and general managers, but also on other senior officers including the chief financial officer and secretary to the board;
- Shares issued outside China may be in the form of warrants or other derivatives subject to the approval of the State Council Securities Commission. An over-allotment option of up to 15% of the total issue may be granted by an issuer to the underwriters;
- Dividends on overseas foreign shares should be declared in *renminbi*

and paid in foreign currency;
- The register of holders of foreign invested shares listed outside China may be kept abroad and maintained by an agent.

Cooperation between Hong Kong and mainland stock market regulators started in 1993 when the issuance of H-shares on Hang Seng Stock Exchange was first proposed. By 1994 Hong Kong was able to update its legislation on listing requirements of PRC issuers. In November 1994, legislators added to Chapter 19 of Hong Kong Stock Exchange Ordinance a sub-clause known as Chapter 19a, which was solely devoted to PRC issuers. Once listed on the Hang Seng Stock Exchange, a PRC issuer is subject to all relevant Hong Kong laws and requirements, including the Hong Kong code on takeovers and mergers.

2.4.1.4 *Red Chip Listing*

Red-chip companies are those incorporated in Hong Kong and listed on the Hong Kong Stock Exchange but with controlling shareholders from mainland Chinese entities. In the early stage of development in Chinese stock markets, some companies had successfully bypassed the official listing channels and gotten listed either through a backdoor listing or by acquiring a Hong Kong "shell" company. After the CSRC was established, mainland and Hong Kong regulators started to cooperate and coordinate on red chip issues. Both sides agreed that before granting listing to a mainland Chinese company, each side would inform the other of the nature of the listing, company type and other related information. Nowadays red chip companies are generally diversified conglomerates which have grown rapidly by the injection of assets from their parent companies in mainland China. Red-chip companies include China Telecom, Beijing Enterprises Holdings, China Everbright, Shanghai Industrial Holdings, China Resources Enterprises and the "window-companies" or "International Trust and Investment Corporations (ITICs)" of provincial governments.

Until very recently, red-chip companies did not, strictly speaking, fall within the supervision of mainland Chinese authorities. Therefore, they were able to conduct restructuring and raise funds from overseas for new investments easily. In June 1997, the CSRC in conjunction with the State Council introduced the *Notice on Further Strengthening the Administration of the Listing and Issuing of Shares Overseas* (also called the "Red Chip Notice"). The purpose of the Red Chip Notice was to protect domestic assets from being channeled overseas and from being sold off indirectly to overseas investors at a discount. This is accomplished by purporting to more stringent requirements for reporting to, and obtaining approval from, Chinese authorities. The Red Chip Notice targets both listed and unlisted companies registered outside mainland China.

The main content of the Red Chip Notice is as follows:

- If a foreign listed company is registered and controlled by Chinese shareholders and is undertaking a spin-off listing or additional issue of shares, it is subject to the supervision of the CSRC and the majority shareholder must report to the CSRC.
- Domestic shareholders that have held foreign and domestic assets for three years or more who seek to inject their assets to a red chip company may do so provided that prior consent is obtained from the local provincial government or relevant department of the State Council. Domestic assets held for less than three years may not be used in connection with foreign share issues unless there are special circumstances that the CSRC deems to be appropriate.
- Consent on restructuring and subsequent equity offerings must be obtained from the provincial government or relevant State Council department and a report must be made to the CSRC for examination and final approval.
- Acquisition, share swap or other methods of injecting assets into a foreign Chinese holding company require similar relevant consent from the CSRC.[7]

2.4.2 *Procedures for Stock Listing*

Although the capital markets in China has developed rapidly over the past seven years, the central government still commands considerable authority over many structural aspects of market operations. A key element of this authority is the listing requirements and procedures which the CSRC controls. Together with the State Planning Commission, the State Council, the State Commission for Restructuring the Economy, and the Ministry of Finance, the CSRC sets an annual quota for the total value of shares to be brought to market. Once the quota has been established, a share of the

[7]The CSRC has made it clear publicly that its considers asset injections as an unauthorized sale of state assets, and approvals will only be issued in special cases.

total allowance is allocated to each province, which then make their own selections among local companies who have applied for stock issues. The decision of the provincial authorities rests mainly on two factors: the size of the share-capital quota allocated to them and whether or not the company is in a "key industry" which the government has chosen to promote. Having been selected, the selected enterprises are recommended to the CSRC which will then review the selections made by individual provinces for final approval.

This heavily-regulated method of selecting firms that go public has been criticized by many experts as not being in the best interest of the public investors. Critics point out that SOEs with capable management and fundamentally sound balance sheets might be passed over in favor of other less commercially viable firms which happen to be in the government's latest key industry category. Although companies to be listed are required to have earned annual profits of 10% per year for the past three years prior to their initial public offerings and are supposedly the most promising SOEs, those receive permission to issue shares are actually part of the slowest-growing sector of the economy–a sector which accounts for only about 30% of the country's industrial output. Nevertheless, the CSRC has found its control over the supply of shares useful in influencing market conditions and investor sentiment. For example, when key market indices have gone up sharply in June 1996, authorities began voicing their concern over the formation of a bubble in stock valuations. When their warnings did not serve to slow the market's rise towards new highs, the CSRC announced it would double the issue volume in 1997, allowing 30 billion *renminbi* (US$3.6 billion) worth of A and B-shares to be placed. By increasing the supply of stock available for purchase, the CSRC hoped to soak up the speculative demand rampaging in the market, thereby promoting a more stable investing environment.

There are two steps involved in selecting an issuer for A shares. The first stage involves provision of share issue quotas by the CSRC to each provincial government, autonomous zone, municipality directly controlled by the central government, and municipality with a separate economic plan. Factors taken into consideration when allocating share issue quotas include (1) the development of the economy of a particular province or a specific industry, which is typically a result of the macroeconomic conditions at that time; (2) applications by prospective A-share issuers to the local municipal government or the relevant industrial department of the State Council; (3)

recommendation by local municipal government or the relevant industrial department of the State Council to the CSRC; (4) preliminary examination by the relevant departments of the CSRC; (5) opinion of the relevant ministry which governs the industry in which the prospective A-share issuer has made the petition; and (6) issues exceeding US$30 million must be approved directly by the State Council.

The second stage involves gaining initial approval from the relevant local government or State Council ministry, submission of formal application materials to the CSRC, review and approval by the issuing department of the CSRC, and examination by the issuing examination committee of the CSRC. Once the issuing examination committee approves the A-share issue, the CSRC decides the specific timing of the IPOs and will issue a formal approval certificate.

The selection and approval process for B-share issuers is pretty much the same as that for A-shares. The selection process involves recommendation by the local municipal government or relevant industrial department of the State Council and pre-selection by the CSRC. The approval process involves initial examination by local municipal government or the relevant industrial department of the State Council, submission of application materials to the international business department of the CSRC, examination and approval by the international business department of the CSRC, and examination by the issuing examination committee of the CSRC.

All foreign listings must be approved by the CSRC and the foreign stock exchanges on which listings are sought before any listing application is made. In the past, Chinese companies have been approved by the CSRC in batches. The latest (the 5th) batch of Chinese companies when this book is written included Wenzhou Infrastructure, Ningbo Port, Zhejiang Tourism, Hebei Expressway, Shandong Expressway, Guangdong Agriculture, Heilongjiang Agriculture, and Beijing Capital Airport.

In addition to the CSRC approval, any Chinese company seeking to list its shares on an overseas stock exchange may have to receive approvals from the State Council, the State Assets Bureau, the Ministry of State Land and Resources, the State Development and Planning Commission, the State Economic and Trade Commission, the prospective issuer's supervising ministry, and the overseas stock exchange on which the securities will be listed. Typically the issuers' advisors will undertake the preparation work for the public offering before all of the aforementioned approvals have been issued.

A Chinese company seeking to issue and list foreign investment shares outside China must complete a three stage procedure. The first stage involves making an application to the local municipal government or the ministry or department-in-charge of the relevant industry, which will review the application and if the company is deemed appropriate, its application will be sent to the CSRC. The second stage will involve a selection process conducted by the CSRC in consultation with the relevant local municipal governments or ministry or department-in-charge. A short list of successful companies will be notified and then released to the public. The final stage comprises the examination and approval by the CSRC during which the CSRC will review prescribed documents in accordance with applicable securities laws and regulations.

2.5 Market Microstructure

2.5.1 *Registration of Stock Dealers*

One of the most successful pieces of reform recently enacted by the State Council included regulations to establish standards within the brokerage industry. In addition to formally prohibiting insider trading and requiring that all companies publicly disclose news which could affect share prices, the *Management Regulations for Securities Industry* imposed the following provisions on all securities firms dealing with A-shares trading:

- 5% of all profits must be kept as reserves or margins.
- Adequate risk-monitoring systems must be developed.
- No more than 80% of a firm's assets can be held in stocks.
- Two-thirds of a securities firm's managers must be certified by the CSRC.
- No securities firm can buy more than 20% of the outstanding float of a listed company during any given trading day.

Regulations for securities firms doing business in B-shares and H-shares have also been issued recently. An important part of the regulation is to require companies that have already listed their B-shares to undergo an annual financial auditing based on International Accounting Standards (IAS). Under these regulations, both foreign and domestic brokerage firms must meet the following criteria to do business in China:

- Stockbrokers must have assets of at least 50 million *renminbi* (or U.S. \$6.0 million).
- They must have suitable trading sites and an extensive network of sales and research staff.
- Overseas brokers must be licensed by the CSRC every two years.
- Domestic brokers must be authorized by the State Administration of Foreign Exchange (SAFE) to do business involving foreign currency transactions.

In addition to regulating the market by imposing rules on brokerage houses, securities authorities have recently launched a crack-down on illegal practices by investors, particularly at the Shenzhen exchange. The CSRC now officially prohibits the ownership of B-shares by P.R.C. citizens, although many continue to mask such purchases by routing them through a series of accounts at different banks. In a further attempt to prevent the rampant speculation in A-share markets, the PBOC has prohibited all forms of margin trading.[8]

2.5.2 *General Rules for Trading*

Securities that have been approved for listing and trading must be quoted and traded on stock exchanges, and trading must be conducted by a public, centralized post at competing prices. Securities firms cannot provide loans or lend securities to their customers. Officers and employees of stock exchanges, securities firms, securities registration and clearing companies, and securities regulatory authorities may not engage in stock trading, whether directly or indirectly.[9] Similarly, professionals who issue documents in connection with a share issue (e.g., audit reports, legal opinions, and so forth) may not purchase or sell shares during and six months after the offering period.

A company applying to list its shares must first be approved by the CSRC, and the CSRC may authorize the stock exchanges to verify and

[8]Under the current P.R.C. law, margin trading is a criminal offense punishable as embezzlement. Although the Chinese securities industry is not really governed by criminal law at present, this ruling is particularly harsh as the embezzlement of more than 20,000 *renminbi* (US\$2,400) carries the death penalty.

[9]The *P.R.C. Securities Law may* appear draconian to have imposed such a restriction, but in fact similar regulations had appeared in various regulations enacted in 1993.

approve applications for listing of shares in accordance with statutory conditions and procedures. The stock exchanges will verify and decide on applications and will, within six months after the applications have been received, arrange for the shares in successful applications to be listed. The government may encourage new listings of qualified enterprises in key industrial sectors it deems appropriate. If a listed company ceases to meet the conditions for listing prescribed in the *P.R.C. Company Law*, the listing of its shares will be suspended or terminated. Furthermore, the CSRC may authorize the stock exchanges to suspend or terminate listings in accordance with the law.

After a company is listed in a stock exchange, it is required to prepare and announce interim reports and annual reports. If a major event not known to investors has occurred that may have serious impact on the price of shares of a listed company, the listed company must immediately submit a report to the CSRC and the relevant stock exchange detailing the occurrence of the event. Examples of major events include:

- a major change in the companys business policies or scope of business;
- a decision by the company on a major investment or asset purchase; or
- conclusion of a material contract that may have a major effect on the companys assets, liabilities, rights, interests or business results.

There is an exception under which a listed company having sufficient reason to believe that the disclosure may harm its interests and that non-disclosure will not lead to major fluctuations in the share price, is not required to make disclosure subject to the consent of the relevant stock exchange.

The *P.R.C. Securities Law* strictly prohibits people with knowledge of inside information on securities trading from carrying out securities transactions by making use of that information.[10] No person with knowledge of inside information on securities trading, and no person who has illegally

[10]The term "inside information" means information, not known to the public, that relates to the companys business or financial affairs or that may have a major effect on the price of the companys securities. The description "people with knowledge of inside information on securities trading" refers to: (1) directors, supervisors, managers, deputy managers and other senior management personnel of a listed company; (2) shareholders holding 5% or more of the shares in a company; (3) people who are able to obtain company information concerning the trading of its securities by virtue of their

obtained inside information, can purchase or sell securities of the relevant company, divulge such information or counsel another person to purchase or sell such securities.

Under the present *Securities Law*, the actual knowledge of inside information is irrelevant in determining whether a person is a "person with knowledge of inside information". In other words, a person is deemed a "person with knowledge of inside information" by virtue of the positions and offices the person holds, and the duties and functions the person performs, in listed companies, professional intermediary firms and securities regulatory authorities. However, this interpretation of the definition creates an anomalous result when applied to the article of the *Securities Law* that imposes an absolute prohibition on sale and purchase of securities by a "person with knowledge of inside information". Thus, a person who is able to obtain company information concerning the trading of its securities by virtue of the position held in the company but who has not actually obtained such information is prohibited to purchase or sell securities of the company. It is doubtful whether this anomalous result is indeed intended by the legislators.[11]

Apart from the prohibition on insider dealings, the *P.R.C. Securities Law* also prohibits market manipulation activities, the making of false statements in the trading of securities, and activities amounting to deception of clients. Further, the new law prohibits state-owned and state-controlled enterprises from engaging in share speculation.

Because the SHSE and SZSE are located in the same time zone, trading takes place in more or less the same hours, with only little differences in each other's opening, mid-session and closing times. The official trading hours of the SHSE are from 9:30 AM to 11:30 AM and 13:00 PM to 15:00 PM for stock trading; 10:15 AM to 11:45 AM and 13:00 PM to 15:30 PM

positions in the company; (4) personnel of the CSRC and other regulatory bodies; and (5) relevant personnel of professional intermediary firms and securities registration and clearing institutions who participate in or oversee securities trading.

[11] At present, insider dealing activities are regulated by the *Provisional Measures on the Prohibition of Deceptive Securities Dealing Activities* (the *Deceptive Dealing Measures*) of 1993. All firms and individuals are prohibited from engaging in the issue and trading of securities by making use of inside information with a view to making profits or avoiding losses. Actual knowledge and use of inside information must be present for an act of insider dealing to occur. The *Deceptive Dealing Measures* does not contain an absolute prohibition on sale and purchase of securities in terms as broadly defined as those of the*P.R.C. Securities Law*.

for treasury bond; and 13:00 PM to 15:30 PM for treasury bond futures. Trading holidays include January 1, the New Year's Day; Chinese lunar New Year's week-long holidays; May 1, the International Labor Day; and October 1-2, the National Day holidays. The official trading hours of the SZSE are from 9:30 AM to 11:30 AM and 13:00 PM to 15:00 PM. The SZSE has the same holiday schedule as the SHSE.

The trading cost is approximately 1.05% of the total value of the transaction on the SHSE. This includes a brokerage fee of 0.7% of the gross consideration (with a minimum trading fee of *renminbi* 5), a transfer fee of 0.1% of face value (minimum US$1), stamp duty of 0.3% of the gross consideration, and a clearing fee of US$4 per execution for individuals and corporations (US$8 for custodians). There is no registration fee. The trading cost is 1.00% of the total value of the transaction on the SZSE, a bit less than the SHSE.

According to China's securities regulations, the listed securities in the SHSE and SZSE must be traded through the centralized competitive method. The securities exchanges are entitled to formulate trading rules which become effective after approved by the State Council's. Under these rules, investors who want to participate in the centralized competitive trading must follow the procedure of opening accounts, entrustment, conclusions, clearing and delivery, and transfer of accounts.[12]

To trade in the SHSE and SZSE one must open separate securities and cash accounts. At the end of a trade, adjustments on the amount of securities and cash will be made in those accounts. Investors must apply for accounts directly through the registration department of the securities exchanges or their securities dealers. However, both domestic and foreign investors may entrust domestic and foreign securities dealers or agencies to open an account of *renminbi* special share. The capital account is issued for deposit of cash, clearing and receiving dividend. It must be opened by the investors at the selected securities dealer's business place. The cash in the account is deposited in a bank by the dealers as current deposit, and the interests will be automatically put in the account. Investors have a magnetic card and a deposit card for their securities account and cash

[12]The method of non-centralized competitive trading refers to the process under which investors trade their securities through buying and selling, bid or auction in the recognized markets outside the exchanges. Non-centralized competitive trading markets include securities dealer's business counters, local securities exchange centre and securities offering price system.

account.

In buying and selling securities, the commission principal (investor) shall fill in the commission sheet. The commission sheet is printed by the dealers according to the requirements set forth by the exchanges. The commission sheet shall list the name of the commission principal, shareholder's code number, the date and time of commission, the kind of securities, the volume and face price, the commission price, effective date, etc.. The commission may be made through written form, by telephone, fax, cable, etc.. In Shanghai and Shenzhen, securities dealers are prohibited from accepting the full commission which delegates the dealers with the power to decide the kind, volume and price of the traded securities. Securities dealers are also prohibited from accepting the commission of trust trading.

Although both the SHSE and SZSE use computer systems to reach conclusion through centralized competitive price, they have some differences carrying out orders. On the SHSE, the representatives of the dealers, who sit in the exchange hall, are the actual operators who make the conclusion through the computer system. On the SZSE, despite that there are representatives of the dealers who sit in the exchange, the actual operators are the dealers themselves who may enter the orders from their business place outside the exchange through the computer system. The centralized competitive price method adopts the principle of price priority and time priority.

After conclusion, the buyer and seller shall pay cash and securities through their dealers. This process includes two steps: In the first step, the volume and value of the same stock will be calculated through an affiliated or independent clearing house. The dealers will only pay the net different value. In the second step, stocks are delivered and payments are cleared between investors and their dealers. Because of the centralized preservation and non-paper trade adopted by the SHSE and SZSE, the transfer of accounts on the underlying securities is made through keeping changes in accounts during the day and completing the transfer automatically via the computer system at the end of the trading day. In August 1995, the SZSE and the Securities Registration Corporation have adopted a unified securities account card which preserved transfer, distribution and subscription of shares, unified share statements, and reduced transaction costs.[13]

[13]On the SHSE and SZSE, B-shares are traded in paperless form using an automatic transfer and computerized system. Buy/sell orders are matched automatically by

2.5.3 *Takeover of Listed Companies*

The *P.R.C. Securities Law* provides that listed companies may be taken over by means of takeover by offer or takeover by agreement.

When an investor has acquired, through securities trading at a stock exchange, five percent of the issued shares of a listed company, the investor must, within three days after the five percent threshold shareholding is reached, submit a written report to the CSRC and the stock exchange, notify the listed company, and make a public announcement. During the initial three-day period, the investor may not purchase or sell shares of the listed company being acquired. Thereafter, this reporting obligation is triggered every time the shareholding of the investor increases or decreases by an amount equivalent to five percent of the issued shares of the listed company.

After the investor has acquired, through securities trading at a stock exchange, thirty percent of the issued shares of a listed company, and if the investor continues to acquire shares of that company, the investor must make a takeover offer to all the shareholders of the listed company, unless the CSRC grants an exemption. The offer period must last for at least thirty days but not more than sixty days. During the offer period the offer must remain irrevocable.

If upon expiration of the offer period the number of shares in the target company that has been acquired by an investor exceeds seventy-five percent of the total shares outstanding of the company, the listing of the target company must be terminated. If this number has exceeded ninety percent of the total shares outstanding of the target company, the shareholders who have not yet accepted the offer will have the right to sell their shares to the investor on the same terms as those of the offer and the investor must take up those shares.

Where a takeover involves shares held by state-controlled enterprises, approval must be obtained from the relevant authority in charge. In the case of takeover by agreement, the investor may acquire shares from shareholders of the target company by entering into an agreement with them. The investor must, within three days after the agreement is reached, submit

computer, based on price priority followed by time priority, and confirmation is relayed to investors on the same day. Foreign brokers with special exchange seats are permitted to execute their orders directly, without passing through local brokers as they used to before 1993.

a written report on the agreement to the CSRC and the relevant stock exchange, and make a public announcement. The takeover agreement cannot be completed until the announcement has been made.

It is important to realize that determining the extent of application of the "takeover by agreement" option under the current *Securities Law* is difficult and involves at least the following problems. The *Securities Law* seems to suggest that the initial thirty percent stake of an investor in a target company must be built up by buying shares incrementally at the relevant stock exchange. This interpretation of the law is consistent with the more fundamental requirement that securities that have been approved for listing and trading must be quoted and traded on stock exchanges. This begs the question: Does the "takeover by agreement" option override this requirement and make it possible for shares of a target company normally required to be traded on a stock exchange to be acquired by agreement by an investor intending to take over the company? If the answer is no, does it then mean that the option extends only to the acquisition of domestic shares that are not required to be publicly traded, e.g. the Chinese legal person shares? If indeed the application of the option is restricted to non-publicly traded shares, is the option available from the very beginning when the investor starts to build up its stake, or is it available only after the investor has acquired at least a thirty percent shareholding by buying shares at the relevant stock exchange and has then obtained from the CSRC an exemption from the obligation to make a general takeover offer? These questions await to be resolved in the *Securities Law*.

With regard to the takeover of a company that has, in addition to domestic shares, issued B-shares or H-shares, the *Securities Law* does not provide an explanation on how enforce the takeover provisions. Because of ownership restrictions, an investor cannot buy and hold both domestic shares and B- or H-shares simultaneously, the specific requirement on an investor to make a takeover offer to acquire all the shares in the largest company is simply not feasible. A similar problem exists with regard to the state-owned shares of a target company as those shares cannot be purchased by private investors. The detailed *Implementing Securities Regulations* to be formulated under the *P.R.C. Securities Law* will need to address these problems.

2.5.4 *Settlement, Clearing and Payment System*

The securities exchanges and trading centers do not utilize a system of specialists as is done on the New York and American Stock Exchanges. Rather, orders are transmitted through a broker to a clerk on the exchange floor. The clerk then inputs the order into a central computer which matches buy and sell orders. Customer accounts are held by the stock exchange, rather than brokerage house. While the brokerage house opens the account and executes order for customers, the exchange physically maintains the account and ensure settlement and clearing of accounts.[14]

Seeking to comply with the Group of Thirty (G30) Standards, Hong Kong Securities Clearing Company Limited now operates the Central Clearing and Settlement System (CCASS) as the central depository body for the settlement of trading. The CCASS provides T+1 matching for brokers who trade and requires T+2 affirmation of settlements by custodian banks. In the SHSE, settlement time for A shares is now three days (T+3) but for B shares remains T+1. Turnaround trading time for A-shares on the SHSE is the same day. The SHSE adopts only the qualified DVP/RVP (delivery versus payment/receipt versus payment) model. It uses a central depository system through a company called the Shanghai Securities Central Clearing and Registration Corporation (SSCCRC), which also serves as a clearing house. However, there is so far no payment in same-day funds. The SHSE is now updating its payment system to keep its technological superiority. The new system, known as the central Real Time Gross Settlement payment system (RTGS), will promise more risk reduction possibilities for the clearing houses, such as payment clearing facilities through RTGS system. The SHSE promises to be more technically capable in securities trading in the future.

The SZSE is more or less in line with its big brother exchange in Shanghai. The clearing and depository house is called the Shenzhen Securities Central Clearing Company Ltd.(SSCC). The settlement period is T+3 for both A- and B-shares. The securities settlement and income, paid in Hong Kong dollars, can be freely repatriated. Short-selling and over-the-counter

[14]This is no margin trading or short selling in Chinese securities markets. It normally takes 5,000 *renminbi* to open an account. Large investors, with accounts generally over 500,000 *renminbi*, have greater access to information available through the brokerage houses and have greater ability to execute trades. Small investors, who constitute the bulk of the market in China, generally trade in one hundred and two hundred share lots.

trading are illegal. Market entry requires obtaining a unique foreign investor code prior to trading.

2.5.5 *Accounting System*

China employed an accounting system established in the centrally planned economy for more than 40 years. This old accounting system adopted different accounting rules for different types of ownership (state-owned, collectively-owned and privately owned) since the 1950s. There was no law on accounting rules until 1985 when the National Congress passed its first *Accounting Law*, which unified different accounting practices.[15] Since then, several major modifications have been updated to adapt to the market-based economy in the country but there are still a number of significant differences with the standard international accounting practice.

Because securities markets had developed rapidly from the beginning of the 1990s, especially from 1992 when the government decided to establish the socialist market economy and transform the SOEs. The influence of stock markets on Chinese accounting practices was manifested by changes in accounting objectives stated by the Ministry of Finance. More and more people from both the accounting profession and outside support the idea of providing accounting information to investors, creditors and the public. In order to provide better information about profitability, financial performance and financial stability of listed companies, the SHSE transformed the 1992 annual financial reports of the earliest 8 listed companies into reports in accordance with international reporting standards. The financial reports of these 8 listed companies were originally produced from different Chinese accounting regulations, because the companies belonged to different industries. This provided practical experience for the standard financial reporting that took place later in 1993. At the same time, China issued the first B-share stock on the SHSE in 1992 and the first H-share stock in the Hong Kong Security Exchange in 1993. Companies which issued B- and H-shares were required to publish accounting reports which were not only

[15]For instance, the *Accounting Law* unified three methods of book-keeping. The debit/credit system was typically used in state owned industrial enterprises, joint ventures and international trade companies. During the Cultural Revolution this system had often been replaced by the increase/ decrease method and this continued to be used by many commercial enterprises. Many banks, some collective enterprises and budgetary government units used the receipt/payment method.

in accordance with Chinese accounting rules, but also in accordance with international accounting standards. This gave Chinese accountants more opportunity to exchange ideas with accountants from outside the country. Against this background, the Ministry of Finance issued *An Accounting Regulation for the Experimental Listed Company* in July 1992. The accountants in listed companies were required to follow international accounting practice and to use the double-entry method in book-keeping. The implied premises and principles in the named regulation provided a basis for the *Basic Accounting Standards for Enterprise* issued in November 1992 followed by 13 new accounting regulations for different industries. This was a remarkable change to unify accounting systems used by different industries and to move financial accounting forward in line with international accounting practice.[16]

[16]The *Basic Accounting Standards* is the first accounting standard in Chinese accounting history. It consists of 10 chapters: general standards; general principles; assets; liabilities; owners equity; revenues; expenses; profit; financial reports and appendix. The basic accounting standards have simplified over 40 old regulations for different ownership and different industries. Particular aspects of the new accounting system include: (1) The government sets the basic and special accounting standards, then sets the practical accounting regulations on the basis of the standards. (2) Accounting entity, going concern, periodicity, and monetary cost measurement are the underlying accounting premises (concepts) in the basic accounting standards. (3) A series of general accounting principles have been established in the standards. These are objectivity, relevance, comparability, consistency, timeliness, clarity, materialism, accrual, matching, prudence, historical cost and differentiation of revenue and capital expenditure. These 12 principles are used as the criteria for guaranteeing the quality of accounting information and provide the means for determining and measuring economic transactions. (4) The terms: assets, liabilities, owners equities, revenues, expenses, and profits are defined as accounting elements. Consequently, the old accounting equation has been replaced by the new accounting equation: assets = liabilities + owners equities. The new accounting system is able to provide more relevant information about enterprises proprietorship, solvency, financial adaptability and profitability. (5) The formats and components of financial statements have been standardized. The new external financial reporting system includes the balance sheet, the income statement and the statement of financial position. Therefore, the financial reports are able to provide more relevant, comparable, understandable and complete financial information to the readers. (6) The capital maintenance principle has been stressed to protect the investors equity. Capital accounts including issued capital stock have been set up to record and protect investors equity. Realized gains or losses on assets and depreciation of long-term fixed assets are included in the profit and loss account but these no longer increase or reduce investment (different kinds of funds provided by the government under the planned economy) as before. This makes property rights and investors equity clear in the accounts. (7) The total cost method has been changed into the manufacturing costing method in accordance with internationally applied costing

China's accounting reforms have been going deeper since 1993 through the efforts of the Ministry of Finance and accounting professionals. The new accounting standards are being improved and developed into a fully-fledged accounting system that meets the increasing needs of the socialist market economy. The transformation of SOEs and the development of securities markets have further influenced the accounting reform. Since 1992, more and more SOEs have been transformed into joint-stock companies and listed on the stock market. Many practical accounting issues such as how to account for mergers and reorganization, valuing SOEs, goodwill and other intangible assets have arisen and required research. On the other hand, the increase in public stock holders and the growth of the stock market require the listed companies to provide true, fair and reliable accounting information to the users of financial reports. Thus the state Security Supervision and Administration Commission issued the *Detailed Practical Rules and Regulations of Disclosing Information for Listed Company* in June 1993 and the *Format and Content of Annual Reports and Mid-term Reports* in 1994. These regulations further standardized accounting practices and improved the quality of financial information.

By the end of 1998, the Ministry of Finance had issued 8 specific accounting standards, including standards for cash flow statement, enterprise investment, rearrangement of liabilities, revenues, construction contracts, post-balance sheet transactions, income statement, and accounting policy, accounting estimation and correction of accounting errors. The *Accounting Standards for Enterprises: Cash Flow Statement* has been put into practice in the listed companies from the accounting year of 1998 and the others were implemented in listed companies from January 1, 1999. All these have firmly proved the determination of accounting reform by the government. Along with the diversity of investors and the increase in the number of shareholders, transparent, open, complete and comparative accounting information together with external auditing have become more and more important.

Accounting reform and improvements in accounting information have provided favorable conditions for economic transformation and development of the capital market in China. Disclosing accounting information on

practice. (8) The three methods of book-keeping have been unified as the international double-entry method. (9) Enterprises have been allowed to use the prudence principle. This permits enterprises to use accounts receivable and the last-in-first-out method in inventory pricing.

stock market listed companies has become an important issue because of its significant influence on the security market. There is strong evidence that disclosed accounting profits have conveyed information to the market with subsequent effects, which indicates a kind of rational investment power based on the nature of capital in the Chinese securities markets.

2.5.6 *Taxes and Fees*

The main goals of the financial reform include expanding the share of central government's fiscal income, transforming state specialized banks into profit-making and risk-taking institutions, and strengthening the role of the central bank in issuing money, managing basic monetary instruments, and regulating and controlling total credits and interest rates. The new tax reform system that became effective in 1994 aimed at unifying the tax code, simplifying the tax system and its administration, and strengthening the overall control capability of central Government by enlarging the central-local tax revenue ratio of 45:55 in 1992 to 60:40, a pattern more in line with that in other countries.[17]

The old tax (consolidated industrial and commercial tax) was replaced by a new value-added tax at 17 percent standard rate supplemented by a consumption tax (mainly for luxury goods) and a business tax (mainly for the service sector). A single personal income tax was also introduced. The tax rate for all enterprises was equalized at 33 percent with some special treatment allowed–27 and 18 percent respectively for the first two years for high-tech companies. Along with tax reforms there were also reforms in accounting and auditing systems as mentioned above.

There are two types of securities taxes for Chinese investors: the withholding tax on dividends and the capital gains tax on securities traded. Withholding tax is imposed on interest, rent, royalties and capital gains received by non-residents. The statutory rate of withholding tax is 20%.

[17]China has implemented a new tax law and regulation system from January 1, 1994. The new tax law has made big changes in major taxes such as value-added-tax and income tax. The related accounting regulations on purchase costs, revenue recording, accounting for tax payable, income tax accounting and the contents of the income statement were adjusted in response to the new tax law system. Accounting practice adapts to tax changes but accounting keeps its objective as providing information to investors, creditors and the public rather than serving the government only. The accounting standards and regulations have maintained some independence from the tax law system, though accounting practice submitted to taxation in the past decades.

It is reduced to 10% for income derived from specially designated zones in China. It could also be reduced under double tax treaties. Dividends from a foreign investment enterprise to a foreign shareholder are exempt from tax. In Hong Kong, dividends are treated as having been paid out of taxed profits and are thus not subject to further taxation. In particular, there are no Hong Kong taxes imposed on foreign shareholders receiving Hong Kong dividends, and there are no withholding taxes on dividends paid by Hong Kong companies.

In Shanghai and Shenzhen, buyers and sellers are subject to as much as 0.3% securities trading tax based on the value of trade. The securities trading tax must be paid or deducted by the clearing and settlement firm. In addition to securities trading tax, individuals have to pay 20% income tax for securities dividend they received according to the *Individual Income Tax Law* of the P.R.C.. Enterprises have to pay additional income tax for the dividend they receive according to the *Income Tax Law of the P.R.C. Concerning Enterprises with Foreign Investment and Foreign Enterprises*, and to the *Enterprises Income Tax Provisions.* However, there is no capital income tax in Shanghai and Shenzhen.

Securities trading fees are the fees the trade participants shall pay in accordance with securities regulations and rules made by the exchanges. There are two types of securities trading fees: listing fees and service fees. Listing fees include an initial listing fee payable in sum and a monthly fee. Both types of fees are paid by the issuer to the exchanges. According to the rule of the SHSE, 0.03% and 0.1% of the issued value is charged for A- and B-share listings, respectively. Initial listing fees must be paid no later than 3 days before listing. The monthly fee is 0.001% of the issued value for A- and B-shares, and must be paid from the next month of the listing day until the monthly listing is terminated.

Service fees are paid by investors and consist primarily the commission paid to dealers. In the SHSE, the standard commission is 0.4% and 0.6% of the value of trade with a minimum of 10 *renminbi* and 20 U.S. dollars for A- and B-shares, respectively. The commission may be reduced for B-share transactions if the trading volume is large. In the SZSE, both the buyer and the seller must pay 0.35% of the value of trade to their dealers as the commission with a minimum of 5 *renminbi* for A-shares. The commission is 0.6% of the value of trade with no minimum service fee for B-shares. There is no commission if the stocks are not trade according to the buyers' or sellers' orders.[18]

In addition, member dealers of an exchange have to pay an entry-place fee which includes the fees paid by both dealers to the exchange according to a certain rate after the conclusion of the trading. The fee is generally 0.1% of the value of trade for A- and B-shares plus an account transfer fee in the SZSE. The fee is 0.03% of the value of trade in the SHSE.

Appendix B summarizes different types of taxes in China.

2.5.7 *Suspension and Termination of Listed Companies*

After a stock is listed, it is supervised by the securities organs in charge and the exchange. When a listed company fails to meet the listing requirement because of the change of social economic conditions or its own business difficulty, its qualification for listing will be cancelled and all future trades will be terminated. According to Article 157 of the *P.R.C. Company Law*, the events which cause suspension of a listed stock include:

(1) a company's total capital and share distribution has been changed to an extent below the standard of listing requirement;
(2) a company fails to disclose its financial situation or produces a false accounting statement;
(3) a company is involved in some serious illegal activity;
(4) a company has made continuous losses for the previous three years.

Article 158 of the *Company Law* stipulates that when either condition (2) or (3) occurs and the investigation proves, the circumstances are especially serious. When either condition (1) or (4) lasts longer than the required period of time, the listed stocks shall be terminated.

In addition to the above regulations, the SHSE and SZSE require that if a listed company plans to reorganize, to replace old stocks with new ones, to provide additional shares for raising more capital, or to distribute special share dividends, it must inform the exchange for suspension of the listed stocks. Suspension of a listed stock cannot exceed a certain period

[18]Securities trading fees cover the fees paid by the listed companies, dealers and investors. In the past, securities trading fees and service fees charged by the SZSE were higher than those by the SHSE. But since October 4, 1995, the fees have been reduced by approximately 60% on the SZSE. In fact, the service fees charged by the SZSE is now 12.5% lower than that by the SHSE. Moreover, the SZSE has adopted a number of measures to reduce the securities fees for B-share transactions.

of time.[19] When the aforementioned activities have been concluded, the listing for the company must be renewed.

Termination of a listed stock happens when the listed stock fails to meet the minimum listing requirement or when suspension time is due but the causes of suspension have not disappeared. Termination of a company is determined and approved by the relevant securities authorities. The following events may cause suspension and termination of a listed stock:

- failure to meet the minimum requirement to maintain its listing, e.g., grossly violating the share distribution procedures, keeping very little capital, or having a very small trading volume in the listed exchange;
- the listed company is involved in some illegal activity;
- a listed company has serious business problem, e.g., a listed company incurs continuous losses and is faced with bankruptcy because of high financial distress or a listed company is declared bankrupted by the court which leads to the termination of the listed stock;
- other illegal activities such as failure to pay the listing fee.

The Shanghai and Shenzhen Exchanges are entitled to make decision of suspension and termination, and the decisions shall be filed or approved by the securities organ in charge. Since the *Company Law* became effective in 1994, suspension and termination of a listed stock based on legal events shall be made by the securities organ in charge, and be enforced by the stock exchanges. Suspension and termination of the listed stocks based on the situation under which the companies are dismissed, ordered to close, or declared bankrupt shall be decided by the security organ in charge. After termination of a listed stock, the stock may still be traded at a non-concentrated competitive trading place authorized by the law.

[19] According to the rules and regulations of the SHSE, the suspension for a listed company cannot exceed nine months.

Chapter 3

Risk, Return and Regulation in Chinese Stock Markets

3.1 Introduction

In the realm of financial studies, the concept of risk and return as well as the relationship between risk and return is of primary interest. When studying financial markets, the notion of risk and volatility are synonymous. Risk (volatility) is the key parameter of interest in studying option pricing, risk management, portfolio management, the Capital Asset Pricing Model (CAPM), and the Arbitrage Pricing Model (APT). Empirically, it has been observed that the level of risk of a financial asset changes over time. In this chapter, we follow Su and Fleisher (1998a, 1999b) in examining the risk and return behavior in Chinese stock markets. We will pay particular attention on how changes in government regulations affect stock-market volatility.

Understanding stock-market risk and return behavior is very important, because in a market consisting of risk-averse investors, greater volatility (risk) would lead investors to demand a higher risk premium, creating higher cost of capital, which impedes investment and slows economic development. We investigate the following questions:

(1) What characterize the risk and return behavior in Chinese stock markets?
(2) How well do Chinese stock markets function relative to other developed and emerging markets?
(3) Can we predict stock-market returns using local and global information variables?
(4) What are some important causes of the high stock-market return volatility?

(5) Are there causality relationship and volatility spill-over effects between Chinese stock markets and stock market of similar economic and geographical conditions?

In Section 3.2, we lay out the basic pattern of returns and volatility in Chinese stock markets. In Section 3.3, we explore whether the distribution of stock returns is identical for all days of the week. In Section 3.4, we investigate the market efficiency hypothesis using variance ratio tests and residual-based cointegration tests. In Section 3.5, we establish an empirical model that captures the effects of local and global information variables on the conditional mean of weekly stock-market returns. We characterize the conditional variance of returns using three alternative formulations of the error-generating process. In Section 3.6, we select the best formulation of the empirical model and report the econometric results. We then apply the best-fitted model to examine the effect of exogenous government policy variables on stock-market return volatility in Section 3.7. In Section 3.8, we examine volatility asymmetry and how the volatility of Chinese stock markets is related to Hong Kong market. We conclude the chapter with a summary of findings in Section 3.9.

3.2 Stock-Market Return and Volatility Pattern

As we have mentioned earlier, there are two categories of shares traded in the stock markets in mainland China: A-shares are available only for Chinese citizens and B-shares can be purchased only by foreign investors. Both A- and B-shares are traded in the two official exchanges in China, Shanghai and Shenzhen. A-shares dominate Chinese stock markets in terms of market capitalization and level of activity. (The number of B-shares listed on the two exchanges is less than one-third of the number of A-shares. B-shares amount to less than 5% of the A-shares' market capitalization and 4% of the A-shares' annual trading value from 1992 to 1998.) Additional categories of shares include H-shares and N-shares, which are available only to foreign investors and are traded in the Hong Kong Stock Exchange and New York Stock Exchange, respectively. The analysis in this chapter is only based on the A- and B-shares data from the first-day of market trading until December 31, 1996.

We first analyze stock-market volatility and returns to investors using

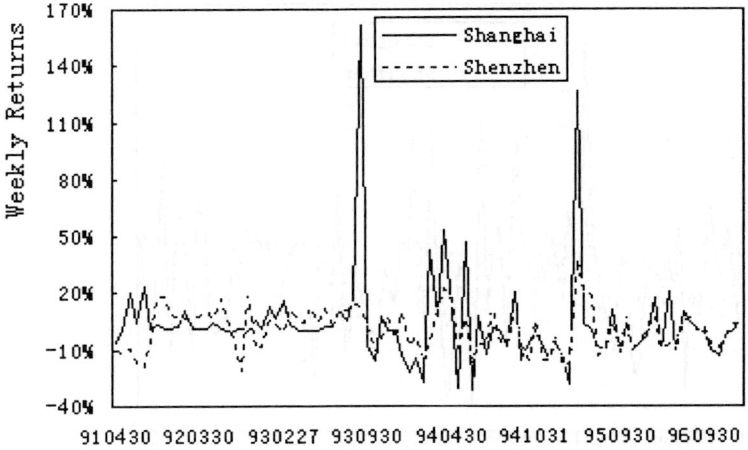

Fig. 3.1 Weekly Returns for A-share Indices in Shanghai and Shenzhen

data of daily stock market indices for A-and B-shares for both the Shanghai and Shenzhen securities exchanges. We relate trading in these shares to daily market indices representing more mature stock markets, including indices of the MSCI world market, the NYSE and the Hong Kong Stock Exchange. The daily market indices are based on value-weighted portfolios of securities and do not reflect dividends.

Figures 3.1 and 3.2 plot time-series of daily stock-market returns for A- and B-shares in Shanghai and Shenzhen. Table 3.1 presents some sample distributional statistics for the stock-market indices included in this chapter. Statistics include:

(i) daily and weekly risk-unadjusted sample mean returns, which are computed as

$$r_{j,t} = \frac{I_{j,t} - I_{j,t-1}}{I_{j,t-1}},$$

where $I_{j,t}$ is the value of jth market index at time t and $I_{j,t-1}$ is the value of jth market index at time $t-1$;

(ii) Sharpe ratio, which is the mean excess stock return divided by the sample standard deviation;

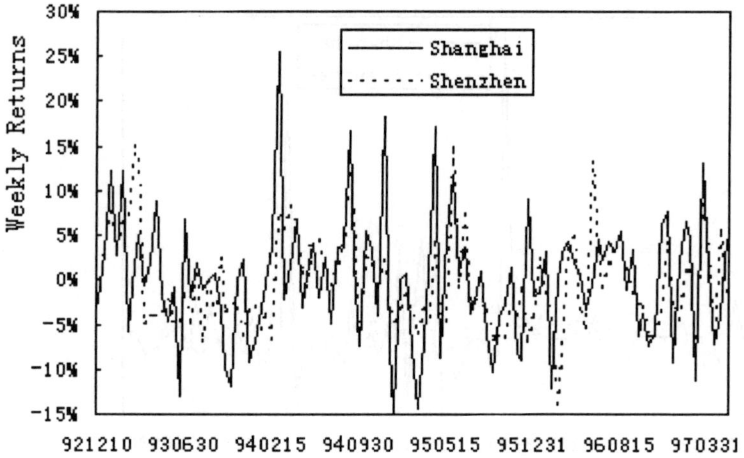

Fig. 3.2 Weekly Returns for B-share Indices in Shanghai and Shenzhen

(iii) coefficients of skewness, which is

$$\frac{T^2}{(T-1)(T-2)} \frac{\frac{1}{T}\sum_{t=1}^{T}(r_{j,t}-\bar{r}_j)^3}{\left[\frac{1}{T-1}\sum_{t=1}^{T}(r_{j,t}-\bar{r}_j)^2\right]^{3/2}};$$

(iv) coefficients of kurtosis, which is

$$\frac{T(T+1)\sum_{t=1}^{T}(r_{j,t}-\bar{r}_j)^4 - \frac{3(T-1)}{T^2}\left[\sum_{t=1}^{T}(r_{j,t}-\bar{r}_j)^2\right]^2}{(T-1)(T-2)(T-3)\left[\frac{1}{T-1}\sum_{t=1}^{T}(r_{j,t}-\bar{r}_j)^2\right]^2}; \text{ and}$$

(v) Ljung-Box portmanteau statistics, which is

$$T(T+2)\left[\sum_{m=1}^{M}\frac{\varepsilon_{j,m}^2}{T-m}\right],$$

where $\varepsilon_{j,m}$ is the m-th order autocorrelation of the residuals for the j-th time series. M is the number of autocorrelation used.

The coefficients of skewness and kurtosis are jointly estimated with the mean and variance. The Ljung-Box Q(12) statistic is used to test the significance of serial correlation up to lag 12.

We find that:

(1) Mean returns on A-shares in Shanghai and Shenzhen securities exchanges are higher than those of U.S., Hong Kong and MSCI world indices, but the standard deviations of returns are also higher. Risk-adjusted mean returns (Shape ratios) are lower in Chinese stock markets.
(2) Mean returns for A-shares in the Shanghai Securities Exchange have been higher than in the Shenzhen Securities Exchange.
(3) Returns on B-shares have been lower than those on A-shares for both exchanges.[1]
(4) The skewness parameters are significantly positive, indicating that the stock-market returns are not symmetrically distributed.
(5) Coefficients of kurtosis are generally higher in Chinese stock markets than those in more developed equity markets, suggesting that "big surprises" are more frequently observed in Chinese markets.

Next, we characterize volatility and risk patterns in Chinese stock markets. We calculate estimates of the variance of daily stock returns over the entire sample period. Important features of the markets' volatility (as can be shown in Figures 3.1 and 3.2) include:

(1) The volatility of stock-market returns is higher in China than in other developed markets.
(2) A-share markets in Shanghai and Shenzhen exhibit far greater volatility than B-share markets.
(3) Extreme price volatility exists in both exchanges. For example, the Shanghai A-share index more than doubled in a single day, from 636.56 on May 22, 1992 to 1341.11 on May 23, 1992; by November 17, 1992, it had fallen by over 70%, to 369.94. The Shanghai A-share index rose from about 400 in July 1994 to more than 1,000 in September.
(4) The size of price "jumps", measured by the percentage change in the price index, are smaller for Shenzhen A-shares than for Shanghai A-shares.

[1] International investors who bought heavily into B shares in the first two years after B-shares were listed and traded in 1992 have become disillusioned by the low returns and have started moving their investment elsewhere.

Table 3.1 Distributional Characteristics of Stock-Market Returns in China and Other World Markets

	Shanghai A share	Shanghai B share	Shenzhen A share	Shenzhen B share	MSCI world	NYSE index	Hong Kong Hang Seng
Daily retn	0.11%	0.065%	0.16%	0.08%	0.053%	0.041%	0.1%
Std. dev.	4.33%	1.65%	3.71%	2.24%	0.52%	0.45%	1.58%
Shape ratio	1.49%	-0.48%	2.03%	1.41%	6.73%	5.11%	5.19%
Minimum	-21.41%	-19.26%	-32.81%	-14.27%	-3.25%	-3.99%	-10.06%
Maximum	82.75%	12.59%	20.18%	15.44%	3.13%	6.58%	13.51%
Skewness	6.27*	0.8*	1.37*	1.69*	-0.156*	-0.313*	0.54*
Kurtosis	33.21*	8.97*	13.01*	21.69*	2.3*	3.86*	7.24*
Ljung-Box $Q(12)$	25.374*	83.016*	31.17*	90.5*	21.41†	21.465†	19.408
Weekly retn	0.513%	0.121%	0.522%	0.305%	0.262%	0.204%	0.485%
Std. dev.	10.69%	4.93%	7.57%	5.59%	1.18%	1.23%	3.34%
Shape ratio	3.28%	-0.83%	4.76%	2.56%	14.58%	9.27%	11.83%
Minimum	-20.7%	-14.09%	-29.07%	-17.37%	-2.79%	-3.81%	-9.62%
Maximum	113.04%	29.31%	57.43%	29.23%	3.43%	4.58%	10.63%
Skewness	5.96*	2.216*	2.36*	2.09*	-0.1467	-0.3467*	0.187*
Kurtosis	28.36*	10.89*	16.5*	10.1*	0.0538	1.2*	0.743*
Ljung-Box $Q(12)$	6.952	12.388†	14.6†	22.95*	10.82	13.7	15.91

*Statistically significant at the 5% level.
†Statistically significant at the 10% level.

Third, we use the daily values of A- and B-share market indices to estimate the monthly variance of stock market returns in Shanghai and Shenzhen. The monthly variance estimates use only non-overlapping sample returns in that month, and allow time-varying volatility change.

Because of the existence of autocorrelation, we follow Merton (1980) in estimating the variance of the monthly return for the A and B share market indices as the sum of the squared daily returns plus twice the sum of the products of the adjacent returns,

$$\sigma_{j,t}^2 = \sum_{i=1}^{N_t} r_{i,t}^2 + 2 \sum_{i=1}^{N_{t-1}} r_{i,t} r_{i+1,t}, \tag{3.1}$$

where there are N_t daily returns, $r_{i,t}$, in month t. I do not subtract the sample mean from each daily return in calculating the variance because the adjustment is very small.

The monthly standard deviation estimates for A- and B-share returns in Shanghai and Shenzhen highlight the variation of estimated volatility in China's stock markets. The major features of the monthly standard deviation estimates include:

(1) There is strong evidence of time-varying volatility change in both share categories in both exchanges.
(2) Periods of high and low volatility tend to cluster, and volatility shows mild persistence.
(3) "Big surprises", or high return volatility, are often observed in Chinese stock markets.
(4) The mean and standard deviation of the stock-market return standard deviation estimates are higher for A-shares than for B-shares.

We briefly summarize the price and return behavior of Chinese stock markets as follows:

- Risk-adjusted returns to investors are low;
- The degree of variability of these returns as evidenced by a conventional measure of volatility is very high;
- Volatility is time-varying, leptokurtotic and is mildly persistent. Volatility of A-share markets is far greater than that of B-share markets in both Shanghai and Shenzhen;

3.3 Day-of-the-Week Effect

Because Monday's return is calculated over three calendar days rather than one single trading day and unfavorable information tends to be released over the weekend, French (1980) and Rogalski (1984) found significant negative average returns for Monday using the S&P 500 and Dow Jones Industrial Average (DJIA) index, respectively.[2] Since then, much research has uncovered day-of-the-week effect for a number of countries in Europe and Asia. For example, Japanese indices show negative returns on Tuesday, London Stock Exchange and the Paris Bourse exhibit negative returns on Monday, and Canada, Hong Kong, and Switzerland display negative returns on Monday and Tuesday. It appears that the day-of-the-week effect is related to market institutions and trading mechanisms (e.g., the extent of non-synchronous trading), and therefore is likely to differ across countries. In this section, we examine whether the distribution of stock returns is identical for all days of the week for Chinese markets. We do so with and without adjusting for the seasonal component of each day-of-the-week return.

3.3.1 *Analysis of Variance Approach*

Assuming that daily stock returns are normal and identically and independently distributed (*i.i.d.* normal), we can test the day-of-the-week effect using simple analysis of variance approach. Our data consist of daily values of A- and B-share market indices in Shanghai and Shenzhen from December 6, 1992 to December 6, 1996. Daily returns are computed as follows:

$$r_{j,t} = 100 \times \ln \frac{I_{j,t}}{I_{j,t-1}}$$

where $I_{j,t}$ is the value of jth stock-market index (j=Shanghai A-, Shanghai B-, Shenzhen A-, and Shenzhen B-share market) at time day t. Monday re-

[2]Cross (1973) first documented that the performance of stocks, as measured by mean returns, was significantly higher on Fridays than on Mondays. More specifically, the average return for Monday, calculated from Friday's closing price to Monday's closing price, was negative. French (1980) examined the day-of-the-week effect using both calendar-time and trading-time models. He concluded that the negative returns from Friday close to Monday close were primarily incurred during the non-trading period, i.e., weekend effect. Intraday studies of stock price behavior, such as Harris (1986a), show that aggregation, while adding to generality of the results, reduces the precision necessary to infer a particular price behavior.

turns are calculated as the difference in logarithmic prices between Tuesday opening and Monday opening.

The equality of daily mean returns is tested with Hotelling's T^2-statistic where $\boldsymbol{\mu}$ is the multivariate normal vector of daily returns. Hotelling's T^2 test is the most common, traditional test where there are two groups formed by the variables that are homoskedastic and linearly independent. If the overall F-test shows the centroid (vector) of means of the dependent variables is not the same for all the groups formed by the categories of the independent variables, tests of group differences are used to explore the nature of the group differences. Significance tests for multiple dependents (e.g., Hotelling, Wilks, or Pillai tests) all follow the F distribution and so an F value and corresponding significance level are printed out for each of these tests in SPSS, in the section labeled "Analysis of Variance". The following joint hypothesis is tested:

$$\begin{aligned} H_0 &: \mu_1 = \mu_2 = \mu_3 = \mu_4 = \mu_5 \\ H_A &: \mu_i \neq \mu_j, \forall i, j \in 1, 2, \cdots, 5 \text{ and } i \neq j \end{aligned}$$

where μ_i is the expected return on day i.

As shown in Table 3.2, the day-of-the-week effect is significant at the 5% level for all four stock indices. In particular, all four share indices have negative returns on Monday and positive returns on Tuesday, Wednesday and Thursday. Shanghai A-share and Shenzhen A- and B-share markets show positive returns on Friday while Shanghai B-share market exhibits negative returns on Friday. The day-of-the-week effect is statistically significant at the 1% level for A-share markets in Shanghai and Shenzhen and at the 5% level for B-share markets. These findings strongly support the hypothesis of a Monday's effect on Chinese stock markets.

3.3.2 *Moving Average Approach*

Although analysis of variance can be employed to detect any abnormal returns in a given trading day, this methodology is not satisfactory because of *i.i.d.* (i.e., identically and independently distributed) and normal assumptions on the return generation process. A better approach is to treat daily returns as time series rather than independent observations selected from

Table 3.2 Day-of-the-Week Effect (Analysis of Variance)

	Shanghai A Share[a]	Shanghai B Share	Shenzhen A Share	Shenzhen B Share
Monday	-0.116	-0.129	-0.155	-0.102
Tuesday	0.313	0.296	0.283	0.194
Wednesday	0.941	0.117	0.586	0.301
Thursday	0.578	0.092	0.731	0.136
Friday	0.207	-0.075	0.197	0.048
T^{2}[b]	21.96*	11.27†	24.16*	9.35†

[a]All figures are in percentage terms.

[b]* and † denote H_0 (daily mean returns are equal) is rejected at the 1% and 5% level, respectively.

a random sample.[3]

Let $r_{m,n}$ be the logarithmic return of an index on day m of week n. Assume that the data generation process for $r_{m,n}$ is as follows:

$$r_{m,n} = DS_m + RT_{m,n} + \sigma_m \epsilon_{m,n} \tag{3.2}$$

where

m = Monday, Tuesday, Wednesday, Thursday, and Friday;
DS_m is the seasonal component of daily returns and

$$\frac{1}{2q+1}\sum_{s=-q}^{q} DS_{m+s} = 0;$$

$RT_{m,n} = RT_t$ is the random trend component of daily returns;
σ_m is the standard deviation for all day m returns; and
$\epsilon_{m,n} = \epsilon_t$ is a *i.i.d.* $N(0,1)$.

Because negative average returns on Monday could arise from a negative market trend, we calculate daily returns using the moving average approach.

[3]Using a sphericity-test (Andersen, 1984, p. 427), we strongly reject independence and homoskedasticity for all market indices during the sample period.

Table 3.3 Day-of-the-Week Effect (Moving Average Seasonal Component)

	Shanghai A Share[a]	Shanghai B Share	Shenzhen A Share	Shenzhen B Share
Monday	-0.139	-0.101	-0.128	-0.083
Tuesday	0.261	0.255	0.202	0.217
Wednesday	1.030	0.164	0.362	0.515
Thursday	0.627	0.128	0.685	0.073
Friday	-0.036	-0.104	0.138	0.021
T^{2}[b]	16.05*	14.82*	10.72†	8.16

[a]All figures are in percentage terms.

[b]* and † denote H_0 (daily mean returns are equal) is rejected at the 1% and 5% level, respectively.

The moving average smoothes the trend of daily returns which are not assumed to be constant over time.

$$
\begin{aligned}
MR_{m,n} = M_t &= \frac{1}{5}\sum_{s=-2}^{2} r_{t+s} \\
&= \frac{1}{5}\sum_{s=-2}^{2} RT_{t+s} + \frac{1}{5}\sum_{s=-2}^{2} \sigma_{m+s}\epsilon_{t+s} \qquad (3.3)
\end{aligned}
$$

After eliminating the trend from the daily return data, we obtain the moving average return for day t (MR_t). MR_t consists of a seasonal component and a white noise.

Table 3.3 presents empirical results of mean daily returns and Hotelling's T^2 statistics for seasonal components of each indices. The main conclusion from Section 3.3.1 is by and large still valid. All stock indices, except Shenzhen B-share index, exhibit significant Monday effect. The values of Hotelling's T^2 statistics, except that of Shanghai B-share index, are smaller under the moving average approach than those under the analysis of variance approach.

3.4 Market Efficiency Hypothesis

The fundamental insight of the market efficiency hypothesis is that security prices reflect optimal use of all available information. It is well known that the Chinese government intervenes its domestic stock markets in an unpredictable way from time to time. For example, the Chinese government suddenly removed the 1% daily price change limit on May 2, 1992 and removed the 5% daily price change limit on May 22, 1992. The Shanghai A-share index doubled on May 23, 1992. In July 1994, the China Securities Regulatory Committee (CSRC) announced a series of "market support" policies to restrict the new supply of shares. The Shanghai A-share index nearly tripled in two months. More recently, the CSRC announced the imposition of a 10% limit in the daily movement of any individual share price on December 13, 1996. If stock markets in China are efficient now, then there is probably no reason to change current security market regulations. But if inefficiencies exist, then policies designed to influence the stock markets may be inappropriate and the government should change or reduce its control or intervention in the stock markets.

The following two conditions describe efficient stock markets:

(1) Stock prices (in logarithmic form) follow a random walk with drift, i.e., any new information arriving between this and next period creates only a random deviation from this period's best forecast so that price will vary randomly around trend.
(2) Stock prices (in logarithmic form) between markets (e.g., Shanghai and Shenzhen security exchanges) are not cointegrated, i.e., no historical information on past stock prices at one market can improve the forecastability of stock prices in the other market.

3.4.1 *Random Walk Hypothesis*

The random walk hypothesis says that stock price sequences vary randomly over time around trend, and new information has no predictable components.

$$\ln P_{j,t+1} = \alpha_j + \ln P_{j,t} + \epsilon_{j,t} \tag{3.4}$$

or equivalently,

$$r_{j,t} = \alpha_j + \epsilon_{j,t} \tag{3.5}$$

where $r_{j,t}$ is the rate of return on jth market index. Equation (3.5) implies that the increments of the variance of stock-market returns are proportional to the observation interval. That is, the variance of $r_t - r_{t-s}$ is s times as much as the variance of $r_t - r_{t-1}$. Therefore, we can test the random walk hypothesis using a variance ratio test. The null hypothesis is that the disturbances $\varepsilon_{j,t}$ are uncorrelated, allowing for quite general forms of heteroskedasticity.

Lo and MacKinlay (1988) have a detailed discussion of the statistical properties of the heteroskedastic increments null hypothesis. They show that the variance ratio statistic is asymptotically equivalent to the following expression:

$$\mathcal{VR}_j(q) = 1 + M_j(q) \stackrel{a}{=} 1 + \sum_{l=1}^{q-1} \frac{2(q-l)}{q} \hat{\rho}_j(l) \tag{3.6}$$

where q is the observation interval of alternative variance estimators and is any integer greater than 1 and $\hat{\rho}_j(l)$ denotes the lth-order autocorrelation coefficient estimator of $r_{j,t}$.

$$\gamma_j(l) \equiv Cov(r_{j,t}, r_{j,t+l}).$$

$$\rho_j(l) \equiv \frac{Cov(r_{j,t}, r_{j,t+l})}{Var(r_{j,t})} = \frac{\gamma_j(l)}{\gamma_j(0)}.$$

$$\hat{\gamma}_j(l) = \frac{1}{T} \sum_{t=1}^{T-l} (r_{j,t} - \bar{r}_{j,T})(r_{j,t+l} - \bar{r}_{j,T}), \qquad 0 \le l < T.$$

$$\hat{\rho}_j(l) = \frac{\hat{\gamma}_j(l)}{\hat{\gamma}_j(0)}.$$

$$\bar{r}_{j,T} \equiv \frac{1}{T} \sum_{t=1}^{T} r_{j,t}.$$

$M_j(q)$ is an unbiased variance ratio estimator and is asymptotically zero under the random walk null hypothesis. Therefore, we only need to compute the standardized asymptotic variance of $M_j(q)$ to derive statistical inference.

The heteroskedastic-consistent standardized test statistic is:

$$\mathcal{Z}_j(q) \equiv \frac{\sqrt{nq}M_j(q)}{\sqrt{\hat{\theta}_j(q)}} \tag{3.7}$$

where $\hat{\theta}_j(q)$ is the asymptotic variance of $M_j(q)$. Lo and MacKinlay (1988) show that

$$\hat{\theta}_j(q) = 4\sum_{l=1}^{q-1}\left(1 - \frac{l}{q}\right)^2 \hat{\delta}_l,$$

$$\hat{\delta}_l = \frac{nq\sum_{t=l+1}^{nq}(p_{j,t} - p_{j,t-1} - \hat{\mu}_j)^2(p_{j,t-l} - p_{j,t-l-1} - \hat{\mu}_j)^2}{\left[\sum_{t=1}^{nq}(p_{j,t} - p_{j,t-1} - \hat{\mu}_j)^2\right]^2},$$

and

$$\hat{\mu}_j = \frac{1}{nq}\sum_{t=1}^{nq}(p_{j,t} - p_{j,t-1}).$$

Despite the presence of general heteroskedasticity, the standardized test statistic $\mathcal{Z}_j(q)$ is still asymptotically standard normal.

$$\mathcal{Z}_j(q) \overset{a}{\sim} N(0,1).$$

Table 3.4 contains values of the variance ratio test statistics $\mathcal{VR}_j(q)$ with heteroskedasticity robust standardized test statistics $\mathcal{Z}_j(q)$ in parentheses.

For Chinese stock markets, the random walk null hypothesis is strongly rejected at the 5% level of significance when daily observations are used and at the 10% level when weekly observations are used. Strong rejection of the random walk hypothesis using variance ratio tests suggests that Chinese stock markets are inefficient.[4] By comparison, for major world equity market indices, such as the MSCI, NYSE and Hong Kong indices, random

[4]The rejection of random walk hypothesis using variance ratio test also indicates that stock-market returns in China are mean-reverting, which is another piece of evidence of market inefficiency. See Fama and French (1988), Poterba and Summers (1988).

Table 3.4 Variance Ratio Tests for Random Walk Hypothesis for the Logarithm of Stock Market Indices

	nq	Number q of base observations aggregated to form variance ratio			
		2	4	8	16
		Daily stock market indices			
Shanghai A	1761	1.069*	1.167*	1.2696*	1.3277*
Shares		(2.4991)	(3.2257)	(3.278)	(2.6604)
Shanghai B	1466	1.2519*	1.3761*	1.4872*	1.6016*
Shares		(8.2841)	(6.3498)	(5.1205)	(4.1895)
Shenzhen A	1720	1.044	1.1207*	1.2375*	1.3523*
Shares		(1.5605)	(2.2811)	(2.8009)	(2.7775)
Shenzhen B	1260	1.2083*	1.3827*	1.5626*	1.7282*
Shares		(6.0101)	(5.7386)	(5.24)	(4.4433)
MSCI World	1310	1.0929*	1.0893†	1.101	1.0941†
Index		(3.376)	(1.7217)	(1.2261)	(1.7649)
NYSE	1750	1.0166	1.0196	1.0453	1.0394
Composite		(0.1345)	(0.7047)	(0.8705)	(0.477)
Hong Kong	1807	0.9168*	0.8864*	0.8976	0.9549
Hang Seng		(-3.0686)	(-2.227)	(-1.2637)	(-0.371)
		Weekly stock market indices			
Shanghai A	374	1.1009†	1.1227	1.1669	1.1671
Shares		(1.6689)	(1.0684)	(0.9001)	(0.5866)
Shanghai B	312	1.1486*	1.2921*	1.4022†	1.5735†
Shares		(2.1798)	(2.2277)	(1.8939)	(1.8273)
Shenzhen A	362	1.1185†	1.196†	1.323†	1.2702
Shares		(1.9181)	(1.6674)	(1.7095)	(0.9299)
Shenzhen B	274	1.2889*	1.4496*	1.6539*	1.8571*
Shares		(3.9365)	(3.0685)	(2.7414)	(2.3965)
MSCI World	373	1.0139	1.0397	1.0234	0.9978
Index		(0.2275)	(0.3478)	(0.1313)	(-0.0079)
NYSE	372	1.0134	1.1013	1.1256	1.2632
Composite		(0.2186)	(0.8865)	(0.6947)	(0.9278)
Hong Kong	377	0.9808	1.0755	1.0978	1.1388
Hang Seng		(-0.3259)	(0.6615)	(0.5365)	(0.492)

* and † denote statistically significant at the 5% and 10% level, respectively.

walk is rejected, but not strongly, for daily observations and can not be rejected at any reasonably level of significance for weekly observations.

3.4.2 *Cointegration-Based Market Efficiency*

Central to the cointegration-based test of market efficiency is the relationship between cointegration and error correction models. Denote the logarithm of stock prices for Shanghai A-shares market and Shenzhen A-shares market as $p^{sh}_{a,t}$ and $p^{sz}_{a,t}$, respectively. If $p^{sh}_{a,t}$ and $p^{sz}_{a,t}$ are cointegrated, then there must exist an error correction representation of the following form (Engle and Granger, 1987, and MacDonald and Kearney, 1987):

$$\begin{pmatrix} \Delta p^{sh}_{a,t} \\ \Delta p^{sz}_{a,t} \end{pmatrix} = \begin{pmatrix} \alpha_1 \\ \alpha_2 \end{pmatrix} (p^{sh}_{a,t-1} - \beta_2 p^{sz}_{a,t-1}) + \sum_{k=1}^{K} \Gamma_k \begin{pmatrix} \Delta p^{sh}_{a,t-k} \\ \Delta p^{sz}_{a,t-k} \end{pmatrix} + \begin{pmatrix} \varepsilon_{1,t} \\ \varepsilon_{2,t} \end{pmatrix} \tag{3.8}$$

and $\alpha_1 + \alpha_2 \neq 0$.

The intuition behind the error-correction equations is that if stock prices in Shanghai and Shenzhen are cointegrated, knowledge of the lagged linear combination of price levels in Shanghai and Shenzhen must improve the forecastability of returns in at least one of the markets. If stock prices are determined in efficient markets, then they should have incorporated all available information. Hence, given the past stock prices in Shanghai (Shenzhen), no other information should be of use in explaining the changes in its stock prices. In particular,

$$E(p^{sh}_{a,t} \mid \Omega^{sh}_{t-1}) = E(p^{sz}_{a,t} \mid \Omega^{sh,sz}_{t-1})$$

where

$$\Omega^{sh}_{t-1} = \{p^{sh}_{a,t-1}, p^{sh}_{a,t-2}, p^{sh}_{a,t-3}, \cdots\cdots\}.$$

$$\Omega^{sh,sz}_{t-1} = \{p^{sz}_{a,t-1}, p^{sz}_{a,t-2}, p^{sz}_{a,t-3}, \cdots\cdots, p^{sh}_{a,t-1}, p^{sh}_{a,t-2}, p^{sh}_{a,t-3}, \cdots\cdots\}.$$

We test for cointegration as follows: first, We test the null hypothesis of a unit root in the time series of $p^{i}_{j,t}$ $(i = sh, sz; j = a, b)$ against the stationary alternative for the following three specifications:

$$p_{j,t} = \hat{\rho}_j p_{j,t-1} + \hat{\epsilon}_{j,t} \tag{3.9}$$

$$p_{j,t} = \alpha^*_j + \rho^*_j p_{j,t-1} + \epsilon^*_{j,t} \tag{3.10}$$

$$p_{j,t} = \tilde{\alpha}_j + \tilde{\beta}_j (t - T/2) + \tilde{\rho}_j p_{j,t-1} + \tilde{\epsilon}_{j,t} \tag{3.11}$$

Table 3.5 Tests for Unit Roots for the Logarithm of Daily Stock Market Prices

H_0	Test statistic[a]	Shanghai A shares	Shanghai B shares	Shenzhen A shares	Shenzhen B shares
$\hat{\rho}_j = 1$	$Z(t_{\hat{\rho}_j})$	-0.745	-1.3166	-0.036	-1.2064
$\rho_j^* = 1$	$Z(t_{\rho_j^*})$	-2.2641	-2.2262	-1.3089	-0.2084
$\rho_j^* = 1$, $\alpha_j^* = 0$	$Z(\Phi_1)$	3.0678	3.1914	0.8617	0.7357
$\tilde{\rho}_j = 1$	$Z(t_{\tilde{\rho}_j})$	-1.1316	-2.5849	-1.1377	-2.0043
$\tilde{\rho}_j = 1$, $\tilde{\alpha}_j = 0$, $\tilde{\beta}_j = 0$	$Z(\Phi_2)$	2.019	2.8259	0.7605	2.2132
$\tilde{\rho}_j = 1$, $\tilde{\beta}_j = 0$	$Z(\Phi_3)$	2.523	3.5279	1.1357	2.6017

[a]Source for critical values: Fuller (1976, p. 373) and Dickey-Fuller (1981, p. 1063).

Critical values	$Z(t_{\hat{\rho}_j})$	$Z(t_{\rho_j^*})$	$Z(\Phi_1)$	$Z(t_{\tilde{\rho}_j})$	$Z(\Phi_2)$	$Z(\Phi_3)$
1%	-2.58	-3.43	6.43	-3.96	6.09	8.27
5%	-1.95	-3.12	4.59	-3.41	4.68	6.25
10%	n/a	-2.57	3.78	-3.12	4.03	5.34

All tests are based on Phillips-Perron Unit Root Tests, with size 4 Barlett Window. The Phillips-Perron test statistics share the same limiting distributions as those of Dickey-Fuller test statistics. The test results in Table 3.5 show that unit root hypothesis can not be rejected for any of the daily price time-series. Therefore $p_{j,t}^i$ is $I(1)$, $\forall i$ and j.

Next, we test the null hypothesis of no pairwise cointegration in stock prices between Shanghai and Shenzhen security exchanges for both A- and B-shares. The first step involves estimating the following cointegration regression by OLS:

$$p_{j,t}^{sh} = \alpha_{j,0} + \alpha_{j,1} p_{j,t}^{sz} + \sum_{s=-m}^{m} \alpha_{j,s} \Delta p_{j,t-s}^{sz} + \mu_{j,t} \tag{3.12}$$

where $\Delta p_{j,t-s}^{sz}$ are leads and lags of $\Delta p_{j,t}^{sz}$. The estimation results in Table 3.6, Panel (I) indicate that the slope coefficient for the cointegration re-

Table 3.6 Tests for Cointegration

Panel (I) OLS estimation for the cointegration regression[a] $p^{sh}_{j,t} = \alpha_{j,0} + \alpha_{j,1} p^{sz}_{j,t} + \sum_{s=-m}^{m} \alpha_{j,s} \Delta p^{sz}_{j,t-s} + \mu_{j,t}$			
	$\hat{\alpha}_{j,0}$	$\hat{\alpha}_{j,1}$	$\bar{R}^2$
A shares	0.0002	0.9126	0.4246
	(0.0253)	(14.19)	
B shares	-0.002	0.125	0.0218
	(-0.3533)	(1.4792)	
Panel (II) Residual-based cointegration test (ADF test) for $\hat{\mu}_{j,t}$[b] $\Delta\hat{\mu}_{j,t} = \gamma_{j,0} + \gamma_{j,1}\hat{\mu}_{j,t-1} + \sum_{k=1}^{K} \gamma_{j,k}\Delta\hat{\mu}_{j,t-k} + \nu_{j,t}$			
	ADF test statistic	Critical value[c]	$Q(K)$
A shares	-18.2696	-2.8649	$Q(2) = 16.3798$ [0.1744]
B shares	ADF test fails to find the value K in which $\nu_{j,t}$ is serially uncorrelated.		

[a]Figures in parentheses are t-statistics and figures in brackets are p-values.

[b]ADF test determines the appropriate number of lagged differences K by adding lags until a Lagrange Multiplier test fails to reject no serial correlation in $\nu_{j,t}$ at 5% level of significance.

[c]The critical values are computed by MacKinnon (1991, p. 267-276).

gression is close to one and significantly positive for A-share markets, but is insignificantly different from zero for B-share markets.

The second step is to test for a unit root on the estimated residuals, $\hat{\mu}_{j,t}$, as a proxy for the true residuals. Since OLS estimation procedure tends to make the estimated residuals become stationary, an augmented Dickey-Fuller unit root test should be applied:

$$\Delta\hat{\mu}_{j,t} = \gamma_{j,0} + \gamma_{j,1}\hat{\mu}_{j,t-1} + \sum_{k=1}^{K} \gamma_{j,k}\Delta\hat{\mu}_{j,t-k} + \nu_{j,t} \tag{3.13}$$

The specific hypothesis is:

$$H_0 \; : \; \gamma_{j,1} = 0$$
$$H_A \; : \; \gamma_{j,1} \neq 0$$

Table 3.6, Panel (II) gives the ADF test statistic with $K = 5$ for A-share markets. The null hypothesis of no cointegration between Shanghai and Shenzhen A-share prices is rejected at 5% level of significance. The Ljung-Box portmanteau statistic $Q(5)$ is not significant at the 10% level, indicating that $\nu_{a,t}$ is white noise. Therefore, we can safely conclude that Chinese A-share markets are inefficient. For B-share markets, ADF fails to generate a t-statistic with white noise $\nu_{b,t}$. Therefore, there is no evidence that Shanghai and Shenzhen B-share markets are cointegrated. International investors can not use past B-share price information on one exchange to predict B-share price movement on the other. According to market efficiency concepts developed by Fama (1991), Chinese B-share markets are at least weak-form efficient.

3.5 GARCH Models

In this section, we follow Su and Fleisher (1998a) and explore the distributional characteristics of the stock-market variance process and analyze the predictability of the stock-market returns using a set of local and global information variables. In particular, we establish an empirical model that captures the deterministic components of the variation in the stock-market returns and characterize the second order conditional moments using three error generation processes. We first specify a baseline Generalized Autoregressive Conditional Heteroskedasticity model, or GARCH(1,1) model, that expresses the time series of weekly stock-market returns, $r_{j,t}$ on a set of lagged local and global information variables $\mathbf{Z}_{t-1}$. Then we combine the baseline model with three types of error distributions in formulating a conditional variance process for Chinese stock markets. Finally, we specify a set of local and global information variables to explain the variation of the conditional mean in the baseline model.

3.5.1 *Model Specification*

Let $r_{j,t}$ denote the return on a market index at time t and $\mathbf{Z}_{j,t-1}$ represent a set of lagged local and global information variables that affect the conditional mean,

$$r_{j,t} = \boldsymbol{\delta}_j' \mathbf{Z}_{j,t-1} + \epsilon_{j,t}, \tag{3.14}$$

$$\epsilon_{j,t} = \sigma_{j,t} z_{j,t} \tag{3.15}$$

$$z_{j,t} | \boldsymbol{\Omega}_{t-1} \sim \phi(0, 1, \nu), \tag{3.16}$$

$$\sigma_{j,t}^2 = \omega_j + \alpha_j \sigma_{j,t-1}^2 + \beta_j \epsilon_{j,t-1}^2, \tag{3.17}$$

where $\sigma_{j,t}^2$ is the conditional variance, $z_{j,t}$ is the standardized residual formed by dividing the residual, $\epsilon_{j,t}$ by the standard deviation, $\sigma_{j,t}$, $\boldsymbol{\Omega}_{t-1}$ is the set of information available at the beginning of time t, $\phi(\cdot)$ denotes a conditional density function, and ν denotes a vector of parameters besides conditional mean and conditional variance that may be needed to fully characterize the probability distribution. Since equation (3.17) defines a variance, a nonnegativity constraint must be imposed on α and β, and the sum $(\alpha + \beta)$ must be less than 1 for the volatility process to be covariance stationary (Bollerslev, 1986).

The GARCH(1,1) model has a distinctive feature, i.e., a set of lagged local and global information is used to explain the returns on a market index, and at the same time, conditional variance is modeled to capture volatility clustering and temporal dependence of market returns. As Nelson and Cao (1992) point out, a possible misspecification of the mean equation (3.14) is not of great concern, because the conditional variance estimates obtained from a GARCH model are robust to an incorrect specification of conditional mean.

3.5.2 *Characterizing Variance in Chinese Stock Markets*

The exact form of the error distribution plays an important role in estimating the GARCH(1,1) formulation. Our findings in Section 3.2 indicate that the time series of stock returns in China are not independent processes; large changes tend to be followed by large changes of either sign, and small changes tend to be followed by small changes. To capture this type of volatility clustering and temporal dependence of stock returns, we consider three different functional forms of the conditional density $\phi(\cdot)$. They are: Gaussian normal distribution, standardized Student t-distribution, and Stable distribution.[5]

3.5.2.1 *Normal Distribution*

Under a Gaussian standard normality assumption, (3.16) becomes:

$$z_{j,t}|\mathbf{\Omega_{t-1}} \sim N(0,1), \tag{3.18}$$

The Gaussian GARCH model can accommodate volatility clustering, but it is not sufficient to account for all the leptokurtosis, or fat tail in the return distribution, that appears in the Chinese data. The large number of very high and very low returns observed suggests that a fatter-tailed distribution than normal distribution might better characterize the error process for Chinese stock-market returns.

3.5.2.2 *Standardized t-distribution*

The conditional density function for $z_{j,t}$, under the standardized Student t-distribution with mean 0, variance 1 and degrees of freedom ν, can be written as:

$$\begin{aligned} z_{j,t}|\mathbf{\Omega}_{t-1} &= \Gamma\left(\frac{\nu+1}{2}\right)\Gamma\left(\frac{\nu}{2}\right)^{-1}(\nu-2)^{-1/2} \\ &\quad \times\left(1+z_{j,t}^2(\nu-2)^{-1}\right)^{-(\nu+1)/2}, \\ &\qquad \nu > 2. \end{aligned} \tag{3.19}$$

It is well known that the parameter ν can be interpreted as the degree of leptokurtosis. Large values of ν are associated with the absence of leptokurtosis while small values are associated with some degree of leptokurtosis.

[5]Other possible parametric densities include normal-Poisson mixture distribution in Jorion (1988), the power exponential distribution in Baillie and Bollerslev (1989), the normal-lognormal mixture distribution in Hsieh (1989), and the generalized error distribution, or GED, in Nelson (1991). The application of these densities in the above empirical model is beyond the scope of this chapter and can be further exercise for researchers.

As $1/\nu$ approaches 0, the Student t -distribution approaches a standard normal distribution, but when $1/\nu > 0$, the t-distribution has "fatter tails" than the corresponding normal distribution.

3.5.2.3 *Stable Distribution*

Under the Gaussian normal distribution, the length and height of the extreme tails are fixed. Assuming a stable distribution density function for the error term in the baseline model allows us to explicitly estimate the tail length and height. Moreover, McCulloch (1997) argues that the stable non-Gaussian distribution generalizes the Central Limit Theorem to cases where the second moments of the underlying variables do not exist. It is especially useful in modeling financial asset returns that exhibit strong leptokurtosis.

We standardize the residual by using the following transformation:

$$\epsilon_{j,t} = (\sigma_{j,t}^2)^{1/\nu} z_{j,t}, \tag{3.20}$$

where $z_{j,t}$ is specified to have a symmetric standard stable density with both a skewness parameter and location parameter equal to zero. Since the standard Stable distribution does not have a simple mathematical description, the log of the characteristic function is used instead:

$$\log[E(e^{iXt})] = -|t|^{\nu}, \tag{3.21}$$

where ν ($\nu \in (0, 2]$) is the characteristic exponent to be estimated from the model. When $\nu = 2$, the standard stable distribution becomes the stable standard normal distribution. When $\nu < 2$, absolute moments of order less than ν exist, but those of order greater than or equal to ν do not, so that variance is infinite. For example, when $\nu = 1$, the stable distribution becomes the Cauchy distribution, for which the mean is also infinite.

3.5.3 *World Versus Local Factors in Volatility*

In the baseline model, $r_{j,t} = \boldsymbol{\delta}_j^{'} \mathbf{Z}_{j,t-1} + \epsilon_{j,t}$, weekly market returns, $r_{j,t}$, are regressed on a set of lagged local and global information variables that may influence the conditional mean of stock-market index returns.

Local information variables include:

- lagged one-week market return, $r_{j,t-1}$;
- lagged change in the exchange rate between Chinese *renminbi yuan* and U.S. dollar, $\Delta RMBUS_{t-1}$;
- lagged change in exchange rate between Hong Kong dollar and U.S. dollar, $\Delta HKUS_{t-1}$;
- lagged change in weekly turnover rate, $\Delta TO_{j,t-1}$;

World information variables include:

- lagged MSCI world index return in excess of the 30-day U.S. Treasury Bill rate, $MSCI_{t-1}$;
- lagged Hong Kong Hang Seng index return in excess of the 30-day U.S. Treasury Bill rate, HS_{t-1};
- lagged NYSE index return in excess of the 30-day U.S. Treasury Bill rate, $NYSE_{t-1}$;
- lagged change in term structure spread (The yield on Long-term U.S. Government Security minus the 30-day U.S. Treasury Bill rate), TS_{t-1};
- lagged change in the 30-day U.S. Treasury Bill rate, ΔTB_{t-1}.

We initially include only lagged local information variables in the baseline model, assuming GARCH(1,1), TGARCH(1,1) and SGARCH(1,1) error generation processes in estimating the parameters. In doing this, we treat the market as fully segmented in the sense that common shocks to world equity markets do not influence the stock markets in China and there are no covariance dynamics. To test the hypothesis that global as well as local factors influence the conditional mean returns in Chinese stock markets, we subsequently include both lagged local and lagged world information variables in the baseline model and estimate all the parameters again. we use constrained maximum likelihood (CMLE) application module with Sequential Quadratic Programming method in estimating the model. Both BFGS (Broyden, Fletcher, Goldfarb and Shanno) and NR (Newton and Raphson) algorithms have been tried to obtain the maximum likelihood estimates.

3.6 Estimation and Empirical Results

We first carefully estimate the GARCH(1,1) model under three alternative formulations of error-generation process. Then we perform a battery of residual diagnosis tests using the Ljung-Box Q(8) portmanteau statistics and the likelihood ratio test statistics and choose the error distribution that is best supported by data. Finally we analyze parameter estimates of the best-fitted model. Our objective is to seek the best statistical model through rigorous econometric analysis and use the model to study the effect of exogenous government policy changes have on the stock-market return volatility.

3.6.1 *Model Comparison*

We estimate the Gaussian GARCH(1,1), TGARCH(1,1) and SGARCH(1,1) models, with and without global information variables.[6] To choose among the alternative error-distribution formulations for the best fit to Chinese stock-market data, we first compare the Ljung-Box portmanteau test statistics for serial correlation with 8 lags on standardized residuals ($\hat{z}_{j,t} = \hat{\epsilon}_{j,t}\hat{\sigma}_{j,t}^{-1}$) for each time series and test the null hypothesis of no autocorrelation up to lag 8. The purpose of this test is to evaluate whether each model fully accounts for all autocorrelation of stock-market returns.

As the results in Tables 3.7–3.9 show, there is evidence of serial correlation for all time series under the Gaussian normal GARCH assumption, as the Ljung-Box Q(8) statistics are significant at the 5% level. The Bera-Jarque test for normality strongly rejects the null hypothesis of normally distributed standardized residuals under the Gaussian normal GARCH model. The skewness and kurtosis in the standardized residuals indicate the inappropriateness of the assumption of conditional normality in the error distribution. Under TGARCH and SGARCH assumptions, there is no evidence of serial correlation in the residuals, as the Ljung-Box Q(8) statistics are not significant even at the 10% level for most of the return series. Moreover, the Ljung-Box Q(8) statistics are not significant at the 5% level for six out of eight time series under the SGARCH formulation, while they meet this level of significance for only three out of eight time series under the TGARCH formulation. This indicates that the SGARCH model outperforms the TGARCH model.

The second phase of residual diagnosis is to determine whether the results under the assumption of the t- and stable distributions are statistically

[6]For brevity, we only include estimation results for the best-fitted model. Estimation results on other models are available upon request.

Table 3.7 Residual Diagnostic Tests for Gaussian GARCH Model

	Shanghai A-Shares	Shanghai B-Shares	Shenzhen A-Shares	Shenzhen B-Shares
	with only local information variables[a]			
$Q_8(\epsilon_j/\sigma_j)$	3.9437	7.1712	5.2187	6.9842
	[0.8522]	[0.5183]	[0.734]	[0.5383]
Skewness	2.3545	3.4975	6.6258	2.1448
	(0.825)	(1.3)	(2.0366)	(0.7225)
Kurtosis	8.6215	14.6961	54.6961	7.6324
	(2.1323)	(2.7522)	(10.3288)	(2.0119)
Bera-Jarque	2159.25	14084.7	1469785	868.83
	with both local and global information variables			
$Q_8(\epsilon_j/\sigma_j)$	4.0904	4.6341	3.5229	4.1608
	[0.8489]	[0.7959]	[0.8974]	[0.8423]
Skewness	2.4393	2.1461	1.7991	1.9583
	(0.8626)	(0.6984)	(0.3644)	(0.4487)
Kurtosis	9.0803	7.2489	4.661	6.799
	(4.1425)	(2.588)	(1.5642)	(2.1139)
Bera-Jarque	2754.83	812.56	186.25	486.98

[a]Figures inside the parentheses are heteroskedasticity-consistent standard errors and figures inside the brackets are p-values. $Q_8(\epsilon_j/\sigma_j)$ denotes the Ljung-Box Q statistic for serial correlation tests with 8 lags on standardized residuals. Bera-Jarque (1982) statistic is used to test for normality, and is calculated as: $\frac{T}{6}Skewness^2 + \frac{T}{24}(Kurtosis - 3)^3$, which is distributed as Chi-square with 2 degrees of freedom. The critical value for $\chi^2(2)$ at 1%, 5% and 10% levels are 9.21, 5.991 and 4.605.

different from those obtained under the normal distribution. To do this, we compute likelihood ratio statistics to test the null hypothesis that the tail-thickness parameter $1/\hat{\nu} \to 0$ against the one-sided alternative that $1/\hat{\nu} > 0$ for the TGARCH formulation, and I test the null hypothesis that the tail thickness and length parameter $\hat{\nu} = 2$ against the one sided alternative that $\hat{\nu} < 2$ for the SGARCH formulation. The values for the likelihood ratio test statistics are reported in Tables 3.8 and 3.9.

Table 3.8 Residual Diagnostic Tests for TGARCH Model

	Shanghai A-Shares	Shanghai B-Shares	Shenzhen A-Shares	Shenzhen B-Shares
	with only local information variables[a]			
$Q_8(\epsilon_j/\sigma_j)$	3.6026	2.7382	5.8249	5.4158
	[0.8911]	[0.9497]	[0.6663]	[0.7124]
Skewness	1.4621	1.4037	2.0193	1.4501
	(0.4852)	(0.4755)	(0.6331)	(0.4751)
Kurtosis	4.2055	20.2045	7.2603	4.4762
	(2.004)	(5.3781)	(2.1141)	(1.8775)
$LR_{1/\nu\to 0}$	73.43	33.78	57.6	39.14
	with both local and global information variables			
$Q_8(\epsilon_j/\sigma_j)$	2.4277	2.3334	4.6341	3.8026
	[0.965]	[0.969]	[0.7959]	[0.8745]
Skewness	1.054	1.2572	1.6154	1.46
	(0.3572)	(0.4083)	(0.4833)	(0.4755)
Kurtosis	1.6593	2.1504	4.623	3.7825
	(1.2108)	(1.3253)	(1.6774)	(1.621)
$LR_{1/\nu\to 0}$	65.93	39.14	54.78	35.11

[a]Figures inside the parentheses are heteroskedasticity-consistent standard errors and figures inside the brackets are p-values. $Q_8(\epsilon_j/\sigma_j)$ denotes the Ljung-Box Q statistic for serial correlation tests with 8 lags on standardized residuals. Bera-Jarque (1982) statistic is used to test for normality, and is calculated as: $\frac{T}{6}Skewness^2 + \frac{T}{24}(Kurtosis - 3)^3$, which is distributed as Chi-square with 2 degrees of freedom. The critical value for $\chi^2(2)$ at 1%, 5% and 10% levels are 9.21, 5.991 and 4.605.

Under the null hypothesis that $1/\hat{\nu} \to 0$ in the TGARCH formulation and $\hat{\nu} = 2$ in the SGARCH formulation, neither the $LR_{1/\hat{\nu}\to 0}$ nor the $LR_{\hat{\nu}=2}$ statistic is distributed as $\chi^2(1)$ because they do not meet the standard regularity conditions for asymptotic χ^2 distribution. McCulloch (1997) calibrates the Monte Carlo critical values for the symmetric stable likelihood ratio statistic when $\nu = 2$. Since all the $LR_{\hat{\nu}=2}$ statistics for the Chinese stock-market indices are highly significant compared with the Monte Carlo

Table 3.9 Residual Diagnostic Tests for SGARCH Model

	Shanghai A-Shares	Shanghai B-Shares	Shenzhen A-Shares	Shenzhen B-Shares
	with only local information variables[a]			
$Q_8(\epsilon_j/\sigma_j)$	3.436	1.8537	5.4158	1.4501
	[0.9041]	[0.9852]	[0.7124]	[0.9935]
Skewness	1.1663	1.4037	1.3532	1.5609
	(0.401)	(0.7359)	(0.4752)	(1.0622)
Kurtosis	2.5621	2.2952	3.1783	3.9651
	(0.9888)	(1.478)	(1.3528)	(1.6742)
$LR_{1/\nu=2}$	59.76	39.76	48.64	2.352
	with both local and global information variables			
$Q_8(\epsilon_j/\sigma_j)$	2.3438	0.8201	6.6658	2.361
	[0.9686]	[0.9991]	[0.5731]	[0.9679]
Skewness	0.5988	1.2258	1.4946	1.7991
	(0.3427)	(0.5107)	(0.5158)	(0.3667)
Kurtosis	0.4073	2.1443	3.8174	5.4245
	(0.4899)	(1.3888)	(1.4282)	(2.0366)
$LR_{1/\nu=2}$	53.33	44.08	50.43	2.352

[a]Figures inside the parentheses are heteroskedasticity-consistent standard errors and figures inside the brackets are p-values. $Q_8(\epsilon_j/\sigma_j)$ denotes the Ljung-Box Q statistic for serial correlation tests with 8 lags on standardized residuals. Bera-Jarque (1982) statistic is used to test for normality, and is calculated as: $\frac{T}{6}Skewness^2 + \frac{T}{24}(Kurtosis-3)^3$, which is distributed as Chi-square with 2 degrees of freedom. The critical value for $\chi^2(2)$ at 1%, 5% and 10% levels are 9.21, 5.991 and 4.605.

critical values, the null hypothesis of normality under SGARCH model is strongly rejected.[7]

McCulloch also points out that the Monte Carlo critical values are smaller than the critical values under χ^2 distribution for the null hypothe-

[7]The Monte Carlo critical values are 0.243, 1.12 and 4.764 for 10%, 5% and 1% level of significance, respectively.

sis of normality. $LR_{1/\hat{\nu}\to 0}$ statistics are all highly significant using critical values under $\chi^2(1)$ distribution. Therefore, the null hypothesis of normality under TGARCH model is also rejected.

Since the TGARCH and SGARCH models are not nested, a likelihood ratio test can not be used to distinguish these two models. However, the Ljung-Box portmanteau statistics seem to support SGARCH formulation better than TGARCH formulation.

Summing up, the residual diagnosis tests indicate that the GARCH model with conditional normal errors does not fully capture the leptokurtosis and the serial correlation of the standardized residuals. The GARCH model with Stable error distributions fits the time-series data the best.[8]

3.6.2 *Parameter Estimates*

The parameter estimates for the SGARCH(1,1) model is presented in Table 3.10. The conditional standard deviations are plotted in Figures 3.3 and 3.4. When only local variables are included in the model, lagged one-week return exhibits a strong influence on market return. This is probably because of nonsynchronization of trading and clearing and thinness of the markets. The constant terms in the conditional mean equations are all very small and not statistically significant at any level. The coefficient estimates for the lagged change in weekly turnover rate are also small and insignificant for all the series. Furthermore, the coefficient estimates for the lagged change in the U.S. dollar-Chinese yuan and U.S. dollar-Hong Kong dollar exchange rates are both statistically insignificant.

When the global information variables are added to the conditional mean, the coefficient estimates for the lagged change in the U.S. dollar-Hong Kong dollar exchange rate become statistically significant in three out of the four series. Since both China and Hong Kong enforce fixed exchange rate regimes, we are puzzled by this result.[9] Among the global information variables, the lagged Hong Kong Hang Seng weekly index return variable

[8] It remains an open question whether other conditional error distributions would provide a better fit. Another interesting question is whether higher order GARCH models might provide an even better description. We leave the answers to all of these questions for future research.

[9] The exchange rate between Hong Kong dollar and U.S. dollar fluctuates within a 1% narrow range, while the exchange rate between Chinese yuan and U.S. dollar seldom fluctuates over the sample period, except that a few "jumps" are observed.

Table 3.10 Maximum Likelihood Estimates of the SGARCH(1,1) Model

	Shanghai A-Shares[a]	Shanghai B-Shares	Shenzhen A-Shares	Shenzhen B-Shares
With only local information variables				
constant	-0.004	-0.006	-0.007	-0.004
$r_{j,t-1}$	0.287*	0.202*	0.15*	0.291*
$\Delta RMBUS_{t-1}$	-0.013	-0.012	-0.037	-0.002
$\Delta HKUS_{t-1}$	0.266	0.57	0.152	0.237
ΔTO_{t-1}	0.006	-0.001	0.018	-0.002
$\hat{\omega}_j$	0.018*	0.003	0.024*	0.017*
$\hat{\alpha}_j$	0.615*	0.318*	0.74*	0.743*
$\hat{\beta}_j$	0.107*	0.189*	0.214*	0.205*
ν	1.551*	1.54*	1.676*	1.58*
Mean log likelihood	1.309	1.769	1.296	1.845
With local and global information variables				
constant	-0.007	-0.005	-0.01	0.002
$r_{j,t-1}$	0.268*	0.191*	0.153*	0.242*
$\Delta RMBUS_{t-1}$	-0.012	-0.018	-0.036	-0.036
$\Delta HKUS_{t-1}$	0.342*	0.071	0.744*	0.32*
ΔTO_{t-1}	0.004	0.001	0.014	-0.001
$MSCI_{t-1}$	0.03	0.198	0.345*	-0.002
HS_{t-1}	-0.06	-0.29*	0.094	0.087
$NYSE_{t-1}$	-0.31*	-0.22	-0.35*	-0.074
TS_{t-1}	0.433	-0.094	0.175	-0.239
ΔTB_{t-1}	-5.937	0.03	-12.22	1.233
$\hat{\omega}_j$	0.033*	0.004	0.011*	0.02*
$\hat{\alpha}_j$	0.619*	0.552*	0.688*	0.732*
$\hat{\beta}_j$	0.121*	0.164*	0.169*	0.224*
ν	1.506*	1.493*	1.7666*	1.567*
Mean log likelihood	1.322	1.828	1.311	1.887

[a]* denotes 5% level of significance according to the Wald Confidence Limits.

is significant for the Shanghai B-share return series. The weekly MSCI world index return variable is significant for the Shenzhen A-share return series. The lagged NYSE weekly return variable is significant for both Shanghai and Shenzhen A-share return series. The coefficient estimates for the lagged change in the U.S. 30-day Treasury Bill rate are large in two cases, but none of the estimates is statistically significant. Neither do the U.S. term structure spread variables have any explanatory power.

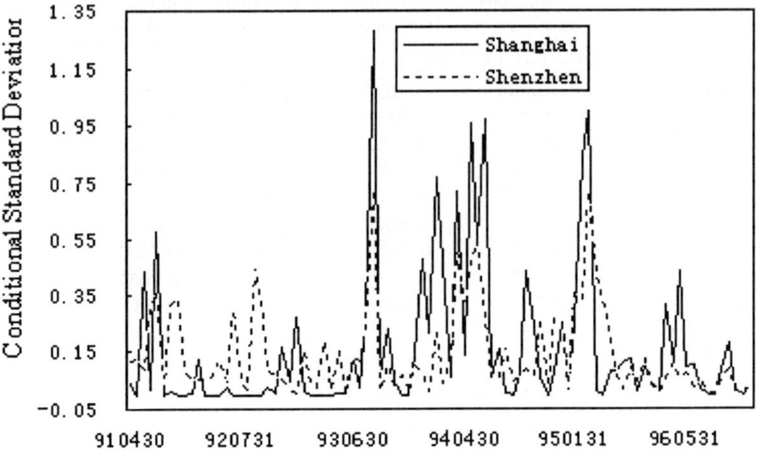

Fig. 3.3 Conditional Standard Deviation from the SGARCH Model (Shanghai and Shenzhen A-Shares)

To test the importance of the set of world factors in the conditional mean equation, I use likelihood ratio statistics to test the joint hypothesis that the estimated coefficients for the global information variables are all zero. For the Shanghai A- and B-share, Shenzhen A- and B-share series, the $LR_{\hat{\delta}_{j,5}=\hat{\delta}_{j,6}=\hat{\delta}_{j,7}=\hat{\delta}_{j,8}=\hat{\delta}_{j,9}=0}$ statistics are 3.48, 12.15, 3.84 and 7.06 under the SGARCH formulation. The critical values for the 1%, 5% and 10% level of significance are 15.09, 11.07 and 9.24, respectively. Hence, the joint null hypothesis that the estimated coefficients for the global information variables are all zero can not be rejected at the 1% significance level, but it can be rejected for the Shanghai B share series at the 5% level of significance.

We conclude that local and global information variables do explain some of the variation in Chinese stock-market returns, but evidence that China's stock markets are integrated into the world financial network is at present rather weak.

The empirical results shown in Table 3.10 indicate that A-share returns in Shanghai and Shenzhen tend to respond similarly to common news and economic factors, as the coefficient estimates in the empirical models are very similar in terms of the values and statistical significance. For example, the coefficient estimates for lagged one-week return, lagged change in the

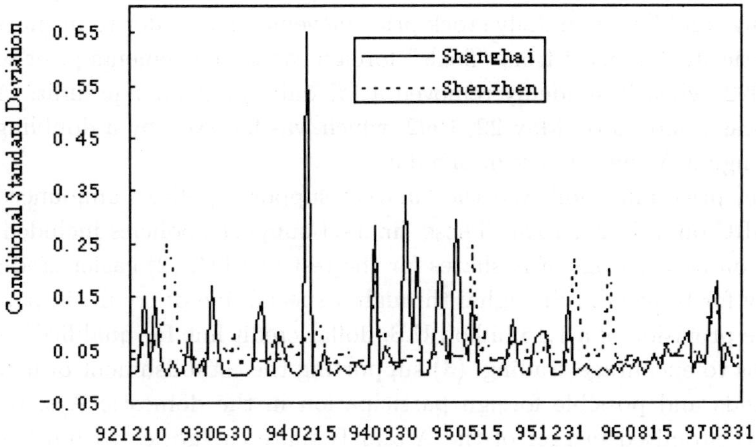

Fig. 3.4 Conditional Standard Deviation from the SGARCH Model (Shanghai and Shenzhen B-Shares)

exchange rate between U.S. dollar and Hong Kong dollar, and the lagged NYSE excess return are 0.268, 0.342 and -0.31 for Shanghai A shares and 0.153, 0.744 and -0.35 for Shenzhen A shares. These coefficient estimates are all significant at the 5% level according to the Wald confidence limits. This implies that:

(1) Even though the Shanghai and Shenzhen securities exchanges are still largely regional exchanges, there is currently potential for them to become a fully integrated national stock market.
(2) The dissimilarity of coefficient estimates for the information variables between the A and B share market return series imply that domestic and international investors have very different investment sentiment and risk-aversion.

3.7 Government Regulation and Market Volatility

We now apply the best-fitted empirical model to study the high stock-market return volatility in China. We observe that Chinese stock markets are very sensitive to government regulations. For example, the Chinese government has expressed the belief that the volatility of "hot money" introduces "excessive" volatility in stock market prices. It therefore imposed price ceilings and floors on daily stock price movements in order to insulate the domestic stock market from "fickle" foreign capital movements prior to May 5, 1992, when it suddenly removed a 1% daily price change limit. A 5% limit was removed on May 22, 1992, which was followed by a doubling of the Shanghai A share index in one day.

Another price jump followed the "market support" policies announced by the CSRC on July 29, 1994. These "market support" policies included: (1) A ban on new listings of A shares for the rest of 1994; (2) easier credit availability for brokers in Shanghai through a special line of credit, in particular, the provision of a 1.15 billion U.S. dollar credit line for qualified security firms to encourage trading; (3) supporting the establishment of new mutual funds and possible foreign participation in the domestic A share market; (4) promised merger of the A and B share categories within five years. Within two months following the announcement of these policies, the Shanghai A share index nearly tripled.

We test the hypothesis that the government's stock-market liberalization policies adopted in May, 1992 led to increased stock-market volatility.[10] We include a policy dummy variable in the best fitted model–SGARCH(1,1) formulation, so that the conditional variance equation becomes

$$\sigma_{j,t}^2 = \omega_j + \eta_j D_t + \alpha_j \sigma_{j,t-1}^2 + \beta_j \epsilon_{j,t-1}^2, \tag{3.22}$$

where

$$D_t = \begin{cases} 0 & : \text{ before the removal of the 5\% daily price change limits} \\ 1 & : \text{ after the removal of the 5\% daily price change limits.} \end{cases}$$

Under the assumption that the conditional volatility process is covariance stationary, i.e., $(\hat{\alpha}_j + \hat{\beta}_j) < 1$, equation (3.17) implies that the unconditional variance of $\epsilon_{j,t}$ is equal to $\frac{\hat{\omega}_j}{1-\hat{\alpha}_j-\hat{\beta}_j}$ before the market liberalization

[10]Because the impact of the stock-market liberalization policy in May 1992 lasted for a long time, and we are unable to separate this effect from the impact of the stock-market support policy in July 1994, we do not conduct a formal test on whether the stock-market volatility increased after the July 1994 announcement at this point. The effect of July 1994 announcement on market volatility will be investigated later in this section.

policies were announced. If the unconditional variance of stock returns changed with the removal of daily price change limits, then the coefficient η_j should be statistically significant and the unconditional variance should become $\frac{\hat{\omega}_j+\hat{\eta}_j}{1-\hat{\alpha}_j-\hat{\beta}_j}, \hat{\eta}_j > 0$.

Another test of the hypothesis that a change in policy regimes led to increased stock-market return volatility is to divide the sample into two sub-periods, one containing the observations before the removal of daily price change limits and the other representing the post-removal period. We then use an SGARCH(1,1) framework to estimate these two sub-samples separately. If market liberalization policies contributed to increased stock-market volatility, then the unconditional variance $\frac{\hat{\omega}_j^1}{1-\hat{\alpha}_j^1-\hat{\beta}_j^1}$ should be smaller than $\frac{\hat{\omega}_j^2}{1-\hat{\alpha}_j^2-\hat{\beta}_j^2}$.

The results of the two tests are shown in Tables 3.11 and 3.12. The coefficient estimates of the dummy variable, $\hat{\eta}_j$ are statistically significant for both the Shanghai and Shenzhen A-share market returns.[11] We note that $\hat{\eta}_j$ is about 28% larger for Shanghai than for Shenzhen, suggesting that volatility in the Shanghai A-share market was influenced to a greater extent by the removal of daily price-change limits. Moreover, the likelihood ratio test results in Tables 3.11 and 3.12 also indicate that the null hypothesis $\hat{\eta}_j = 0$ is strongly rejected at the 5% level of significance for both Shanghai and Shenzhen.

When we estimate the SGARCH(1,1) model using two sub-samples, we find that the unconditional standard deviations are 0.1162 and 0.1237 for the first sub-sample and 0.1685 and 0.1483 for the second sub-sample, respectively, indicating that stock-market volatility increased by more than 45% for Shanghai but by only 20% for Shenzhen after the removal of daily price change limits. Moreover, the null hypothesis that $\frac{\hat{\omega}_j^1}{1-\hat{\alpha}_j^1-\hat{\beta}_j^1} < \frac{\hat{\omega}_j^2}{1-\hat{\alpha}_j^2-\hat{\beta}_j^2}$, is strongly rejected at the 5% level of significance for both the Shanghai and Shenzhen sub-samples. Even though additional factors other than the removal of daily price change limits may have affected the volatility of stock-market returns over time, we conclude that a volatility increase

[11] We do not use the B-share market return data because the Shanghai B-share market started trading on February 21, 1992, which was too close to May 5, 1992, when the price limits were removed. B shares were not traded in Shenzhen until December 2, 1992.

Table 3.11 Maximum Likelihood Estimates of the SGARCH(1,1) Model with Policy Dummy Variable

	Shanghai A-Shares[a]	Shenzhen A-Shares
constant	-0.0064	-0.0091
$r_{j,t-1}$	0.3574*	0.1014*
$\Delta RMBUS_{t-1}$	0.0482	-0.0199
$\Delta HKUS_{t-1}$	-0.7565*	-0.1944
ΔTO_{t-1}	0.003	-0.0024
$MSCI_{t-1}$	-0.134	0.2589
HS_{t-1}	0.4154*	0.0114
$NYSE_{t-1}$	0.0108	0.3399*
TS_{t-1}	-0.1505	0.0045
ΔTB_{t-1}	-4.3147*	-2.4379
$\hat{\omega}_j$	0.0013*	0.0061*
$\hat{\eta}_j$	0.085*	0.0613*
$\hat{\alpha}_j$	0.5532*	0.4561*
$\hat{\beta}_j$	0.3169*	0.4789*
ν	1.5587*	1.6013*
Mean log likelihood	2.0502	2.1156
$LR_{\hat{\eta}_j=0}{}^b$	17.061	5.3915
$Q_8(\epsilon_j/\sigma_j)^c$	2.3788	4.3003
	[0.9671]	[0.8291]

[a]Figures inside the brackets are p-values and * denotes 5% level of significance according to the Wald Confidence Limits.

[b]Likelihood ratio statistics is used to test the null hypothesis that $\hat{\eta}_j = 0$, and is asymptotically distributed as Chi-square with 1 degree of freedom. The critical value for $\chi^2(1)$ at the 5% level of significance is 3.8415.

[c]$Q_8(\epsilon_j/\sigma_j)$ denotes the Ljung-Box Q statistic for serial correlation tests with 8 lags on standardized residuals.

of the magnitude observed could not have occurred without the observed exogenous change in government policy. We can only speculate at this point whether reimposing daily price change limits would improve the functioning of Chinese stock markets and enhance their role in the capital market mobilization process. It is interesting to note that the security regulatory

Table 3.12 Maximum Likelihood Estimates of the SGARCH(1,1) Model Using Subsamples

	Shanghai A-Shares[a]		Shenzhen A-Shares	
	First sample	Second sample	First sample	Second sample
constant	-0.0158	-0.0107	-0.0089	0.0023
$r_{j,t-1}$	0.672*	0.2409*	0.528*	0.1126*
$\Delta RMBUS_{t-1}$	-0.2109	0.0682	-0.0495	0.0223
$\Delta HKUS_{t-1}$	-0.7789*	-0.4907*	-0.0716	-0.3576
ΔTO_{t-1}	0.002	0.0137	-0.0006	-0.0023
$MSCI_{t-1}$	-0.0691	-0.674*	0.146	-0.0963
HS_{t-1}	0.0395	0.3973*	-0.274	-0.0222
$NYSE_{t-1}$	0.0669	-0.0339	0.253	0.3092*
TS_{t-1}	0.06119	-0.08545	2.616*	-0.34
ΔTB_{t-1}	-4.3269*	3.5378	2.537	-2.8475
$\hat{\omega}_j$	0.0051*	0.0024*	0.0037*	0.0063*
$\hat{\alpha}_j$	0.5113*	0.6301*	0.4053*	0.4232*
$\hat{\beta}_j$	0.1109*	0.2855*	0.3527*	0.2903*
ν	1.7576*	1.6929*	1.7615*	1.5995*
Mean log likelihood	3.6207	1.8917	3.5542	2.0785
$\frac{\omega_j}{1-\alpha_j-\beta_j}$	0.0135	0.0284	0.0153	0.022
LR^b	23.301		11.85	

[a]* denotes 5% level of significance according to the Wald Confidence Limits.

[b]Likelihood ratio statistics is used to test the null hypothesis that $\frac{\omega_j^1}{1-\alpha_j^1-\beta_j^1} = \frac{\omega_j^2}{1-\alpha_j^2-\beta_j^2}$, and is asymptotically distributed as Chi-square with 3 degrees of freedom. The critical value for $\chi^2(3)$ at the 5% level of significance is 7.8147.

authorities reimposed a 10% daily price-change limit on any individual stock on December 13, 1996 in order to curb volatility.

Four volatility spikes common to Shanghai and Shenzhen securities exchanges are observed after the removal of daily price change limits: during December 1992 and January 1993; in January 1994; during July and August 1994; and in June 1995. Each of these spikes can be associated with major changes in regulation. For example, the Shanghai and Shenzhen stock-market indices reached their lowest historical values on November 17, 1992. To stimulate the market demand for shares, the central bank eased the borrowing limits for brokers in both Shanghai and Shenzhen through a special line of credit. At the same time, newly established closed-end mutual funds started issuing and trading shares. In December 1992, the market indices rose to an historical high level in both exchanges. In January 1994, the State Planning Committee announced an annual quota of 700 million U.S. dollars for new issues in that year, which was much lower than the market had anticipated. In addition, the CSRC temporarily prohibited new issue and trading of legal entity shares, which were held by many state-owned enterprises and accounted for more than 15% of total market capitalization. These events were accompanied by a volatility spike in January 1994. On July 19, 1994, the CSRC announced a series of aforementioned "market support and market liberalization" policies. Within two months following the announcement of these policies, the Shanghai A share index nearly tripled. In June 1995, the CSRC suspended market trading of futures on government bonds and at the same time, the central bank set an interest rate ceiling for corporate and municipal bonds. As a consequence, a large amount of funds were transferred from the bond markets into the stock markets.

In order to examine whether there are structural breaks in the stock-market volatility process, we introduce the following five dummy variables to break the time-series into five segments:[12]

$$D_t^0 = \begin{cases} 1 & : \text{ between May 5, 1992 and October 31, 1992} \\ 0 & : \text{ otherwise;} \end{cases}$$

$$D_t^1 = \begin{cases} 1 & : \text{ between November 1, 1992 and November 31, 1993} \\ 0 & : \text{ otherwise;} \end{cases}$$

$$D_t^2 = \begin{cases} 1 & : \text{ between December 1, 1993 and May 31, 1994} \\ 0 & : \text{ otherwise;} \end{cases}$$

[12]Due to investors' anticipation, stock-market volatility may be affected prior to the date of the policy change announcement. We allow about two months for such anticipation.

$$D_t^3 = \begin{cases} 1 & : \text{ between June 1, 1994 and April 30, 1995} \\ 0 & : \text{ otherwise;} \end{cases}$$

$$D_t^4 = \begin{cases} 1 & : \text{ between May 1, 1995 and September 4, 1996} \\ 0 & : \text{ otherwise.} \end{cases}$$

We add D_t^1, D_t^2, D_t^3, and D_t^4 variables in the conditional variance equation (3.17) and estimate the SGARCH(1,1) model. The conditional variance equation becomes

$$\sigma_{j,t}^2 = \omega_j + \sum_{l=1}^{4} \eta_{l,j} D_t^l + \alpha_j \sigma_{j,t-1}^2 + \beta_j \epsilon_{j,t-1}^2, \tag{3.23}$$

The maximum likelihood estimation results are presented in Table 3.13. None of the estimated coefficients for the above dummy variables is statistically significant, although the changes in the magnitude of the coefficients suggest that the unconditional variances decreased in Shanghai but increased in Shenzhen after the announcement of stock-market liberalization policies in July 1994. The null hypothesis that $\hat{\eta}_{1,j} = \hat{\eta}_{2,j} = \hat{\eta}_{3,j} = \hat{\eta}_{4,j} = 0$ can be rejected for Shanghai but not for Shenzhen, indicating that volatility became smaller over time in Shanghai while it remained basically unchanged in Shenzhen after the daily price-change limits were removed.

3.8 Volatility Asymmetry and Spill-over

The GARCH-type of models delineates the volatility as a symmetric response in that information absorption is the same to good news as to bad news. The partial adjustment model of Amihud and Mendelson (1987), Domodaran (1993), and Koutmos (1998) is of the asymmetric volatility type in that the volatility response to good news is different from the bad news.

Amihud and Mendelson (1987) examine the role of different market mechanisms in inducing stock return autocorrelation by means of a partial adjustment price model. They find that stock returns are more persistent, i.e., they exhibit greater autocorrelation when securities are traded in a call market as opposed to a continuous auction market. Damodaran (1993) also uses the partial adjustment model and finds that stocks listed in NASDAQ adjust slower to new information than those listed in NYSE/AMEX. Koutmos (1998) tests the hypothesis that both the conditional mean and

Table 3.13 Maximum Likelihood Estimates of the SGARCH(1,1) Model with Dummy Variables

	Shanghai A-Shares[a]	Shenzhen A-Shares
constant	0.0063	0.0044
$r_{j,t-1}$	0.4816*	0.1153*
$\Delta RMBUS_{t-1}$	0.0168	0.0223
$\Delta HKUS_{t-1}$	-0.1217	-0.3103
ΔTO_{t-1}	-0.002	0.0006
$MSCI_{t-1}$	-0.5788*	-0.1731
HS_{t-1}	0.2856*	-0.0049
$NYSE_{t-1}$	-0.0393	0.4052*
TS_{t-1}	-0.0498	-0.3774
ΔTB_{t-1}	-2.1456	-2.6475
$\hat{\omega}_j$	0.0064*	0.0063*
$\hat{\eta}_j^1$	0.1946	0.0774
$\hat{\eta}_j^2$	0.1717	0.1171
$\hat{\eta}_j^3$	0.1571	0.1129
$\hat{\eta}_j^4$	0.1253	0.1292
$\hat{\alpha}_j$	0.5196*	0.6638*
$\hat{\beta}_j$	0.2931*	0.3537*
ν	1.8062*	1.736*
Mean log likelihood	1.9563	2.1165
$LR_{\hat{\eta}_j=0}$[b]	13.3076	7.828
$Q_8(\epsilon_j/\sigma_j)$[c]	2.5536	0.0691
	[0.9592]	[0.9999]

[a]Figures inside the brackets are p-values and * denotes 5% level of significance according to the Wald Confidence Limits.

[b]Likelihood ratio statistics is used to test the null hypothesis that $\hat{\eta}_{1,j} = \hat{\eta}_{2,j} = \hat{\eta}_{3,j} = \hat{\eta}_{4,j} = 0$, and is asymptotically distributed as Chi-square with 4 degrees of freedom. The critical value for $\chi^2(4)$ at the 5% level of significance is 9.49.

[c]$Q_8(\epsilon_j/\sigma_j)$ denotes the Ljung-Box Q statistic for serial correlation tests with 8 lags on standardized residuals.

the conditional variance of index stock returns are asymmetric functions of past information and finds that the conditional mean is an asymmetric function of past returns and the conditional variance rises more proportionately during market declines (the so-called "leverage effect").

In this section, we test whether the stock-market returns in China adjust to their intrinsic values through partial adjustment with asymmetries and study the possible spill-over effects between China and Hong Kong.

3.8.1 *A Partial Adjustment Model with Asymmetries*

The price adjustment process is assumed to be self-adapted from the intrinsic value as follows:

$$P_t - P_{t-1} = (1-\theta)(V_t - P_{t-1}) \tag{3.24}$$

where P_t is the observed equity price and V_t is the intrinsic value, both expressed in natural logarithmic form. The adjustment cost gives rise to the friction parameter, θ. The greater the value of θ, the slower the adjustment process. As a result, the adjustment speed can be measured by $(1-\theta)$.[13] The intrinsic value of a stock index is assumed to follow a random walk with drift,

$$V_t = \pi + V_{t-1} + e_t \tag{3.25}$$

where $\{e_t\}$ is an i.i.d. process with zero mean and π stands for the expected daily intrinsic value. Equations (3.24) and (3.25) imply that the return

[13] As described in Koutmos (1998), an economic justification for equation (3.24) can be based on the assumption that market price, P_t, is arrived at through minimization of the following cost function:

$$C = a(P_t - V_t)^2 + b(P_t - P_{t-1})^2,$$

where $a(P_t - V_t)^2$ measures the cost of being out of equilibrium, and $b(P_t - P_{t-1})^2$ measures the cost of making the adjustment. Minimization of the above equation implies that:

$$P_t - P_{t-1} = a(a+b)^{-1}(V_t - P_{t-1}),$$

which is essentially equation (3.24) with speed of adjustment given by $a(a+b)^{-1}$.

process follows an autoregressive process of order one,[14] i.e.,

$$r_t = \beta + \theta r_{t-1} + \epsilon_t \tag{3.26}$$

where $r_t = P_t - P_{t-1}$, $\beta = (1-\theta)\pi$, and $\epsilon_t = (1-\theta)e_t$. Estimates of the friction parameter, θ, can be obtained by simply estimating the AR(1) process given in equation (3.26). However, if adjustment costs are asymmetric, then equation (3.24) has to changed as follows:

$$P_t - P_{t-1} = (1-\theta^+)(V_t - P_{t-1})^+ + (1-\theta^-)(V_t - P_{t-1})^- \tag{3.27}$$

in which $(V_t - P_{t-1})^+ = \max\{(V_t - P_{t-1}), 0\}$ and $(V_t - P_{t-1})^- = \min\{(V_t - P_{t-1}), 0\}$. For $\theta^+ = \theta^- = \theta$, equation (3.27) reverts back to the symmetric model. Equations (3.26) and (3.27) imply that stock returns follow an autoregressive process of order one, given by:

$$r_t = \beta + \theta^+ r^+_{t-1} + \theta^- r^-_{t-1} + \epsilon_t \tag{3.28}$$

where $r^+_{t-1} = \max\{r_{t-1}, 0\}$ and $r^-_{t-1} = \min\{r_{t-1}, 0\}$. As can be seen, the asymmetric autoregressive process given in equation (3.28) utilizes two different filters, one for positive and another for negative previous stock returns. Again, when $\theta^+ = \theta^- = \theta$, the price process is symmetric and the $\{r_t\}$ sequence follows the usual symmetric autoregressive process. As a result, the optimal one-step ahead forecast will be $E(r_t|\Omega_{t-1}) = \beta + \theta r_{t-1}$. However, when $\theta^+ \neq \theta^-$, the $\{r_t\}$ sequence will exhibit more complex behavior. The optimal one-step ahead forecast will depend on the sign of r_{t-1}, i.e.,

$$E(r_t|\Omega_{t-1}) = \begin{cases} \beta + \theta^+ r^+_{t-1} & \text{for} \quad r_{t-1} \geq 0 \\ \beta + \theta^- r^-_{t-1} & \text{for} \quad r_{t-1} \leq 0 \end{cases} \tag{3.29}$$

[14]From equation (3.24), we get P_t as follows:

$$P_t = (1-\theta)V_t + \theta P_{t-1}.$$

And then,

$$\begin{aligned} r_t &= P_t - P_{t-1} \\ &= \theta(P_{t-1} - P_{t-2}) + (1-\theta)(V_t - V_{t-1}) \\ &= \theta(P_{t-1} - P_{t-2}) + (1-\theta)(e_t + \pi) \\ &= (1-\theta)\pi + \theta(P_{t-1} - P_{t-2}) + (1-\theta)e_t \\ &= \beta + \theta r_{t-1} + \epsilon_t \end{aligned}$$

The error process, $\{\epsilon_t\}$, is assumed to be conditionally heteroskedastic with time-varying conditional standard deviation given by:

$$\sigma_t = \alpha_0 + \alpha_1^+ \epsilon_{t-1}^+ - \alpha_1^- \epsilon_{t-1}^- + \phi\sigma_{t-1} \tag{3.30}$$

where $\epsilon_{t-1}^+ = \max(0, \epsilon_{t-1})$ and $\epsilon_{t-1}^- = \min(0, \epsilon_{t-1})$. This model is introduced in Zakoian (1994) as the Threshod GARCH or TGARCH model. The advantage of a TGARCH specification is that the conditional variance is allowed to be leptokurtotic and the probabilistic properties of σ_t are more complicated. In order to make sure that the conditional volatility is non-negative, $\alpha_0 > 0$, $\alpha_1^+ \geq 0$, $\alpha_1^- \geq 0$, and $\phi \geq 0$ non-negativity constraints need to be imposed on equation (3.37). Using Generalized Error Distribution, we employ the maximum likelihood method to estimate the specified model while allowing the distribution parameter, ν, to be estimated from the data. The probability density function of the Generalized Error Distribution is given by:

$$f(\mu_t, \sigma_t, \nu) = \frac{\nu}{2}\left[\Gamma\left(\frac{3}{\nu}\right)\right]^{\frac{1}{2}}\left[\Gamma\left(\frac{1}{\nu}\right)\right]^{-\frac{3}{2}}\left(\frac{1}{\sigma_t}\right)\exp^{\left[\frac{\Gamma(\frac{3}{\nu})}{\Gamma(\frac{1}{\nu})}\right]^{\frac{\nu}{2}}\left|\frac{\epsilon_t}{\sigma_t}\right|^{\nu}} \tag{3.31}$$

where $\Gamma(\cdot)$ is the gamma function and ν is the degree of freedom to be estimated endogenously. When $\nu = 2$, the GED distribution is reduced to the normal distribution and when $\nu = 1$ it yields the Laplace or double exponential distribution. Given initial values for ϵ_t and σ_t^2, the parameter set $\mathbf{\Theta} = (\beta, \theta^+, \theta^-, \alpha_0, \alpha_1^+, \alpha_1^-, \phi, \nu)$ can be estimated by maximizing the log-likelihood over the sample period. The log-likelihood can be expressed as:

$$L(\mathbf{\Theta}) = \sum_{t=1}^{T} \log f(\mu_t, \sigma_t, \nu) \tag{3.32}$$

where μ_t represents the conditional mean. When estimated using the model described above, we may add moving average terms into the return equation (3.28) to alleviate the problem of error distribution.

Furthermore, to understand whether the volatility equation is well-specified for the underlying asset returns, we employ a battery of diagnostic tests proposed by Engle and Ng (1993) to check the fit of the model. These diagnostic statistics are the sign bias test (SBT), the negative size bias test

(NSBT), the positive size bias test (PSBT), and the joint test (JT):

$$\text{SBT:} \quad \left(\frac{\epsilon_t}{\sigma_t}\right)^2 = a + bS_{t-1}^- + \eta_t \tag{3.33}$$

$$\text{NSBT:} \quad \left(\frac{\epsilon_t}{\sigma_t}\right)^2 = a + bS_{t-1}^- \epsilon_{t-1} + \eta_t \tag{3.34}$$

$$\text{PSBT:} \quad \left(\frac{\epsilon_t}{\sigma_t}\right)^2 = a + b(1 - S_{t-1}^-)\epsilon_{t-1} + \eta_t \tag{3.35}$$

$$\text{JT:} \quad \left(\frac{\epsilon_t}{\sigma_t}\right)^2 = a + b_1 S_{t-1}^- + b_2 S_{t-1}^- \epsilon_{t-1} + b_3(1 - S_{t-1}^-)\epsilon_{t-1} + \eta_t \tag{3.36}$$

where ϵ_t/σ_t is the standard deviation and $S_{t-1}^- = 1$ if $\epsilon_{t-1} < 0$, and $S_{t-1}^- = 0$ otherwise. For SBT, NSBT, and $PSBT$ tests, the t-statistic of b is insignificant if volatility estimation is well-specified. On the other hand, the joint test is to test the hypothesis that $b_1 = b_2 = b_3 = 0$. The test statistic for the joint test is the product of the number of observations and R^2 and is distributed as $\chi^2(3)$.

3.8.2 *Asymmetric Behavior on Returns and Volatility*

We estimate the partial adjustment model with asymmetries for daily indices of A- and B-shares in Shanghai and Shenzhen. Table 3.14 presents the coefficient estimates. As shown on the table, the A- and B-share markets strongly react to good and bad news in Shanghai. The reaction to negative news is larger than that to positive news in the A-share market because $\theta^+ < \theta^-$ and the likelihood ratio tests reject the equality of them. This indicates that in general, price adjustment to intrinsic value for good news is a little faster than for bad news in A-share market in Shanghai. However, B-share market in Shanghai seems to respond to good and bad news symmetrically during the sample period. This reflects the nature of the B-share market that it opens only to international investors who probably have better access to higher quality news and can analyze news better than domestic Chinese investors.

In contrast to the findings in Shanghai markets, the return reaction to good or bad news is not statistically significant in Shenzhen A-share market. This implies that the A-share market in Shenzhen may not be asymmetric in terms of return responses to information arrival. However, the coefficient estimates for positive and negative returns are all significant

Table 3.14 Estimates of Partial Adjustment Model with Asymmetries

	Shanghai A-share	Shanghai B-share	Shenzhen A-share	Shenzhen B-share
β	0.017*	-0.092*	0.010†	-0.084†
	(0.008)	(0.0288)	(0.006)	(0.053)
θ^{+}	0.852*	0.347*	0.472*	0.306*
	(0.064)	(0.031)	(0.089)	(0.065)
θ^{-}	0.729*	0.186*	0.029	0.074*
	(0.093)	(0.051)	(0.033)	(0.024)
α_0	0.135*	0.188*	0.171*	0.129*
	(0.046)	(0.085)	(0.070)	(0.058)
α_1^{+}	0.427*	0.601*	0.205*	0.196*
	(0.103)	(0.175)	(0.084)	(0.079)
α_1^{-}	0.271*	0.492*	0.266*	0.148*
	(0.066)	(0.108)	(0.058)	(0.040)
ϕ	0.681*	0.735*	0.699*	0.618*
	(0.052)	(0.068)	(0.054)	(0.049)
ν	0.926*	1.305*	0.891*	1.056*
	(0.042)	(0.061)	(0.38)	(0.049)
$LR_{\theta^{+}=\theta^{-}}$	13.97*	1.75	10.06*	1.04
$LR_{\alpha_1^{+}=\alpha_1^{-}}$	363.15*	1.09	496.22*	5.87*
Ljung-Box(12)	24.83	76.40*	28.91	84.35*

* and † denote significance at the 5% and 10% level, respectively.

for the B-share market in Shenzhen, and the coefficient estimate of positive return is larger than that of the negative return. Therefore, the asymmetric return response to news is present in the B-share market in Shenzhen.

Furthermore, our empirical results show that the volatility exhibits asymmetric behavior for both A- and B-share markets in Shanghai and Shenzhen. This implies that past information, including both good and bad news, can influence the information assimilation process no matter whether the returns are eventually affected. The degree of asymmetry, calculated as $\alpha_1^{-}/\alpha_1^{+}$, varies from 0.5 to 1.3. This suggests that Chinese markets are very sensitive to negative news.

Table 3.15 Specification Tests for Volatility Asymmetries

	Shanghai A-share	Shanghai B-share	Shenzhen A-share	Shenzhen B-share
SBT	-1.188	1.472	-1.305	-2.206[†]
NSBT	2.37*	2.163*	1.286	1.047
PSBT	0.625	0.891	-1.974[†]	0.835
JT	3.306	2.924	2.558	3.179

* and † denote significance at the 5% and 10% level, respectively.

Table 3.15 presents specification tests for volatility asymmetries (or the news impact tests). The SBT, NSBT, PSBT, and JT statistics show that the model captures the volatility asymmetry very well. Therefore, the partial adjustment model with asymmetries can well-describe the absorption of information in the Chinese stock markets.

3.8.3 *Stock-Market Volatility Spill-over Between Mainland China and Hong Kong*

To understand volatility spill-over from one market to another, we need to modify the partial adjustment model with asymmetries to account for volatility transmission. In particular,

$$r_{i,t} = \delta + \gamma r_{i,t-1} + \phi_1 r_{j,t} + \phi_2 r_{j,t-1} + \phi_3 r_{j,t-2} + \epsilon_{i,t} \tag{3.37}$$

$$h_{i,t} = \omega + \alpha\epsilon^2_{i,t-1} + \lambda\epsilon^2_{i,t-1}d_{t-1} + \beta h_{i,t-1} + \rho_1 r^2_{j,t} + \rho_2 r^2_{j,t-1} + \rho_3 r^2_{j,t-2} \tag{3.38}$$

$$d_{t-1} = \begin{cases} 1 & \text{if } \epsilon_{i,t-1} < 0 \\ 0 & \text{otherwise} \end{cases}$$

$$\epsilon_{i,t} \sim N(0, h_{i,t})$$

The modified partial adjustment model with asymmetries explicitly considers the impact of current and past innovations of market j have on return and volatility of market i. If market j indeed has impacts on the current

Table 3.16 Partial Adjustment Model with Asymmetric Volatility Spill-over from Shanghai and Shenzhen to Hong Kong

	Shanghai A-share	Shanghai B-share	Shenzhen A-share	Shenzhen B-share
γ	0.067*	0.048†	0.074*	0.062*
	(0.031)	(0.026)	(0.038)	(0.032)
ϕ_1	0.012	0.128†	0.022	0.018
	(0.019)	(0.038)	(0.020)	(0.017)
ϕ_2	0.007	0.022	0.016	0.004
	(0.015)	(0.026)	(0.014)	(0.012)
ϕ_3	0.006	0.002	0.006	0.009
	(0.011)	(0.013)	(0.011)	(0.010)
α	0.102†	0.064*	0.048	0.091
	(0.059)	(0.021)	(0.037)	(0.088)
λ	0.148*	0.382*	0.207*	0.195*
	(0.036)	(0.087)	(0.064)	(0.049)
β	0.427*	0.292*	0.338*	0.401*
	(0.129)	(0.087)	(0.081)	(0.166)
ρ_1	-0.096	-0.053	-0.108	0.004
	(0.088)	(0.061)	(0.115)	(0.007)
ρ_2	-0.008	-0.013	-0.026	-0.017
	(0.014)	(0.026)	(0.041)	(0.083)
ρ_3	-0.002	-0.001	-0.003	-0.001
	(0.003)	(0.004)	(0.005)	(0.002)
Ljung-Box(12)	14.82	19.05	13.60	15.12

* and † denote significance at the 5% and 10% level, respectively.

return and volatility of market i, the coefficient estimates for ϕ_1, ϕ_2, ϕ_3, ρ_1, ρ_2, and ρ_3 will be statistically significant.

Tables 3.16 and 3.17 present parameter estimates for the partial adjustment model with asymmetric volatility spill-over. As shown in the table, there is no obvious influence of return and volatility spill-over from Shanghai and Shenzhen to Hong Kong except the B-share market in Shanghai. This is probably because the market capitalization and trading volume of the B-share market in Shanghai is larger than those of the B-share market

Table 3.17 Partial Adjustment Model with Asymmetric Volatility Spill-over from Hong Kong to Shanghai and Shenzhen

	Shanghai A-share	Shanghai B-share	Shenzhen A-share	Shenzhen B-share
γ	0.157*	0.108*	0.083†	0.184*
	(0.062)	(0.041)	(0.054)	(0.066)
ϕ_1	0.008	0.195*	0.012	0.163*
	(0.010)	(0.082)	(0.009)	(0.069)
ϕ_2	0.072	0.102	0.095	-0.019
	(0.063)	(0.085)	(0.071)	(0.011)
ϕ_3	-0.017	0.039	-0.028	-0.005
	(0.014)	(0.027)	(0.024)	(0.009)
α	1.783*	4.061*	2.682*	1.933*
	(0.429)	(0.974)	(0.488)	(0.643)
λ	0.217*	0.183*	0.406*	0.320*
	(0.094)	(0.055)	(0.116)	(0.087)
β	0.387*	0.501*	0.515*	0.559*
	(0.062)	(0.091)	(0.096)	(0.078)
ρ_1	-0.017	-0.011	-0.072	0.009
	(0.025)	(0.019)	(0.069)	(0.008)
ρ_2	-0.014	-0.019	-0.016	-0.010
	(0.019)	(0.016)	(0.014)	(0.007)
ρ_3	-0.028	-0.047	-0.016	-0.025
	(0.023)	(0.039)	(0.020)	(0.028)
Ljung-Box(12)	22.15	72.37*	17.40	58.26*

* and † denote significance at the 5% and 10% level, respectively.

in Shenzhen.

In contrast to the spill-over effect from Shanghai and Shenzhen to Hong Kong, the spill-over of return from Hong Kong to Shanghai and Shenzhen is statistically significant while the spill-over of volatility is not. The current and past stock returns in Hong Kong have significant impact on the Shanghai and Shenzhen securities exchanges, but for B-shares only. A possible explanation is that international traders who include B-share indices as part of their global diversification portfolios place a significant portion of their other types of China investment funds in Hong Kong market. As a consequence, their investment adjustment decisions on B-share indices will depend on their investment decisions on Hong Kong market. However, the current and lagged stock-market volatility in Hong Kong has little or no impact on the volatility in Shanghai and Shenzhen. An explanation is that the overall liquidity is lower in Shanghai and Shenzhen than that of Hong Kong.

3.9 Summary

In this chapter, we analyze the dynamic behavior of risks and returns in Chinese stock markets. We find that the risk-adjusted mean stock returns are low and the volatility of stock-market returns is high in China relative to developed markets. Moreover, returns are positively autocorrelated to greater extent in Chinese stock markets than in developed markets. The famous Monday effect exists in both domestic and foreign share markets, even if market trend is removed from daily return data. We find that the random walk hypothesis is rejected for Chinese stock markets using variance ratio tests while it can not be rejected for developed markets. A residual-based cointegration test shows that the daily A share market indices in Shanghai and Shenzhen tend to move together, but the daily B share market indices do not.

We also establish an empirical model to capture the deterministic components of the variation in the stock-market returns and characterize the second order conditional moments using three error generation processes. We find that the variance of stock-market returns is time-varying, mildly persistent, leptokurtotic and is influenced by exogenous variables representing government market liberalization policies. We also find that the Shanghai B-share market is more integrated with the world equity markets than any other Chinese market, although even here the degree of integration appears to be weak. A share returns in Shanghai and Shenzhen tend to respond similarly to common news and economic factors, leading me to believe that there is potential for them to become a fully integrated national stock market. Encouraging cross-listing and eliminating the distinction between different classes of shares will improve stock-market liquidity and enhance capital mobilization.

In addition, we find that government's market liberalization policies have contributed to the high stock-market volatility in China. We also conjecture that market segmentation, both across different stock exchanges and across different share types, and extraordinary large IPO underpricing may have contributed to the high stock-market volatility as well.

Finally, we investigates the partial adjustment process with asymmetries on stock indices in China. We find that stock-market returns and volatility exhibit asymmetric adjustment behavior in all markets except the A-share market in Shenzhen. The adjustment speed is faster for bad news than for good news. We also find that current and past returns and volatility in Hong Kong stock market have significant impact on B-share markets in Shanghai and Shenzhen. Our empirical results are consistent with Chui and Kwok (1998), who find significant cross-correlation between the B-share markets in China and Hong Kong market.

The empirical model used in this chapter is a univariate model. Therefore, some interesting questions are left unexplored. For example, what are the sources of differences in expected returns and volatility in A- and B-share markets? Has the degree of integration among Chinese stock markets and world markets improve over time? Analyzing these questions requires exploiting a multivariate factor asset pricing model with time-varying world market integration.

Chapter 4

Ownership Restrictions and Foreign Shares Discount

4.1 Introduction

It is widely documented that ownership restrictions and market segmentation result in price differentials among classes of shares in many emerging stock markets. For example, Eun and Jankiramanan (1986) examine a two-country model in which investors from each country attempt to maximize the expected utility of wealth subject to a one-way investment barrier on foreign investors and domestic investors can have no limits on security holding internationally. Errunza and Losq (1985) study a special case of Eun and Jankiramanan model in which foreign ownership is completely banned in one country and domestic investors are not subject to restrictions in the other country. Hietala (1987) develops a single-period capital asset pricing model (CAPM), incorporating specific investment restrictions imposed by Finnish government (Finnish people must hold at least 80% of domestic shares). Bailey and Jagtiani (1994) examine the effects of investment barriers in Thailand and find that cross-sectional differences in local and foreign share prices are correlated with proxies for foreign ownership limits, liquidity and information availability. Stulz and Wasserfallen (1995) use Hietala's model with added implication. They develop and test a price discrimination model assuming domestic country is relatively small, relaxing the holding restriction will not affect foreign investor's required return and will therefore not affect the free share price. Johnson (1995) introduces a multi-period model to explain the existence of a time-varying premium between free and restricted shares in the case of Sweden, assuming free shares are available only for domestic investors and restricted shares are available for both domestic and foreign investors.

The price differential raises two questions: First, what economic factors determine domestic and foreign investors' portfolio choices under ownership restrictions? Second, why do firms issue both types of shares, if one type sells at a higher price than the other?

In this chapter, we extend Stulz and Wasserfallen's one-period price discrimination model to multiple domestic firms that issue A and B shares at the same time, assuming A shares are only available to domestic investors and B shares can only be owned by foreign investors, a case that mostly resembles the restrictions in the Chinese stock markets. The model posits that cross-sectional variations in the expected return between two classes of shares—those purchased and traded by domestic and foreign investors, respectively, are determined by the shares' own market betas and betas with respect to the international financial markets. We also formulate an Intertemporal Capital Asset Pricing Model (ICAPM), assuming domestic investors have a smaller investment opportunity set than foreign investors, as is the case in China. The solution of the ICAPM also clearly shows that cross-sectional variations in the expected return between domestic and foreign shares are determined by the shares' own market betas and betas with respect to the international financial markets. Given that we reach the same results using two different theoretical models, we firmly believe that we have solid ground for further empirical work. After testing the predictions from both models using appropriate econometric techniques, we find that:

- Cross-sectional excess of domestic over foreign shares' average returns are positively related to domestic shares' market betas and negatively related to both foreign shares' market betas and betas with the Hong Kong Hang Seng index.
- The variance of shares' returns and the firm size do not appear to influence cross-sectional return differences.

These results strongly support both price discrimination model and the ICAPM formulation.

The rest of the chapter proceeds as follows: In Section 4.2, we describe the effects ownership restrictions have on stock prices in China. In Section 4.3, we develop a price discrimination model with effective market segmentation. In Section 4.4, we analyze the ICAPM under ownership restrictions. In Section 4.5, we derive some testable implications from both models. In Section 4.6, we describe the methodology in empirical tests and present the empirical results. We conclude this chapter in Section 4.7 with a summary of findings.

4.2 Ownership Restrictions in Chinese Stock Markets

Chinese stock markets are segmented in two aspects. First, dual listing is not allowed so that each company's issue is restricted to one of the two exchanges. In this way, the domestic and international share markets remain distinct. In other words, a company officially listed in one exchange cannot be listed in another exchange. Second, a listed company in either exchange can issue to two types of shares: A-shares for domestic investors and B-shares for foreign investors. Chinese citizens are only permitted to trade A-shares, while international investors, including overseas Chinese residing in Hong Kong, Macau, or Taiwan, can only participate in the trading of B-shares in mainland China.

China's stock markets opened to international investors on February 21, 1992, when Shanghai Vacuum Electronics began issuing B-shares in Shanghai Securities Exchange. This was quickly followed by the listing of China Southern Glass B-shares in Shenzhen Securities Exchange on February 28, 1992. For each company, A- and B-shares are entitled to the same rights and dividends. Henceforth, international investors were allowed to participate in Shanghai and Shenzhen exchanges, but only in B-shares.[1]

Column one in Tables 4.1–4.4 list the companies that have issued B shares in either Shanghai or Shenzhen securities exchange by the end of August 1995. Column four of the tables report the initial public offering prices for A- and B-shares. A-share prices are converted to either U.S. dollar prices or Hong Kong dollar prices for the ease of comparison. As shown in the tables, A-shares are generally sold at substantially higher prices than B shares.

[1] In 1993, China created an additional class of stock to facilitate the direct listings of Chinese companies on foreign stock exchanges, known as H-shares (for Hong Kong Stock Exchange) and N-shares (for New York Stock Exchange). H-shares and N-shares carry the same rights and obligations as A- and B-shares, but they can only be traded on stock exchanges outside of China.

Table 4.1 Profiles for Companies Issuing Both A and B Shares in the Shanghai Securities Exchange (As of August 1995)

Company	Code	Number of A-Shares[‡]	Price (in USD)
Shanghai Vacuum Electro.	901	12139	1.14
Shanghai Erfangji	902	5882.8	3.14
Dazhong Taxi	903	1300	2.55
Yongsheng Stationery	904	600	3.5
China First Pencil	905	1320	1.86
China Textile Machinery	906	2340	1.71
Shanghai Rubber Belt	907	660	1.99
Shanghai Chlor Alkai	908	2300	0.92
Shanghai Tire & Rubber	909	2080	2.49
Shanghai Refrigerator	910	1300	1.06
Jinqiao Export & Import	911	7500	1.7
Outer Gaoqiao	912	1950	2.56
Lianhua Fiber	913	900	2.06
Shanghai Jin Jiang Tower	914	2400	1.96
Forever Bicycle	915	1300	1.18
Phoenix Bicycle	916	2000	1.57
Shanghai Haixian Group	917	1100	2.0
Yaohua Pilkington Glass	918	2500	1.69
Dajiang Group	919	1950	1.72
Shanghai Diesel Engine	920	1800	1.95
Hero Pen	921	1300	1.48
Sanmao Textile	922	1000	1.18
Shanghai Friendship Store	923	1204	1.46
Industrial Sewing Machine	924	1200	1.58
Shang-Ling Refrigerators	925	1800	1.22
Shanghai Steel Tube	926	1320	1.1
Shanghai Merchandise Trading	927	1100	1.95
Shanghai Automated Machine	928	2420	1.34
Communication Equipment	930	1300	2.62
Shuixian Electronics	931	1595	1.39
Lujia Development	932	6300	2.99
Huaxin Cement	933	1300	0.56
Shanghai Xinya Group	934	1200	1.39

[‡]: in 10,000 shares

Table 4.2 Profiles for Companies Issuing Both A and B Shares in the Shanghai Securities Exchange (As of August 1995)

Company	Number of B-Shares‡	IPO Date for B Share	IPO Price (in USD)
Shanghai Vacuum Electro.	14250	Feb. 12, 1992	0.72
Shanghai Erfangji	19250	July 1, 1992	0.59
Dazhong Taxi	7800	July 22, 1992	0.652
Yongsheng Stationery	3000	July 22, 1992	0.835
China First Pencil	6600	July 28, 1992	0.525
China Textile Machinery	10920	July 28, 1992	0.61
Shanghai Rubber Belt	3300	July 28, 1992	0.53
Shanghai Chlor Alkai	33600	Aug. 20, 1992	0.798
Shanghai Tire & Rubber	22100	Aug. 28, 1992	1.1
Shanghai Refrigerator	6500	Nov. 16, 1992	0.461
Jinqiao Export & Import	14300	May 21, 1993	0.344
Outer Gaoqiao	16575	July 29, 1993	0.39
Lianhua Fiber	3600	Oct. 18, 1993	0.3792
Shanghai Jin Jiang Tower	9243	Oct. 18, 1993	0.3792
Forever Bicycle	6000	Nov. 12, 1993	0.405
Phoenix Bicycle	10000	Nov. 12, 1993	0.68
Shanghai Haixian Group	3850	Dec. 10, 1993	0.7
Yaohua Pilkington Glass	10000	Dec. 10, 1993	0.72
Dajiang Group	4500	Dec. 15, 1993	0.4023
Shanghai Diesel Engine	11000	Dec. 28, 1993	0.523
Hero Pen	4550	Dec. 28, 1993	0.439
Sanmao Textile	3300	Dec. 31, 1993	0.3425
Shanghai Friendship Store	4800	Jan. 5, 1994	0.44
Industrial Sewing Machine	7500	Jan. 18, 1994	0.42
Shang-Ling Refrigerators	7900	Jan. 31, 1994	0.75
Shanghai Steel Tube	8800	Mar. 15, 1994	0.75
Shanghai Merchandise	5500	Mar. 30, 1994	0.258
Shanghai Automated Mac.	7700	Apr. 29, 1994	0.248
Communication Equipment	6000	Nov. 10, 1994	0.52
Shuixian Electronics	10000	Nov. 10, 1994	0.265
Lujia Development	20000	Nov. 22, 1994	0.668
Huaxin Cement	4500	Dec. 9, 1994	0.233
Shanghai Xinya Group	10000	Dec. 9, 1994	0.35

‡: in 10,000 shares

Table 4.3 Profiles for Companies Issuing Both A and B Shares in the Shenzhen Securities Exchange (As of August 1995)

Company	Code	Number of A-Shares‡	Price (in USD)
Shenzhen Vanke Co.	2002	5673	23.77
Gintian Industry	2003	6877.6	19.65
Property & Resource Devel.	2011	4150	23.3
China Southern Glass	2012	2030	19.85
Shenzhen Petroch. Co	2013	2350	18.15
Shenzhen Zhonghao Co.	2015	5972.2	9.74
Konka Electronics	2016	3015	20.01
Shenzhen China Bicycles	2017	3280	11.6
Victor Onward Textile	2018	5972.2	9.74
Shenbao Industry	2019	1940	8.85
Shenzhen Huafa Electronics	2020	2963	13.33
Chiwan Wharf Holdings	2022	4600	13.15
China Merchants Shekou Co.	2024	9975	11.24
Tellus Machinery	2025	2598	10.54
Fiyta Holdings	2026	3350	12.67
Yili Mineral Water	2028	3000	12.56
SEZ Real Estate	2029	11200	9.65
Shenzhen Lionda Holdings	2030	4350	10.67
Shenzhen Nanshan Power	2037	4350	11.3
China Marine Containers	2039	1776	10.08
Shenzhen Textile	2045	8200	5.93
Hainan Pearl River Ent.	2505	11340.5	3.89
Lizon Pharmaceutical Co.	2513	4978.3	3.47
Guangdong Electric Power	2539	9855	4.44
Foshan Electric Lighting	2541	55566	8.22
Jiangling Motors	2550	35324	3.88

‡: in 10,000 shares

All firms can issue A-shares, but as discussed further below, firms must apply for permission to issue B-shares. To limit foreign ownership, the Chinese government allows no more than 25% of an enterprise's convertible shares to be B-shares. Unlike Indonesia and Thailand, where individuals are permitted to purchase local shares and have them registered as foreign shares through a foreign sponsor, Chinese investors are allowed to purchase and trade only A-shares while foreign investors can purchase and trade only B-shares. Firms that issue B-shares are entitled to favorable tax treatment

Table 4.4 Profiles for Companies Issuing Both A and B Shares in the Shenzhen Securities Exchange (As of August 1995)

Company	Number of B-Shares‡	IPO Date for B Share	IPO Price (in USD)
Shenzhen Vanke Co.	4500	May 28, 1993	10.53
Gintian Industry	3800	June 29, 1993	10.71
Property & Resource Devel.	3000	Mar. 30, 1992	5.3
China Southern Glass	1600	Feb. 28, 1992	5.3
Shenzhen Petroch. Co	1500	May 6, 1992	4.28
Shenzhen Zhonghao Co.	2000	June 16, 1992	2.50
Konka Electronics	1000	Mar. 27, 1992	5.5
Shenzhen China Bicycles	2550	Mar. 31, 1992	5.3
Victor Onward Textile	2000	June 16, 1992	2.5
Shenbao Industry	1800	Oct. 12, 1992	3.6
Shenzhen Huafa Electronics	2350	Apr. 28, 1992	2.69
Chiwan Wharf Holdings	4000	May 5, 1993	2.83
China Merchants Shekou Co.	5000	June 7, 1993	3.23
Tellus Machinery	2000	June 21, 1993	4.03
Fiyta Holdings	1500	June 3, 1993	3.48
Yili Mineral Water	2000	Aug. 9, 1993	3.17
SEZ Real Estate	10000	Jan. 10, 1994	3.5
Shenzhen Lionda Holdings	3000	Sept. 29, 1993	3.5
Shenzhen Nanshan Power	3000	Sept. 29, 1993	3.5
China Marine Containers	1300	Mar. 23, 1994	7.54
Shenzhen Textile	2500	Aug. 15, 1994	2.39
Hainan Pearl River Ent.	5750	June 29, 1995	2.56
Lizon Pharmaceutical Co.	2132.5	June 28, 1995	4.29
Guangdong Electric Power	9000	June 28, 1995	4.29
Foshan Electric Lighting	50000	Aug. 8, 1995	5.61
Jiangling Motors	17400	Sept. 29, 1995	1.1919

‡: in 10,000 shares

and more freedom to import and export goods.

Although A- and B-shares represent claims to the same cash flow rights, B-shares are generally sold and traded at substantially lower prices than A-shares. Define A-share premium as $(P_A - P_B)/P_B$, where P_A is the price for A-share and P_B is the price for the corresponding B-share. Tables 4.5 and 4.6 present the time-series average weekly A-share premia for 27 Shanghai firms and 20 Shenzhen firms that issued both A- and B-shares before April 1994. The sample period is between April 1994 and October 1998. Define

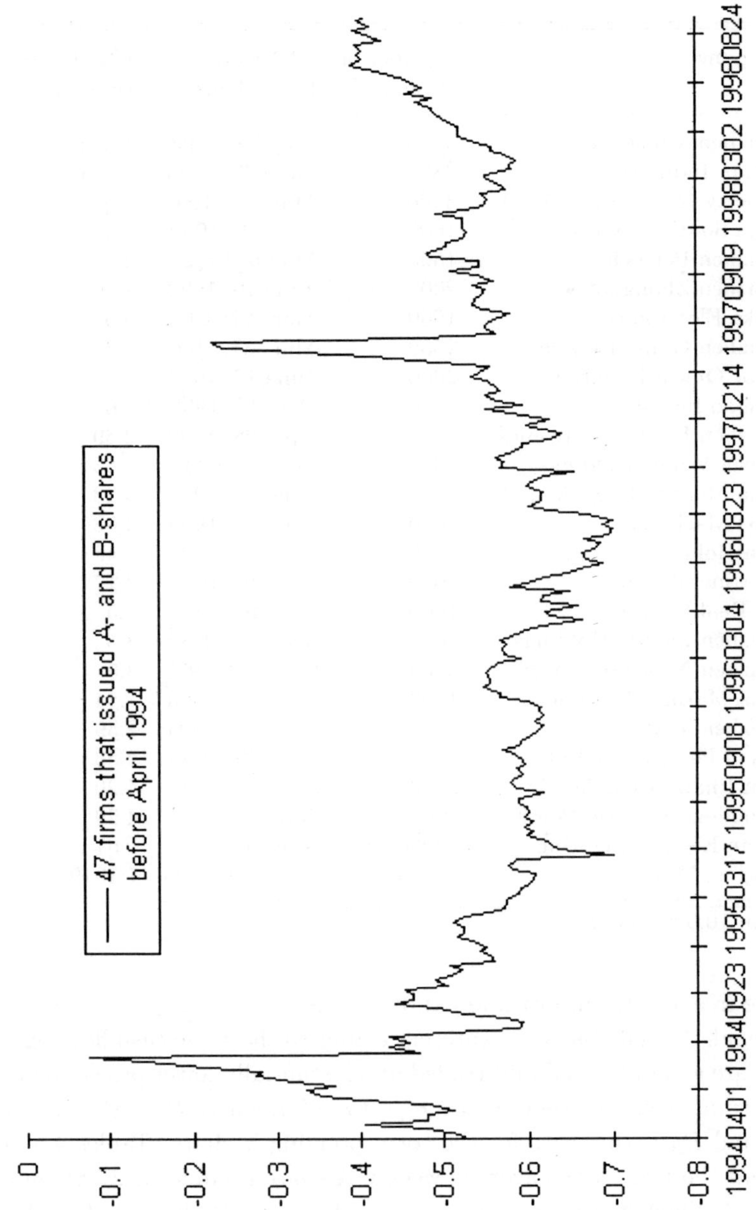

Fig. 4.1 Equally-Weighted Average Weekly B-Share Discount (April 1994–October 1998)

Table 4.5 Sample Statistics for A-share Premia for Shanghai Companies That Issued A- and B-shares Before April 1994 (Sample Period: April 1, 1994–October 31, 1998)

Company	Mean	Std. Dev.	Minimum	Maximum
Shanghai Vacuum Electronics	0.95	0.51	0.13	1.64
Shanghai Erfangji	0.56	0.31	-0.11	1.25
Dazhong Taxi	1.26	0.53	0.15	1.93
Yongsheng Stationery	0.61	0.39	-0.26	1.16
China First Pencil	0.75	0.23	0.33	1.30
China Textile Machinery	0.87	0.47	-0.35	1.66
Shanghai Rubber Belt	1.31	0.61	0.25	2.38
Shanghai Chlor Alkai	0.63	0.37	0.20	1.26
Shanghai Tire & Rubber	0.56	0.34	0.11	1.09
Shanghai Refrigerator	0.98	0.43	0.17	1.76
Jinqiao Export & Import	0.56	0.34	-0.09	1.23
Outer Gaoqiao	0.62	0.38	-0.19	1.46
Lianhua Fiber	0.92	0.39	-0.05	1.83
Shanghai Jin Jiang Tower	0.79	0.38	0.24	1.62
Forever Bicycle	0.61	0.36	0.08	0.97
Phoenix Bicycle	0.68	0.29	0.30	1.14
Shanghai Haixian Group	1.51	0.63	0.42	2.75
Yaohua Pilkington Glass	0.88	0.34	0.21	1.92
Dajiang Group	0.61	0.38	-0.04	1.27
Shanghai Diesel Engine	0.55	0.28	0.09	0.96
Hero Pen	0.73	0.36	-0.13	1.37
Sanmao Textile	1.38	0.49	0.26	2.12
Shanghai Friendship Store	0.85	0.48	-0.25	1.63
Industrial Sewing Machine	1.49	0.54	0.16	2.24
Shang-Ling Refrigerators	0.62	0.36	0.12	1.27
Shanghai Steel Tube	1.25	0.46	0.28	2.10
Shanghai Merchandise Trading	0.75	0.32	-0.06	1.27

B-share discount as $(P_B - P_A)/P_A$. Figure 4.1 plots the unweighted average weekly B-share discount for these firms during the sample period. As shown in the figure, the magnitude of the discount is persistently large but varies over time. The average B-share discount over the entire sample period is 59.18%, with the spreads in Shenzhen about half of those in Shanghai.

A complete analysis of this price difference would explain both why different investor groups pay different prices and why firms sell both shares when their price differ. Any attempt to model firm's behavior would en-

Table 4.6 Sample Statistics for A-share Premia for Shenzhen Companies That Issued A- and B-shares Before April 1994 (Sample Period: April 1, 1994–October 31, 1998)

Company	Mean	Std. Dev.	Minimum	Maximum
Shenzhen Vanke Co.	0.43	0.21	0.08	0.87
Gintian Industry	0.62	0.27	0.09	1.08
Property & Resource Devel.	0.32	0.18	-0.05	0.68
China Southern Glass	0.36	0.20	0.04	0.83
Shenzhen Petroch. Co	0.58	0.34	0.11	1.07
Shenzhen Zhonghao Co.	0.49	0.31	-0.06	1.12
Konka Electronics	0.26	0.15	-0.18	0.62
Shenzhen China Bicycles	0.28	0.19	-0.23	0.75
Victor Onward Textile	0.69	0.37	0.09	1.41
Shenbao Industry	0.74	0.39	0.14	1.57
Shenzhen Huafa Electronics	0.24	0.16	-0.17	0.70
Chiwan Wharf Holdings	0.28	0.16	-0.14	0.69
China Merchants Shekou Co.	0.14	0.17	-0.58	1.06
Tellus Machinery	0.08	0.16	-0.24	0.46
Fiyta Holdings	0.04	0.32	-0.57	0.80
Yili Mineral Water	0.85	0.27	0.04	1.27
SEZ Real Estate	0.87	0.28	-0.09	1.56
Shenzhen Lionda Holdings	0.33	0.20	-0.14	0.93
Shenzhen Nanshan Power	0.45	0.24	-0.28	0.76
China Marine Containers	0.13	0.22	-0.24	0.53

counter a number of difficult issues. Stulz and Wasserfallen (1995) use a one-period CAPM to analyze the price differentials between restricted and unrestricted shares in the Swiss case, in which firms choose ownership restrictions voluntarily. They argue that price differentials can arise when a representative domestic firm maximizes its value by discriminating domestic and foreign investors.

To apply their framework to the Chinese case, we note that there is enough evidence from the initial public offering process and daily trading activities that domestic demand for A-shares is enormous while the foreign demand for B-shares is weak and A- and B-share markets are effectively segmented. The amount of new shares issued in each year is determined by a national quota set by the State Planning Committee and the CSRC. The quota is distributed to individual provinces and then to individual firms. When a firm is approved for a listing, it usually sets an IPO price so that the price-earning ratio is around 15 to 25. To issue foreign shares, firms must obtain special approval from the CSRC and local security regulatory authorities. An issuer of B-shares must, besides satisfying requirements stated in the securities regulations, meet the following conditions:

(1) It must have obtained approval from the relevant authorities for its use of foreign investment or for its conversion into a foreign-funded enterprise.
(2) It must have a stable source of adequate foreign exchange income and the total amount of its annual foreign exchange income must be sufficient to pay the annual dividend.
(3) The proportion of B-shares to the total number of shares, in a company which has been restructured from a state enterprise into joint-venture or private enterprise, must not exceed the ceiling determined by the relevant authority.

The aggregate amount of shares is fixed in each year and the total number of firms allowed to issue foreign shares is also limited.

There are a few limitations on price discrimination approach: First, assumptions are needed on whether firms are engaged in Cournot competition or in cartel competition in allocating A- and B-shares, or whether firms issue foreign shares simply to enhance their reputation. Second, It is unclear whether the allocation of shares may result from the government's planning behavior. Third, as Stulz and Wasserfallen (1995, p.1054) note, the price discrimination strategy they describe is likely to be time-inconsistent in a dynamic framework.

In light of these peculiarities, we analyze the price and return differentials using another approach (besides price discrimination approach). We do not model the firms' behavior. Instead, we use asset pricing theory to explain why different investors pay different prices for exogenously determined quantity of shares. Since a stock's price equals the present value of expected future dividends discounted at investors' required rates of return, different shares with the same expected future cash flows should have the same prices unless different investors have different required rates of returns due to different valuation of risks. B-share investors are primarily foreign investors who are likely to have different risk exposure or altitude toward risks in Chinese financial markets than domestic investors do. For example, in a simple dividend growth model, $P_i = D_0(1+g)/(r_i - g)$ where P_i is the price

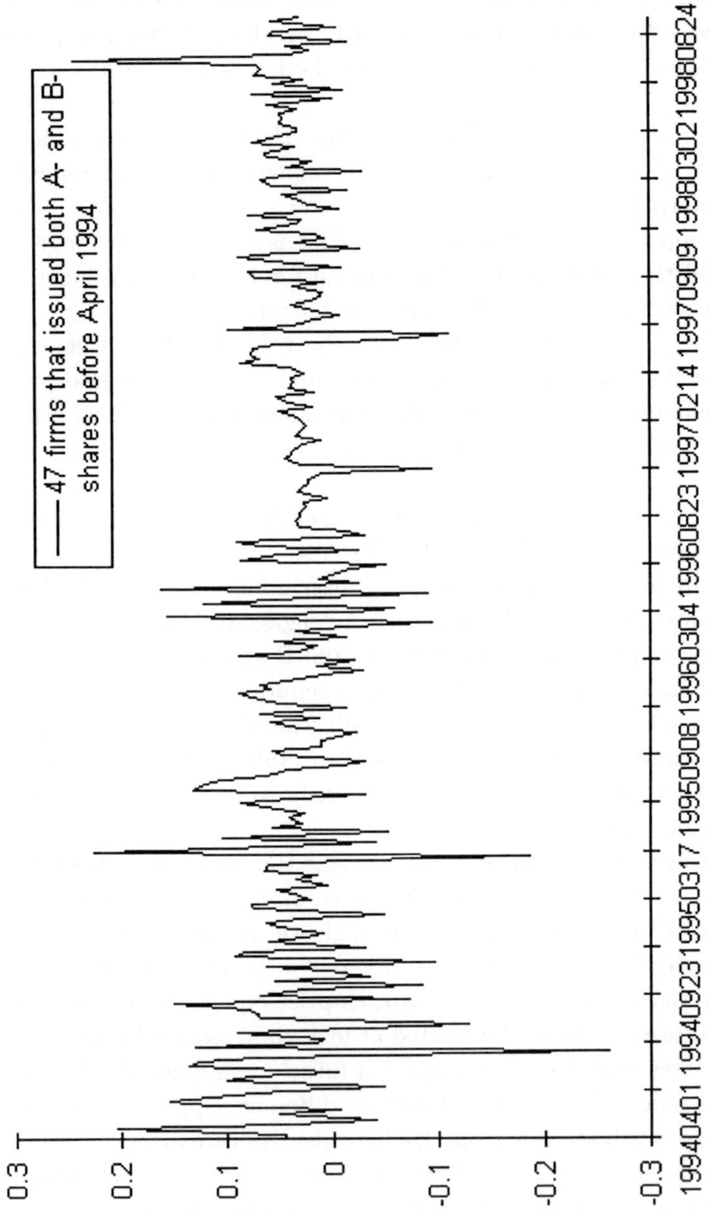

Fig. 4.2 Time-Series Differences in Average Weekly Returns Between B and A Shares (April 1994–October 1998)

for a specific type of share, g is the dividend growth rate (assumed as constant) and r_i is the investor's required rate of return for that type of share. From simple manipulation, $(P_B - P_A)/P_A = (r_A - r_B)/(r_B - g)$. If dividend growth rate is assumed to be zero, then $(P_B - P_A)/P_A = (r_A - r_B)/r_B$. The cum dividend average returns for A- and B-shares are 8.27% and 18.79% in the sample period, respectively. These return figures are consistent with an average B-share discount of 59.18%. Figure 4.2 plots the time-series differences in average weekly returns between B- and A-shares during the sample period, As shown in the figure, B-share returns are on average 57.44% higher than their A-share counterparts.

4.3 A Price Discrimination Model

In this section, we describe a one-period partial equilibrium model for stock pricing and portfolio behavior in a two-country world economy with investment restrictions across countries. This one-period model is a variation of the price discrimination model of Stulz and Wasserfallen (1995) in the sense that there are multiple domestic firms who issue different types of shares and domestic investors are not allowed to hold foreign securities. It is still a static partial equilibrium model because the total supply of domestic A- and B-shares are assumed to be a constant S and the rates of return for domestic and foreign risk-free assets are assumed to be fixed and do not depend upon the investor's maximization problem. The purpose of this model is to demonstrate the difference in the prices for B-shares and the corresponding A-share prices. The model also explains the difference in the holding for premium-priced A-shares by domestic investors and discount-priced B-shares by foreign investors in the presence of domestic ownership restrictions.

4.3.1 *Modeling Ownership Restrictions*

Throughout this section, we assume that there are only two countries in the world, the domestic country D $(D = D_1 \cup D_2)$ and the foreign country F $(F = F_1 \cup F_2)$. An investor i is a domestic investor (foreign investor) if $i \in D_1$ $(i \in F_1)$. D_1 and F_1 are the sets of investors in domestic and foreign countries, respectively, and $D_1 \equiv (1, \cdots\cdots, N)$, $F_1 \equiv (1, \cdots\cdots, M)$. A firm j is a domestic firm (foreign firm) if $j \in D_2$ $(j \in F_2)$. D_2 and F_2 are the sets of firms in domestic and foreign countries, respectively. I assume there are Q domestic firms who issue two different types of shares but there is only one foreign firm who issue a single type of shares. Therefore $D_2 \equiv (1, \cdots\cdots, Q)$ and $F_2 \equiv (1)$.

A representative firm in the domestic country issues a single stock but in two types of shares: A- and B-shares. A-shares are sold to domestic citizens only while B-shares are sold solely to foreign investors. A domestic firm has to decide whether it is optimal to charge different prices for A- and B-shares given the fact that markets for A- and B-shares are entirely segmented. It will be shown later that a necessary and sufficient condition for the representative domestic firm to price discriminate is that domestic and foreign investors have different demand functions for the firm's stock. A representative firm in the foreign country issues a single type of stock: C-shares. C-shares are only available to investors residing in foreign countries. A risk-free debt instrument (L_D, L_F) exists in each country. The following ownership restrictions exist in the world economy:

(1) Domestic investors $(i \in D_1)$ are prohibited from buying B- and C-shares;
(2) Foreign investors $(i \in F_1)$ are prohibited from buying A-shares;
(3) No short selling of A- and B-shares are allowed in domestic country.

Under the above situation, domestic investors face a smaller investment opportunity set than foreign investors. Therefore it is likely that domestic investor's demand for A-shares is less elastic than the foreign investor's demand for comparable B-shares. A domestic firm can choose to price discriminate between these two groups of investors in order to maximize the proceed from selling its stocks.

Denote $P_{j,k}$ as the price for type-k stock j at time 0, $\tilde{P}_{j,k}$ as the payoff of type-k stock j at time 1, r_D as the rate of return on the domestic risk-free debt instrument L_D at time 1, and r_F as the rate of return on the foreign risk-free debt instrument L_F at time 1. $\tilde{P}_{j,k}$ includes capital gain and dividend. It is unknown to investors at time 0 and is therefore itself random variables.

Also let $D_{i,j,k} \equiv D_i(P_{j,k})$ as the demand function for type-k stock j for investor i and is differentiable with respect to $P_{j,k}$. Also denote $S_{j,k}$ as the supply for type-k stock j. Market equilibrium implies that $S_{j,k} = \sum_i D_{i,j,k}$.

4.3.2 *Investors' Maximization Problems*

A domestic investor i chooses the optimal amount of A-share stocks to maximize the indirect utility from her end-of-period wealth:

$$\max_{\{D_{i,A}\}} \quad E[U(W_i(1))] = E[W_i(1)] - \tfrac{1}{2}\lambda_D Var(W_i(1)) \tag{4.1}$$

$$s.t. \qquad W_i(0) = D_{i,A}^{'} P_A + L_D \tag{4.2}$$

$$W_i(1) = D_{i,A}^{'} \tilde{P}_A + (1 + r_D) L_D \tag{4.3}$$

where $D_{i,A}$ is a $(1 \times Q)$ demand vector for A shares for Q domestic firms and $D_{i,A}^{'} = (D_{i,1,A}, D_{i,2,A}, \cdots\cdots, D_{i,Q,A})$. $D_{i,j,A} \geq 0$, i.e., the holding of a domestic firm's share cannot be negative. P_A is a $(Q \times 1)$ price vector for all A-shares at time 0 and $P_A^{'} = (P_{1,A}, P_{2,A}, \cdots\cdots, P_{Q,A})$. $\tilde{P}_A$ is a $(Q \times 1)$ vector for A share payoffs at time 1 and $\tilde{P}_A = (\tilde{P}_{1,A}, \tilde{P}_{2,A}, \cdots\cdots, \tilde{P}_{Q,A})$. λ_D is the coefficient for absolute risk aversion for a domestic investor i. $W_i(0)$ is her initial wealth and $W_i(1)$ is her end-of-period wealth.

$$E[W_i(1)] - \frac{1}{2}\lambda_D Var(W_i(1)) = D_{i,A}^{'} E(\tilde{P}_A) + (1 + r_D)[W_i(0) - D_{i,A}^{'} P_A] + \frac{1}{2}\lambda_D D_{i,A}^{'} V_{AA} D_{i,A} \tag{4.4}$$

where V_{AA} is the variance-covariance matrix of the A-share payoffs for all Q firms at time 1. The solution to the above wealth maximization problem yields the following demand vector for A-shares for domestic investor i:

$$D_{i,A} = \frac{1}{\lambda_D} V_{AA}^{-1} \left[E(\tilde{P}_A) - (1 + r_D) P_A \right] \tag{4.5}$$

or,

$$D_{i,A} = \phi_D - \psi_D P_A \tag{4.6}$$

where

$$\phi_D = \frac{1}{\lambda_D} V_{AA}^{-1} E(\tilde{P}_A), \quad \text{and} \tag{4.7}$$

$$\psi_D = \frac{1 + r_D}{\lambda_D} V_{AA}^{-1}. \tag{4.8}$$

Therefore, the demand for A-shares depends on domestic investor's absolute risk aversion coefficient, future A-share payoff, the variance-covariance matrix of A-share payoffs and the risk-free rate in the domestic country.

In equilibrium, the aggregate demand for A-shares for all N domestic investors must equal to the aggregate supply of A-shares by Q domestic firms. Hence,

$$S_A = ND_{i,A} = N(\phi_D - \psi_D P_A) \tag{4.9}$$

$$P_A = \frac{E(\tilde{P}_A)}{1+r_D} - \frac{\lambda_D V_{AA}}{(1+r_D)N} S_A \tag{4.10}$$

A foreign investor chooses the optimal amount of B- and C-shares to maximize the indirect utility from her end-of-period wealth:

$$\max_{\{D_{i,B}, D_{i,C}\}} \quad E[U(W_i(1))] = E[W_i(1)] - \tfrac{1}{2}\lambda_F Var(W_i(1)) \tag{4.11}$$

$$s.t. \quad W_i(0) = D'_{i,B} P_B + D_{i,C} P_C + L_F \tag{4.12}$$

$$W_i(1) = D'_{i,B} \tilde{P}_B + D_{i,C} \tilde{P}_C + (1+r_F) L_F \tag{4.13}$$

where $D_{i,B}$ is a $(Q \times 1)$ demand vector for B-shares for Q domestic firms, $D_{i,j,B} \geq 0$, and $D'_{i,B} = (D_{i,1,B}, D_{i,2,B}, \cdots\cdots, D_{i,Q.B})$. P_B is a $(Q \times 1)$ price vector for all B-shares at time 0, $P'_B = (P_{1,B}, P_{2,B}, \cdots\cdots, P_{Q,B})$ and $\tilde{P}_B$ is a $(Q \times 1)$ vector for B-share payoffs at time 1. $D_{i,C} \equiv D_{i,j,C}$, $P_C \equiv P_{j,C}$ and $\tilde{P}_C \equiv \tilde{P}_{j,C}$ because it is assumed that there is only one foreign firm that issues C-share. And λ_F is the coefficient for foreign investor's absolute risk aversion.

$$\begin{aligned} E[U(W_i(1))] &= E[W_i(1)] - \frac{1}{2}\lambda_F Var(W_i(1)) \\ &= D'_{i,B} E(\tilde{P}_B) + D_{i,C} E(\tilde{P}_C) \\ &\quad + (1+r_F)(W_i(0) - D'_{i,B} P_B - D_{i,C} P_C) \\ &\quad - \frac{1}{2}\lambda_F \Big(D'_{i,B} V_{BB} D_{i,B} + D^2_{i,C} \sigma^2_C \\ &\quad + 2D'_{i,B} \bar{\beta} \sigma^2_C D_{i,C} \Big) \end{aligned} \tag{4.14}$$

where V_{BB} is the $(Q \times Q)$ variance-covariance matrix of B-share payoffs for all domestic firms at time 1. β is the $(Q \times 1)$ vector of β-coefficients of the B-share payoffs with respect to the C-share payoffs, i.e., $\bar{\beta}' = (\beta_1, \beta_2, \cdots\cdots, \beta_Q)$ and $\beta_j = Cov(\tilde{P}_{j,B}, \tilde{P}_C)/\sigma_C^2$.

The solution to the above representative foreign investor's maximization problem yields the following demand vector for B-shares:

$$\begin{aligned} D_{i,B} &= \frac{1}{\lambda_F}\left(V_{BB}' - \frac{V_{BC}V_{BC}'}{\sigma_C^2}\right)^{-1}\Big\{E(\tilde{P}_B) - (1+r_F)P_B \\ &\quad -\bar{\beta}\Big[E(\tilde{P}_C) - (1+r_F)P_C\Big]\Big\} \end{aligned} \tag{4.15}$$

or,

$$D_{i,B} = \phi_F - \psi_F P_B \tag{4.16}$$

where

$$\begin{aligned} \phi_F &= \frac{1}{\lambda_F}\left(V_{BB}' - \frac{V_{BC}V_{BC}'}{\sigma_C^2}\right)^{-1} \\ &\quad \cdot\Big\{E(\tilde{P}_B) - \bar{\beta}\Big[E(\tilde{P}_C) - (1+r_F)P_C\Big]\Big\} \end{aligned} \tag{4.17}$$

$$\psi_F = \frac{1+r_F}{\lambda_F}\left(V_{BB}' - \frac{V_{BC}V_{BC}'}{\sigma_C^2}\right)^{-1} \tag{4.18}$$

and V_{BC} is a $(Q \times 1)$ vector of covariances of B-shares payoffs with C-shares payoffs at time 1.

Therefore, the demand for B-shares depends upon the foreign investor's absolute risk aversion coefficient, future B-shares and foreign C-share payoffs, variance-covariance matrix of B-shares payoffs, covariances between B-share payoffs and C-share payoffs, β-coefficients of the B-share payoffs with respect to C-share payoffs, and risk-free rate in foreign country.

In equilibrium, the aggregate demand for B-shares by all M foreign investors must equal to the aggregate supply of B-shares by Q domestic firms. Hence,

$$S_B = MD_{i,B} = M(\phi_F - \psi_F P_B) \tag{4.19}$$

$$P_B = \frac{E(\tilde{P}_B) - \beta\left[E(\tilde{P}_C - (1+r_F)P_C\right]}{1+r_F} - \frac{\lambda_F(V'_{BB} - V_{BC}V'BC)}{(1+r_F)M}S_B \tag{4.20}$$

To find out whether the demand functions for A- and B-shares are the same or not, we calculate the ratio of the slope coefficients and the ratio of the constant terms from the two demand functions:

$$\phi_D\phi_F^{-1} = \frac{\lambda_F}{\lambda_D}\left[V_{AA}^{-1}E(\tilde{P}_A)\right]\left(V'_{BB} - \frac{V_{BC}V'_{BC}}{\sigma_C^2}\right) \cdot\left\{E(\tilde{P}_B - \beta\left[E(\tilde{P}_C) - (1+r_F)P_C\right]\right\}^{-1} \tag{4.21}$$

$$\psi_D\psi_F^{-1} = \frac{\lambda_F}{\lambda_D}\left(\frac{1+r_D}{1+r_F}\right)V_{AA}^{-1}\left(V'_{BB} - \frac{V_{BC}V'_{BC}}{\sigma_C^2}\right) \tag{4.22}$$

The implication of equations (4.21) and (4.22) can be summarized in the following proposition:

Theorem 4.1 *A necessary and sufficient condition for all domestic firms to price discriminate between domestic and foreign investors is* $\phi_D\phi_F^{-1} \neq \bar{1}$ *and* $\psi_D\psi_F^{-1} \neq \bar{1}$, *where* $\bar{1}$ *is a* $(Q \times 1)$ *vector of 1.*

Since A- and B-shares are identical except there are restrictions on ownership, i.e., domestic investors can only own A-shares and foreign investors can only hold B-shares, the expected payoffs on A- and B-shares should be the same. It is also reasonable to assume that the present value of the expected payoff on C-shares is greater than the time-0 price and foreign investors are more risk-averse than domestic investors in investing in Chinese shares ($\lambda_D < \lambda_F$). Bailey (1994) provides empirical evidence that the β-coefficients of the B-share payoffs with respect to the foreign share (i.e., C-share) payoffs in Chinese stock markets are very close to 0. If the rates of return on domestic and foreign risk-free debt instruments are the same ($r_D = r_F$), and if variance-covariance matrices of the payoffs of A- and B-shares are the same ($V_{AA} = V_{BB}$), then from equations (4.21) and (4.22), it is not difficult to derive that $\phi_D\phi_F^{-1} > e$ and $\psi_D\psi_F^{-1} > e$.

Therefore, it is optimal for domestic firms to charge higher prices for A-shares than for B-shares, despite the fact that A- and B-shares are entitled to the same type of ownership and liability of the firms' assets. Of course, in order for a firm to price discriminate between two investor groups, the firm has to be able to prevent resale (Carlton and Perloff, 1994).

4.3.3 *Firms' Maximization Problems*

A representative domestic firm faces identical domestic investors in their demand for A-shares and identical foreign investors in their demand for B-shares. It has to decide the optimal amount of A- and B-shares issued in order to maximize its proceed from selling the stocks taken as given the amount of A- and B-shares other firms issue. The equilibrium prices for A- and B-shares will then be determined by domestic and foreign investors' demand functions.

$$\begin{aligned}
\max_{\{S_A,S_B\}} Z &= \sum_{i=1}^{N} D_{i,A}P_A^{'} + \sum_{i=1}^{M} D_{i,B}P_B^{'} \\
&= ND_{i,A}P_A^{'} + MD_{i,B}P_B^{'} \\
&= S_A\psi_D^{-1}\frac{N\phi_D^{'} - S_A^{'}}{N} + S_B\psi_F^{-1}\frac{M\phi_F^{'} - S_B^{'}}{M} \qquad (4.23) \\
s.t. \quad & S_A + S_B = S \\
& S_A \geq \underline{0} \\
& S_B \geq \underline{0}
\end{aligned}$$

where Z is a $(A \times 1)$ vector of firms' proceeds from selling the stocks, S_A and S_B are $(Q \times 1)$ vectors of firms' supply for A- and B-shares, respectively. $\underline{0}$ is a $(Q \times 1)$ vector of zeros.

To get equation (4.23), we simply use equations (4.6), (4.16) and the market equilibrium condition that aggregate demand for a firm's shares equals aggregate supply, and make necessary transformations. The solution to the firms' maximization problems yields the following vector on optimal amount of A- and B-shares issued:

$$S_A^{*} = \frac{1}{2}NM(M\psi_F + N\psi_D)^{-1}\left(\psi_F\phi_D^{'} - \psi_D\phi_F^{'} + \frac{2}{M}\psi_D S^{'}\right) \qquad (4.24)$$

$$S_B^* = \frac{1}{2}NM(M\psi_F + N\psi_D)^{-1}\left(\psi_D\phi_F' - \psi_F\phi_D' + \frac{2}{D}\psi_F S'\right) \quad (4.25)$$

The above solution to the firm's maximization problem is an interior solution. In the next section, we prove that this interior solution is almost guaranteed given reasonable assumptions on risk-free rates and covariances of the B-shares payoffs with respect to the C-share payoff.

Substituting the inverse demand vector equations (4.8) and (4.18) into equations (4.24) and (4.25) yields the following equilibrium price vectors for A- and B-shares:

$$P_A^* = \phi_D\psi_D^{-1} - \frac{1}{2}M(M\psi_F + N\psi_D)^{-1}\left(\psi_F\phi_D'\psi_D^{-1} - \phi_F' + \frac{2}{M}S'\right) \quad (4.26)$$

$$P_B^* = \phi_F\psi_F^{-1} - \frac{1}{2}M(M\psi_F + N\psi_D)^{-1}\left(\psi_D\phi_F'\psi_F^{-1} - \phi_D' + \frac{2}{N}S'\right) \quad (4.27)$$

After manipulation,

$$P_A^* - P_B^* = \frac{1}{2}\left(\phi_D\psi_D^{-1} - \phi_F\psi_F^{-1}\right) \quad (4.28)$$

or,

$$P_A^* - P_B^* = \frac{1}{2}\left[\frac{E(\tilde{P}_A)}{1+r_D} - \frac{E(\tilde{P}_B)}{1+r_F} + \frac{\bar{\beta}[E(\tilde{P}_C - (1+r_F)P_C]}{1+r_F}\right] \quad (4.29)$$

The price discounts on B-shares is determined by the expected payoffs for A-, B- and C-shares, the β-coefficients of the B-share payoffs with respect to C-share payoff, and the rates of return of domestic and foreign risk-free debt instruments. The following proposition summarizes the result:

Theorem 4.2 *A necessary and sufficient condition for all domestic firms to charge higher prices for A shares is*
$(\phi_D\psi_D^{-1} - \phi_F\psi_F^{-1}) > \underline{0}$ *or*

$$\left[\frac{E(\tilde{P}_A)}{1+r_D} - \frac{E(\tilde{P}_B)}{1+r_F} + \frac{\bar{\beta}[E(\tilde{P}_C - (1+r_F)P_C]}{1+r_F}\right] > \underline{0}$$

Taking the first derivative of $(P_A^* - P_B^*)$ with respect to various right-hand variables generates:

$$\frac{\partial(P_A^* - P_B^*)}{\partial(E(\tilde{P}_A))} > \underline{0}, \qquad \frac{\partial(P_A^* - P_B^*)}{\partial(E(\tilde{P}_B))} < \underline{0},$$

$$\frac{\partial(P_A^* - P_B^*)}{\partial(E(\tilde{P}_C))} = \frac{1}{1+r_F}\bar{\beta}, \qquad \frac{\partial(P_A^* - P_B^*)}{\partial(P_C)} = -\bar{\beta},$$

$$\frac{\partial(P_A^* - P_B^*)}{\partial(r_D)} < 0,$$

$$\frac{\partial(P_A^* - P_B^*)}{\partial(r_F)} = \frac{E(\tilde{P}_B) - \bar{\beta}E(\tilde{P}_C)}{(1+r_F)^2}$$

Therefore, the higher the expected payoff on A-shares, the higher the A-share price premium or B-share discount; the higher the expected payoff on B-shares, the smaller the B-share discount. If the β-coefficients of the B-share payoffs with respect to the C share payoff are nonnegative, i.e., $\beta \geq \underline{0}$, then $\partial(P_A^* - P_B^*)/\partial(E(\tilde{P}_C)) \geq \underline{0}$ and $\partial(P_A^* - P_B^*)/\partial(P_C) \leq \underline{0}$. The higher the expected payoffs on C-shares, the smaller (if not unchanged) the B-share discount; the higher the price for C-share, the smaller (if not unchanged) the B-share discount. And finally, the higher the domestic risk-free rate, the smaller the B-share discount. The effect of a change in foreign risk-free rate on B-share discount is ambiguous.

Again, since A- and B-shares are identical except restrictions on ownership, the expected payoffs on A- and B-shares should be the same for the same firm. Employing the same assumption as before, i.e., $E[\tilde{P}_C/(1+r_F)] > P_C$ and $r_D = r_F$, then it is quite obvious that $P_A^* > P_B^*$. Therefore, given proper assumption on domestic and foreign risk-free rates, as well as the assumption that the present value of the expected payoff on foreign C-shares exceeds its initial issuing price, there will be a discount on B-share price.

4.3.4 *Corner Solutions for Domestic Firms' Maximization Problems*

It is of concerns on whether there will be corner solutions to the price discrimination model under the one-way domestic ownership restrictions. We show below that given the original conditions of the model (equations (4.20)–(4.23)) and some reasonable assumptions, interior solution (4.24) and (4.25) are guaranteed.

Consider the representative firm's maximization problem, to simplify the expressions, we get rid of M and N in the equations by assuming a composite domestic investor and a composite foreign investor with risk-aversion coefficients λ_D and λ_F, respectively,

$$\frac{1}{\lambda_D} = \frac{\sum_{i=1}^{N} \frac{1}{\lambda_{i,D}}}{N}, \qquad \frac{1}{\lambda_F} = \frac{\sum_{i=1}^{M} \frac{1}{\lambda_{i,F}}}{M},$$

Further assume that the variance-covariance matrices of A- and B-share payoffs are the same, i.e., $V_{AA} = V_{BB} = V$, and the expected payoffs on A- and B-shares are the same, i.e., $E(\tilde{P}_A) = E(\tilde{P}_B = \mu$. A representative domestic firm chooses the optimal amount of A- and B-shares to maximize its proceeds from selling the stocks taken as given the amount of A- and B-shares other firms issued:

$$\begin{aligned}\max_{\{S_A\}} Z &= D_{i,A}P_A^{'} + D_{i,B}P_B^{'} \\ &= S_A\psi_D^{'-1}(\phi_D^{'} - S_A^{'}) + (S - S_A)\psi_F^{'-1}[\phi_F^{'} - (S^{'} - S_A^{'})]\end{aligned}$$

Note that

$$\phi_D = \frac{1}{\lambda_D}V^{-1}\mu,$$

$$\psi_D = \frac{1 + r_D}{\lambda_D}V^{-1},$$

$$\phi_F = \frac{1}{\lambda_F}\left(V^{'} - \frac{V_{BC}V_{BC}^{'}}{\sigma_C^2}\right)^{-1}\left\{\mu - \beta\left[E(\tilde{P}_C) - (1 + r_F)P_C\right]\right\},$$

and

$$\psi_F = \frac{1+r_F}{\lambda_F}\left(V' - \frac{V_{BC}V_{BC}'}{\sigma_C^2}\right)^{-1}.$$

Therefore,

$$\begin{aligned} Z &= S_A\left\{\frac{\mu}{1+r_D} - \frac{\mu-\beta\left[E(\tilde{P}_C)-(1+r_F)P_C\right]}{1+r_F}\right. \\ &\quad \left. + \frac{2\lambda_F\left(V-\frac{V_{BC}V_{BC}'}{\sigma_C^2}\right)}{1+r_F}S'\right\} - S_A\left[\frac{\lambda_D V}{1+r_D} + \frac{\lambda_F\left(V-\frac{V_{BC}V_{BC}'}{\sigma_C^2}\right)}{1+r_F}\right]S_A' \\ &\quad +S\left\{\frac{\mu-\beta\left[E(\tilde{P}_C-(1+r_F)P_C\right]}{1+r_F}\right\} + S\left[\frac{\lambda_F\left(V-\frac{V_{BC}V_{BC}'}{\sigma_C^2}\right)}{1+r_F}\right]S' \end{aligned}$$

The first order condition to the above maximization problem yields:

$$\begin{aligned} \frac{\partial Z}{\partial S_A} &= \left\{\frac{\mu}{1+r_D} - \frac{\mu-\beta\left[E(\tilde{P}_C)-(1+r_F)P_C\right]}{1+r_F}\right. \\ &\quad \left. + \frac{2\lambda_F\left(V-\frac{V_{BC}V_{BC}'}{\sigma_C^2}\right)}{1+r_F}S\right\} - 2\left[\frac{\lambda_D V}{1+r_D} + \frac{\lambda_F\left(V-\frac{V_{BC}V_{BC}'}{\sigma_C^2}\right)}{1+r_F}\right]S_A \\ &= 0 \end{aligned}$$

This gives the optimal amount of A-shares issued:

$$S_A^* = \frac{1}{2}\left[\frac{\lambda_D V}{1+r_D} + \frac{\lambda_F\left(V-\frac{V_{BC}V_{BC}'}{\sigma_C^2}\right)}{1+r_F}\right]^{-1}\left\{\frac{\mu}{1+r_D}\right.$$

$$-\frac{\mu - \beta\left[E(\tilde{P}_C) - (1+r_F)P_C\right]}{1+r_F} + \frac{2\lambda_F\left(V - \frac{V_{BC}V_{BC}'}{\sigma_C^2}\right)}{1+r_F}S\right\}$$

Further assume that the risk-free rates are the same across countries, i.e., $r_D = r_F = r$, the above expression can be reduced to:

$$\begin{aligned} S_A^* &= \frac{1}{2}\left[\lambda_D V + \lambda_F\left(V - \frac{V_{BC}V_{BC}'}{\sigma_C^2}\right)\right]^{-1}\left\{\beta\left[E(\tilde{P}_C - (1+r)P_C\right]\right. \\ &\quad \left. +2\lambda_F\left(V - \frac{V_{BC}V_{BC}'}{\sigma_C^2}\right)S\right\} \end{aligned}$$

If B-share payoffs are uncorrelated with C-share payoff, i.e., $V_{BC} = \underline{0}$, and the β-coefficients of the B-share payoffs with respect to C-share payoffs are approximately 0, then

$$S_A^* = \frac{\lambda_F}{\lambda_D + \lambda_F}S$$

Therefore, interior solution is guaranteed as long as the risk-averse coefficients for domestic and foreign composite investors are not too different. However, if foreign composite investor is very risk-averse (λ_F is a very large number) while domestic composite investor is risk-neutral, then domestic firms will only issue A shares for domestic investors ($S_A^* = S$) and pay them risk-free rate for owning the firms' equities. On the other hand, if domestic composite investor is very risk-averse (λ_D is a very large number) while foreign composite investor is risk-neutral, then domestic firms will only issue B-shares ($S_A^* = 0$). These two cases are too extreme and contradict to reality.

4.3.5 *Relaxing Ownership Restrictions*

An interesting question arises concerning the effect on price differentials for A- and B-shares when ownership restrictions are entirely or partially removed. If domestic investors are allowed to purchase foreign C shares, then domestic investors' investment opportunity sets expand and their wealth functions will also include C-shares. Equation (4.5) becomes:

$$D_{i,A} = \frac{1}{\lambda_D}\left(V_{AA}^{-1} - \frac{V_{AC}V_{AC}^{'}}{\sigma_C^2}\right)^{-1}\left\{E(\tilde{P}_A) - (1+r_D)P_A \right.$$
$$\left. -\bar{\beta}^*\left[E(\tilde{P}_C) - (1+r_D)P_C\right]\right\} \tag{4.30}$$

where $\bar{\beta}^*$ is the $(Q \times 1)$ vector of β-coefficients of the A-share payoffs with respect to the C-share payoffs, V_{AA} is the $(Q \times Q)$ variance-covariance matrix of A-share payoffs of all domestic firms at time 1 and V_{AC} is the $(Q \times 1)$ covariance vector of A-shares payoffs with C-shares payoffs at time 1. Equations (4.21) and (4.22) become:

$$\phi_D\phi_F^{-1} = \frac{\lambda_F}{\lambda_D}\left(V_{AA}^{-1} - \frac{V_{AC}V_{AC}^{'}}{\sigma_C^2}\right)^{-1}\left\{E(\tilde{P}_A)\right.$$
$$\left. -\beta^*\left[E(\tilde{P}_C) - (1+r_D)P_C\right]\right\}\left(V_{BB}^{'} - \frac{V_{BC}V_{BC}^{'}}{\sigma_C^2}\right)$$
$$\cdot\left\{E(\tilde{P}_B - \beta\left[E(\tilde{P}_C) - (1+r_F)P_C\right]\right\}^{-1} \tag{4.31}$$

$$\psi_D\psi_F^{-1} = \frac{\lambda_F}{\lambda_D}\left(\frac{1+r_D}{1+r_F}\right)\left(V_{AA}^{-1} - \frac{V_{AC}V_{AC}^{'}}{\sigma_C^2}\right)^{-1}$$
$$\cdot\left(V_{BB}^{'} - \frac{V_{BC}V_{BC}^{'}}{\sigma_C^2}\right) \tag{4.32}$$

Therefore, given the same assumptions as those with complete ownership restrictions, domestic and foreign investors will have the same demand functions for domestic Chinese firm's stocks if $\lambda_D = \lambda_F$, $\bar{\beta} = \bar{\beta}^*$ and $V_{AC} = V_{BC}$. However, if the risk-averse coefficients are not the same across domestic and foreign investors, or if the covariances of A-shares payoffs with C-share payoff are not equal to the covariances of B-shares payoffs with C-share payoff, it is still optimal for domestic firm to price discriminate between domestic and foreign investors. Otherwise, price discrimination will no longer exist. The results can be summarized in the following proposition:

Theorem 4.3 *The sufficient conditions for the elimination of B-share discount are: (1) removal of ownership restrictions; (2) domestic and foreign investors have the same absolute risk-averse coefficients; (3) the covariance of B-share payoffs with respect to C-share payoff are identical to the covariance of A-share payoffs with respect to C-share payoff.*

In the next section, we show that the difference in the expected return for domestic and foreign investors can be predicted from the equilibrium asset pricing theory. A general equilibrium model accounting for the supply side economy would certainly be an interesting extension to this chapter.

4.4 An Intertemporal Capital Asset Pricing Model

In this section, we formulate an ICAPM to model the optimal portfolio selection for domestic and foreign investors under ownership restrictions and effective market segmentation. Our objectives are: (1) to explain the cross-section spread in expected returns for A- and B- shares; (2) to draw testable implications from the model; and (3) to compare the empirical predictions of ICAPM with those of price discrimination model.

4.4.1 *Stock Price and Return Dynamics*

Denote the cum dividend price of a type h stock i at time t as $P_{h,i}(t)$ ($h = A, B, C$), and assume that $P_{h,i}(t)$ follows a diffusion process with constant proportional mean and variance (geometric Brownian motion).

$$dP_{h,i}(t) = \mu_{h,i} P_{h,i}(t)dt + \sigma_{h,i} P_{h,i}(t) dz_{h,i}(t) \tag{4.33}$$

where $\mu_{h,i}$ and $\sigma^2_{h,i}$ are the mean and variance of the return on type h stock i and $dz_{h,i}(t)$ is a standard diffusion (Wiener) process.

Therefore, the distribution of stock price is log-normal and the rate of return is

$$r_{h,i}(t) = \frac{dP_{h,i}(t)}{P_{h,i}(t)} = \mu_{h,i}dt + \sigma_{h,i} dz_{h,i}(t) \tag{4.34}$$

The assumption of lognormal returns is a simplification of the actual process, which has some serial correlation as discussed by Su and Fleisher

(1998).

4.4.2 *Intertemporal Maximization by Domestic Investors*

We assume that a composite domestic consumer-investor is infinitely lived and has state-independent isoelastic utility of consumption,[2]

$$U(C,t) = \frac{C(t)^{1-\gamma_D}}{1-\gamma_D} \tag{4.35}$$

where $C(t)$ is the composite domestic investor's consumption at time t and γ_D is the measure of her constant relative risk aversion. This investor maximizes

$$V(W,t) = \max_{\{C(t),w_{a,i}(t)\}} E_0 \left[\int_{t=0}^{\infty} e^{-\rho t} U(C,t)dt \right] \tag{4.36}$$

where ρ is the rate of pure time preference, $w_{a,i}(t) \equiv N_{a,i}(t)P_{a,i}(t)/W(t)$ is the fraction of wealth invested in the ith A-share stock at time t, $i = 1, 2, \cdots\cdots, N$. In particular, $w_{a,N+1}(t)$ is the fraction invested in safe asset. $N_{a,i}(t)$ is the number of ith A-share stock investor k owns, and $W(t)$ is his total wealth.

The investor's wealth accumulation equation is

$$dW(t) = \sum_{i=1}^{N+1} w_{a,i}(t)W(t)dr_{a,i}(t) - C(t)dt \tag{4.37}$$

Since there are N different A-share stocks and one riskless domestic asset with time-invariant risk-free interest rate r_D, substituting $r_{a,i}(t)$ from (4.34) and using $\sum_{i=1}^{N+1} w_{a,i}(t) = 1$, equation (4.37) can be rewritten as,

$$dW(t) = \left[\sum_{1}^{N} w_{a,i}(t)(\mu_{a,i} - r_D) + r_D \right] W(t)dt$$

[2] A composite investor's risk-aversion coefficient is the harmonic mean for all K individual investors' risk-aversion coefficients, $\frac{1}{\gamma_D} = \frac{\sum_{k=1}^{K} \frac{1}{\gamma_{k,D}}}{K}$.

$$+\sum_{1}^{N} w_{a,i}(t)W(t)\sigma_{a,i}dz_{a,i}(t) - C(t)dt \qquad (4.38)$$

Equations (4.36) and (4.38) constitute a continuous-time portfolio optimization problem of the form solved by Merton (1971, 1973). The Bellman equation yields the following optimality condition,

$$\begin{aligned} 0 \;=\; & \max_{\{C(t),w_{a,i}(t)\}} \left[U(C,t) + \frac{\partial V^*}{\partial t} + \frac{\partial V^*}{\partial W} \right. \\ & \left[\left(\sum_{1}^{N} w_{a,i}(t)(\mu_{a,i} - r_D) + r_D(t) \right) W(t) - C(t) \right] \\ & \left. + \frac{W(t)^2}{2} \frac{\partial^2 V^*}{\partial W^2} \sum_{1}^{N} \sum_{1}^{N} w_{a,i}(t) w_{a,j}(t) \sigma_{a,i,j} \right] \end{aligned} \qquad (4.39)$$

where $\sigma_{a,i,j}$ are the instantaneous covariance between the returns on the ith and jth A-share stock. Now, following Merton (1971, 1973), conjecture that the value function V^* is of the form

$$V^*(W(t)) = Ye^{-\rho t}\frac{W(t)^{1-\gamma_D}}{1-\gamma_D},$$

where Y is a constant. The choice variables are consumption and the portfolio weights and the corresponding first-order conditions are:

$$\frac{\partial U}{\partial C} = \frac{\partial V^*}{\partial W} \qquad (4.40)$$

$$\frac{\partial V^*}{\partial W} W(t)(\mu_{a,i} - r_D) + \frac{\partial^2 V^*}{\partial W^2} W(t)^2 \sum_{1}^{N} w_{a,j}(t)\sigma_{a,i,j} = 0 \qquad (4.41)$$

Equation (4.40) is the familiar envelope condition equating the marginal utility of consumption to the shadow value of wealth and (4.41) is the standard set of linear equations in the mean-variance portfolio problem. Substituting in the conjectured value function yields the following optimal portfolio selection for domestic composite investor,[3]

[3]We assume $\rho > \max\left\{0, \gamma_D\left[r_D + \frac{1}{2}\left(\frac{\mu_{a,i}-r_D}{\sigma_{a,i,j}}\right)^2\left(\frac{1}{1-\gamma_D}\right)\right]\right\}$, which is necessary for a well-defined solution. This restriction ensures that an investor cannot achieve infi-

$$\mu_{a,i} - r_D = \gamma_D \sum_{j=1}^{N} w_{a,j}(t)\sigma_{a,i,j}, \tag{4.42}$$

The optimal portfolio choice is time-invariant because the investor's risk-aversion and the means, variances and covariance of asset returns are constant over time. Moreover, the optimal portfolio choice is independent of the domestic investor's wealth, consumption, and time preference. The greater the risk aversion, the lower the expected return, the higher the risk-free interest rate, or the higher the risk, the less will be held in A-share stocks.

The equilibrium (domestic market) portfolio is mean-variance efficient. Therefore the equilibrium return for stock i satisfies the classical capital asset pricing model (CAPM). To show this, note that $\sum_{j=1}^{N} w_{a,j}(t)\sigma_{a,i,j} = \sigma_{a,i,M}$ and $\sum_{i=1}^{N} w_{a,i}(t)\sigma_{a,i,M} = \sigma^2_{a,M}$, where $\sigma_{a,i,M}$ is the covariance of the ith A-share return with the return on A-share market portfolio and $\sigma^2_{a,M}$ is the variance of A-share market portfolio return. Then (4.42) can be rewritten as $\mu_{a,i} - r_D = \gamma_D \sigma_{a,i,M}$, which implies $\mu_{a,M} - r_D = \gamma_D \sigma^2_{a,M}$. Therefore,

$$\begin{aligned} \mu_{a,i} - r_D &= \gamma_D \frac{\sigma_{a,i,M}}{\sigma^2_{a,M}} \sigma^2_{a,M} \\ &= \beta_{a,i,M}(\mu_{a,M} - r_D), \end{aligned} \tag{4.43}$$

which is the familiar single-beta CAPM.

4.4.3 *Intertemporal Maximization by Foreign Investors*

I assume a composite foreign consumer-investor who is also infinitely lived and has state-independent isoelastic utility of consumption,

$$U(C,t) = \frac{C(t)^{1-\gamma_F}}{1-\gamma_F} \tag{4.44}$$

This foreign composite investor maximizes

nite expected utility by any plan. For example, if $\rho < 0$, which does not satisfy this restriction, $U(C,\infty) = \infty$ for any consumption plan with $C > 0$.

$$V(W,t) = \max_{\{C(t),w_{b,i}(t),w_{c,j}(t)\}} E_0 \left[\int_{t=0}^{\infty} e^{-\rho t} U(C,t) dt \right] \tag{4.45}$$

subject to

$$\begin{aligned} dW(t) &= \sum_{i=1}^{N+1} w_{b,i}(t) W(t) dr_{b,i}(t) \\ &\quad + \sum_{j=1}^{M} w_{c,j}(t) W(t) dr_{c,j}(t) - C(t) dt \end{aligned} \tag{4.46}$$

where $w_{b,i}(t) \equiv N_{b,i}(t)P_{b,i}(t)/W(t)$ and $w_{c,j}(t) \equiv M_{c,j}(t)P_{c,j}(t)/W(t)$ are the fractions of wealth invested in the ith B-share stock and jth C-share stock at time t, respectively, $i = 1, 2, \cdots\cdots, N$, $j = 1, 2, \cdots\cdots, M$, $N_{b,i}(t)$ and $M_{c,j}(t)$ are the number of ith B-share stock and the number of jth C-share stock investor k owns.

There are N different B-shares, M different C-shares and one risk-free foreign debt instrument with interest rate r_F, which is assumed to be time-invariant. Without loss of generality, number the safe asset as $N+1$. Since $\sum_{i=1}^{N+1} w_{b,i}(t) + \sum_{j=1}^{M} w_{c,j}(t) = 1$, (4.46) can be rewritten as:

$$\begin{aligned} dW(t) &= \left[\sum_{1}^{N} w_{b,i}(t)(\mu_{b,i} - r_F) + \sum_{1}^{M} w_{c,j}(t)(\mu_{c,j} - r_F) + r_F \right] \\ &\quad \cdot W(t) dt + \sum_{1}^{N} w_{b,i}(t) W(t) \sigma_{b,i} dz_{b,i}(t) \\ &\quad + \sum_{1}^{M} w_{c,j}(t) W(t) \sigma_{c,j} dz_{c,j}(t) - C(t) dt \end{aligned} \tag{4.47}$$

The optimality conditions for the foreign investor's maximization problem are

$$0 = \max_{\{C(t),w_{b,i}(t),w_{c,j}(t)\}} \left\{ U(C,t) + \frac{\partial V^*}{\partial t} + \frac{\partial V^*}{\partial W} \right.$$

$$\left[\left(\sum_{1}^{N} w_{b,i}(t)(\mu_{b,i} - r_F) + \sum_{1}^{M} w_{c,j}(t)(\mu_{c,j} - r_F) + r_F(t)\right)W(t)\right.$$
$$\left.-C(t)\right] + \frac{W(t)^2}{2}\frac{\partial^2 V^*}{\partial W^2}\left[\sum_{1}^{N}\sum_{1}^{N} w_{b,i}(t)w_{b,j}(t)\sigma_{b,i,j}\right.$$
$$\left.\left.+\sum_{1}^{M}\sum_{1}^{M} w_{c,i}(t)w_{c,j}(t)\sigma_{c,i,j} + \sum_{1}^{N}\sum_{1}^{M} w_{b,i}(t)w_{c,j}(t)\sigma_{b,c,i,j}\right]\right\} \tag{4.48}$$

where $\sigma_{b,i,j}$ ($\sigma_{c,i,j}$) are the instantaneous covariance between the returns on the ith and jth A-share (B-share) stock, and $\sigma_{b,c,i,j}$ are the instantaneous covariance between the returns on the ith A-share and the jth B-share. The corresponding first-order conditions with respect to the portfolio weights are given by (4.49) and (4.50):

$$\begin{aligned} 0 &= \frac{\partial V^*}{\partial W}W(t)(\mu_{b,i} - r_F) + \frac{\partial^2 V^*}{\partial W^2}W(t)^2 \\ &\quad \cdot\left[\sum_{1}^{N} w_{b,j}(t)\sigma_{b,i,j} + \sum_{1}^{M} w_{c,j}(t)\sigma_{b,c,i,j}\right] \end{aligned} \tag{4.49}$$

$$\begin{aligned} 0 &= \frac{\partial V^*}{\partial W}W(t)(\mu_{c,i} - r_F) + \frac{\partial^2 V^*}{\partial W^2}W(t)^2 \\ &\quad \cdot\left[\sum_{1}^{M} w_{c,j}(t)\sigma_{c,i,j} + \sum_{1}^{N} w_{b,j}(t)\sigma_{b,c,i,j}\right] \end{aligned} \tag{4.50}$$

The value function takes the form $V^*(W(t)) = Ye^{-\rho t}\frac{W(t)^{1-\gamma_F}}{1-\gamma_F}$, so (4.49) can be rewritten as

$$\mu_{b,i} - r_F = \gamma_F\left[\sum_{j=1}^{N} w_{b,j}(t)\sigma_{b,i,j} + \sum_{j=1}^{M} w_{c,j}(t)\sigma_{b,c,i,j}\right] \tag{4.51}$$

The optimal holdings of B-shares are

$$w_{b,i}(t) = \frac{1}{\gamma_F}\left[\sum_{1}^{M}\sum_{1}^{N}\frac{(\mu_{b,j} - r_F)\sigma_{c,i,j}}{\sigma_{b,i,j}\sigma_{c,i,j} - \sigma^2_{b,c,i,j}}\right.$$

$$-\sum_{1}^{M}\sum_{1}^{N}\frac{(\mu_{c,j}-r_F)\sigma_{c,i,j}\sigma_{b,c,i,j}}{\sigma_{b,i,j}\sigma^2_{c,i,j}-\sigma^2_{b,c,i,j}}\Bigg] \tag{4.52}$$

Therefore, the foreign composite investor's optimal portfolio choice is also time-invariant and is independent of his wealth, consumption and time preference. The greater the risk aversion, the lower the expected return on B-shares, the higher the expected return on C shares, or the higher the risk on B-shares, the less will be held in B-share stocks. Moreover, less wealth will be allocated to B-shares if the correlation between B- and C-share stocks is higher.

To show that the CAPM holds under continuous time portfolio optimization problem for the foreign investors, denote $\sigma_{b,i,M}$ as the covariance of returns between an ith B-share stock and the B-share market portfolio, $\sigma^2_{b,M}$ as the variance of returns on B-share market portfolio, $\sigma_{b,i,c,M}$ as the covariance of returns between an ith B-share stock with a C-share market portfolio and $\sigma^2_{c,M}$ as the variance of returns on C-share market portfolio, since

$$\sum_{j=1}^{N} w_{b,j}(t)\sigma_{b,i,j} = \sigma_{b,i,M},$$

$$\sum_{i=1}^{N} w_{b,i}(t)\sigma_{b,i,M} = \sigma^2_{b,M},$$

$$\sum_{j=1}^{M} w_{c,j}(t)\sigma_{b,c,i,j} = \sigma_{b,i,c,M},$$

and $$\sum_{i=1}^{M} w_{c,i}(t)\sigma_{b,i,c,M} = \sigma^2_{c,M},$$

(4.51) becomes,

$$\mu_{b,i} - r_F = \beta_{b,i,M}\gamma_F\sigma^2_{b,M} + \beta_{b,i,c,M}\gamma_F\sigma^2_{c,M}. \tag{4.53}$$

4.5 Testable Implications From the Models

To derive testable implications from the price discrimination model, we express the share price equations (4.10) and (4.20) in expected return format for individual stocks as follows:

$$E(R_j^A) - r_D = a_D + \left(\frac{\lambda_D \Pi_j^A \sigma_{m,A}^2}{N} \right) \beta_{j,A} \tag{4.54}$$

$$E(R_j^B) - r_F = a_F + \left(\frac{\lambda_F \Pi_j^B \sigma_{m,B}^2}{M} \right) \beta_{j,B} + \left[E(R^C) - r_F \right] \sigma_C^2 \beta_{j,C} \tag{4.55}$$

where a_D and a_F are constants, $E(R_j^A), E(R_j^B)$ and $E(R^C)$ are expected returns on individual A-, B- and C-shares, respectively, $\Pi_j^A = P_{j,A} S_{j,A}$ and $\Pi_j^B = P_{j,B} S_{j,B}$ are market values for the jth stock. $\sigma_{m,A}^2$ and $\sigma_{m,B}^2$ are variances of the A- and B-share market returns. Note that in equations (4.54) and (4.55), the coefficients that come before $\beta_{j,A}$ and $\beta_{j,B}$ contain Π_j^A and Π_j^B, respectively, hence they are not constant over j. The reason for this lies in the choice of the constant **absolute** risk aversion utility for domestic and foreign investors. With the constant **relative** risk averse utility, it follows that $\lambda_D \Pi_j^A / N \approx \lambda_D W_i(0) \equiv \lambda_D^*$, where λ_D^* is investor's coefficient of constant relative risk aversion. It is clear that λ_D^* is independent of j. After combining equations (4.54) and (4.55), we obtain

$$[E(R_j^B) - r_F] - [E(R_j^A) - r_D] = \alpha_0 + \alpha_1 \beta_{j,A} + \alpha_2 \beta_{j,B} + \alpha_3 \beta_{j,C} + \epsilon_j \tag{4.56}$$

Therefore, according to the price discrimination model, the explanation for the differences in A- and B-share prices can be framed in terms of a model that explains the differences in expected returns for these two types of shares.

To derive the testable implications from the ICAPM formulation, we combine (4.43) and (4.53) and obtain the following equation for the variation of expected return between A- and B-shares:

$$\begin{aligned} (\mu_{a,i} - r_D) - (\mu_{b,i} - r_F) &= \beta_{a,i,M}(\mu_{a,M} - r_D) - \beta_{b,i,M} \gamma_F \sigma_{b,M}^2 \\ &\quad - \beta_{b,i,c,M} \gamma_F \sigma_{c,M}^2 \end{aligned} \tag{4.57}$$

Regressions (4.56) and (4.57) decompose the B-share return premium into two components: The first component, $\alpha_1 \beta_{j,A} + \alpha_2 \beta_{j,B} + \alpha_3 \beta_{j,C}$, represents the part of B-share return premium that is related to cross-sectional structure of risks, as measured by A-share market beta, B-share market beta and betas with respect to the international market returns. The second component, $\alpha_1 + \epsilon_j$, is the sum of residuals and intercept which is uncorrelated with measures of risk. The lower the A-share market beta, the higher the B-share market beta, or the higher the beta of an individual B-share with respect to international financial market returns, the higher the foreign investor's required B-share premium. Therefore, both (4.56) and (4.57) provide a basis for testing the linear relationship between the difference in the expected return for A- and B- shares and the market risk factors in the Chinese stock markets.

Note that no other variables, such as the variance of returns or firm size, appears in (4.56) or (4.57). Therefore, another testable implication of the model is that the betas are complete measure of the stock risks.

4.6 Empirical Results

4.6.1 *Estimating Betas*

The Chinese data consist of time-series of weekly A- and B-share market indexes and weekly stock prices for all 47 firms that issued both domestic A-shares and foreign B-shares before April 1994. 27 firms are listed in Shanghai and 20 firms are listed in Shenzhen. The sample period is from April 1994 to October 1998 with a total of 235 observations for each firm.

In calculating the rates of return on individual shares, we make the following adjustments to account for dividend payoffs, stock splits and rights issued:

(1) The amount of cash dividend per share is added to the stock price on the date it is paid.

(2) When there is a stock split at time t, P_t is divided by the split ratio so that

$$r_{t-1} = [(P_t/SR) - P_{t-1}]/P_{t-1},$$

where SR is the stock split ratio. The rate of return between t and $t+1$ is calculated as usual.

(3) When shares begin trading ex-rights, the theoretical stock price falls by the intrinsic value of rights. To consider the effect of rights issued on the rate of return of a share, the following adjustment is

made to the market price at the time trading ex-rights begins: Take the number of rights required to buy one new share, multiply by the market price per share before the ex-date, plus the subscription price and then divide the result by 1 plus the number of rights required to buy one new share.

Because A-shares are listed in Chinese *renminbi yuan* while Shenzhen B-shares are listed in Hong Kong dollar and Shanghai B-shares in U.S. dollar, we use the weekly exchange rates between the Chinese yuan, U.S. dollar and Hong Kong dollar to convert all share prices to U.S. dollars. Returns are calculated using U.S. dollar prices. The rate of return for the six-month Chinese Treasury Bond is used as the risk-free rate for domestic investors and the yield on the one-month U.S. T-bill is used as foreign risk-free rate. Stock indexes for Hong Kong Hang Seng market, MSCI world equity market, NASDAQ and NYSE are also obtained from April 1994 to October 1998.[4]

To test equations (4.56) and (4.57), I estimate betas for each company from the following time-series regressions,

$$r_{i,t} - r_{f,t} = \omega_i + \beta_{i,l}(r_{M,l,t} - r_{f,t}) + \nu_{i,t}, \tag{4.58}$$

where $r_{i,t}$ is the rate of return for stock i in week t, $r_{f,t}$ is the corresponding risk-free interest rate, $r_{M,l,t}$ is the rate of return for lth market index at time t, $\beta_{i,l}$ is the market beta for stock i with respect to type l market, and $\nu_{i,t}$ is the error term. Six beta estimates, namely, $\hat{\beta}_{i,A}$, $\hat{\beta}_{i,B}$, $\hat{\beta}_{i,NASDAQ}$, $\hat{\beta}_{i,NYSE}$, $\hat{\beta}_{i,MSCI}$ and $\hat{\beta}_{i,HS}$, are obtained for all companies. Tables (4.7) and (4.8 present the beta estimates.

Many of the Chinese firms whose stocks have significant betas with international financial markets are well-established world-class companies with strong international connections. For example, Sanmao Textile (code 900922), which has a significant beta with respect to the Hong Kong market, produces world-famous "SB" brand wool and its products are exported to the U.S., Europe, Middle East, Japan and Hong Kong. Shanghai Phoenix Bicycle (code 900916), which has significant betas with respect to the MSCI and Hong Kong markets, owns state-of-the-art production lines and also is-

[4]The data on Chinese stock prices are obtained from Shenyin International Securities, Xiamen Branch. The dividend, stock split and rights issued information is obtained from "Chinese Stocks and Futures Encyclopedia" on a compact disc produced by Shanghai Xian Zi Information Co., Ltd. and from China Securities Weekly magazine.

Table 4.7 Beta Estimates for 28 Firms that Issue A- and B-shares in Shanghai

Code	$\beta_{j,A}$	$\beta_{j,B}$	$\beta_{j,NASDAQ}$	$\beta_{j,NYSE}$	$\beta_{j,MSCI}$	$\beta_{j,HS}$
900901	1.1935*	0.8495*	0.4455	-0.2472	0.0913	2.3292*
900902	1.3070*	1.2242*	0.0613	-1.1188	-0.1853	0.5589†
900903	1.2090*	0.8525*	0.2201	-1.2434	-0.1089	0.1833
900904	0.8340*	0.7177*	0.9719*	-1.1257	0.9776	0.4780
900905	1.2325*	0.6826*	0.0752	-0.8016	-0.5958	0.1167
900906	1.1456*	0.8163*	0.2541	-1.1800	-0.3151	0.2789
900907	1.1780*	0.8565*	0.2890	-1.273	-0.3996	0.1499
900908	1.2925*	1.0348*	0.1819	-0.9815*	-0.9015*	0.2772
900909	1.0574*	1.1499*	0.3294	-1.0379	0.0992	0.3632
900910	0.8165*	0.6009*	0.0754	-1.0806	0.0871	0.3759
900911	0.9733*	1.1079*	0.2117	0.2336	0.7002	0.3666
900912	0.7780*	1.0583*	0.4058†	-0.1731	0.4511	0.2105
900913	1.1365*	0.5538*	0.1840	-0.0315	0.0432	-0.1964
900914	1.2409*	1.1381*	0.2599	-0.3709	0.7236	0.4688*
900915	0.8813*	0.8732*	0.0190	0.0718	0.0857	0.1323
900916	1.5244*	1.2782*	0.3094	-0.4234	1.0074*	0.7258*
900917	0.8859*	0.4777*	0.2818	0.5562	0.583	0.0749
900918	0.9004*	0.8159*	0.3719	0.2326	0.4647	0.3544*
900919	0.9685*	0.6332*	-0.1381	0.5799	-0.0365	0.1674
900920	1.0776*	0.9866*	-0.0136	-0.6957†	0.4105	0.2879†
900921	1.0321*	0.6260*	0.0403	0.1610	0.1765	-0.0932
900922	1.0816*	0.2031	0.0485	-0.0897	0.235	-0.1963*
900923	1.1830*	0.6218*	0.1293	0.1071	0.6271†	0.3454*
900924	1.0953*	0.5589*	0.0263	-0.3797	0.2491	-0.0084
900925	0.9475*	1.0164*	0.0857	0.0286	0.26	0.3782*
900926	1.2173*	0.9253*	0.1744	-0.2255	0.3117	0.4345*
900927	0.9910*	0.6291*	0.1691	0.1905	0.0049	0.1643
900928	1.1303*	0.9782*	0.1244	-0.8847*	1.3602*	0.3062†

*, †: Statistically significant at 5% and 10% level, respectively.

sues Euro-dollar denominated B-share stock convertible bonds. Shanghai Chlor Alkali (code 900908), which has significant beta with respect to the NYSE and MSCI world market, is the biggest chemical manufacturer in China and East Asia. It also issues H-shares which are listed on the Hong Kong Stock Exchange and some of its B-shares have been traded on the New York OTC market in the form of level ADR. Shenzhen Property & Resource Development (code 2011), which has a significant beta with respect

Table 4.8 Beta Estimates for 19 Firms that Issue A- and B-shares in Shenzhen

Code	$\beta_{j,A}$	$\beta_{j,B}$	$\beta_{j,NASDAQ}$	$\beta_{j,NYSE}$	$\beta_{j,MSCI}$	$\beta_{j,HS}$
2002	1.0536*	0.8246*	0.1940	-0.2188	0.3041	-0.0989
2003	0.9882*	0.9494*	-0.0581	-0.5975	-0.3401	0.0065
2011	1.0503*	0.8515*	0.7717*	-0.1537	0.2275	0.2232
2012	1.1240*	0.7203*	0.3178	-0.4439	-0.1169	-0.0574
2013	1.1258*	0.7451*	-0.3533	-1.0418*	0.1725	0.0533
2015	1.1905*	1.0442*	0.6263	-0.9906	0.7404	0.0521
2016	0.9872*	0.6120*	0.0557	0.5724	0.0292	-0.0837
2017	1.0827*	1.1580*	0.0594	0.1389	-0.3561	-0.0314
2018	1.1707*	1.0497*	0.5214	-0.9496†	0.9303	-0.1157
2019	1.1656*	0.8618*	0.2938	-1.1016†	0.7119	0.0757
2022	1.1087*	1.0550*	0.0936	-0.3743	0.0614	0.0784
2024	1.1068*	1.1574*	0.0533	-0.6759	0.3936	0.1863
2025	1.1616*	0.3598	-0.6407	-0.6910	-1.1334	-0.4887†
2026	1.0567*	0.8809*	0.4690	-0.1622	0.2148	-0.2265
2028	1.0342*	1.0536*	0.2440	-0.7823†	0.3909	-0.0058
2029	1.0305*	0.7722*	0.1702	-0.3739	0.6258	0.0002
2030	1.1953*	1.2391*	0.3190	-0.3210	0.7026	-0.0140
2045	1.1132*	1.1991*	0.2255	-1.0039	0.027	0.0416
2513	1.0958*	0.4934*	-0.0436	-0.4910†	0.0738	0.2036†

*, †: Statistically significant at 5% and 10% level, respectively.

to the NASDAQ market, always has the largest A- and B-share market capitalization on the Shenzhen Securities Exchange and is one of the most actively traded stocks by international investors. Lizon Pharmatheutical (code 2513), which has significant betas with respect to the NYSE and Hong Kong Stock Exchange, has also issued level ADR on the New York OTC market.

As described above, the price discrimination model and ICAPM formulation predict that these firms will have higher B-share returns. Now, we proceed with cross-section studies to test whether this prediction is valid.

4.6.2 *Errors-in-Variables and Tests for B-share Premiums*

To test hypothesis on B-share return premiums, we proceed in three steps. First, we test the validity of equations (4.43) and (4.54) by estimating the following cross-section regression:

Table 4.9 Cross-section Regression For Average A-Share Excess Returns

$\hat{\delta}_0{}^a$	$\hat{\delta}_1$	$\hat{\delta}_2$	$\hat{\delta}_3$	$\bar{R}^2$	F
-0.0705	0.0737*	0.0348	0.0425*	0.2962	3.2265
(-1.3591)	(2.1428)	(0.8441)	(1.9878)		[0.0406]
	{ 1.9890}				

[a]Figures in parentheses are t-statistics for the GLS estimates. Figures in braces are EIV-adjusted t-statistics. Figures in brackets are p-values. * and † denote statistically significant at the 5% and 10% level, respectively.

$$\frac{\sum_{t=1}^{T}(r_{a,i,t} - r_{D,t})}{T} = \delta_0 + \delta_1 \hat{\beta}_{i,A}^{SW} + \delta_2 (\hat{\beta}_{i,A}^{SW})^2 + \delta_3 D_i + \xi_i \tag{4.59}$$

where $\sum_{t=1}^{T}(r_{a,i,t} - r_{D,t})/T$ is the average excess return for the i-th A-share, D_i is a location dummy variable,

$$D_i = \begin{cases} 0 & : \text{ if firm } i \text{ is listed in Shanghai} \\ 1 & : \text{ if firm } i \text{ is listed in Shenzhen.} \end{cases}$$

and $\delta_1 = \gamma_D \sigma_{a,M}^2$.

In estimating regression (4.59), it is necessary to recognize that betas estimated from (4.58) are measured with error. To correct for the errors-in-variables (EIV) problem (specifically non-synchronous trading) and obtain a consistent estimator for $\beta_{i,A}$, we follow Scholes and Williams (1977) and use the lag, current and lead market returns to construct $\hat{\beta}_{i,A}^{SW}$. In particular,

$$\hat{\beta}_{i,A}^{SW} = \frac{\hat{\beta}_{i,A,-1} + \hat{\beta}_{i,A} + \hat{\beta}_{i,A,+1}}{1 + 2\rho_A}$$

where ρ_A is the first-order autocorrelation coefficient of the A-share market return. The variable $(\hat{\beta}_{i,A}^{SW})^2$ is included in (4.59) to test for linearity.

Table 4.9 presents the parameter estimates using Generalized Least Squares (GLS). As shown in the table, $\hat{\delta}_1$ is significantly positive at the 5% level, suggesting that A-share market beta is a good measure of risk for an individual firm's share.[5] Both $\hat{\delta}_0$ and $\hat{\delta}_2$ are statistically insignificant,

[5]Using principle component analysis (Campbell, Lo and MacKinlay, 1997), we find only

implying that non-beta risk does not affect the average returns across firms and the relationship between individual firm's excess return and its A-share market beta is linear. Furthermore, the representative domestic investor's absolute risk aversion coefficient, γ_D, is $\hat{\delta}_1/\sigma^2_{a,M} = 0.0737/0.0328 = 2.25$.

However, the EIV problem treated by Scholes and Williams remains in the cross-section regression standard errors, i.e., $\hat{\delta}_1$ is not N-consistent.[6] To adjust for the small sample bias in the cross-section regression estimates due to measurement errors in the betas, we follow Shanken (1992) and compute an EIV adjustment term from the sample covariance matrix of market risk factors, $\hat{c}$, which is positively related to the price of market risk factor and inversely related to the variance of market risk factor.[7] In cross-sectional regression (4.59), $\hat{c} = 0.21$. Then we compute the EIV-adjusted standard error for $\hat{\delta}_1$ as:

$$\sqrt{1.21\left[\left(\frac{0.0737}{2.1428}\right)^2 - \frac{0.0328}{235}\right] + \frac{0.0328}{235}} = 0.0372$$

where 0.0737 is $\hat{\delta}_1$, 2.1428 is the unadjusted t-statistic for $\hat{\delta}_1$, 0.0328 is the variance of A-share market excess return, $\sigma^2_{a,M}$, and $T = 235$ is the number of weekly observations. The EIV-adjusted t-statistic is $0.0737/0.0372 = 1.9890$ with p-value of 0.4902, as reported in the braces in Table 4.9. Therefore, $\hat{\delta}_1$ is still statistically significant at the 5% level after adjusting for the EIV problem.

Second, we test the validity of equations (4.53) and (4.55) by estimating the following cross-sectional regression:

$$\begin{aligned}\frac{\sum_{t=1}^{T}(r_{b,i,t} - r_{F,t})}{T} &= \theta_0 + \theta_1\hat{\beta}^{SW}_{i,B} + \theta_2\hat{\beta}^{SW}_{i,c} + \theta_3(\hat{\beta}^{SW}_{i,B})^2 \\ &\quad + \theta_4(\hat{\beta}^{SW}_{i,c})^2 + \theta_5 D_i + \xi_i. \end{aligned} \tag{4.60}$$

one common factor affecting A-share excess returns among firms.

[6] It is not consistent when the time-series length is fixed and the number of assets, N, is allowed to vary (Shanken, 1992).

[7] Given a single market risk factor, $\hat{c}$ is just the squared value of the famous Sharpe ratio (Shanken, 1992).

Table 4.10 Cross-section Regression for Average B-Share Excess Returns

$\hat{\theta}_0{}^a$	-0.0726	-0.0527	-0.0651	-0.0367
	(-1.3920)	(-1.0869)	(-1.1738)	(-1.0244)
$\hat{\theta}_1$	0.0551*	0.0636*	0.0573*	0.0755*
	(2.3806)	(2.6301)	(2.1433)	(2.2062)
	{ 2.2642}	{ 2.4714}	{ 1.9338}	{ 1.9290}
$\hat{\theta}_{2,NYSE}$	0.0239			
	(1.1528)			
	{ 1.070}			
$\hat{\theta}_{2,NASDAQ}$		0.0215		
		(0.9430)		
		{ 0.8941}		
$\hat{\theta}_{2,MSCI}$			0.0355	
			(1.5826)	
			{1.3254}	
$\hat{\theta}_{2,HS}$				0.1583*
				(2.7408)
				{ 2.3991}
$\hat{\theta}_3$	0.0396	0.0406	0.0462	0.0308
	(1.0261)	(0.8990)	(0.9860)	(0.8101)
$\hat{\theta}_{4,NYSE}$	0.0093			
	(0.3028)			
$\hat{\theta}_{4,NASDAQ}$		0.0068		
		(0.9233)		
$\hat{\theta}_{4,MSCI}$			0.0318	
			(0.6109)	
$\hat{\theta}_{4,HS}$				0.0269
				(0.9547)
$\hat{\theta}_5$	-0.0012	-0.0015	0.0008	0.0011
	(-0.1866)	(-0.7862)	(0.4133)	(0.2550)
$\bar{R}^2$	0.1688	0.1803	0.1526	0.3257
F	2.6759	2.8747	2.4982	3.7909
	[0.0843]	[0.07960]	[0.0931]	[0.0186]

[a]Figures in parentheses are t-statistics for the GLS estimates. Figures in braces are EIV-adjusted t-statistics. Figures in brackets are p-values. * and † denote statistically significant at the 5% and 10% level, respectively.

where $\sum_{t=1}^{T}(r_{b,i,t} - r_{F,t})/T$ is the average excess return for the i-th B-share, $\hat{\beta}_{i,B}^{SW}$ and $\hat{\beta}_{i,c}^{SW}$ are the Scholes-Williams consistent estimators for B-share market beta and B-share beta with respect to c-th foreign market ($c \in \{NYSE, NASDAQ, MSCI, HS\}$), respectively. According to equation (4.53), $\theta_1 = \gamma_F \sigma_{b,M}^2$ and $\theta_2 = \gamma_F \sigma_{c,M}^2$.

Table 4.10 presents the GLS parameter estimates. Using the usual t-statistics, $\hat{\theta}_1$ is significantly positive at the 5% level in all four regressions. Using the EIV-adjusted t-statistics, it is still significant at the 5% level (with p-value of 0.031, 0.018, 0.057, and 0.039, respectively), suggesting that B-share own market beta is a good measure of risk for B-shares. In addition, none of the foreign-market betas chosen in this study is statistically significant except the B-share beta with respect to the Hong Kong Hang Seng index, which is significant at the 5% level even under the EIV-adjusted t-statistic. This result may be explained the geographical proximity of Hong Kong to mainland China (and hence more rapid transmission of news) and the high proportion of B-share investors residing in Hong Kong. The estimated parameters $\hat{\theta}_0$, $\hat{\theta}_3$ and $\hat{\theta}_{4,HS}$ are all statistically insignificant, implying that non-beta risk does not affect the cross-section variation in the average B-share excess returns and that the relationship between B-share excess returns and B-share market beta and B-share beta with respect to the Hong Kong market is linear. The representative foreign investor's absolute risk aversion coefficient, γ_F, can be computed in two ways: $\hat{\theta}_1/\sigma_{b,M}^2 = 0.0755/0.0128 = 5.90$ or $\hat{\theta}_1/\sigma_{HS,M}^2 = 0.1583/0.0271 = 5.84$, implying that international investors are two-and-a-half times more risk-averse towards Chinese shares than domestic Chinese investors.

Finally, we estimate the following cross-section regression:

$$\left(\frac{\sum_{t=1}^{T}(r_{a,i,t} - r_{D,t})}{T}\right) - \left(\frac{\sum_{t=1}^{T}(r_{b,i,t} - r_{F,t})}{T}\right) = \alpha_0 + \alpha_1\hat{\beta}_{i,A}^{SW} + \alpha_2\hat{\beta}_{i,B}^{SW} + \alpha_3\hat{\beta}_{i,HS}^{SW} + \alpha_4 D_i + \epsilon_i \quad (4.61)$$

Regression (4.61) decomposes the differences in average returns for A- and B-share into two components: The first component, $\alpha_1\hat{\beta}_{i,A}^{SW} + \alpha_2\hat{\beta}_{i,B}^{SW} + \alpha_3\hat{\beta}_{i,HS}^{SW}$ represents the part of the average return difference between A- and B-shares that is related to the cross-section structure of risks, as measured by consistent estimates of A-share market beta, B-share market beta, and B-share beta with respect to the Hong Kong Hang Seng index. The sec-

Table 4.11 Cross-section Test for B-share Return Premiums

$\hat{\alpha}_0$ [a]	$\hat{\alpha}_1$	$\hat{\alpha}_2$	$\hat{\alpha}_3$	$\hat{\alpha}_4$	$\bar{R}^2$	F
0.0841	0.1238†	-0.1733*	-0.2095*	0.1118	0.3662	4.2869
(1.2508)	(1.8044)	(-2.3108)	(-2.9668)	(0.7925)		[0.0053]
	{1.5174 }	{ -1.9453}	{-2.5579 }			

[a]Figures in parentheses are t-statistics for the GLS estimates. Figures in braces are EIV-adjusted t-statistics. Figures in brackets are p-values. * and † denote statistically significant at the 5% and 10% level, respectively.

ond component, $\alpha_0 + \epsilon_i$, is the sum of residuals and an intercept which is uncorrelated with measures of risk.

Table 4.11 reports the GLS parameter estimates of equation (4.61). The coefficient estimates for the three market-risk factors are not only of right sign but also statistically significant using the conventional t-statistics. In addition, the constant terms are not significantly different from zero, suggesting that the smaller the A-share market beta, the higher the B-share market beta, or the higher the B-share beta with respect to the Hong Kong Hang Seng market, the smaller the difference in average returns between A- and B-shares. Using the EIV-adjusted t-statistics, A-share market beta becomes marginally significant (with p-value of 0.1503), B-share market beta becomes significant only at the 10% level, but the B-share beta against the Hong Kong Hang Seng market is still statistically significant at the 5% level. Therefore, the cross-section results support the price discrimination model and ICAPM formulation, although the empirical evidence is not overwhelming strong after adjusting for the EIV problem.

4.6.3 *Idiosyncratic Variance Effect and Firm Size Effect*

To test the hypothesis that the betas are complete measures of risk and that there are no systematic effects of non-beta risks on the difference in expected excess returns for A- and B-shares, we estimate the following two cross-section regressions:

$$\left(\frac{\sum_{t=1}^{T}(r_{a,i,t} - r_{D,t})}{T}\right) - \left(\frac{\sum_{t=1}^{T}(r_{b,i,t} - r_{F,t})}{T}\right) = \alpha_0 + \alpha_1 \hat{\beta}_{i,A}^{SW}$$

$$+\alpha_2\hat{\beta}^{SW}_{i,B} + \alpha_3\hat{\beta}^{SW}_{i,HS} + \alpha_4 D_i + \alpha_5(\hat{\sigma}^2_{a,i} - \hat{\sigma}^2_{b,i}) + \epsilon_i, \quad (4.62)$$

$$\left(\frac{\sum_{t=1}^{T}(r_{a,i,t} - r_{D,t})}{T}\right) - \left(\frac{\sum_{t=1}^{T}(r_{b,i,t} - r_{F,t})}{T}\right) = \alpha_0 + \alpha_1\hat{\beta}^{SW}_{i,A}$$

$$+\alpha_2\hat{\beta}^{SW}_{i,B} + \alpha_3\hat{\beta}^{SW}_{i,HS} + \alpha_4 D_i + \alpha_6(\ln MV_i) + \epsilon_i, \quad (4.63)$$

where $\hat{\sigma}^2_{a,i}$ and $\hat{\sigma}^2_{b,i}$ are the sample variances of A- and B-share returns, respectively, and $\ln MV_i$ is the logarithm of the sum of the average daily outstanding market capitalization of A- and B-shares for firm i.

If the price discrimination approach or ICAPM formulation is valid in explaining the cross-section differences in average returns, the variance of share returns should not have any explanatory power and $\hat{\alpha}_5$ should not be statistically significant. Both approaches also imply that firm size should not have any power in explaining the cross-section variation of asset returns, after controlling for risks. Therefore, $\hat{\alpha}_6$ should not be statistically significant either.

The regression results in Tables 4.12 and 4.13 show that neither $\hat{\alpha}_5$ nor $\hat{\alpha}_6$ is statistically significantly different from zero. Therefore, after the betas are controlled for, the variance of returns and firm size do not systematically affect the difference in expected returns for A- and B-shares in Chinese stock markets. It is interesting to note that the EIV-adjusted t-statistics for $\hat{\delta}_1$, $\hat{\delta}_2$ and $\hat{\delta}_3$ are smaller than the conventional t-statistics, which weaken evidence for the price discrimination and ICAPM formulations. Nevertheless, smaller t-statistics for $\hat{\delta}_5$ and $\hat{\delta}_6$ after adjusting for the EIV problem indicate that there are no idiosyncratic variance effect and firm size effect, thus render further support to both approaches.

4.7 Summary

In this chapter, we formulate a one-period price discrimination model under ownership restrictions to explain the discounts on foreign-owned Chinese B-shares relative to the prices of domestic A-shares. Under the one-period price discrimination model, the differences in prices for A- and B-shares for the same firm can be expressed in terms of the differences in their expected excess returns. The model posits that cross-section variations in expected

Table 4.12 Idiosyncratic Variance Effect

$\hat{\alpha}_0$[a]	$\hat{\alpha}_1$	$\hat{\alpha}_2$	$\hat{\alpha}_3$
0.0301	0.1055†	-0.1863*	-0.1927*
(0.4419)	(1.6886)	(-2.4511)	(-2.7230)
	{ 1.4089}	{ -2.0426}	{ -2.3271}
$\hat{\alpha}_4$	$\hat{\alpha}_5$	$\bar{R}^2$	F
0.4708	0.2899	0.3347	3.9715
(1.2336)	(0.1755)		[0.0107]
	{0.1438}		

[a]Figures in parentheses are t-statistics for the GLS estimates. Figures in braces are EIV-adjusted t-statistics. Figures in brackets are p-values. * and † denote statistically significant at the 5% and 10% level, respectively.

Table 4.13 Firm Size Effect

$\hat{\alpha}_0$[a]	$\hat{\alpha}_1$	$\hat{\alpha}_2$	$\hat{\alpha}_3$
-0.0275	0.1806*	-0.1604*	-0.2205*
(-0.2488)	(2.1169)	(-2.1033)	(-3.2008)
	{ 1.8052}	{ -1.8001}	{ -2.8202}
$\hat{\alpha}_4$	$\hat{\alpha}_6$	$\bar{R}^2$	F
0.3955	-0.0836	0.3751	4.5058
(1.0460)	(-0.8735)		[0.0018]
	{-0.8168}		

[a]Figures in parentheses are t-statistics for the GLS estimates. Figures in braces are EIV-adjusted t-statistics. Figures in brackets are p-values. * and † denote statistically significant at the 5% and 10% level, respectively.

excess returns between A- and B-shares depend on shares' own market betas and betas with respect to the international equity markets.

Then we combine the ICAPM with circumstances peculiar to China to explain the discounts on B-shares again. Under the assumption of infinite investment horizon and representative consumer-investor, we formulate an ICAPM with restrictions on share ownership. With the one-instant ICAPM, the differences in prices for A- and B-shares for the same firm are again expressed in terms of the differences in their expected excess returns. As the prediction of the one-period price discrimination model, the ICAPM posits that cross-section variations in expected excess returns between A- and B-shares are related to shares' own market betas and betas with respect to the global equity markets.

Empirical tests of the models using the conventional GLS t-statistics indicate that cross-section excess A-share over B-share average return is positively related to A-share market betas and is negatively correlated to B-share own market betas and betas with respect to Hong Kong Hang Seng market. After correcting for the EIV problem using Shanken's method, we find that these relationships are somewhat weak. Nevertheless, non-beta risk variables, such as the variance of returns and firm size do not systematically affect returns. Therefore, the empirical results by and large support the hypothesis of effective market segmentation and price discrimination as well as the ICAPM formulation in explaining the price differentials and return spread between domestic A-shares and foreign B-shares.

We have only investigated the investors' side of the problem in this chapter. A natural extension would be to account for the supply side as well as the demand side in a general equilibrium multi-period asset pricing framework.

Chapter 5

Excess Volatility in Domestic Share Markets

5.1 Introduction

In this chapter, we attempt to resolve an intriguing problem in Chinese stock markets: Why is return volatility for domestic A-shares so much higher than for foreign B-shares, even though the two share categories are entitled to identical rights and dividends within the same company?

Chinese stock markets are segmented in the sense that A-shares are available only to Chinese citizens and B-shares can only be purchased by foreign investors. Both types of shares are traded in the Shanghai and Shenzhen exchanges, but companies are not cross-listed. Bailey (1994) provides evidence that B-shares are sold and traded at various discounts relative to their A-share counterparts. Su and Fleisher (1998a) find that the volatility of stock-market return is much higher for A-shares than for B-shares. In the sample used in the current paper, the unweighted means of daily returns were 0.0303% and 0.0516% while the standard deviations were 6.0146% and 3.8916%, for A- and B-shares, respectively.

Su (1999a, 1999b) analyzes the B-share discounts and finds that foreign investors require a larger risk premium for holding B-shares than domestic investors do for holding A-shares. Moreover, the differences in the average excess returns for A- and B-shares are related to the shares' market risks in a manner predicted by the price discrimination model and Intertemporal Capital Asset Pricing Model. However, the sources of the volatility differences between A- and B-shares remain a puzzle.

To explore the sources of volatility differences in A- and B-share markets, we specify a model under the Mixture of Distribution Hypothesis

(MDH) as modified by Andersen (1996) in which stock returns and trading volumes are assumed to be contemporaneously dependent on an underlying mixing variable representing the non-uniform intensity over time (relative to an unobserved benchmark level) of the information flow. Since we do not observe the actual level of the latent information flow, we assume (realistically we believe) that the unobserved benchmark flow of information to (domestic) A-share investors is no less than that to (foreign) investors in B-shares.

The empirical model posits that the volatility of stock returns is identical to the latent information flow, and trading volume fluctuates in response to news. To model positive autocorrelation in news arrival, we specify that the latent information flow follows a stochastic autoregressive process. We estimate the dynamic system relating stock returns and trading volume using Generalized Method of Moments (GMM) and obtain parameter estimates characterizing the distribution of the unobservable daily information arrival for 24 companies that issue both A- and B-shares. We find that news arrival (1) is on average 49.45% larger for A-shares than for B-shares; (2) is more highly correlated with trading for A-shares than for B-shares; and (3) displays larger persistence in A-shares than in B-shares. We conclude that trading volume is a good approximation for the news flowing into the stock markets and that the differences in news levels and fluctuations as reflected in trading volume, as well as the way markets process news, can explain the difference in the return volatility between A- and B-shares.

The rest of this chapter is divided into four sections. In Section 5.2, we discuss the mixture of distribution theory and specify our empirical model. In Section 5.4, we describe the data and detail the adjustment procedure to remove long-run trend and other systematic calendar effects for stock prices and volume data. In Section 5.5, we present our empirical results. We summarize our findings in Section 5.6.

5.2 A Modified Mixture of Distribution Approach

We hypothesize that the main source of stock price movements is changes in the flow of information perceived by market participants. Market microstructure theory suggests that trading volume, number of transactions, and bid-ask spreads are related to the stock-return volatility. It is observed that market volatility is linked to phenomena associated with information arrival such as trading volume, quote spreads, market closures and forecastable events such as dividend announcements and macroeconomic data releases. The MDH posits that the joint distribution of daily returns and volume can be modeled as a mixture of bivariate normal distributions, specifically that they are contemporaneously dependent on an underlying mixing variable representing the flow of information,

$$R_t|K_t \sim N(\mu_1 K_t, \sigma_1^2 K_t) \tag{5.1}$$

$$V_t|K_t \sim N(\mu_2 K_t, \sigma_2^2 K_t), \text{and} \tag{5.2}$$

$$Cov(R_t, V_t|K_t) = 0 \tag{5.3}$$

where R_t is the stock return on day t, V_t is the trading volume on day t, and K_t is a mixing variable, usually interpreted as the unobserved flow of underlying information pertaining to the future dividends and/or the liquidation value of a particular stock.

The MDH was first developed by Clark (1973), and has been extended and tested by Epps and Epps (1976), Tauchen and Pitts (1983), Harris (1986, 1987), Lamoureux and Lastrapes (1990). These authors find evidence to support the hypothesis that trading volume is a good proxy for the latent information arrival process and is significantly correlated with the volatility of stock returns. However, recent and more comprehensive work by Richardson and Smith (1994), Lamoureux and Lastrapes (1994) and Gallant, Rossi and Tauchen (1992) provide more mixed evidence on the validity of the MDH. In particular, these studies find that the normality assumption for the trading volume is unrealistic because trading volume cannot be negative. In the simulation exercise of Lamoureux and Lastrapes (1994), the distribution of the error term is truncated in order to accommodate strictly nonnegative values of K_t.

Anderson (1996) proposed an improved characterization of the return volatility by assuming a time-invariant Poisson distribution for the trading volume, ruling out negative values *a priori*. Anderson's modified MDH (MMDH) can be modeled as

$$R_t = \mu + Z_t\sqrt{K_t} \tag{5.4}$$

$$\hat{V}_t | K_t \sim c \cdot Po(m_0 + m_1 K_t) \tag{5.5}$$

where Z_t is a standard normal random variable, $\hat{V}_t$ is the detrended, stationary trading volume series, m_0 is the daily arrival intensity of noise trading, m_1 is the proportion of trading volume that fluctuates in response to the underlying information flow (or news), c is a scaling parameter for the level of the trading volume, and σ_1^2 (equation 5.1) is normalized to be 1. In equations (5.4) and (5.5), the volatility of daily returns is the latent information flow itself.

We adapt Anderson's MMDH to model China's A- and B-share markets. Suppose that a company has higher A-share volatility than B-share volatility. If the expected value of K_t^A and/or the estimate of cm_1^A are larger than for K_t^B and cm_1^B, respectively, we can take this as evidence that a greater magnitude of news arrival, operating through trading volume, explains the company's "excess" A-share volatility.

In the spirit of Andersen (1996), we specify a dynamic process governing information arrivals, K_t, assuming that news arrivals are positively autocorrelated and follow a lognormal stationary stochastic autoregressive process in the following form:

$$\ln \sqrt{K_t} = \alpha + \beta \ln \sqrt{K_{t-1}} + \gamma u_t, \text{ and } K_t \geq 0 \tag{5.6}$$

where $0 \leq \beta < 1$, $\alpha > 0$, $\gamma > 0$, $u_t > 0$, and $u_t \sim i.i.d. N(0, 1)$. Note that, in (5.6), the information arrival process generating the dynamics of return volatility displays positive conditional dependency similar to GARCH-type models, which have been shown to be a reasonable representation of stock-market return volatility in China by Su and Fleisher (1998a).

It follows from equation (5.6) that

$$E(\ln \sqrt{K_t}) = \alpha/(1-\beta),$$

$$Var(\ln \sqrt{K_t}) = \gamma/(1-\beta^2),$$

and

$$Cov(\ln \sqrt{K_t}, \ln \sqrt{K_{t-j}}) = \beta^j Var(\ln \sqrt{K_t}) = (\beta^j \gamma)/(1-\beta^2).$$

The unconditional moments for K_t are:

$$
\begin{aligned}
E(\sqrt{K_t^n}) &= \exp\left[nE(\ln\sqrt{K_t}) + \frac{n^2}{2}Var(\ln\sqrt{K_t})\right] \\
&= \exp\left[\frac{n\alpha}{1-\beta} + \frac{n^2\gamma}{2(1-\beta^2)}\right], \qquad (5.7)
\end{aligned}
$$

$$
\begin{aligned}
E\left(\sqrt{K_t^n}\cdot\sqrt{K_{t-j}^m}\right) &= E\left(\sqrt{K_t^n}\right)\cdot E\left(\sqrt{K_{t-j}^m}\right) \\
&\quad \cdot\exp\left[mnCov\left(\ln\sqrt{K_t}, \ln\sqrt{K_{t-j}}\right)\right] \\
&= \exp\left[\frac{(n+m)\alpha}{1-\beta} + \frac{(n^2+m^2+2mn\beta^j)\gamma}{2(1-\beta^2)}\right],
\end{aligned}
\qquad (5.8)
$$

where n can be any positive integer.

5.3 Estimation: Generalized Method of Moments

Our dynamic system consists of equations (5.4)-(5.6). The parameterization of the system involves seven unknown coefficients, $\boldsymbol{\theta} = (\mu, \alpha, \beta, \gamma, c, m_0, m_1)$, which can be estimated by the GMM developed by Hansen (1982).

Let $\mathbf{v_t}$ be an $(p \times 1)$ vector of variables that are observed at date t, $\boldsymbol{\theta}$ be an unknown $(q\times 1)$ vector of coefficients, $\mathbf{h}(\boldsymbol{\theta}, \mathbf{v_t})$ be an $(r\times 1)$ vector-valued function where $\mathbf{h} : (\mathbf{R^p} \times \mathbf{R^q}) \to \mathbf{R^r}$, and $\boldsymbol{\theta_0}$ be the true parameter vector. Then the r orthogonality conditions can be written as $E[\mathbf{h}(\boldsymbol{\theta_0}, \mathbf{v_t})] = \mathbf{0}$. Let $\mathbf{y} = (\mathbf{v_1'}, \cdots, \mathbf{v_T'})$ be a $(Tp \times 1)$ vector containing all the observations in a sample of size T, then the vector of sample moments can be denoted as $\mathbf{g}(\boldsymbol{\theta}, \mathbf{y}) = (\sum_{t=1}^{T} \mathbf{h}(\boldsymbol{\theta}, \mathbf{v_t}))/T$. The GMM estimator $\hat{\boldsymbol{\theta}}_T$ is obtained by choosing $\boldsymbol{\theta}$ to minimize the scalar

$$
Q(\boldsymbol{\theta}, \mathbf{y}) = [\mathbf{g}(\boldsymbol{\theta}, \mathbf{y})]'\mathbf{W}_T[\mathbf{g}(\boldsymbol{\theta}, \mathbf{y})] \qquad (5.9)
$$

so that the sample moments are as close as possible to the population moment. $\mathbf{W}_T$ is a $(r \times r)$ positive definite weighting matrix that is a function of the data $\mathbf{y}$. Hansen (1982) shows that $\mathbf{g}(\boldsymbol{\theta}, \mathbf{y}) \xrightarrow{p} E[\mathbf{h}(\boldsymbol{\theta_0}, \mathbf{v_t})]$ if $\mathbf{v_t}$ is strictly stationary and $\mathbf{h}(\cdot)$ is continuous. Thus the value of $\hat{\boldsymbol{\theta}}_T$ that minimizes (5.9) offers a consistent estimate of $\boldsymbol{\theta_0}$.

The following unconditional moments can be exploited to estimate the unknown coefficients:

$$E(R_t) = \mu \tag{5.10}$$

$$E(\hat{V}_t) = cm_0 + cm_1 E(K_t) = \bar{V} \tag{5.11}$$

$$Var(R_t) = E(K_t) \tag{5.12}$$

$$Var(\hat{V}_t) = c^2 m_1^2 Var(K_t) \tag{5.13}$$

$$E(R_t, \hat{V}_t) = \mu(cm_0 + cm_1 E(K_t)) = \mu\bar{V} \tag{5.14}$$

$$E(|R_t - \mu|) = \sqrt{\frac{2}{\pi}} E(\sqrt{K_t}) \tag{5.15}$$

$$E[(R_t - \mu_1)^2 \hat{V}_t] = cm_0 E(K_t) + cm_1 E(K_t^2) \tag{5.16}$$

$$E(|R_t - \mu|\hat{V}_t) = cm_0 \sqrt{\frac{2}{\pi}} E(\sqrt{K_t}) + cm_1 \sqrt{\frac{2}{\pi}} E(\sqrt{K_t^3}) \tag{5.17}$$

$$E[(R_t - \mu)^2 (R_{t-j} - \mu)^2] = \frac{2}{\pi} E(K_t, K_{t-j}) \tag{5.18}$$

$$E[(\hat{V}_t - \bar{V})(\hat{V}_{t-j} - \bar{V})] = c_1^2 m_1^2 Cov(K_t, K_{t-j}) \tag{5.19}$$

$$E(|R_t - \mu||R_{t-j} - \mu|) = \frac{2}{\pi} E(\sqrt{K_t}, \sqrt{K_{t-j}}) \tag{5.20}$$

where $j = 1, \cdots, 6$. Our dynamic system has a total of 26 moment conditions and 7 unknown parameters and therefore 19 overidentifying restrictions.

Denote $\mathbf{\Pi}$ as the asymptotic variance-covariance matrix of the sample mean of $\mathbf{h}(\boldsymbol{\theta}_0, \mathbf{v_t})$. Then $\mathbf{\Pi} = \lim_{T\to\infty} T \cdot E\{[\mathbf{g}(\boldsymbol{\theta}_0, \mathbf{y})][\mathbf{g}(\boldsymbol{\theta}_0, \mathbf{y})]'\}$. Assuming that $\mathbf{h}(\boldsymbol{\theta}_0, \mathbf{v_t})$ is serially uncorrelated,

$$\hat{\mathbf{\Pi}}_T = (1/T) \sum_{t=1}^{T} [\mathbf{h}(\hat{\boldsymbol{\theta}}_\mathbf{T}, \mathbf{v_t})][\mathbf{h}(\hat{\boldsymbol{\theta}}_\mathbf{T}, \mathbf{v_t})]' \xrightarrow{p} \mathbf{\Pi}$$

for any consistent estimate for $\boldsymbol{\theta_0}$. Then our optimal weighting matrix is given by $\mathbf{W}_T = \hat{\boldsymbol{\Pi}}_T^{-1}$. To ensure that $\mathbf{W}_T$ is positive semidefinite, we follow Newey and West (1987) to estimate $\boldsymbol{\Pi}$:

$$\hat{\boldsymbol{\Pi}}_T = \hat{\boldsymbol{\Gamma}}_0 + \sum_{\nu=1}^{l} \left[1 - \frac{\nu}{(l+1)}\right] (\hat{\boldsymbol{\Gamma}}_\nu + \hat{\boldsymbol{\Gamma}}'_\nu) \tag{5.21}$$

where

$$\hat{\boldsymbol{\Gamma}}_\nu = \frac{1}{T} \sum_{t=\nu+1}^{T} [\mathbf{h}(\boldsymbol{\theta}, \mathbf{v_t})][\mathbf{h}(\boldsymbol{\theta}, \mathbf{v_{t-\nu}})]' \tag{5.22}$$

and l is a parameter representing the maximal order of autocorrelation for $\mathbf{v_t}$.

5.4 Data Adjustments

The raw data consists of daily closing prices and trading volume for all 24 companies represented by both A- and B- share issues for the period August 6, 1993 through September 25, 1997 for a total of 1021 observations. Cum-dividend returns are computed using $\ln(P_t + D_t) - \ln P_{t-1}$. Tables 5.1 and 5.2 present summary statistics for the percentage returns. As shown in the tables, average daily returns are uniformly higher for B-shares than for A-shares, but the volatility of returns, as measured by the standard deviation of daily stock returns, is higher for A-shares than for B-shares. Most of the return series are skewed to the right, although 5 of 24 A-shares and 10 of 24 B-shares exhibit negative skewness. All return series display excess kurtosis, meaning that large one-day returns are frequently observed. Tables 5.3–5.4 reports the autocorrelation of daily returns up to lag 8. The Ljung-Box portmanteau statistics for 12-th order autocorrelation in returns and squared returns are all statistically significant at the 1% level.

Table 5.1 Summary Statistics for Daily Returns for A- and B-Shares in Shanghai

Company		Mean (%)	Std. Dev. (%)	Skewness	Kurtosis
Vacuum	A	0.0189	5.5104	1.1417*	9.3754*
Electronics	B	0.0426	4.3738	0.0646	1.8447*
Shanghai	A	0.0235	6.8080	0.8821*	7.2607*
Erfangji	B	0.0330	4.1857	0.6738*	3.9148*
Dazhong Taxi	A	0.0214	4.8206	-5.6027*	106.15*
	B	0.0715	4.0776	-3.1307*	56.639*
Yongsheng	A	0.0523	5.1929	1.2784*	42.506*
Stationery	B	0.0728	3.6338	-0.2321*	5.2527*
China	A	0.0282	4.4095	-0.4829*	22.052*
First Pencil	B	0.0470	3.7804	-0.6932*	11.684*
China Textile	A	0.0577	4.5440	0.6768*	16.318*
Machinery	B	0.1006	3.7172	0.6592*	9.6953*
Shanghai	A	0.0397	4.3691	0.9262*	10.082*
Rubber Belt	B	0.0400	4.1637	-0.6671*	9.8001*
Shanghai	A	0.0306	4.3436	1.2151*	10.936*
Chlor Alkali	B	0.0493	3.2005	-0.1058	3.0754*
Shanghai Tire	A	0.0120	4.1982	1.1762*	9.0307*
& Rubber	B	0.0228	3.4573	0.1220	3.3694*
Shanghai	A	0.0024	4.2352	0.3674*	11.293*
Refrigerator	B	0.0129	3.6603	-0.855*	8.276*
Jinqiao Export	A	0.0181	4.4087	-2.3892*	56.288*
& Import	B	0.0495	3.1875	0.4043*	4.1316*
Outer Gaoqiao	A	0.0170	3.8895	-1.2698*	25.579*
	B	0.0943	3.2147	-0.4841*	16.294*

*: Statistically significant at the 5% level.

Table 5.2 Summary Statistics for Daily Returns for A- and B-Shares in Shenzhen

Company		Mean (%)	Std. Dev. (%)	Skewness	Kurtosis
Shenzhen	A	0.0144	3.9284	-0.15223*	10.8596*
Vanke Co.	B	0.0268	3.368	0.9935*	28.684*
Property &	A	0.0624	8.8933	-0.0514	326.05*
Resource Devel.	B	0.0717	3.9288	0.3238*	6.1907*
China	A	0.0326	23.6045	0.0700	93.6294*
Southern Glass	B	0.0393	4.1852	0.4169*	16.698*
Shenzhen	A	0.0469	4.3663	0.5319*	11.479*
Petroch. Co.	B	0.0493	3.7285	-1.0372*	15.375*
Shenzhen	A	0.0547	9.0626	0.0505	245.95*
Zhonghao Co.	B	0.0631	4.5195	0.8339*	8.8355*
Konka	A	0.0549	4.3610	-0.8690*	164.91*
Electronics	B	0.0674	3.7465	-1.1687*	22.921*
Shenzhen	A	0.0573	4.3966	0.1085	9.5413*
China Bicycles	B	0.1431	4.2169	1.4624*	33.141*
Victor Onward	A	0.0323	4.5932	1.0872*	9.0665*
Textile	B	0.0330	4.3152	0.6208*	24.753*
Shenbao	A	0.0021	4.9079	0.5246*	7.5238*
Industry	B	0.0049	4.5281	0.3851*	10.766*
Chiwan Wharf	A	0.0168	4.0620	0.9916*	8.4955*
Holdings	B	0.0352	3.6050	-0.2657*	9.8367*
China Merchants	A	0.0079	9.7604	0.6713*	384.20*
Shekou Co.	B	0.0191	4.0811	1.5517*	18.538*
Tellus	A	0.0237	5.6844	0.8061*	71.997*
Machinery	B	0.0480	4.5225	0.7864*	7.161*

*: Statistically significant at the 5% level.

Table 5.3 Autocorrelation for Daily Returns for A- and B-Shares in Shanghai

Company		Lag 1	Lag 2	Lag 3	Lag 4	Lag 5	Lag 6
Vacuum	A	-0.2168	-0.1493	0.0262	0.1560	0.0118	-0.1718
Electronics	B	-0.2064	-0.1538	0.0265	0.1626	0.0036	-0.1698
Shanghai	A	-0.2285	-0.1430	0.0261	0.1492	0.0044	-0.1583
Erfangji	B	-0.2016	-0.1491	0.0234	0.1588	0.0055	-0.1723
Dazhong Taxi	A	-0.2084	-0.1537	0.0220	0.1658	0.0052	-0.1772
	B	-0.2071	-0.1570	0.0245	0.1632	0.0043	-0.1731
Yongsheng	A	-0.2071	-0.1554	0.0221	0.1674	0.0065	-0.1763
Stationery	B	-0.2215	-0.1887	0.0099	0.2003	0.0039	-0.2066
China	A	-0.2058	-0.1557	0.0209	0.1626	0.0043	-0.1780
First Pencil	B	-0.2079	-0.1566	0.0219	0.1647	0.0061	-0.1776
China Textile	A	-0.2072	-0.1557	0.0219	0.1666	0.0052	-0.1768
Machinery	B	-0.1866	-0.1289	0.0216	0.1327	0.0112	-0.1457
Shanghai	A	-0.2068	-0.1553	0.0262	0.1628	0.0035	-0.1702
Rubber Belt	B	-0.2285	-0.1445	0.0257	0.1487	0.0048	-0.1599
Shanghai	A	-0.2043	-0.1514	0.0221	0.1581	0.0045	-0.1732
Chlor Alkali	B	-0.2084	-0.1534	0.0217	0.1656	0.0056	-0.1771
Shanghai Tire	A	-0.2074	-0.1555	0.0264	0.1639	0.0041	-0.1696
& Rubber	B	-0.2264	-0.1444	0.0270	0.1511	0.0051	-0.1589
Shanghai	A	-0.2207	-0.1883	0.0100	0.1999	0.0037	-0.2061
Refrigerator	B	-0.2071	-0.1545	0.0218	0.1618	0.0039	-0.1770
Jinqiao Export	A	-0.2077	-0.1581	0.0214	0.1653	0.0063	-0.1766
& Import	B	-0.2075	-0.1552	0.0216	0.1665	0.0060	-0.1769
Outer Gaoqiao	A	-0.2274	-0.1868	0.0121	0.1939	0.0074	-0.2049
	B	-0.2065	-0.1541	0.0258	0.1635	0.0042	-0.1727

Table 5.4 Autocorrelation for Daily Returns for A- and B-Shares in Shenzhen

Company		Lag 1	Lag 2	Lag 3	Lag 4	Lag 5	Lag 6
Shenzhen	A	-0.2284	-0.1445	0.0253	0.1481	0.0052	-0.1593
Vanke Co.	B	-0.2036	-0.1504	0.0224	0.1579	0.0040	-0.1735
Property	A	-0.2162	-0.1494	0.0258	0.1564	0.0107	-0.1712
Development	B	-0.2074	-0.1544	0.0265	0.1636	0.0041	-0.1699
China	A	-0.2268	-0.1450	0.0255	0.1496	0.0045	-0.1584
S. Glass	B	-0.2186	-0.1865	0.0099	0.1984	0.0040	-0.2039
Shenzhen	A	-0.2055	-0.1532	0.0224	0.1630	0.0042	-0.1778
Petroch. Co.	B	-0.2084	-0.1571	0.0207	0.1654	0.0063	-0.1765
Shenzhen	A	-0.2060	-0.1556	0.0216	0.1664	0.0068	-0.1765
Zhonghao Co.	B	-0.2264	-0.1849	0.0122	0.1936	0.0066	-0.2035
Konka	A	-0.2054	-0.1546	0.0214	0.1620	0.0046	-0.1773
Electronics	B	-0.2273	-0.1440	0.0189	0.1534	0.0067	-0.1653
China	A	-0.2036	-0.1506	0.0219	0.1582	0.0044	-0.1733
Bicycles	B	-0.2182	-0.1488	0.0253	0.1562	0.0116	-0.1722
Victor	A	-0.2070	-0.1530	0.0268	0.1627	0.0041	-0.1704
Textile	B	-0.2282	-0.1443	0.0255	0.1491	0.0051	-0.1584
Shenbao	A	-0.2021	-0.1480	0.0222	0.1573	0.0047	-0.1701
Industry	B	-0.2042	-0.1532	0.0221	0.1637	0.0048	-0.1767
Chiwan Wharf	A	-0.2079	-0.1556	0.0214	0.1654	0.0058	-0.1767
Holdings	B	-0.2067	-0.1550	0.0212	0.1670	0.0070	-0.1758
China	A	-0.2217	-0.1875	0.0100	0.1998	0.0040	-0.2068
Merchants	B	-0.2060	-0.1560	0.0208	0.1631	0.0044	-0.1774
Tellus	A	-0.2087	-0.1543	0.0214	0.1644	0.0073	-0.1780
Machinery	B	-0.2030	-0.1510	0.0217	0.1585	0.0040	-0.1745

Tables 5.5 and 5.6 present summary statistics for the raw daily trading volumes corrected for stock splits. As shown in the tables, the mean and standard deviation of trading volume are much larger for A-shares than for B-shares. Tables 5.7 and 5.8 report the autocorrelation in the logarithm of trading volume up to lag 6. The autocorrelation coefficients are large and decay only slowly.[1] This behavior is very typical for non-stationary moving average process. Since the MMDH is built on the assumption that trading volume is stationary, we test the null hypothesis of a unit root in the time-series of logarithm of trading volume against the trend-stationary alternative using Phillips-Perron unit root tests. The test results show that unit root hypothesis can be strongly rejected for all the trading volume series. (The Phillips-Perron unit root test results are available upon request.) Moreover, the time-series plots of the logarithm of trading volume clearly indicate a constant upward trend for all A- and B-shares. Therefore, we believe that the Chinese trading volume data are trend stationary.

To detrend the trading volume time-series, we follow Gallant, Rossi and Tauchen (1992) and use the following set of dummy and time-trend variables in the adjustment regression:

- Day-of-the-week dummies (Tuesday through Friday).
- Dummy variables for the number of non-trading days preceding the current trading day (dummies for each of 1, 2, 3 and 4 and more days preceding the current trading day). These dummy variables capture the systematic effects of weekends and holidays.
- Dummy variables for each month (January, and March through December).
- Dummy variables for each year (1994 to 1997).
- A time trend variable $= 1, \cdots, 1021$.

[1] Obviously, the presence of zero-values for some observations on B-share volume presents a problem here. In performing all estimation procedures involving log volume we have set $\log\ 0 = 0$.

Table 5.5 Summary Statistics for the Raw Trading Volume for A- and B-Shares in Shanghai

Company		Mean ($\times 10^3$)	Std. Dev. ($\times 10^3$)	Skewness	Kurtosis
Vacuum	A	32.114	46.575	2.9166*	10.2976*
Electronics	B	2.5204	4.042	3.3309*	14.4421*
Shanghai	A	11.787	17.586	3.2307*	13.1728*
Erfangji	B	4.7763	6.6654	3.0039*	11.9879*
Dazhong Taxi	A	4.6959	7.1137	3.1867*	13.3447*
	B	2.3143	3.3539	3.2553*	16.3812*
Yongsheng	A	2.2968	4.4025	6.5944*	68.6105*
Stationery	B	0.4547	1.5289	11.1901*	184.148*
China	A	3.4404	5.1296	2.8465*	9.5381*
First Pencil	B	1.6512	3.2055	7.5157*	104.426*
China Textile	A	7.3257	12.7792	4.2259*	26.9474*
Machinery	B	2.2739	5.9229	10.5660*	171.536*
Shanghai	A	2.2419	4.5986	6.9131*	72.2882*
Rubber Belt	B	0.563	1.1667	4.2031*	22.6308*
Shanghai	A	5.1942	9.7279	4.5083*	28.623*
Chlor Alkali	B	5.9343	7.4490	3.0992*	15.2082*
Shanghai Tire	A	3.7693	6.7162	4.3760*	27.0091*
& Rubber	B	4.5577	6.2202	3.9702*	25.6410*
Shanghai	A	3.3995	5.4373	3.8467*	21.5183*
Refrigerator	B	3.8023	5.3126	2.8662*	10.5796*
Jinqiao Export	A	22.0144	44.8383	5.4912*	40.0738*
& Import	B	4.6155	5.6830	3.3453*	19.8269*
Outer Gaoqiao	A	4.2763	8.9029	8.8738*	142.068*
	B	5.0448	5.6617	2.7272*	10.3127*

*: Statistically significant at the 5% level.

Table 5.6 Summary Statistics for the Raw Trading Volume for A- and B-Shares in Shenzhen

Company		Mean ($\times 10^3$)	Std. Dev. ($\times 10^3$)	Skewness	Kurtosis
Shenzhen	A	29.4483	45.5784	2.7029*	9.0481*
Vanke Co.	B	1.1971	2.8022	5.5819*	42.3339*
Property	A	15.1792	24.2258	3.4490*	16.8830*
Development	B	0.9688	3.5524	10.7562*	145.704*
China	A	17.088	29.8682	3.6385*	17.9250*
S. Glass	B	3.2343	8.4756	7.1944*	75.4146*
Shenzhen	A	11.5309	19.4081	3.1606*	12.1630*
Petroch. Co.	B	0.4597	1.4796	7.8157*	78.2487*
Shenzhen	A	7.7190	11.2185	2.9985*	11.5989*
Zhonghao Co.	B	0.6052	1.4470	4.8237*	27.7306*
Konka	A	15.4057	22.1406	2.4938*	7.8229*
Electronics	B	0.6391	2.2242	9.4728*	118.868*
China	A	18.8657	30.3878	2.8935*	10.0227*
Bicycles	B	4.6383	10.8935	4.8382*	27.1395*
Victor	A	5.0691	8.4574	3.6083*	18.0816*
Textile	B	0.6896	2.3477	7.8718*	90.5425*
Shenbao	A	7.2486	12.3383	3.5413*	15.7309*
Industry	B	0.9655	3.2586	9.7383*	139.379*
Chiwan Wharf	A	10.9633	15.7688	2.8565*	9.9275*
Holdings	B	1.6686	4.4655	7.7874*	87.0522*
China	A	8.7451	11.4356	2.4407*	6.9676*
Merchant	B	2.3985	5.3088	6.6242*	72.4576*
Tellus	A	10.1318	16.1771	3.2258*	13.0613*
Machinery	B	1.1188	2.9569	7.5704*	90.6199*

*: Statistically significant at the 5% level.

Table 5.7 Autocorrelation for the Log of Daily Trading Volume for A- and B-Shares in Shanghai

Company		Lag 1	Lag 2	Lag 3	Lag 4	Lag 5	Lag 6
Vacuum	A	0.7042	0.5968	0.5080	0.4086	0.3343	0.2799
Electronics	B	0.6973	0.5996	0.5062	0.4138	0.3360	0.2876
Shanghai	A	0.7019	0.5963	0.4924	0.3912	0.3115	0.2566
Erfangji	B	0.6888	0.5925	0.4998	0.3984	0.3214	0.2759
Dazhong Taxi	A	0.7092	0.6048	0.5156	0.4231	0.3372	0.2865
	B	0.6928	0.5989	0.5044	0.4109	0.3286	0.2850
Yongsheng	A	0.7038	0.5995	0.5089	0.4104	0.3360	0.2817
Stationery	B	0.7029	0.6043	0.5132	0.4149	0.3433	0.2857
China	A	0.7094	0.5983	0.5021	0.4043	0.3368	0.2833
First Pencil	B	0.7141	0.6083	0.5110	0.4136	0.3301	0.2733
China Textile	A	0.7132	0.6091	0.5151	0.4236	0.3490	0.2990
Machinery	B	0.6958	0.5917	0.4990	0.4042	0.3281	0.2728
Shanghai	A	0.7056	0.6039	0.5087	0.4116	0.3422	0.2896
Rubber Belt	B	0.7077	0.6006	0.4941	0.3909	0.3092	0.2500
Shanghai	A	0.6903	0.5950	0.5036	0.4021	0.3251	0.2802
Chlor Alkali	B	0.7061	0.5968	0.5091	0.4208	0.3351	0.2806
Shanghai Tire	A	0.7022	0.6109	0.5152	0.4198	0.3384	0.2940
& Rubber	B	0.7099	0.6039	0.5099	0.4080	0.3291	0.2696
Shanghai	A	0.6982	0.5982	0.5102	0.4169	0.3384	0.2835
Refrigerator	B	0.7090	0.6006	0.5008	0.4000	0.3285	0.2771
Jinqiao Export	A	0.7138	0.6161	0.5253	0.4278	0.3477	0.2938
& Import	B	0.7188	0.6121	0.5150	0.4200	0.3408	0.2855
Outer Gaoqiao	A	0.7023	0.5970	0.5053	0.4075	0.3360	0.2783
	B	0.7100	0.6054	0.5090	0.4103	0.3352	0.2786

Table 5.8 Autocorrelation for the Log of Daily Trading Volume for A- and B-Shares in Shenzhen

Company		Lag 1	Lag 2	Lag 3	Lag 4	Lag 5	Lag 6
Shenzhen	A	0.7243	0.6188	0.5147	0.4135	0.3289	0.2706
Vanke Co.	B	0.6929	0.5982	0.5078	0.4075	0.3308	0.2866
Property	A	0.7069	0.5979	0.5067	0.4143	0.3312	0.2793
Development	B	0.7047	0.6147	0.5197	0.4256	0.3452	0.3017
China	A	0.7087	0.6062	0.5088	0.4069	0.3299	0.2750
S. Glass	B	0.7014	0.6010	0.5092	0.4119	0.3293	0.2755
Shenzhen	A	0.7117	0.6021	0.5098	0.4174	0.3353	0.2857
Petroch. Co.	B	0.7103	0.6144	0.5222	0.4238	0.3446	0.2929
Shenzhen	A	0.7162	0.6107	0.5193	0.4238	0.3472	0.2958
Zhonghao Co.	B	0.7039	0.6000	0.5090	0.4119	0.3411	0.2837
Konka	A	0.7059	0.5947	0.4981	0.4017	0.3343	0.2798
Electronics	B	0.7193	0.6130	0.5132	0.4164	0.3339	0.2787
China	A	0.7005	0.6012	0.5024	0.4042	0.3315	0.2863
Bicycles	B	0.7087	0.6003	0.5088	0.4148	0.3321	0.2778
Victor	A	0.7006	0.6032	0.5049	0.4142	0.3326	0.2880
Textile	B	0.7083	0.6055	0.5086	0.4052	0.3263	0.2723
Shenbao	A	0.6895	0.5939	0.5015	0.4002	0.3235	0.2787
Industry	B	0.7094	0.5990	0.5107	0.4205	0.3393	0.2911
Chiwan Wharf	A	0.6957	0.6018	0.5070	0.4131	0.3298	0.2869
Holdings	B	0.7092	0.6008	0.5138	0.4189	0.3395	0.2878
China	A	0.7065	0.6059	0.5157	0.4176	0.3438	0.2868
Merchants	B	0.7022	0.5910	0.4940	0.3972	0.3295	0.2750
Tellus	A	0.7136	0.6057	0.5087	0.4122	0.3276	0.2723
Machinery	B	0.6996	0.6013	0.5042	0.4076	0.3368	0.2926

We first regress the logarithm of trading volume on the above set of adjustment variables,

$$\ln V_t = \mathbf{X}\boldsymbol{\beta} + \epsilon_t.$$

Each regression produces $\widehat{\ln V_t}$, the trading volume that is assumed to be due to factors not systematically related to news or information arrival. Then we divide each volume observation, $\ln V_t$, by the corresponding "non-constant noise" component, $\widehat{\ln V_t}$, for that day to obtain the detrended volume series.

Table 5.9 presents estimated coefficients of the detrending equation for Shanghai Vacuum Electronics and China Textile Machinery. Monday has a higher volume, which can be seen by noting that the coefficients of all other day-of-the-week dummies are negative. There are seasonal patterns by months of the year, with higher volume in January, March and April. The estimated coefficients for the time trend variable and the year dummies are all significantly positive, indicating that there is a pronounced upward trend in trading volume from 1993 to 1997.

To adjust for infrequent trading, we use a nonparametric kernel estimation procedure based on Gaussian kernel to further smooth the detrended trading volume data. This approach captures a wide variety of nonlinearities in the data without assuming any particular type of functional form. The nonparametric kernel estimator replaces 0 trading volume observation with weighted average of those $\tilde{V}_t$ in a small neighborhood around 0, where the weights decline as the $\tilde{V}_t$'s get farther away from 0. Denote the nonparametric smoothing estimate for the trading volume as $\hat{V}_t$,

$$\hat{V}_t = \frac{1}{T}\sum_{t=1}^{T} \mathcal{K}_h\left(\frac{\tilde{V}^* - \tilde{V}_t}{h}\right) \tag{5.23}$$

where $\mathcal{K}_h(\cdot)$ refers to the kernel, $\tilde{V}^*$ is the reference index (the choice of location of $\tilde{V}_t$), and h is the bandwidth. We use the most popular kernel, the Gaussian kernel, therefore

$$\mathcal{K}_h\left(\frac{\tilde{V}^* - \tilde{V}_t}{h}\right) = \frac{1}{h\sqrt{2\pi}} \exp\left[-\frac{1}{2}\left(\frac{\tilde{V}^* - \tilde{V}_t}{h}\right)^2\right] \tag{5.24}$$

Selecting the optimal bandwidth h is crucial in kernel estimation, since it determines the amount of smoothing undertaken. We use the method of cross-validation with fast Fourier transformation, in which the bandwidth is chosen to minimize a weighted-average squared error of the kernel estimator. (We use np_dens.src, a Gauss code written by Mico Loretan (1996), to compute the kernel estimates of the trading volume series. By plotting the bandwidths against the cross validation scores, which validate the success of the kernel estimator in fitting $\hat{V}_t$ series across $T-1$ subsamples, each with one observation omitted, the bandwidth is chosen to minimize the cross validation score function.)

Tables 5.10 and 5.11 report summary statistics for the detrended volume series $\hat{V}_t$ for A and B shares for 24 companies. The mean is near unity and the standard deviation is stabilized, which is to be expected given the normalization procedure. Skewness is mostly negative for A shares but positive for B shares. However, compared with the skewness and kurtosis parameters for the raw trading volume series, the number of significant parameters is reduced by more than one third in the detrended sample. Table 5.12 and 5.13 report the autocorrelation of the detrend volume. As shown in the tables, the autocorrelation coefficients are much smaller than those in the raw trading volume series and display a smooth decline from lag 1 to lag 4, becoming randomly positive or negative and statistically insignificant. In sum, the detrended volume series appear to be stationary and exhibit the type of characteristics that are required by the empirical model.

Table 5.9 Adjustment Regressions for the Log of Volume for A and B Shares

	Shanghai Vacuum Electronics[a]		China Textile Machinery	
	A	B	A	B
Trend				
Intercept	10.1559*	7.7634*	5.6967*	6.0316*
	(0.7140)	(0.6440)	(0.7711)	(0.7947)
t	0.017*	0.0121*	0.0105*	0.0111*
	(0.0054)	(0.0048)	(0.0058)	(0.0059)
Day of the week				
Tuesday	-0.5697†	-0.1559	0.2678	0.2250
	(0.3337)	(0.3009)	(0.3603)	0.3714)
Wednesday	-0.5517†	-0.0568	0.2701	0.2633
	(0.3332)	(0.3005)	(0.3598)	(0.3708)
Thursday	-0.5528†	-0.1561	0.2807	0.3373
	(0.3328)	(0.3001)	(0.3594)	(0.3704)
Friday	-0.6011†	-0.2358	0.3645	0.8472
	(0.3302)	(0.2978)	(0.3566)	(0.3675)
Number of non-trading days				
One day	-0.2049	0.1517	0.6395	0.8472
	(0.6158)	(0.5554)	(0.6650)	(0.6854)
Two days	0.5790†	0.1570	0.4107	0.3956
	(0.3315)	(0.2990)	(0.3580)	(0.3689)
Three days	0.6971*	0.1075	0.0442	0.3647
	(0.3484)	(0.3142)	(0.3762)	(0.3877)
Four and more days	0.7268†	0.1857	0.044	0.3582
	(0.4206)	(0.3793)	(0.4541)	(0.4681)

(*continue on the next page*)

[a]Standard errors in parentheses and * and † denote significance at the 5% and 10% level, respectively.

(continued)

	Shanghai Vacuum Electronics		China Textile Machinery	
	A	B	A	B
Month				
January	0.6113*	0.8181*	0.2675	0.7069*
	(0.2057)	(0.1855)	(0.1603)	(0.2289)
March	0.4986*	0.7392*	0.7640*	0.3956
	(0.2067)	(0.1864)	(0.2231)	(0.3649)
April	0.1810	0.8062*	0.7061*	0.9862†
	(0.2796)	(0.2522)	(0.3019)	(0.3111)
May	-0.0931	0.3971	0.7550†	0.7434†
	(0.3713)	(0.3349)	(0.4001)	(0.4132)
June	-0.6748	-0.0651	-0.2702	-0.0211
	(0.4685)	(0.4225)	(0.5059)	(0.5214)
July	-1.1874*	-0.3856	-0.6146	-0.4240
	(0.5744)	(0.5181)	(0.6203)	(0.6392)
August	-0.3049	0.4315	0.1391	0.3920
	(0.6846)	(0.6174)	(0.7392)	(0.7619)
September	-0.9524	-0.1924	-0.3383	0.0710
	(0.7916)	(0.7140)	(0.8548)	(0.8811)
October	-1.0678	-0.1780	-0.4755	0.1578
	(0.9110)	(0.8217)	(0.9838)	(1.0140)
November	-1.2164	-0.0251	-0.8339	-0.1852
	(1.0184)	(0.9185)	(1.0997)	(1.1335)
December	-2.2157†	-0.6425	-1.1126	-0.9613
	(1.1329)	(1.0218)	(1.2234)	(1.2609)
Year				
1994	4.0286*	2.2612†	0.6063	1.6064
	(1.3399)	(1.2085)	(1.4470)	(1.4913)
1995	7.9731*	5.3672*	4.2099*	4.850*
	(2.6768)	(2.4143)	(1.8906)	(1.9792)
1996	11.2462*	7.6414*	6.3185*	7.1678*
	(3.9957)	(3.6039)	(3.0148)	(3.4471)
1997	4.9623*	9.5176*	7.8986*	9.4826*
	(1.2940)	(4.7748)	(3.7167)	(4.8920)

Table 5.10 Summary Statistics for the Detrended Trading Volume for A- and B-Shares in Shanghai

Company		Mean	Std. Dev.	Skewness	Kurtosis
Vacuum	A	0.9989	0.3250	0.2782*	0.1451
Electronics	B	1.0014	0.2795	-0.0869	0.0419
Shanghai	A	0.9999	0.2026	0.2813*	0.2407*
Erfangji	B	1.0001	0.2931	0.3691*	2.7334*
Dazhong Taxi	A	1.1097	0.3474	-1.0437*	0.4297*
	B	0.9778	0.2772	0.1209	0.7557*
Yongsheng	A	1.7229	0.7028	-1.2679*	2.1036*
Stationery	B	1.0029	0.4719	0.1704*	0.2073*
China	A	1.1083	0.3367	-0.7865*	0.4380*
First Pencil	B	0.9083	0.3156	-0.039	0.1382
China Textile	A	1.3808	0.520	-0.2591*	0.1198
Machinery	B	0.9930	0.3259	-0.0717	0.4752*
Shanghai	A	1.164	0.3571	-0.1665*	0.1487
Rubber Belt	B	1.009	0.3146	0.590*	0.2374*
Shanghai	A	1.0203	0.2151	-0.1924*	0.3395*
Chlor Alkali	B	0.9097	0.1938	0.2928*	0.490*
Shanghai Tire	A	1.0317	0.2589	-0.1306	0.1198
& Rubber	B	0.9845	0.2288	0.1639*	0.1778*
Shanghai	A	1.0208	0.2978	-0.2250*	0.3276*
Refrigerator	B	0.8841	0.2602	0.419	0.1131
Jinqiao Export	A	1.1058	0.1701	0.1984*	0.2371*
& Import	B	1.0011	0.1579	0.7633*	1.5953*
Outer Gaoqiao	A	1.0029	0.1550	0.1145	0.1367
	B	0.9960	0.1211	0.4793*	1.1669*

Table 5.11 Summary Statistics for the Detrended Trading Volume for A- and B-Shares in Shenzhen

Company		Mean	Std. Dev.	Skewness	Kurtosis
Shenzhen	A	1.2427	0.4526	-0.9507*	2.1414*
Vanke Co.	B	0.8766	0.2995	0.0615	0.1559
Property	A	1.3605	0.5123	-1.1003*	2.7906*
Development	B	0.9723	0.3443	0.1844*	0.0793
China	A	1.2274	0.4501	0.-2286*	0.3429*
S. Glass	B	1.0002	0.3619	0.6686*	0.8692*
Shenzhen	A	1.0957	0.2139	-0.2276*	0.5272*
Petroch. Co.	B	0.9566	0.1663	0.2763*	0.1255
Shenzhen	A	1.1796	0.3223	-0.1129	0.0759
Zhonghao Co.	B	1.0279	0.2957	0.3502*	0.2475*
Konka	A	1.0616	0.1619	-0.1176	0.0809
Electronics	B	0.8915	0.1220	0.2653*	0.3944*
China	A	1.370	0.2235	0.1093	0.1058
Bicycles	B	0.9588	0.1884	0.1992*	0.2953*
Victor	A	1.1822	0.2486	-0.3710*	0.4172*
Textile	B	1.0103	0.1899	0.8209*	0.6215*
Shenbao	A	1.3070	0.2497	-0.1022	0.0857
Industry	B	0.9484	0.1969	-0.0735	0.0391
Chiwan Wharf	A	1.124	0.2898	-0.1181	0.0740
Holdings	B	0.9974	0.2275	0.2418*	0.2472*
China	A	1.1528	0.2003	0.1255	0.1103
Merchants	B	0.9742	0.1814	0.2418*	0.4355*
Tellus	A	1.158	0.2209	0.1021	0.0810
Machinery	B	0.9551	0.1989	0.540*	1.1313*

Table 5.12 Autocorrelation for the Detrended Daily Trading Volume for A and B Shares in Shanghai

Company		Lag 1	Lag 2	Lag 3	Lag 4	Lag 5	Lag 6
Vacuum	A	0.2866	0.1509	0.0507	-0.0792	-0.0269	0.0080
Electronics	B	0.2689	0.1457	0.0409	-0.0885	0.0317	0.0963
Shanghai	A	0.2286	0.1611	0.0159	0.0480	-0.0008	-0.1031
Erfangji	B	0.2208	0.1673	0.1043	0.0157	-0.0069	-0.1829
Dazhong Taxi	A	0.2377	0.1552	0.1121	0.0169	-0.0042	-0.0686
	B	0.2253	0.1933	0.1038	0.0043	-0.0017	-0.1108
Yongsheng	A	0.2172	0.1644	0.1551	0.0130	-0.0052	-0.1889
Stationery	B	0.2941	0.1457	0.1049	0.0142	-0.0699	-0.0977
China	A	0.3091	0.1745	0.1011	0.0441	-0.0723	0.0788
First Pencil	B	0.3229	0.2453	0.1020	0.0435	-0.0882	-0.0229
China Textile	A	0.3204	0.1907	0.0660	-0.0568	-0.0493	0.0396
Machinery	B	0.3434	0.2303	0.1607	0.0665	-0.0240	-0.1009
Shanghai	A	0.3341	0.2277	0.1394	0.0404	-0.0940	-0.0466
Rubber Belt	B	0.3026	0.2324	0.1145	0.0695	-0.0285	-0.0950
Shanghai	A	0.3278	0.1622	0.1125	0.0839	-0.0731	0.0506
Chlor Alkali	B	0.3427	0.2313	0.1138	0.0733	-0.0337	-0.1095
Shanghai Tire	A	0.3615	0.2431	0.1216	0.0838	-0.0492	0.0373
& Rubber	B	0.3451	0.1615	0.0735	0.0070	-0.0693	-0.1364
Shanghai	A	0.3208	0.1865	0.0705	-0.0241	-0.0420	0.0653
Refrigerator	B	0.3316	0.2351	0.1787	0.0541	-0.0436	-0.1570
Jinqiao Export	A	0.2885	0.1593	0.0800	-0.0284	-0.1108	0.0173
& Import	B	0.3395	0.2273	0.1231	0.0371	-0.0417	-0.1307
Outer Gaoqiao	A	0.3002	0.2372	0.1242	0.0673	-0.0752	-0.1206
	B	0.2864	0.1881	0.0520	-0.0531	0.0703	-0.0229

Table 5.13 Autocorrelation for the Detrended Daily Trading Volume for A- and B-Shares in Shenzhen

Company		Lag 1	Lag 2	Lag 3	Lag 4	Lag 5	Lag 6
Shenzhen	A	0.3209	0.2348	0.1470	0.0399	-0.0611	-0.1243
Vanke Co.	B	0.3062	0.2315	0.1438	0.0663	-0.0767	0.0584
Property	A	0.3492	0.2405	0.1084	0.0291	-0.0681	-0.0804
Development	B	0.3318	0.2388	0.1244	0.0666	-0.0240	-0.1201
China	A	0.2682	0.1348	0.0716	-0.0114	0.0647	-0.470
S. Glass	B	0.2271	0.1764	0.0774	0.0265	-0.0532	-0.1145
Shenzhen	A	0.2537	0.1338	0.0422	-0.0488	-0.0101	0.0628
Petroch. Co.	B	0.2480	0.1302	0.0481	-0.0449	0.0549	-0.0200
Shenzhen	A	0.2983	0.1949	0.1239	0.0762	-0.0394	0.0028
Zhonghao Co.	B	0.2722	0.1977	0.1158	0.0561	-0.0125	-0.0655
Konka	A	0.2938	0.1817	0.1243	0.0488	-0.0419	0.0073
Electronics	B	0.3054	0.1865	0.1170	0.0501	-0.0368	-0.0891
China	A	0.3248	0.2393	0.1269	0.0569	-0.0341	0.0843
Bicycles	B	0.3142	0.2117	0.1577	0.0607	-0.0384	-0.0615
Victor	A	0.3299	0.2398	0.1223	0.0421	-0.0518	0.0492
Textile	B	0.2693	0.1529	0.1079	0.0478	-0.0027	-0.0974
Shenbao	A	0.3078	0.1902	0.1366	0.0823	-0.0301	-0.0964
Industry	B	0.2618	0.1783	0.1027	0.0231	-0.0589	0.0180
Chiwan Wharf	A	0.2732	0.1893	0.0994	0.0490	-0.0469	0.0604
Holdings	B	0.2525	0.1624	0.0745	-0.0083	0.0451	0.0992
China	A	0.2687	0.1452	0.0471	-0.0400	0.0451	-0.0187
Merchants	B	0.2630	0.2156	0.1274	0.0545	-0.0208	-0.0834
Tellus	A	0.2730	0.1724	0.1021	0.0241	-0.0584	0.0295
Machinery	B	0.2585	0.1662	0.0743	-0.0210	0.0528	-0.0467

5.5 Empirical Results

In estimating our dynamic return-volume system (5.4)-(5.6) by GMM procedure, the weighting matrix used in the objective function (5.9) is calculated according to Newey and West (1987a).[2] A modification of Durbin's method is used in the procedure to determine the optimal maximal order of autocorrelation in the sample (l) and to obtain the autoregression coefficients from Yule-Walker equations. The weighting matrix and the parameters are iterated until convergence, so the final parameter estimates reflects the optimal value of the weighting matrix. Since we have 26 moment conditions and 7 unknowns, we use a J-statistic suggested by Hansen (1982) to test whether the 19 overidentifying restrictions are needed. In particular,

$$J = \frac{1}{T}[\mathbf{g}(\hat{\boldsymbol{\theta}}, \mathbf{y})]'\mathbf{W}_T[\mathbf{g}(\hat{\boldsymbol{\theta}}, \mathbf{y})] \sim \chi^2_{(19)}. \tag{5.25}$$

Table 5.14 presents the parameter estimates as well as Hansen's J-statistics. As shown in the table, the overidentifying restrictions are rejected for Jinqiao Export & Import, Shenzhen Petrochemical Co. and Shenbao Industry, meaning that our empirical model does not fare well for these three companies. For the remaining 21 companies, the J-statistics are not statistically significant even at the 10% level, suggesting that the MMDH cannot be rejected and our dynamic system is quite informative in studying the stock return and trading volume for these companies.[3] Therefore, we only report the distributional characteristics for return volatility, or the latent information variable, for 21 companies in Tables 5.14 and 5.15.

To see how well the MMDH helps us to understand the greater volatility of returns among Chinese A-shares, we first recall from equation (5.12) that the volatility of returns is the expected value of K_t. Therefore, an estimate of $E(K_t)$ larger across A- than across B-shares may be viewed as supporting our hypothesis that a greater volume of news arrival is a fundamental explanation of the excess of volatility in the A-share markets over the B-share markets. As shown in Tables 5.16 and 5.17, $E(K_t)$ are

[2]We use a GAUSS program written and made publicly available by Hansen, Heaton and Ogaki for the GMM procedure.

[3]We should point out that we have estimated our dynamic system of stock return and volume using different number of moment conditions. Our results are quite robust to the specification of the moment conditions.

Table 5.14 Estimation Results for Return-Volume System for A- and B-Shares in Shanghai

(Standard errors in parentheses and p-values in brackets)

Company		μ	c	m_0	m_1	α	β	γ	χ^2_{19}
Shanghai Vacuum	A	0.000475	0.1921	1.1265	2.8993	0.0561	0.8796	0.1152	13.707
Electronics		(0.000954)	(0.0775)	(0.4049)	(0.9237)	(0.0192)	(0.1883)	(0.0547)	[0.8030]
	B	0.000932	0.4334	0.7562	0.6579	0.0270	0.6420	0.1562	23.065
		(0.002075)	(0.1514)	(0.1968)	(0.2297)	(0.0101)	(0.2278)	(0.0727)	[0.2441]
Shanghai Erfangji	A	0.000132	0.2446	0.9875	2.1218	0.0370	0.7938	0.1360	14.596
		(0.000073)	(0.0864)	(0.1253)	(0.8399)	(0.0104)	(0.2561)	(0.08614)	[0.7604]
	B	0.000124	0.4439	0.8208	0.8504	0.0006	0.5624	0.0523	19.068
		(0.000058)	(0.1751)	(0.2776)	(0.3219)	(0.0002)	(0.2863)	(0.0229)	[0.4335]
Dazhong Taxi	A	0.000563	0.1727	1.6115	2.7234	0.0592	0.7419	0.1788	15.713
		(0.001855)	(0.0545)	(0.5159)	(1.2096)	(0.0136)	(0.1727)	(0.0643)	[0.6922]
	B	0.000718	0.3173	1.0082	1.6180	0.0170	0.5398	0.3019	20.324
		(0.001907)	(0.1422)	(0.3089)	(0.8066)	(0.0057)	(0.1699)	(0.1521)	[0.4017]
Yongsheng	A	0.001308	0.2977	0.8382	1.7669	0.0453	0.7772	0.1899	14.782
Stationery		(0.004492)	(0.0946)	(0.3806)	(0.5026)	(0.0138)	(0.2989)	(0.0885)	[0.7567]
	B	0.001335	0.5232	0.6968	0.9297	0.0153	0.6301	0.1596	19.336
		(0.008662)	(0.1845)	(0.2807)	(0.3553)	(0.0052)	(0.2920)	(0.0684)	[0.4627]

(Continued on the next page)

(*Continued*)

Company		μ	c	m_0	m_1	α	β	γ	χ^2_{19}
China	A	0.000468	0.3983	0.5021	0.4043	0.1368	0.4833	0.2104	22.3862
First Pencil		(0.000160)	(0.1203)	(0.1796)	(0.0807)	(0.1974)	(0.1047)	(0.0652)	[0.2710]
	B	0.000718	0.4083	0.5110	0.4136	0.1301	0.2733	0.2074	26.119
		(0.000356)	(0.1769)	(0.2050)	(0.1836)	(0.0652)	(0.0934)	(0.1015)	[0.1249]
China Textile	A	0.000549	0.3917	0.4990	1.1042	0.0281	0.7728	0.1981	14.602
Machinery		(0.000303)	(0.1116)	(0.1357)	(0.3824)	(0.0095)	(0.2039)	(0.0904)	[0.7582]
	B	0.00103	0.5454	0.4396	0.3608	0.0699	0.6113	0.2831	19.806
		(0.000495)	(0.1708)	(0.1548)	(0.1996)	(0.0104)	(0.2633)	(0.1240)	[0.4482]
Shanghai	A	0.000781	0.3339	0.5087	1.4116	0.0422	0.6896	0.2210	17.035
Rubber Belt		(0.000185)	(0.1412)	(0.2166)	(0.5372)	(0.0164)	(0.1990)	(0.0703)	[0.5448]
	B	0.000955	0.5100	0.6941	0.5909	0.050	0.5884	0.2092	18.821
		(0.000433)	(0.1262)	(0.2195)	(0.1137)	(0.014)	(0.1706)	(0.0711)	[0.4902]
Shanghai	A	0.000564	0.2457	1.0512	2.4070	0.0422	0.7964	0.1136	14.982
Chlor Alkali		(0.000208)	(0.1033)	(0.3144)	(0.7675)	(0.0185)	(0.1309)	(0.0341)	[0.7801]
	B	0.00880	0.5849	0.7068	0.6775	0.0779	0.3951	0.2517	24.988
		(0.00301)	(0.1906)	(0.2612)	(0.2118)	(0.0235)	(0.1499)	(0.0841)	[0.2065]

(Continued on next page)

(Continued)

Company		μ	c	m_0	m_1	α	β	γ	χ^2_{19}
Shanghai Tire	A	0.000469	0.2385	0.9181	2.1420	0.0737	0.6158	0.0865	20.268
& Rubber		(0.000192)	(0.0687)	(0.2407)	(0.8468)	(0.0162)	(0.1891)	(0.0206)	[0.3899]
	B	0.000703	0.3466	1.1745	1.0869	0.0980	0.3717	0.1206	24.841
		(0.000242)	(0.1104)	(0.3563)	(0.2917)	(0.0204)	(0.1608)	(0.0533)	[0.1924]
Shanghai	A	-0.000320	0.3982	0.8102	1.4169	0.0384	0.5835	0.2166	18.705
Refrigerator		(0.000388)	(0.1174)	(0.3705)	(0.6629)	(0.0088)	(0.2083)	(0.0774)	[0.5185]
	B	0.000144	0.6006	0.5008	0.7908	0.0825	0.4771	0.1002	22.850
		(0.000175)	(0.1989)	(0.1627)	(0.2995)	(0.0073)	(0.1299)	(0.0444)	[0.2439]
Jinqiao Export	A	0.000273	0.0433	1.4286	10.8032	0.1285	0.3019	0.0812	74.2219
& Import		(0.000139)	(0.1017)	(0.5338)	(0.5965)	(0.0110)	(0.1862)	(0.0498)	[0.0001]
	B	0.000759	0.0584	0.7329	14.0671	0.1565	0.1927	0.2134	100.3204
		(0.000256)	(0.0649)	(0.3940)	(3.8158)	(0.0042)	(0.1186)	(0.0792)	[0.0001]
Outer Gaoqiao	A	0.000744	0.4091	0.9151	1.4236	0.0490	0.7990	0.1326	14.2
		(0.000267)	(0.1380)	(0.3377)	(0.4891)	(0.0038)	(0,1881)	(0.0592)	[0.7861]
	B	0.001106	0.5667	0.7019	0.4880	0.0150	0.5702	0.1256	18.464
		(0.000152)	(0.1858)	(0.2061)	(0.1332)	(0.0044)	(0.1719)	(0.0409)	[0.4993]

Table 5.15 Estimation Results for Return-Volume System for A- and B-Shares in Shenzhen

(Standard errors in parentheses and p-values in brackets)

Company		μ	c	m_0	m_1	α	β	γ	χ^2_{19}
Shenzhen	A	0.000206	0.2989	1.0636	1.5104	0.0050	0.6228	0.1029	19.201
Vanke Co.		(0.000202)	(0.1046)	(0.3619)	(0.5727)	(0.0008)	(0.1941)	(0.0523)	[0.4286]
	B	0.000423	0.4913	0.8825	0.6094	0.0117	0.4492	0.1360	23.089
		(0.000209)	(0.1481)	(0.2116)	(0.2307)	(0.0038)	(0.1093)	(0.0404)	[0.2655]
Property &	A	0.000851	0.3081	1.0583	1.6192	0.0141	0.7034	0.1799	16.104
Resource Devel.		(0.000391)	(0.1139)	(0.3442)	(0.4919)	(0.0033)	(0.1687)	(0.0612)	[0.6427]
	B	0.000397	0.4389	0.9381	1.147	0.0988	0.6725	0.0580	17.552
		(0.000196)	(0.1117)	(0.2036)	(0.2250)	(0.0241)	(0.1973)	(0.0084)	[0.5208]
China	A	0.000864	0.3292	0.8417	1.6799	0.0511	0.8220	0.1539	13.928
Southern Glass		(0.000435)	(0.1409)	(0.2762)	(0.4990)	(0.0098)	(0.1905)	(0.0482)	[0.7886]
	B	0.000839	0.3825	1.2219	0.8046	0.0481	0.4337	0.2112	23.169
		(0.000431)	(0.1274)	(0.3770)	(0.2855)	(0.0087)	(0.1169)	(0.0812)	[0.2338]
Shenzhen	A	0.000435	0.3085	0.2109	0.5684	0.0633	0.2940	0.1806	42.9838
Petroch. Co.		(0.000197)	(0.1997)	(0.1561)	(0.2874)	(0.0083)	(0.1035)	(0.6169)	[0.0001]
	B	0.000296	0.1003	0.7107	0.4912	0.1052	0.3616	0.1672	49.4439
		(0.000181)	(0.1344)	(0.4228)	(0.2260)	(0.0091)	(0.1159)	(0.1036)	[0.0001]

(*Continued on the next page*)

(Continued)

Company		μ	c	m_0	m_1	α	β	γ	χ^2_{19}
Shenzhen	A	0.000495	0.3662	0.4819	1.2450	0.0316	0.7636	0.1380	15.066
Zhonghao Co.		(0.000217)	(0.1261)	(0.1475)	(0.3927)	(0.0089)	(0.1903)	(0.0424)	[0.7403]
	B	0.000971	0.4838	0.7963	0.5130	0.0605	0.5482	0.1382	20.755
		(0.000308)	(0.1078)	(0.2145)	(0.1609)	(0.0104)	(0.1745)	(0.0577)	[0.4316]
Konka	A	0.001029	0.3110	1.2136	1.3301	0.0733	0.5074	0.1337	20.940
Electronics		(0.000368)	(0.1017)	(0.5338)	(0.5965)	(0.0110)	(0.1862)	(0.0498)	[0.4082]
	B	0.000725	0.5443	1.0755	0.6081	0.0020	0.5837	0.1993	18.711
		(0.000260)	(0.2064)	(0.4438)	(0.2856)	(0.0007)	(0.2145)	(0.0836)	[0.5136]
Shenzhen	A	0.000846	0.3854	0.6512	1.2067	0.0903	0.8074	0.1065	14.225
China Bicycles		(0.000315)	(0.1275)	(0.2369)	(0.3675)	(0.0258)	(0.1363)	(0.0319)	[0.7714]
	B	0.001041	0.8147	0.5310	0.3875	0.0889	0.4063	0.2721	24.311
		(0.00455)	(0.1634)	(0.2511)	(0.1585)	(0.0462)	(0.1807)	(0.0794)	[0.2265]
Victor	A	0.000580	0.2406	0.8119	2.0240	0.0811	0.6094	0.0750	19.862
Onward Textile		(0.000275)	(0.0867)	(0.2074)	(0.6848)	(0.0135)	(0.1798)	(0.0196)	[0.4009]
	B	0.000611	0.3389	1.1477	1.0946	0.0750	0.3622	0.1019	25.401
		(0.000298)	(0.1047)	(0.3365)	(0.2829)	(0.0154)	(0.1806)	(0.0421)	[0.1885]

(Continued on next page)

(*Continued*)

Company		μ	c	m_0	m_1	α	β	γ	χ^2_{19}
Shenbao	A	0.000309	0.1386	0.5961	0.8119	0.1026	0.2750	0.1143	53.6720
Industry		(0.000179)	(0.1074)	(0.3251)	(0.4779)	(0.0283)	(0.1338)	(0.0614)	[0.0001]
	B	0.000157	0.0524	0.6989	5.6237	0.0281	0.3176	0.1608	69.3371
		(0.000163)	(0.0973)	(0.3428)	(1.4662)	(0.0074)	(0.1673)	(0.0645)	[0.0001]
Chiwan Wharf	A	0.000296	0.2419	1.134	1.996	0.0805	0.7768	0.1364	14.557
Holdings		(0.000125)	(0.0715)	(0.3228)	(0.4197)	(0.0120)	(0.1655)	(0.0351)	[0.7288]
	B	0.000470	0.4386	1.2669	0.4931	0.1022	0.380	0.1904	24.685
		(0.000213)	(0.1104)	(0.3174)	(0.1505)	(0.0229)	(0.1063)	(0.0738)	[0.2204]
China Merchants	A	-0.000381	0.1098	2.6224	3.8028	0.0437	0.8615	0.0633	13.622
Shekou Co.		(0.000227)	(0.0414)	(0.7231)	(0.8655)	(0.0096)	(0.1417)	(0.0244)	[0.8125]
	B	0.000352	0.2773	1.4054	1.1127	0.0699	0.4128	0.1350	24.018
		(0.000164)	(0.110)	(0.3125)	(0.2682)	(0.0146)	(0.1054)	(0.0387)	[0.2374]
Tellus	A	0.000199	0.3004	0.8152	1.4663	0.0240	0.7629	0.0835	14.986
Machinery		(0.000103)	(0.0772)	(0.2285)	(0.2979)	(0.0060)	(0.1614)	(0.0217)	[0.7015]
	B	0.000983	0.3608	1.0416	0.7239	0.1020	0.4038	0.1295	24.324
		(0.000315)	(0.1174)	(0.2616)	(0.2035)	(0.0225)	(0.1968)	(0.0342)	[0.2285]

uniformly higher for A-shares than for B-shares, ranging from 1.9187 to 4.7095 with an average of 3.0810 for A-shares, and from 1.1685 to 2.5890 with an average of 2.0615 for B-shares. These estimates imply that daily news arrivals have been on average 49.45% larger across all 21 A-shares than across B-shares. Moreover, the point estimates for $\mu, c, m_0, m_1, \alpha, \beta, \gamma$ also appear to be consistent with the MMDH. The parameter cm_0, representing the average fraction of the daily trading volume unrelated to news arrival (noise trading) ranges from 0.1699 to 0.3774 with an average of 0.2574 for A-shares and from 0.23978 to 0.5854 with an average of 0.3873 for B-shares. This implies, of course, that the proportional importance of informed trading volume is greater for A-shares. Moreover, the parameter cm_1, associated with the proportion of informed trading volume due to news arrival, ranges from 0.161 to 0.5914 with an average of 0.4768 for A-shares and from 0.1968 to 0.5034 with an average of 0.3331 for B-shares, offering further support to the role of information flows in determining A- and B-share relative volatility.

The estimates for persistence in return volatility ($\alpha + \beta$) are large and statistically significantly positive across companies. This is consistent with the findings in Su and Fleisher (1998a), who documented a GARCH effect in the Chinese stock markets using A- and B-share market indices. The persistence in return volatility ranges from 0.5807 to 0.9357 with an average of 0.7749 for A shares and from 0.4034 to 0.7713 with an average of 0.5503 for B shares.

In summary, we find that: (1) News flows more intensively into A-share markets than to B-share markets; (2) News is more highly correlated with trading for A-shares than for B-shares; and (3) News is more persistent for A-shares than for B-shares.

5.6 Cross-Sectional Analysis

It is irresistible to ask why, if rights and dividends are identical across A- and B-shares, information relevant to domestic and foreign investors is not also identically distributed. The answer, we believe, lies in the proximity of domestic investors to their information sources. Moreover, the larger number of and, presumably, higher geographical density, of domestic investors intuitively leads to larger amount of news entering the A-share markets and possibly a more rapid propagation of news, both of which have greater

Table 5.16 Distributional Characteristics for the Mixing Variable in Shanghai

Company		cm_0	cm_1	$E(K_t)$	$Var(K_t)$	Kurtosis
Vacuum	A	0.2164	0.557	3.0286	32.0876	455.2750
Electronics	B	0.3277	0.2851	1.9784	7.4158	16.3885
Shanghai	A	0.2415	0.519	2.9869	29.9097	604.8968
Erfangji	B	0.3644	0.3775	1.1685	1.1685	48.9391
Dazhong	A	0.2783	0.4703	3.5048	48.0010	915.0005
Taxi	B	0.3199	0.5134	2.5243	28.6541	136.4124
Yongsheng	A	0.2495	0.526	3.9190	29.2303	795.4628
Stationery	B	0.3646	0.4864	1.8443	6.4042	161.9072
China	A	0.2	0.161	2.9404	17.2789	181.9652
First Pencil	B	0.2086	0.1689	2.2397	7.2794	102.9925
China Textile	A	0.1955	0.4325	3.0384	27.2149	353.5309
Machinery	B	0.2398	0.1968	2.4247	6.8356	79.0401
Shanghai	A	0.1699	0.4713	3.0486	19.8525	127.9680
Rubber Belt	B	0.4169	0.3549	2.4179	5.1797	32.9673
Shanghai	A	0.3226	0.5642	2.3192	24.6291	358.129
Refrigerator	B	0.3008	0.475	1.7771	2.1483	48.6289
Shanghai	A	0.2583	0.5914	2.2416	38.2823	100.3267
Chlor Alkali	B	0.4134	0.3963	1.9065	7.5179	46.2556
Outer	A	0.3744	0.5824	3.3905	38.3418	396.878
Gaoqiao	B	0.3978	0.2765	1.1365	2.5558	71.2696
Shenzhen	A	0.3179	0.4515	2.4670	3.9808	61.4547
Vanke Co.	B	0.4336	0.2994	2.4372	2.1024	22.5456

impact on A-share trading volume. Higher trading volume that is proportional to news leads to higher A-share volatility, consistent with our results. We should note, though, that the MDH's definition of news is value-free, in the sense that "truth" versus "gossip" and public versus private information are indistinguishable in the MMDH model as specified in Section 5.2. "Information is what information does," and anything leading to non-noise ("non-liquidity") trading is defined to be "information." In an attempt to gain some insight into the nature of the differences in the intensity of information flows to the A- and B-share markets, we examine the cross-sectional variation across firms and across share types for the following variables: (1)

Table 5.17 Distributional Characteristics for the Mixing Variable in Shenzhen

Company		cm_0	cm_1	$E(K_t)$	$Var(K_t)$	Kurtosis
Property	A	0.3261	0.4989	2.2595	15.8543	216.9141
Development	B	0.4117	0.5034	2.2417	2.6924	35.6494
China	A	0.2771	0.553	4.5870	19.3756	744.2686
S. Glass	B	0.4674	0.3078	1.9940	7.2787	153.5039
Shanghai Tire	A	0.1699	0.4713	4.0638	4.8339	75.3546
& Rubber	B	0.354	0.3014	1.9229	3.8033	29.1589
Konka	A	0.3774	0.4137	4.7095	8.9309	156.1073
Electronics	B	0.5854	0.331	2.5890	2.0293	36.2989
Shenzhen	A	0.251	0.4651	2.9304	13.2296	268.1887
China Bicycles	B	0.4326	0.3157	1.8482	7.9808	146.5652
Victor	A	0.1953	0.487	1.9230	2.2616	46.8391
Textile	B	0.389	0.371	1.5996	1.5317	16.5769
Shenzhen	A	0.1765	0.4559	2.2607	2.5196	66.9716
Zhonghao Co.	B	0.3852	0.2482	2.0701	1.8481	27.4972
Chiwan Wharf	A	0.2743	0.4828	4.0927	29.5482	439.4244
Holdings	B	0.5557	0.2163	2.170	6.7597	101.2753
China	A	0.2879	0.4175	3.0713	15.7529	129.9115
Merchants	B	0.3897	0.3086	1.7569	2.8314	29.0362
Tellus	A	0.2449	0.4405	1.9187	4.0782	80.7247
Machinery	B	0.3758	0.2612	1.8257	3.1546	45.8312

$\delta E(K_t)$, which is the return volatility-related expected intensity of information flow; and (2) $cm_1 E(K_t)$, which is the amount of trading volume that fluctuates with the intensity of information arrival, or the amount of informed trading volume. In particular, we test the following hypotheses:

(i) The cross-section variation in the volatility-related expected intensity of information flow is positively related to the standard deviation of profit-per-share, firm size, and the average number of investors over the sample period.
This hypothesis is tested jointly with the supporting hypothesis that news observable by both A- and B-share investors (or publicly available information) is positively correlated with the standard deviation of profit-per-share, firm size and the average number of

investors. The first variable, a firm's profit variation over time, is of obvious interest to investors. It is entirely plausible that the greater variation in current and expected future profits, the more intensely will investors search for and analyze news items about a firm. Given fixed costs of processing and publicizing information about a firm, larger firms are likely to find these expenditures less burdensome than small firms, *cet. par.* Thus, large firms are likely to provide more news than small firms. The larger the number of investors in a stock, the greater is the probability that a given news item will be observed and passed on, or propagated, through the investor pool. Therefore, the intensity with which news is perceived by investors should be positively related to the number of investors in a particular stock.

(ii) The relationship between the volatility-related expected intensity of information flows and the standard deviation of profit-per-share, firm size, and the average number of investors is more intense (greater) for A-shares than for B-shares.
Again, this is a joint test. The supporting hypothesis is that the gap between news observed by informed A-share investors but unobserved by B-share investors is positively correlated with information observable to all investors as proxied by the above variables. The rationale for this hypothesis is that if a firm's time-series of profit-per-share is flat and/or there is little other types of published data about the firm, nobody will find it worthwhile thinking, talking and gossiping about it. But if there is considerably published information and/or actual and potential changes in a firm's future earnings, then it may be worthwhile for investors to acquire information and gossip about the firm. Such communication, it seems to us, is more likely among domestic Chinese than among disparate foreign investors. Furthermore, the larger the size of a firm, the more likely are domestic investors to gossip about it, and the larger is the expected volatility-related intensity of information flow.

To investigate the cross-section pattern of estimated news arrival in greater depth, following the market microstructure theory described in Andersen (1996), we assume that the probability of a single informed investor trading on the arrival of a given amount of information is constant across firms. As a result, cross-section variation in m_1, the expected number of daily trades given a certain amount of benchmark information arrival, should be explainable in terms of the number of a firm's stockholders, which is assumed to be positively related to the number of informed traders. In addition, cross-section variation in $cm_1E(K_t)$, the amount of trading volume that fluctuates with news, should be explainable in terms of variables affecting the proportion of trading volume that fluctuates with news arrival and by proxies for information arrivals as perceived by investors. Therefore, we hypothesize:

(iii) The cross-section variation in the amount of trading volume fluctuating with the intensity of news arrival is positively related to the standard deviation of profit-per-share, firm size, and the average number of investors.[4]

(iv) The relationship between amount of trading volume fluctuating with the intensity of news arrival and the standard deviation of profit-per-share, firm size, and the average number of investors is more intense (greater) for A shares than for B shares.

Tests of the above four hypotheses should also be viewed as joint tests with the following two hypotheses:

(v) Noise trading, or liquidity trading, is uncorrelated with any proxy for information flow.

(vi) The proportion of noise traders is uncorrelated with the number of investors.

To test hypotheses (i) and (ii) empirically, we regress the log of volatility-related expected intensity of information flow ($\ln[\delta E(K_t)]$) on the following variables:

$\ln STDPROF_i^j$ = the logarithm of the standard deviation of calendar year's profit-per-share during 1993-97 ($i = 1, 2, \cdots, 24$, $j \in \{\text{A-share, B-share}\}$).

SD_i^j = a share-type dummy that takes the value of 1 for A shares and 0 for B shares.

[4] Andersen (1996) assumes that the benchmark information flow is time-invariant for an individual firm, but not necessarily invariant across firms.

$\ln INVESTOR_i^j$ = the logarithm of the average daily number of investors during the sample period.

$\ln FIRMSIZE_i^j$ = the logarithm of the average daily stock-market capitalization during the sample period.

ED_i^j = a stock-exchange dummy, $ED_i^j = 0$ if firm i is listed in Shanghai, and $ED_i^j = 1$ if it is listed in Shenzhen.

$$\begin{aligned}\ln[\delta E(K_t)]_i^j &= \phi_0 + \phi_1 \ln STDPROF_i^j + \phi_2 SD_i^j \\ &+\phi_3 (SD \cdot \ln STDPROF)_i^j + \phi_4 \ln INVESTOR_i^j \\ &+\phi_5 \ln FIRMSIZE_i^j + \phi_6 (SD \cdot \ln FIRMSIZE)_i^j \\ &+\phi_7 ED_i^j + \epsilon_i^j \qquad (5.26)\end{aligned}$$

The regressions are estimated using Generalized Least Squares. Table 5.18 presents parameter estimates. As shown in the table, the estimated elasticity of the volatility-related expected intensity of news arrival variable with respect to the standard deviation of profit-per-share is about 0.11, statistically significant at the 5% level. The estimated elasticity of the volatility-related expected intensity of news arrival variable with respect to the number of investors is about 0.06, and is also statistically significant at the 5% level. The variable representing firm size (and assumed negatively related to information asymmetry) is positively related to the volatility-related expected intensity of information flow. The estimated coefficient for this variable is statistically significant at the 10% level without the presence of stock-exchange dummy, but is marginally significant at best when the stock-exchange dummy is included. The stock-exchange dummy is positively related to $\delta E(K_t)$, although it is only marginally significant in the specification in which both the number of investors and firm size are included. Perhaps companies listed in Shenzhen generate a higher degree of intensity of information flow (both publicly available information and private information, or gossip) and volatility, in part because of their proximity to foreign investors. The econometric results reported in table 5.18 imply that hypothesis (i) is not rejected by the data. Cross-section variation in volatility-related expected intensity of information arrival among firms can be explained by cross-section differences in information-related

Table 5.18 Cross-section Analysis on Volatility-Related Information Flow

	$\ln[\delta E(K_t)]$ as dependent variable[a]			
Constant	0.32	$0.42^{\dagger}$	-0.26	0.02
	(1.41)	(1.97)	(-0.55)	(0.04)
$\ln STDPROF$	0.12^{*}	0.12^{*}	$0.09^{\dagger}$	0.11^{*}
	(2.42)	(2.63)	(1.85)	(2.05)
SD	0.05	0.15	0.02	0.02
	(0.26)	(0.84)	(0.03)	(0.03)
$SD \cdot \ln STDPROF$	0.06	0.07	0.06	0.06
	(0.87)	(1.07)	(0.90)	(0.91)
$\ln INVESTOR$	0.09^{*}	0.07^{*}	0.06^{*}	0.06^{*}
	(3.59)	(2.81)	(2.15)	(2.06)
$\ln FIRMSIZE$			$0.03^{\dagger}$	0.02
			(1.93)	(1.11)
$SD \cdot \ln FIRMSIZE$			0.01	0.01
			(0.30)	(0.33)
ED		0.08^{*}		0.05
		(2.57)		(1.23)
$\bar{R}^2$	0.78	0.81	0.81	0.81

[a]We pool both A and B shares for 24 firms in our sample. The regressions are estimated using Generalized Least Squares. Figures in parentheses are t-statistics. * and † denote 5% and 10% levels of significance, respectively.

variables.

The estimated coefficient for $\ln INVESTOR$ suggests that the difference in the number of A- and B-share investors helps account for the difference in the volatility-related expected intensity of news between A- and B-shares. However, the coefficients of the A-share dummy variable (SD) and its interaction terms with $\ln STDPROF$ and $\ln FIRMSIZE$ are quite insignificant. This implies that there are no excluded variables, correlated with stock type, that help explain variation in the dependent variable, $\delta E(K_t)$, and that the effects of $\ln STDPROF$ and $\ln FIRMSIZE$ are no more intense in A-share markets than in B-share markets. Therefore, hypothesis (ii) must be rejected.

To test hypotheses (iii) and (iv), we specify the following regression, relating the amount of trading volume that fluctuates with the expected intensity of news arrival to the same right-hand variables specified for equation (5.26):

$$\begin{aligned}\ln[cm_1 E(K_t)]_i^j &= \rho_0 + \rho_1 \ln STDPROF_i^j + \rho_2 SD_i^j \\ &+\rho_3 (SD \cdot \ln STDPROF)_i^j + \rho_4 \ln INVESTOR_i^j \\ &+\rho_5 \ln FIRMSIZE_i^j + \rho_6 (SD \cdot \ln FIRMSIZE)_i^j \\ &+\rho_7 ED_i^j + \epsilon_i^j \qquad (5.27)\end{aligned}$$

Table 5.19 presents the econometric results. In comparing the coefficient estimates for equation (5.27) with those for equation (5.26), we note that the $\bar{R}^2$, or adjusted R^2, is higher and that the estimated coefficients for $\ln STDPROF$ and $\ln INVESTOR$ are quite robust, both in magnitude and statistical significance. The coefficient for the variable $\ln FIRMSIZE$ remains positive, and is statistically more significant in equation (5.27) than that in equation (5.26). Therefore, hypothesis (iii) cannot be rejected.

In Table 5.19, the coefficient of the A-share dummy variable is significant in the estimation of equation (5.27) when firm size and stock-exchange are both included, suggesting that proxies for public information do not fully explain the differences in $cm_1 E(K_t)$ between A- and B-shares. The coefficients of the interaction terms ($SD \cdot \ln STDPROF$ and $SD \cdot \ln FIRMSIZE$) are insignificant, implying that firm size and profit variation do not differentially affect informed trading volume of A-shares compared to B-shares. Therefore, hypothesis (iv) must be rejected.

We emphasize however, that the estimated coefficient for the A-share dummy in equation (5.27) indicates that something is yet to be learned about the nature of the events that leads A-share investors to engage in trading on news not perceived by owners of B-shares. We conjecture that our ignorance partially lies in the structure and type of information flows perceived by A- and B-share investors. This interesting question awaits further investigation.

In summary, hypotheses (i) and (iii) are not rejected by the data, while hypotheses (ii) and (iv) are rejected. The evidence suggests that differences in volatility-related expected intensity of information flow and differences in how information impacts trading volume across firms can be explained

Table 5.19 Cross-section Analysis on the Proportional of Trading Volume That Fluctuates with News

	$\ln[cm_1 E(K_t)]$ as dependent variable[a]			
Constant	-1.35*	-1.03*	-3.84*	-3.14*
	(-2.81)	(-2.44)	(-4.79)	(-3.68)
$\ln STDPROF$	0.09†	0.09†	0.09†	0.08†
	(1.97)	(1.91)	(1.86)	(1.79)
SD	0.29	0.56†	1.84†	1.83†
	(0.80)	(1.72)	(1.78)	(1.80)
$SD \cdot \ln STDPROF$	0.05	0.08	0.15	0.15
	(0.42)	(0.69)	(1.27)	(1.31)
$\ln INVESTOR$	0.13*	0.08†	0.08†	0.07†
	(2.76)	(1.82)	(1.85)	(1.80)
$\ln FIRMSIZE$			0.13*	0.10*
			(4.27)	(3.05) [3pt]
$SD \cdot \ln FIRMSIZE$			-0.05	-0.05
			(-1.15)	(-1.12) [3pt]
ED		0.20*		0.10†
		(3.69)		(1.65) [3pt]
$\bar{R}^2$	0.80	0.84	0.87	0.87

[a]We pool both A and B shares for 24 firms in our sample. The regressions are estimated using Generalized Least Squares. Figures in parentheses are t-statistics. * and † denote 5% and 10% levels of significance, respectively.

by differences in information-related variables and the intensity with news is propagated among investors in particular stocks. The news-related variables are the standard deviation of profit-per-share, firm size and the number of investors. Since the number of A-share investors is always greater than their B-share counterparts, equations (5.26) and (5.27) do help explain the gap between A-share and B-share volatility. However, the forces proxied by firm size and standard deviation of firm profits do not differentially impact the trading of A- and B-shares.

5.7 Time-Series Analysis

In an attempt to explore further the implications of our hypothesized information-volume-volatility relationship as it pertains to A- and B-share price behavior, we examine whether there exists any time-series relationship between the differences in A- and B-share expected intensity of information flows and the average B-share discounts. The idea is that international investors have less information about Chinese shares than the domestic investors do. The information asymmetry increases international investors' required risk premium for B-shares and reduces their incentives to trade. As a consequence, information-induced B-share trading volume is less than that of A-share, and so is the B-share volatility. To investigate this question, we estimate the relationship between $\delta^A E(K_t^A) - \delta^B E(K_t^B), t = 1, \cdots, T$, and $\frac{1}{T}\sum_{t=1}^{T}\left(\frac{P_t^B - P_t^A}{P_t^A}\right)$, where $\delta^A E(K_t^A) - \delta^B E(K_t^B)$ is the difference in the estimated volatility-related expected intensity of information arrivals between value-weighted A- and B-share portfolios during time period T, and $\frac{1}{T}\sum_{t=1}^{T}\left(\frac{P_t^B - P_t^A}{P_t^A}\right)$ is the average B-share discount during time period T. (P_t^B is the price of the B-share portfolio at time t while P_t^A is the price of the A-share portfolio at time t.) After considering the number of observations T that is required to estimated the MMDH model and the number of moment conditions specified, we choose 10 moment conditions (equations (5.10)–(5.17), and (5.18) and (5.19) without lags) and set $T = 60$. We estimate the MMDH model for the return and trading volume for A- and B-share portfolios to obtain 17 pairs of estimated $\delta^A E(K_t^A)$ and $\delta^B E(K_t^B)$. Then we compute the average B-share discounts in the corresponding 17 time periods. Figure 5.1 plots the average B-share discount against the differences in the volatility-related information flow for A- and B-share portfolios ($\delta^A E(K_t^A) - \delta^B E(K_t^B)$). As shown in the figure, the two time series seem to be positively correlated. In fact, the correlation coefficient between the time-series of the differences in volatility-related expected intensity of information flows and the time-series of the average B-share discounts is 0.59, which means an R^2 of approximately 0.36%. The result suggests that one of the reasons B-shares are priced lower than their corresponding A-shares, even though both share types are entitled to the same rights and dividends, is that the intensity of information arriving at B-share markets is smaller than for A-share markets. The result lends support to the hypothesis that information asymmetry is important in explaining

B-share discounts, which is consistent with the findings of Chakravarty, et. al (1998).

In order to test for the persistence of volatility-related expected intensity of information flow differences between A- and B-share portfolios over time, we estimate the MMDH model (equations (5.5)–(5.6)) using the same 26 moment conditions described in Section 2 (equations (5.10)–(5.20)) for the A- and B-share portfolios over four 255-trading day periods (one calendar year). The econometric results are reported in Table 5.20. They show that the differences in the return volatility persists over the entire sample period, and the MMDH model describes the portfolio return and aggregate trading volume data quite well.

5.8 Summary

The main focus of this paper is to identify the sources of the substantial volatility differences across the Chinese stock markets segmented between domestic (A-share) and foreign (B-share) investors. In the spirit of Anderson's MMDH, we hypothesize that daily stock return and trading volume are contemporaneously dependent on an underlying mixing variable representing daily flow of information, or news. We assume that news follows a lognormal stochastic autoregressive process and is non-uniform through time. Using GMM, we estimate a dynamic system of return and volume equations and find that the MMDH cannot be rejected for 21 out of 24 companies in our sample.

After comparing the parameter estimates that characterize the joint distribution of the news and return variables, we conclude that the differences in return volatility between A and B shares are directly related to differences in the flow of news as reflected in trading volume and the differences in the way news is incorporated into trading decisions. News arrives more intensively for holders of an individual company's A shares than for holders of its B shares, so the volatility of returns is higher for A shares, and a larger fraction of news is incorporated into trading volume for A shares. One may be tempted to ask why, if rights and dividends are identical across A- and B-shares, information relevant to domestic and foreign investors is not also identically distributed. The answer, we believe, lies in the proximity of domestic investors to their information sources. Moreover, the larger number of and, presumably, higher geographical density, of domestic investors intu-

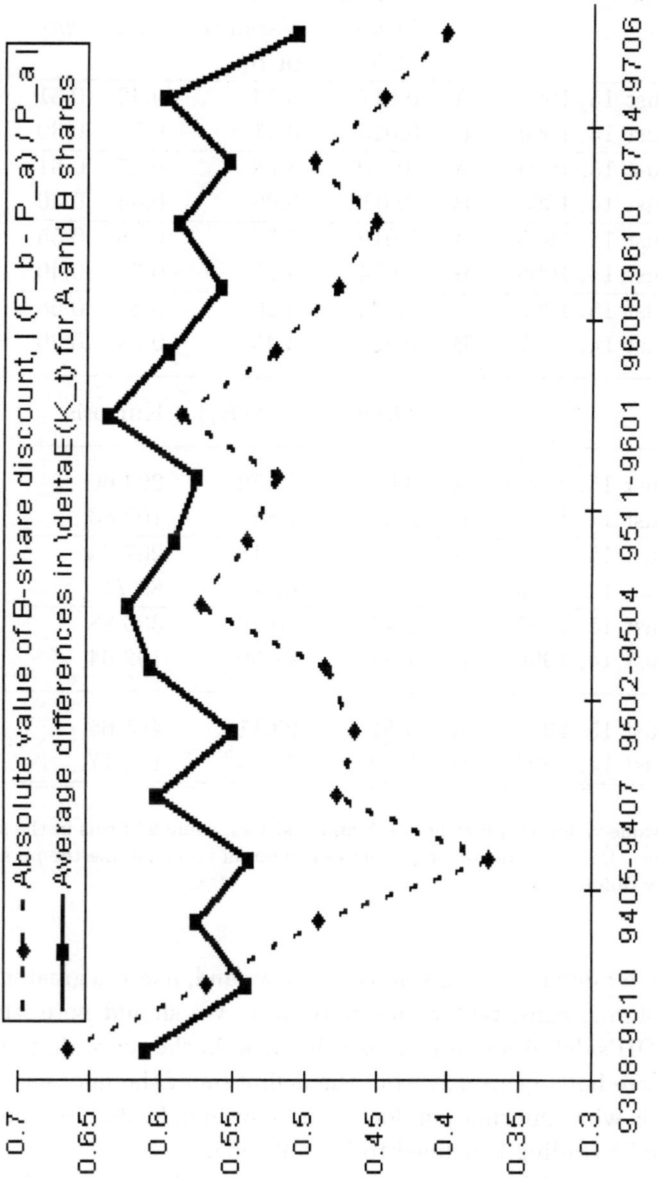

Fig. 5.1 B-Share Discounts and the Differences in Estimated Information Flow Between A- and B-Shares

Table 5.20 Time-series Analysis for the Value-weighted Portfolio

Company[a]		Sample Mean of R_t	Sample Variance of R_t	cm_0	cm_1
August 15, 1993–	A	0.017	3.74	0.42	0.51
August 14, 1994	B	0.023	3.11	0.59	0.30
August 15, 1994–	A	-0.026	3.68	0.27	0.61
August 14, 1995	B	-0.022	3.06	0.44	0.40
August 15, 1995–	A	0.019	3.52	0.38	0.55
August 14, 1996	B	0.024	3.25	0.52	0.40
August 15, 1996–	A	0.022	4.20	0.37	0.58
August 14, 1997	B	0.026	3.46	0.58	0.29
		$\delta E(K_t)$	$Var(K_t)$	Kurtosis	
August 15, 1993–	A	3.09	18.72	294.60	
August 14, 1994	B	2.46	7.85	102.83	
August 15, 1994–	A	2.69	14.18	207.24	
August 14, 1995	B	1.95	6.27	89.71	
August 15, 1995–	A	2.47	20.26	336.88	
August 14, 1996	B	2.05	11.90	192.64	
August 15, 1996–	A	3.51	23.11	445.65	
August 14, 1997	B	2.62	12.40	184.77	

[a]We construct value-weighted portfolio for A and B shares, using 24 firms in the sample. We estimate the MMDH model during a one-year interval and examine the persistence in the volatility differences.

itively leads to a more rapid transmission of news and, likely, a greater affect on trading volume, consistent with our results. We should note, though, that the MMDH's definition of news is value-free, in the sense that "truth" and "gossip" are homogeneous within the definition of the unobserved K_t. "Information is what information does," and anything leading to non-noise ("non-liquidity") trading is defined to be "information."

Our empirical model so far has formally treated A-share and B-shares as independent, but as though they can be compared via estimates of the expected values K_t^A and K_t^B, assuming that the benchmark flow of information the A-share markets is not less than that to B-share markets. In subsequent work, we hope to develop a joint model of the A-share and B-share markets, allowing for the possibility of both common and idiosyncratic information flows. Moreover, our estimation results so far have been obtained under the assumption that the innovation in news process, u_t, is lognormally distributed. It would be worthwhile to consider alternative specifications such as Gamma, Student t and Stable distributions in further studies.

Chapter 6

The Underpricing of Initial Public Offerings

6.1 Introduction

Initial public offering (IPO) underpricing, or high IPO initial return, is a phenomenon common to most stock markets—both in developed and emerging economies (Loughran, Ritter, and Rydquist, 1994). A common perception is that underpricing of IPOs is a contradiction to market efficiency and may hurt emerging firms trying to raise capital for expansion. Therefore it has spawned an extensive literature attempting to explain this apparent financial anomaly. A number of theories of IPO underpricing have been put forth and tested against the data of various stock markets.

This chapter attempts to explain the cross-sectional differences in underpricing of Chinese IPOs using data compiled for 308 firm-commitment new issues from 1987 to 1995. The Chinese case is of particular interest because of the extreme magnitudes observed after market trading of stocks began in late 1990. Defining IPO initial return as $IPORETN = (P_1 - P_0)/P_0$, the mean $IPORETN$ in our sample is 948.6%! In other words, the first-day market closing price was on average almost eleven times as high as the initial price offered to domestic Chinese investors.

A frequent and understandable reaction to the striking statistics for initial returns of Chinese IPOs is that the extraordinarily low IPO prices relative to first-day market prices must represent either irrational behavior or, more likely, give-aways (presumably bribes) to officials who allocate the rights to go public. For instance, Basu and Li (1998) argue that offering the shares of newly privatized enterprises to the bureaucrats that most closely controlled these State-Owned Enterprises was a necessary condition for efficient privatization, because: (1) these bureaucrats were the possessors of inside information on which enterprises would most likely be successful in a world of hard budget constraints; and (2) they (the bureaucrats) would not reveal this information and risk their control over the enterprises under their supervision without compensation (bribes), which took the form of offering them shares at par value. We believe, however, that the bribery, while it may well occur, does not explain underpricing for three reasons. First, underpricing an entire public offering in order to allocate some of the underpriced shares to officials in return for favors is very costly relative to other means of paying illicit bribes. Second, underpricing of shares can be explained as rational behavior under asymmetric information. Third, the bureaucrat-insiders had strong incentives to reveal information about which firms were good prospects; "bribery" and asymmetric information may not be mutually exclusive alternative hypotheses. We believe that the conditions for equilibrium underpricing exist in China, and that high underpricing is caused by basic problems derived from the microeconomic uncertainty and information asymmetry.

Allen and Faulhaber (1989), Grinblatt and Hwang (1989), and Welch (1989) have proposed a class of signaling models in which IPO underpricing is an equilibrium outcome where issuers possess superior information than investors do. As long as the revelation probability for the issuers' quality is neither too large nor too small, there exists a separating equilibrium where high-value issuers signal their quality by retaining a portion of shares and underpricing initial offerings and low-value issuers sell all of their shares and do not underprice. In a pooling equilibrium, no signaling occurs, although high-quality firms will be observed, after the fact, to underprice. Underpricing, averaged over all firms in the pool, will be zero.

Allen and Faulhaber (1989) showed that underpricing in a separating equilibrium implies a shortage of IPO shares, which must be allocated by the issuer or underwriter in some fashion. Granting favored public officials the right to purchase IPO shares may be one of the allocation methods chosen, just as an underwriter may favor long-term customers with purchase rights. In this sense, bribery is a byproduct of underpricing, not a cause. We believe that our econometric results support this view.

The rest of the chapter proceeds as follows. In Section 6.2, we present institutional details of the new-issue offering process in China and describe variables used in our empirical work. In Section 6.3 we test various hypotheses derived from the signaling models against data of Chinese IPOs and subsequent market behavior. In Section 6.4, we consider the hypothesis that IPO underpricing in China is primarily explainable as a means of bribing public officials, and we examine an assertion of the World Bank that allocating IPO shares by lottery has been a cause of extreme underpricing. In Section 6.5, we extend the above approach to examine the difference in initial returns between A shares (available only to Chinese investors) and B shares (available only to foreign investors). We summarize the findings and propose future research in this area in Section 6.6.

6.2 The New-issue and Offering Process

There are several interesting characteristics of the new-issue and offering process in China:

First, the aggregate amount of new shares issued each year is determined by a quota set by the security regulatory authorities, namely, the State Planning Commission, the People's Bank of China (the central bank), and the China Securities Regulatory Committee (CSRC). The quota is then distributed to individual provinces. The stated criteria used for allocation of new issues among provinces reflect the central security regulatory authorities' perceived regional development needs and provincial differences in production structure and industrial base. Within each regional quota, the local security regulatory authorities invite enterprises to request a listing and make a selection based upon enterprise performance and sectoral development objectives. Infrastructure enterprises, especially those specializing in electricity and water supply, are given priority.

Second, the Chinese government has introduced a variety of share categories to allow ownership of state-owned enterprises to be dispersed among the government itself, other state-owned enterprises, firms' own employees, domestic public and foreign investors. There are currently five types of shares: (1) government shares, which are retained in the state institutions and government departments and are non-tradable; (2) legal entity shares, or C shares, which can only be held by other state-owned enterprises. C shares can not be listed in the two official exchanges (Shanghai and Shenzhen Security Exchange), but a very small number are traded on the Security Trading and Automatic Quote System (STAQS) and National Electronic Trading System (NETS); (3) employee shares, which are non-tradable until the firm allows their convertibility; (4) ordinary domestic individual shares, or A shares, which can only be purchased and traded by private Chinese citizens in the two official exchanges in China; (4) foreign individual shares, which can only be purchased and traded by the foreign investors in security exchanges in China (B shares), in Hong Kong (H shares) or in NYSE (N shares).[1]

Sample statistics of the proportion of each kind of share in new-share offerings are shown in Table 6.1. Note that most stock sales are partial sales. The government maintains control in varying degree over many firms. The size of government ownership at the time of IPO ranged from none to 74% with an average of 10%. Only 89 out of 308 issuers going public between December 1986 and January 1996 reported no retained government shares, and even these enterprises reported IPO sizes that did not exceed 50% of firm's intrinsic value, indicating that a large portion of shares were controlled by other state-owned enterprises. The concept of an enterprise's intrinsic value (formally defined to be the discounted value of all future net cash flows) is essential to analysis of the causes of IPO underpricing and to other important aspects of corporate finance. Yet, in world of imperfect, not to mention asymmetric, information, intrinsic value is unobservable to outsiders and, hence to researchers. Our operational definition of intrinsic value is a measure of total market capitalization, measured by the value of the sum of all types of shares from the IPO through all and all subsequent equity offerings.

Third, most stock sales are partial sales. The government still maintains control in varying degree over many firms. The size of government ownership ranges from 10% to 88%. Only 89 out of 308 issuers going public between December 1986 and January 1996 do not report government ownership of shares. However, none of these 89 issuers has reported IPO size that is above 50% of its total market capitalization, which indicates

[1] An issuer of B shares must, besides satisfying requirements stated in the securities regulations, meet the following conditions: (1) It must have obtained approval from the relevant authorities for its use of foreign investment or for its conversion into a foreign-funded enterprise. (2) It must have a stable source of adequate foreign exchange income and the total amount of its annual foreign exchange income must be sufficient to pay the annual dividend. (3) The proportion of B shares to the total number of shares must not exceed the ceiling determined by the relevant authority. The aggregate amount of shares is fixed in each year and the total number of firms allowed to issue foreign shares is also limited. An issuer of H or N shares is not subject to the quota restriction, but is subject to case-by-case approval.

Table 6.1 Sample Statistics for Share Offerings

Variable	Mean	Median	Min.	Max.	Number of Observations
Full sample of 308 firm-commitment IPOs between December 1986 and January 1996 (in million U.S. dollar)					
A Share IPOs	16.83	11.99	0.29	249.40	308
Government shares	15.91	3.66	0	486.09	219
Other State Enterprise	7.10	2.71	0	289.13	264
Employee Shares	0.80	0.36	0	22.89	294
Seasoned Equity	114.42	33.60	0	8513.8	268
B Share Offerings	4.06	2.54	0.82	23.07	57
(as a fraction of firm's intrinsic value, %)					
A Share IPOs	15.02	12:6	0.07	81.25	308
Government shares	10.05	4.41	0	74.27	219
Other State Enterprise	5.81	2.67	0	33.85	264
Employee Shares	0.87	0.39	0	11.09	294
Seasoned Equity	49.93	41.58	0	99.87	268

that a larger portion of its shares are still controlled by other state-owned enterprises.

Fourth, it is also noteworthy in terms of the signaling hypotheses tested in this paper that initial offering size relative to firm's intrinsic value is on average 15%, which is small relative to subsequent seasoned equity offerings (50% on average). Seasoned equity offerings (SEOs) are very frequently observed. About 91% of the Chinese firms that went public before June 30, 1994 have issued subsequent equities. By comparison, in the United States, between 1980 and 1986, only about 20% of firms going public subsequently issued seasoned offerings. (See Jegadeesh, Weinstein and Welch, henceforth JWW, 1993.)

Fifth, average time elapsed between the announcement of an IPO and the first day of market trading is considerable greater in China than in other countries—260 calendar days for A shares and 72 calendar days for B shares. There are a number of steps a firm must take after it is selected for initial public offering and before the market trading begins. Some typical steps include: (1) publication of a prospectus in newspapers and selection of underwriters; (2) purchase of application forms by prospective investors; (3) a lottery to determine which individual and institutional investors will be allowed to purchase new issues at the IPO price; (4) delivery of shares to the lottery winners after payments are made.

Sixth, the offering mechanism adopted by most Chinese firms is quite different from those observed in mature stock markets and has undergone several substantial changes over time. The offer price is chosen months before the market trading starts, and in the great majority of offerings there is no feedback mechanism through market demand that allows adjustment in the offer price. The lottery mechanism, which remains the primary method of share allocation, has undergone several substantial changes. Before 1992, the security regulatory authorities designed a lottery system based on a pre-announced fixed number of application forms. Each retail investor was allowed to purchase a limited number of lottery forms from the central bank and its subsidiaries. Lottery winners were entitled to a certain number of shares per winning form. With the number of lottery forms pre-determined, the odds of winning the lottery was known to investors. In 1993, the security regulatory authorities introduced two new lottery mechanisms: One mechanism was based on an unlimited number of application forms. The central bank sold as many lottery forms as investors were willing to buy. Therefore, the odds of winning the lottery were unknown to investors at the time of lottery. The other lottery mechanism was based on savings deposit certificates. Investors were required to deposit a certain quantity of funds into a special saving account when submitting an application for shares, which could not be withdrawn until the lottery was completed. These special saving accounts were given relatively low interest.

Under the lottery mechanisms, the IPO prices were fixed for all investors. In the early stage of development of Chinese stock markets, some initial issues were even offered at the shares' face values, which were *Renminbi* 1 *yuan*. Companies that went public before January 1991, such as Shanghai Vacuum Electronics, Jinbei Automotive, Phoenix Chemical, China Textile Machinery, Shenzhen Vanke Co., Gintian Industry, Shenzhen Zhenye Co., and Shenyang Materials Development, all offered shares at *Renminbi* 1 *yuan*. Initial IPO returns were over 1000% for these shares.

In 1994, two kinds of auction mechanisms were introduced. Under the first auction mechanism, an issuer set an initial price and investors were required to bid for the price and quantity. The final offer price was set at the level where the accumulative quantities demanded by investors equaled the total number of new shares available. Under the second auction mechanism, the IPO price was fixed and investors were invited to bid for the quantity of shares. In case of oversubscription, all investors were guaranteed a certain amount of shares and the remaining shares were distributed on a pro-rata basis. Lottery mechanisms as described above remained as options, however, so firms could choose either a lottery method of distributing IPO shares or an auction mechanism. The proceeds from the lottery become the property of the state banks that sell shares for the firms.

Seventh, Chinese A-share IPOs are sold to relatively unsophisticated retail investors while B shares are usually sold to international institutional investors such as foreign mutual funds.

6.3 The Role of Financial Variables in the Pricing of IPOs

6.3.1 *The Chinese Data*

We use data of all the firm-commitment IPOs of A-share common stocks occurring between 1987 and 1995. In order to study the effects of subsequent equity offerings on IPO underpricing, we also extract a sub-sample of firms that went public between 1987 and June 1994. The June 1994 cutoff allows 548 days for a firm to issue seasoned equities.

Variables used in our empirical work include:

$IPOSZ$ = the number of shares issued at the time of an IPO, including A- and B-shares.

$IPOVALUE$ = $IPOSZ \times$ offer price, or the proceeds from an IPO (in U.S. dollars).

$LNIPOSZ$ = logarithm of $IPOVALUE$.

$SEOSZ_q$ = the number of shares issued at the time of an SEO, $q = 1, 2, 3. \sum_q SEOSZ_q = SEOSZ$

$SEOVALUE$ = $\sum_q SEOSZ_q \times \text{offer price}_q$, or the proceeds from all SEOs.

$TOTALSHA$ = $IPOSZ + SEOSZ +$ government shares + employee shares +state enterprises shares, or the total number of shares outstanding.

$LNTOSIZE$ = logarithm of the sum of IPO and SEO values.

$LNGOVNT$ = logarithm of the value of government shares.

$LNEMPLOY$ = logarithm of the value of employee shares.

$INTRINSC$ = $IPOVALUE + SEOVALUE +$ stated, or face, value of government shares, employee shares and other state enterprises shares.

$PROFIT$ = past calendar year's profit at the time of IPO. (in U.S. dollars).

$INFORMED$ = the sum of government shares, manager and employee shares, and legal entity shares divided by $TOTALSHA$, or the percentage of shares held by insiders and institutional investors.

AGE = age of the firm at the date of its IPO.

$TIMEIPO$ = number of days elapsed between announcement of an IPO and first-day of market trading.

$AFTRETN1$ = after-market return based on closing prices from the closing of the first day of trading to the end of the second week of trading.

$AFTRETN2$ = after-market return between the closing prices from the beginning of the third week of trading to the end of the fourth week.

$EARNINGS$ = earnings forecast dummy, $EARNINGS = 1$ if the issuer provides earnings forecast in the prospectus, $EARNINGS = 0$ otherwise.

$LEVERAGE$ = the book value of pre-IPO debt (short term and long term) divided by the book value of all assets.

$MKTRUNUP$	$=$	cumulative daily returns on the Shanghai or Shenzhen security exchange 30 trading days before an IPO, an indicator for the market conditions surrounding a new issue.
$PREMSTD$	$=$	standard deviation of daily returns on the Shanghai or Shenzhen security exchange 30 trading days before an IPO, an indicator for the market uncertainty surrounding a new issue.
STD	$=$	standard deviation of daily after-market returns estimated over a 100-trading day period after inception of market trading.
EXD	$=$	stock exchange dummy, $EXD = 1$ for a company that is listed on the Shanghai Securities Exchange, $EXD = 0$ for a company that is listed on the Shenzhen Securities Exchange.
$SIC(k)$	$=$	six industry dummies: durable goods ($SIC1$), non-durable goods ($SIC2$), transportation and public utilities ($SIC3$), finance, insurance and real estate ($SIC4$), services including restaurants, department stores and hotels ($SIC5$) and domestic and foreign trade ($SIC6$).
$YEAR(t)$	$=$	IPO year dummies, $t = 1$ if a firm went public before January 1, 1991; $t = 2 \cdots 5$ for going public in the years 1992 through 1995.

Descriptive statistics for some of the above variables are presented in Tables 6.2 and 6.3. The correlation matrix for some of the variables is presented in Table .

Table 6.2 Descriptive Statistics for Variables to Explain IPO Initial Returns

Variable	Mean	Median	Std. dev.	Min.	Max.
A-share full sample with 308 firm-commitment IPOs between December 1986 and January 1996					
$IPORETN$	948.59%	231.25%	2967.7%	-18.58%	38300%
$AFTRETN1$	-0.0264	-0.054	0.2428	-0.9268	1.7039
$AFTRETN2$	-0.0275	-0.045	0.1841	-0.9173	0.9444
$\ln P_0$	1.1966	1.335	0.6352	0	2.5938
$LNIPOSZ$	9.0781	9.2053	0.9955	5.4806	12.241
$LNTOSIZE$	10.681	10.628	1.0975	7.1701	15.772
$LNAGE$	2.4849	2.7701	0.8929	0.6931	4.4773
$TIMEIPO$	260.12	135	341.24	3	1868
$LNGOVNT$	6.0294	8.0194	4.0055	0	12.908
$LNEMPLOY$	5.6087	5.7038	1.5882	0	9.8522
$IPOVALUE$	16.83	11.99	22.56	0.29	249.40
$PROFIT$	466.58	221.99	98.13	2.77	3788.3
STD	5.89%	4.74%	5.11%	0.65%	51.27%
$INTRINSC$	161.23	86.01	237.43	2.61	1856.4
$\frac{IPOSZ}{INTRINSC}$	15.02%	12.6%	11.22%	0.07%	81.25%

6.3.2 *A Benchmark Regression*

As an empirical exercise to analyze the cross-sectional differences in IPO underpricing among Chinese firms, we estimate the following baseline cross-sectional regression using ordinary least squares (OLS) for the full sample and sub-sample of firms.

$$\begin{aligned} IPORETN_i &= \alpha_0 + \alpha_1 RCPIPO_i + \alpha_2 LNIPOSZ_i \\ &\quad + \alpha_3 PROFSHA_i + \alpha_4 LNTOSIZE_i \\ &\quad + \alpha_5 LNAGE_i + \alpha_6 TIMEIPO_i \\ &\quad + \alpha_k SIC(k) + \alpha_t YEAR(t) + \epsilon_i \end{aligned} \tag{6.1}$$

The OLS regression estimates for A-share IPOs presented in Table 6.4 show that:

(1) The smaller the IPO price, the larger is the IPO initial return.
(2) The smaller the size of initial offering, the higher is the IPO initial

Table 6.3 Descriptive Statistics for Variables to Explain IPO Initial Returns

Variable	Mean	Median	Std. dev.	Min.	Max.
A-share sub-sample with 268 firm-commitment IPOs between December 1986 and June 1994					
$IPORETN$	1043.1%	271.24%	3166.3%	-10%	38300%
$AFTRETN1$	-0.2171	-0.0215	0.2519	-0.9268	1.704
$AFTRETN2$	-0.0712	-0.0375	0.1684	-0.9173	0.693
$\ln P_0$	1.1805	1.315	0.6271	0	2.3253
$LNIPOSZ$	9.0635	9.177	1.0099	5.4806	12.241
$LNTOSIZE$	10.77	10.678	1.0583	8.2295	15.772
$LNAGE$	2.7743	2.6391	0.9016	0.6931	4.477
$TIMEIPO$	251.04	142	305.98	3	1831
$LNGOVNT$	6.0898	8.0283	4.0101	0	12.908
$LNEMPLOY$	5.6935	5.7038	1.3461	0	9.852
$IPOVALUE$	16.89	11.65	23.61	0.29	249.40
$PROFIT$	430.64	211.13	83.64	2.77	3788.3
STD	6.01%	4.74%	5.42%	0.65%	51.27%
$INTRINSC$	160.03	88.59	236.72	2.61	1856.4
$TIMEIPO$	251	142	306	3	1831
$\frac{SEOSZ}{INTRINSC}$	49.93%	43.85%	28.95%	0	99.87%
$TIMESEO$	284	220	217	0	1217

return; the larger the size of total offerings, which is the sum of IPO and all SEOs, the higher is the IPO initial return. These findings imply that firms with small IPOs relative to their total offerings have a relatively high degree of IPO underpricing.

(3) Time elapsed between the announcement of an IPO and the first-day market trading does not affect the IPO underpricing. This contradicts Chowdhry and Sherman (1996), who show that IPO underpricing is positively related to the time period between IPO date and first trading date.

(4) The age of the firm and the profit per share variables do not seem to be related to the IPO initial return, indicating that available information about a firm at the time of the IPO is not related to IPO underpricing. This is in contrast to that of Ritter (1991), who found significant negative relationship between IPO underpricing and past information for the U.S. firms.

Table 6.4 OLS Regression Estimates for the Baseline Empirical Model

	Constant	RCPIPO	LNIPOSZ	PROFSHA	LNAGE
Full[a]	-69.6048*	22.9758*	-5.0583*	-4.1638	2.3892
	(-3.0612)	(3.4019)	(-2.4754)	(-1.4312)	(1.4162)
Sub	-93.6159*	25.1627*	-4.1532†	-4.4099	2.5793
	(-3.7446)	(3.4513)	(-1.8391)	(-1.4059)	(1.3741)
	LNTOSIZE	TIMEIPO	SIC1	SIC2	SIC3
Full	10.0695*	-0.0172	7.8147†	10.7099*	1.6218
	(6.1995)	(-1.0161)	(1.7232)	(2.1654)	(0.2802)
Sub	11.1672*	-0.0141	9.9033†	14.0239*	3.2262
	(5.9527)	(-1.2724)	(1.9049)	(2.4707)	(0.4773)
	SIC4	SIC5	YEAR1	YEAR2	YEAR3
Full	2.8004	5.0636	43.5243*	-7.6043	0.6983
	(0.4782)	(0.9657)	(3.3936)	(-0.8122)	(0.0868)
Sub	3.8525	8.193	44.4975*	-8.5893	-0.9173
	(0.5565)	(1.384)	(3.3733)	(-1.0246)	(-0.1385)
	YEAR4	YEAR5	$\bar{R}^2$		
Full	-3.9135	0.7963	0.3581		
	(-0.5362)	(0.1014)			
Sub	-3.6153		0.3757		
	(-0.6443)				

[a]The dependent variable is the IPO initial return. The independent variables are the reciprocal of IPO price ($RCPIPO$), logarithm of IPO size ($LNIPOSZ$), profit per share ($PROFSHA$), logarithm of the age of the firm ($LNAGE$), logarithm of the size of total offerings ($LNTOSIZE$), time elapsed between the offer date and the first trading date ($TIMEIPO$), industry dummies ($SIC(k)$) and IPO year dummies ($YEAR(t)$). Figures in parentheses are t-statistics. *, † denote 5% and 10% level of significance, respectively.

(5) Durable and non-durable goods industries have larger IPO underpricing than other industries, suggesting that the proportion of high-value firms going public is larger in durable and non-durable goods industries than in other industries.

(6) IPO initial returns were significantly higher at the early stage of

development of Chinese stock markets.

Since the $LNIPOSZ$, $TIMEIPO$ and $\ln P_0$ variables are endogenous, OLS estimation gives inconsistent estimates for the coefficients for these variables. Therefore, I use the instrumental variables (IV) approach in estimating the structural equation (6.1).

To instrument the $LNIPOSZ$, $LNTIMEIPO$ and $\ln P_0$ variables, we regress them against the exogenous variables $LNAGE$, $LNPROFIT$, $SIC(k)$ and $YEAR(t)$ using OLS, and obtain the fitted values $LN\widehat{IPOSZ}$, $LNTI\widehat{ME}IPO$ and $\widehat{\ln P_0}$. As will be shown in subsequent sections, IPO prices are determined from firms' value-maximization problem and first-day market prices reveal whether a firm is of high-value or not. There is no compelling reason for the IPO price and first-day market price to depend upon industry and IPO year dummies. Therefore, $SIC(k)$ and $YEAR(t)$ variables are excluded from the structural equation (6.1).

The results from the 2SLS regression presented in Table 6.5 show that:

(1) The smaller the IPO price, the larger the IPO initial return.
(2) The smaller the size of initial offering, the higher the IPO initial return. This implies that firms with small IPOs have higher degree of IPO underpricing.
(3) Time elapsed between the announcement of an IPO and the first-day market trading is positively related to the degree of IPO underpricing. This is consistent with Chowdhry and Sherman (1996).
(4) The age of the firm and the past profit variables are positively related to the IPO initial return. This implies that firms with better performance and low-priced new issues have higher-priced shares after market trading begins.

The benchmark model successfully relates the cross-sectional differences in IPO underpricing to some economic variables. In the next section, I test signaling hypotheses that may help explain the extraordinarily high A-share IPO underpricing that characterizes the Chinese markets.

6.4 The Adverse-Selection Models

Rock (1986) and Beatty and Ritter (1986) propose that there is information asymmetry between informed and uninformed investors. Because quantity rationing instead of price adjustment occurs when there is excess demand

Table 6.5 2SLS Regression Estimates for the Benchmark Model

Variable	Full Sample[a]	Sub-Sample
Constant	210.4286*	271.942*
	(3.1832)	(3.2998)
$\widehat{\ln P_0}$	-120.1951†	-146.3093†
	(-1.753)	(-1.901)
$LN\widehat{IPOS}Z$	-43.7689*	-53.3934*
	(-4.2017)	(-4.2471)
$LNPROFIT$	20.9588*	25.223*
	(4.4772)	(4.5008)
$LNAGE$	5.8186*	6.8196*
	(3.1548)	(3.2696)
$LNT\widehat{IME}IPO$	13.9308†	14.3106†
	(1.9101)	(1.7707)
$\bar{R}^2$	0.2415	0.2561

[a]The dependent variable is the IPO initial return. The independent variables are the instrument for the logarithm of IPO price variable ($\widehat{\ln P_0}$), instrument for the logarithm of IPO size variable measured in dollars ($LN\widehat{IPOS}Z$), logarithm of past year's profit at the time of IPO ($LNPROFIT$), logarithm of the age of the firm ($LNAGE$) and instrument for the logarithm of time elapsed between the offer date and the first trading date ($LNT\widehat{IME}IPO$). $\widehat{\ln P_0}$, $LN\widehat{IPOS}Z$ and $LNT\widehat{IME}IPO$ are obtained by regressing $\ln P_0$, $LNIPOSZ$, and $LNTIMEIPO$ on $LNAGE$, $LNPROFIT$, industry dummies ($SIC(k)$) and IPO year dummies ($YEAR(t)$). Figures in parentheses are t-statistics. *, † denote 5% and 10% level of significance, respectively.

for shares, the informed investors crowd out the uninformed investors for allocations of profitable issues. The allocations received by uninformed investors are biased toward less-profitable issues. Therefore, in order to attract uninformed investors to participate in the IPO market, firms must underprice their IPOs sufficiently to allow uninformed investors a reasonable return for their *ex ante* uncertainty, and to enable them to recover the losses resulting from their purchase of overpriced securities. There are two important empirical implications: (1) Issues in which the public have *a priori* knowledge that insiders and institutional investors have little or no participation will be less underpriced. The reason is that uninformed investors will not face winner's curse and allocation disadvantage, and underpricing will not be required to induce them to participate in the IPO markets. (2) Expected underpricing increases in the *ex ante* uncertainty surrounding an issue.

To examine cross-section variations in the underpricing of Chinese IPOs, we regress the degree of IPO underpricing ($IPORETN$) against a number of proxies for *ex ante* uncertainty. That is, we test the joint hypotheses that there is a positive relationship between risks and the degree of IPO underpricing and proxies used in the following regression are adequate measures of risks.

$$\begin{aligned} IPORETN_i &= \alpha_0 + \alpha_1 \left(\frac{1}{IPOVALUE} \times 1,000,000 \right)_i \\ &\quad + \alpha_2 EARNINGS_i + \alpha_3 USAGE_i \\ &\quad + \alpha_4 INFORMED_i + \alpha_5 PROFSHA_i \\ &\quad + \alpha_6 LEVERAGE_i + \alpha_7 \ln AGE_i \\ &\quad + \alpha_8 MKTRUNUP_i + \alpha_9 PREMSTD_i \\ &\quad + \alpha_{10} STD_i + \alpha_{11} \ln TIMEIPO_i \\ &\quad + \alpha_{12} LD_i + \alpha_{13} EXD_i + \alpha_{14} TIME_i \\ &\quad + \alpha_k SIC(k)_i + \epsilon_i \end{aligned} \tag{6.2}$$

$1/IPOVALUE$ is the inverse of proceeds raised in an A-share IPO expressed in terms of 1993 purchasing power. It reflects the maintained hypothesis that smaller offerings are more speculative, on average, than larger offerings (Beatty and Ritter, 1986). This implies that α_1 is positive. In general, firms are unwilling to give out detailed information on what they will do with the net proceeds from IPOs because of increasing legal liability and exposure to competitors. However, the China Security Regulatory Committee (CSRC) requires highly speculative issues to provide future earnings forecasts and disclose IPO funds usage in their prospectus. As a result of this regulation, issues that list earnings forecasts and usage of IPO funds are associated with greater *ex ante* uncertainty.[2] α_2 and α_3, the coefficients for $EARNINGS$ and $USAGE$, should both be positive. The percentage of shares held by insiders and institutional investors ($INFORMED$), a proxy for the severity of the winner's curse problem, is hypothesized to be positively related to underpricing.

In addition, information on the past performance of a firm, such as

[2] For example, it is well known that Tsing Tao Brewery stated one use of its proceeds in the prospectus and then use the money for other purposes, which turned out to yield very disappointing returns to investors.

calendar year's profit prior to an IPO divided by the number of IPO shares ($PROFSHA$), debt-to-total assets ratio ($LEVERAGE$) and the age of the issuing firm ($\ln AGE$), is related to the *ex ante* information asymmetry (Ritter, 1991, and Su, 2000d). In particular, the higher the past profit per-share, the better is a firm's growth potential. α_5 should be negative. Su (2000c) argues that a high pre-IPO leverage ratio raises *ex ante* uncertainty about the financial strength of a firm, because debt financing for investment projects is not a viable choice for imposing a hard budget constraint on management, while a small pre-IPO leverage conveys good news to the market. This suggests that α_6 is negative. Ritter (1991) finds that there is a strong negative relationship between the age of the firm and the IPO initial return, which is consistent with the notion that risky issues require higher average returns and that age is an useful proxy for this risk. Therefore, α_7 should be negative.

Prevailing market conditions ($MKTRUNUP$ and $PREMSTD$) influence the assessment of firm risk. If market returns are high and the variance of returns is low at the time a firm goes public, the IPO initial return will naturally be high. Moreover, risky firms have an incentive to go public when market conditions are favorable. Hence, α_8 should be positive while α_9 should be negative. Furthermore, Ritter (1984) uses the variability of stock returns of the issuing firm in the after-market period as one of the proxies for *ex ante* uncertainty. He finds significant relationship between the variability of after-market returns and the degree of IPO underpricing for a sample of natural resource companies. He interprets his findings as giving support to the claim that the greater the uncertainty about the true price of new shares, the larger is the discount that an issuer must offer in selling IPOs, and that there is no reason to restrict risk proxies to *ex ante* observable characteristics. Therefore, we hypothesize that the degree of IPO underpricing is positively related to $AFTMSTD2$, i.e., α_{10} is positive.

Chowdhry and Sherman (1996) propose that IPO initial returns will be higher if the underwriter gets some direct compensation based on the size of the demand for IPO shares. In addition, when the offer price of an IPO is set many days before the actual issue day, there is a possibility that the first-day price at which the issue would trade in the secondary market may leak to the public. It is well known that most Chinese A-share IPOs are sold through a lottery mechanism and the underwriter (typically a state bank) sells lottery application forms. The revenue from the sale of lottery forms belongs to the underwriter. The IPO price is also set long before shares are sold–49 days on average. The empirical prediction is that the risk of an issue and hence, the degree of underpricing, will be higher if $\ln TIMEIPO$ is larger and/or a lottery mechanism is used in share allocation. This suggests that both α_{11} and α_{12} are positive.

Since most firms listed in Shanghai are formerly large-scale state enterprises while most firms listed in Shenzhen are relatively small joint-venture companies, we add a variable EXD to capture the differential risks of these two types of firms. α_{13} is hypothesized to be positive. Finally, we use $SIC(k)$ and $TIME$ to control for industry-specific risks and risks associated with the year of IPOs.[3]

We note that to raise a given amount of funds from IPO ($IPOVALUE$), a firm can sell a smaller fraction of ownership and thus, retain a larger fraction of shares held by government, managers, employees and other institutions ($INFORMED$). To detect possible simultaneous equation bias, we estimate regression (1) with and without $\frac{1}{IPOVALUE}$ for the entire sample of 371 firms and a sub-sample of 239 firms. All regressions are corrected for heteroskedasticity using the generalized least squares (GLS) procedure. We present regression results of initial-day underpricing on issue characteristics and proxies of informational uncertainty in Table 6.6.

We find that there are only minor differences among the regressions. The explanatory power of the model, as measured by the adjusted-R^2, is between 0.62 and 0.70. The coefficient estimates for $INFORMED$ are significantly positive at the 5% level, indicating that IPO underpricing is smaller for issues in which the public knows *a priori* that government and other institutions have little or no participation. To further investigate the relation between IPO underpricing and the participation of insider and institutional investors, we rank firms in ascending order of $INFORMED$ and group firms into quintiles. Table 6.7 compares IPO initial returns and some fundamental characteristics of firms that are grouped into the lowest and highest quintiles of $INFORMED$. As shown in the table, the mean IPO initial return is significantly larger for the high $INFORMED$ group than for the low $INFORMED$ group. This suggests that the "lemon's problem" is less pronounced in a market in which uninformed investors have

[3]Because firms going public in China typically use large state banks, which in turn use their branch networks, to distribute shares, there is little or no variation in underwriters' reputation. We do not use variables such as investment banker prestige, venture capital backing and the use of warrants to underwriters as proxies for *ex ante* uncertainty.

Table 6.6 GLS Regression Estimates for the Relationship Between IPO Underpricing and Proxies of Uncertainty

	Full-sample		Sub-sample	
Constant	-3.1461**	-4.2073**	-3.9426**	-4.9050**
	(-5.1636)	(-6.5922)	(-6.1407)	(-7.2825)
$\frac{1,000,000}{IPOVALUE}$		10.8424**		12.0629**
		(3.2911)		(4.8463)
EARNINGS	0.8664*	1.4015**	0.7155*	1.3407**
	(2.1883)	(4.0682)	(2.0377)	(3.6299)
USAGE	1.6282*	1.3358*	1.4420*	1.2512*
	(2.3530)	(2.1004)	(2.1646)	(2.0319)
INFORMED	2.5051**	1.7472*	2.3118**	1.4550*
	(3.1630)	(2.4705)	(3.0069)	(2.1504)
LEVERAGE	1.0343*	0.8551†	1.2177*	0.8835†
	(2.1180)	(1.8495)	(2.5099)	(1.9033)
ln *AGE*	-2.5209	-2.6864	-2.7038	-2.7599
	(-1.0216)	(-1.2883)	(-1.3170)	(-1.3656)
MKTRUNUP	4.7535**	3.9609**	5.2459**	4.4620**
	(3.6186)	(2.9301)	(4.1784)	(3.3861)
PREMSTD	-1.4661†	-1.2054	-1.6295†	-1.3305
	(-1.7620)	(-1.5163)	(-1.8942)	(-1.5955)
STD	-1.1442	-1.3059	-1.2684	-1.4117
	(-1.0620)	(-1.2191)	(-1.1742)	(-1.2838)
LD	3.7522**	4.1086**	3.9901**	4.5360**
	(4.1737)	(4.8452)	(4.3174)	(5.2044)
EXD	2.5730*	2.0288†	2.1916*	1.8633†
	(2.3595)	(1.8803)	(2.1066)	(1.7110)
TIME	-6.3106**	-7.7296**	-6.9350**	-8.3260**
	(-7.1883)	(-8.6960)	(-7.8054)	(-9.5414)
SIC(1)	2.0184†	2.3353*	1.7728†	1.9660†
	(1.8695)	(2.0597)	(1.7820)	(1.8204)
SIC(2)	2.9155*	2.5930*	3.2475*	2.7305*
	(2.3472)	(2.1306)	(2.5185)	(2.0608)
adjusted-R^2	0.6240	0.6749	0.6508	0.7033

prior knowledge of a lack of informed investors. This result is consistent with the winner's curse hypothesis but is contradictory to the prediction of the signaling model of Perotti (1995), who argues that underpricing of state-enterprises' IPOs is an equilibrium outcome for a government issuer to signal its future commitment to pro-market privatization policies.

Table 6.7 Comparison of the Characteristics of Firms Grouped Into the Lowest and Highest Quintile of Insider and Institutional Investors' Ownership

	IPORETN	*INFORMED*	*IPOVALUE*	*LEVERAGE*	*PROFSHA*
Lowest Quintile[a]	3.38%	16.85%	57.94	0.36	0.22
Highest Quintile	240.70%	66.25%	85.63	0.29	0.27
t-statistics of the difference	24.820	9.035	1.228	0.386	0.694

[a]A comparison of some fundamental characteristics of firms grouped into the lowest and highest quintile of *INFORMED*, the percentage of shares held by insiders and institutional investors, based on the sample of 371 non-financial firm-commitment domestic IPOs between January 1, 1994 and December 31, 1997. *IPORETN* is the degree of IPO underpricing, *IPOVALUE* is the offer price multiplied by the number of IPO shares in million U.S. dollars, *LEVERAGE* is the pre-IPO debt-to-total assets ratio, and *PROFSHA* is the calendar year's profit prior to the IPO divided by the total number of IPO shares. When calculating t-statistics of the differences in variables, the assumption of unequal variances between the two groups is used if the assumption of equal variance is rejected.

In Table 6.6, the coefficient estimates for $EARNINGS$ and $USAGE$ are both significantly positive at the 5% level, suggesting that firms required to provide earnings forecasts and detailed usage of IPO proceeds experience higher IPO underpricing. The coefficient estimates for the reciprocal of the A-share proceeds from an IPO are significantly positive at the 1% level, indicating that smaller offerings have substantially higher average initial returns. The coefficient estimates for $LEVERAGE$ are significantly positive at least at the 10% level, which implies that investors perceive the debt-to-total assets ratio as a correlate with the *ex ante* uncertainty of the firm, and that the higher the pre-IPO leverage ratio, the larger is the expected initial return. In addition, there is evidence that prevailing market conditions influence the assessment of firm risk because the coefficient estimates for $MKTRUNUP$ are significantly positive at the 1% level and the coefficient estimates for $PREMSTD$ are significantly negative at the 10% level when $\frac{1}{IPOVALUE}$ is not included in the regression. Investors seem to believe that risky firms go public when market conditions are favorable (i.e., the pre-IPO market return is high while the standard deviation of returns is low) and require higher initial returns for risky firms. However, in contrast to empirical findings of the U.S. data by Ritter (1984), the variable $AFTMSTD2$ is not only statistically insignificant, but also of wrong sign. Since we are testing joint hypotheses here, it is possible that the after-market standard deviation of returns is not a very good proxy for the *ex ante* uncertainty of the firm.

Furthermore, we find conflicting evidence from the Chinese data against the theories of Chowdhry and Sherman (1996). The coefficient estimates for LD are significantly positive at the 1% level, indicating that underpricing is higher, on average, for firms that use a lottery mechanism in allocating shares. However, the coefficient estimates for $\ln TIMEIPO$ are insignificant at the conventional level, although it is of right sign. There is lack of evidence that the degree of IPO underpricing is related to the time elapsed between when the IPO price is set and when the issue is actually sold. The coefficient estimates for EXD are significantly positive, suggesting that firms listed in the Shenzhen Securities Exchange are, on average, more risky and have higher expected IPO underpricing. $TIME$, the variable representing the year of an IPO, is significantly negative. This implies that firms going public in the early stages of development of Chinese stock markets were generally perceived as more risky firms, probably because the degree of information asymmetry among investors was larger at that time.

The coefficient estimates for $SIC(1)$ and $SIC(2)$ are significantly positive at the 10% and 5% level, respectively, indicating that durable and non-durable goods industries are underpriced more than the other industries, whose coefficient estimates are insignificant and hence, omitted from Table 6.6 for brevity. Finally, the coefficient estimates for $PROFSHA$ and $\ln AGE$ are of right signs, but are insignificant at the conventional level.

In summary, we find evidence that investors interpret the percentage of insider and institutional investors' ownership, the size of offerings, whether the issuer provides earnings forecast and IPO fund usage in the prospectus, leverage, market conditions prior to IPOs, allocation mechanism, listing exchange, listing time, and the belonging industry as correlates with *ex ante* uncertainty, and that there is a positive relation between *ex ante* uncertainty among investors and expected underpricing. Our empirical results strongly support the winner's curse hypothesis of IPO pricing.

6.5 The Signaling Models

6.5.1 *Empirical Implications from the Signaling Models*

Allen and Faulhaber (1989), Grinblatt and Hwang (1989), Welch (1989) and Chemmanur (1993) have proposed a class of signaling models of IPO underpricing in which issuers have superior information than investors do about the intrinsic value of the firms. The discussion in the remainder of this section draws heavily upon these papers. In the cited models, an issuer maximizes the value of the firm through the IPO and subsequent SEOs. Because they do not have complete information, in the absence of a signal, investors cannot distinguish between "high value" and "low value" firms. In a separating equilibrium, a "high value" issuer signals its quality by underpricing. It can afford to underprice its IPO because it expects to capture larger revenues through SEOs. In contrast, a "low value" issuer does not signal because it does not expect to recoup its investment in underpricing through after-market SEOs. The best a low-value issuer can do is to "take the money and run" when its stock is initially offered. When a separating equilibrium occurs, the average risk-adjusted IPO return over all new issues will be positive, the quantity of shares demanded for underpriced issues will exceed quantity supplied, and shares will be rationed by a mechanism other than the offer price.

The papers mentioned above have somewhat different setups that lead to similar, but not identical, testable hypotheses. In Allen and Faulhaber's framework, as long as the probability that a high-quality firm will remain good after it implements its production technique, product, or whatever it does, is not "very large", the high-value firm will find it advantageous to signal by underpricing its IPO while a low-value firm will not find it worthwhile to underprice. Therefore, underpricing occurs in a separating equilibrium. In Grinblatt and Hwang (1989), if the expected value and the variance of future cash flow for a risk-averse firm is unknown to the investors, then, corresponding to the revelation probability of the firm's intrinsic value (between 0 and 1), there exists an equilibrium signaling schedule relating two signals, fractional holding and IPO underpricing. The firm signals its value to the market by choosing the optimal combination of underpricing and IPO size. In Welch (1989), low-value firms must invest in imitation expenses to appear to be high-value firms, and with non-zero probability this imitation will be discovered between the dates of IPO and SEO. Underpricing by high-value firms at the time of IPO can add sufficient signaling costs to these imitation expenses to induce low-value firm to separate and thus reveal their value voluntarily.

In a recent paper, Chemmanur (1993) models the long held intuition that underpricing motivates the market to produce information about the issuing firm. High value issuers underprice to motivate outsiders to produce information and make informed bids for the IPO. Low value issuers mimic this behavior, but their type will be revealed after the IPO bids. IPO underpricing results from insiders inducing information production to obtain a more precise valuation of their firms in seasoned equity offerings.

The testable implications from the signaling models with separating equilibrium include:

(1) The correlation between the degree of IPO underpricing and IPO proceeds is negative. In the signaling model of Grinblatt and Hwang (1989), there exists a monotonic correspondence between offering price at which the issue is being sold and the degree of IPO underpricing in a separating equilibrium, holding constant the firm's fractional shareholding (or, equivalently, holding constant the fractional size of the IPO). That is, if investors observe an issuer's fractional ownership and can conjecture the value of a benchmark lowest-variance issuer by looking the relative size of its IPO, they can also infer the degree of IPO underpricing for any arbitrary is-

suer given the issuer's initial offering price and relative IPO size.

(2) There is an optimal signaling schedule relating the firm's intrinsic value, the degree of underpricing, and relative IPO size. In particular, the degree of underpricing and the issuer's intrinsic value are positively correlated, holding constant the issuer's fractional ownership and the variance of returns; the degree of underpricing and the project variance are positively correlated, holding constant the issuer's fractional ownership and the variance of returns; the degree of underpricing and the fractional holding are positively related, holding constant the variance of returns and the firm's intrinsic value.

(3) Issuers with a larger degree of IPO underpricing are more likely to return to the secondary market and offer larger amount of SEOs, more quickly than issuers with lower IPO underpricing.

There are various "stories" rationalizing this signaling hypothesis. One linkage between the underpricing signal and SEO behavior is that an issuer gives out "free samples" to the public by underpricing and induces the public to learn more about the issuer. The learning process leads to a higher price on the first day of market trading than would otherwise occur—but for high-value issuers only. This effect on the market price allows a high-value issuer to quickly return to the market with SEOs and thereby reap the return from underpricing its IPO. In another version, investors are more passive and "learning" occurs through exogenous revelation of information after implementation of the firm's innovation. The IPO is underpriced to induce investors to furnish sufficient startup funds to enable implementation of the innovation. Firms are willing to underprice because they expect a higher-than-normal return on their investment.

The alternative to a separating equilibrium is a pooling equilibrium where IPO prices are a weighted average of the present value of high-value and low-value issuers. When information is revealed after market trading starts, price differentiation occurs, but the first-day market price cannot be predicted from the IPO price and there is no risk-adjusted "excess" IPO initial return between the offer date and the first-day market trading for a large sample of firms.

In a pooling equilibrium, high-value firms do issue SEOs, but only in response to market-provided information about their value. That is, the market possesses superior information than the issuers. If the after-market returns are high, then firms will issue seasoned equities. If they are low, then there are no seasoned issues. No equilibrium signaling schedule exists. This is the so called market feedback hypothesis.

6.5.2 *Correlation Between IPO Returns and IPO Proceeds*

The first set of empirical implications in Section 6.4.1 indicates a monotonic negative correspondence between the price of the initial offering and $IPORETN$, holding constant the relative size of the IPO in a separating equilibrium under the signaling hypothesis. In a pooling equilibrium, since the IPO price is a weighted average of the intrinsic value of low- and high-quality firms, there is no implied correspondence between the offering price and realized IPO initial return.

To test this hypothesis empirically, we need to consider that measuring offering price consistently across firms is complicated by the fact that the number of shares a firm declares when it corporatizes is arbitrary. There is no reason, *a priori* why two firms with the same intrinsic value would declare the same number of shares. Ideally, we would measure offering price as the observed offering price per share divided by intrinsic value per share. However, intrinsic value is unobservable. Since we do not observe the firm's intrinsic value, offering prices are measured with error. This measurement error does not affect the variable $IPORETN$, because the unobserved value of intrinsic value per share would appear in both the numerator and denominator, and thus cancels out. Moreover, there could be a spurious negative correlation between the observed offering price and the observed $IPORETN$, even under a pooling equilibrium.

In light of the above complications, we use the following two proxies for the offering price: (1) $\ln IPOVALUE$, which is the logarithm of the product of the number of share issued at the time of an IPO and the observed offering price. (2) $OPTOBOOK$, which is the observed offering price per share divided by the book value per share. To correct for the errors-in-variable (EIV)problem, we adopt a two-stage approach to derive unbiased estimates of the relationship between the logarithm of IPO return, IPO price, and the relative size of IPO (the number of shares offered at the time of the IPO divided by the total number of shares outstanding, the complement of the firm's fractional shareholding). In the first stage, we

Table 6.8 2SLS Regression Estimates for the Correlation Between IPO Underpricing and IPO Price

Variable[a]	Full Sample	Sub-Sample
Constant	15.1907*	13.9522*
	(23.2712)	(20.1465)
$\ln \widehat{IPOSZ}$	-0.8612*	-0.7021*
	(-11.3981)	(-8.5542)
$\widehat{\frac{IPOSZ}{MKTCAP}}$	-11.2312*	-12.3773*
	(-10.4522)	(-10.7187)
$\bar{R}^2$	0.5396	0.5469

[a]The dependent variable is the logarithm of IPO initial return ($\ln IPORETN$). The independent variables are the instruments for the logarithm of IPO proceeds ($\ln \widehat{IPOSZ}$) and the relative size of IPO ($\widehat{\frac{IPOSZ}{MKTCAP}}$). The instruments are obtained by regressing $\ln IPOSZ$ and $\frac{IPOSZ}{MKTCAP}$ on exogenous variables including $\ln AGE$, $\ln PROFIT$, $\ln TIMEIPO$, stock-exchange dummy (EXD), industry dummies ($SIC(k)$) and IPO year dummies ($YEAR(t)$). Figures in parentheses are t-statistics. *, † denote 5% and 10% level of significance, respectively.

regress $\ln IPOVALUE$ or $OPTOBOOK$ against the exogenous variables $\ln AGE$, $\ln PROFIT$, $\ln TIMEIPO$, EXD, $SIC(k)$ and $YEAR(t)$, and obtain the instruments $\ln IPO\widehat{V}ALUE$ or $OPT\widehat{O}BOOK$. In the second stage, we estimate the following regression:

$$\ln IPORETN_i = \beta_0 + \beta_1 \ln IPO\widehat{V}ALUE + \beta_2 \frac{IPOSZ}{TOTALSHA} + \epsilon_i \quad (6.3)$$

We interpret Grinblatt and Huang (1989) to imply that equation (6.3) holds for issuers of given initial wealth. We assume that the issuer is the Chinese government, and therefore the initial wealth in the cross section of issuers is roughly constant and can thus safely be omitted from the regression.

The estimation results reported in Table 6.8 show that: (1) holding constant the relative size of initial offerings, a one percent decline in the price of initial offering is associated with approximately a 1.98 percent increase in IPO initial return and that (2) a one percentage-point increase in relative IPO size is associated with a 6 percent decline in the IPO return. Both coefficients are highly significant.

6.5.3 *Correlations Among IPO Underpricing and Issuer's Intrinsic Value, Fractional Ownership and Project Variance*

The second set of empirical implications in Section 6.4.1 suggests a positive relationship between an issuing firm's IPO return, relative IPO size, variance of future returns, and intrinsic value (under a separating equilibrium). Testing these implications is complicated by the necessity of measuring the variance of future returns and lack of an error-free measure of the issuing firm's intrinsic value. As a proxy for intrinsic value, we use the $INTRINSC$ variable which is the sum of the proceeds from IPO, all SEOs, employee shares, government shares and state enterprises shares. We proxy the variance of future returns with variance of daily A-share returns over the first 100-day period of market trading. Moreover, the complement of the fraction of the firm's value retained by the issuer, the relative size of IPO is determined endogenously. Again, to correct for these EIV and endogeneity problems we estimate the following regression by 2SLS using the same instruments as in equation (6.3) to obtain the fitted values of the regressors:

$$\begin{aligned} \ln IPORETN_i &= \beta_0 + \beta_1 \ln \widehat{INTRINSC} \\ &\quad + \beta_2 \ln \widehat{IPOVALUE} + \beta_3 \widehat{STD} + \epsilon_i \end{aligned} \qquad (6.4)$$

The estimation results reported in Table 6.9 show that: (1) holding constant the firm's intrinsic value and the project variance, a one percent decrease in the size of the initial offering is associated with approximately a two percent increase in the degree of IPO underpricing; (2) holding constant the size of the initial offering and the project variance, a one percent increase in the firm's intrinsic value is associated with approximately a one percent increase in the degree of IPO underpricing; and (3) holding constant the firm's intrinsic value and the size of the initial offering, an increase of one standard deviation in the variation of future returns is associated with almost an eleven percent increase in the degree of IPO underpricing, which implies an elasticity of approximately 0.6 at the mean value of the regressor. All of the coefficients are statistically significant, even at the 1% level.

It should be noted that we have calculated another measure of firm's intrinsic value, which is the outstanding market capitalization as of December 29, 1995. We find that both measures of firm's intrinsic value are

Table 6.9 2SLS Regression Estimates for the Correlation Among IPO Underpricing and Issuer's Intrinsic Value, Fractional Ownership and Project Variance

Variable[a]	Full Sample	Sub-Sample
Constant	-5.1423*	-6.2608*
	(-2.9377)	(-3.1859)
$\ln \widehat{IPOSZ}$	-1.8383*	-1.7676*
	(-19.9304)	(-17.411)
$\ln \widehat{MKTCAP}$	1.1406*	1.1646*
	(12.0549)	(10.9617)
$\widehat{STD}$	10.9575*	10.2704*
	(4.0374)	(3.7736)
$\bar{R}^2$	0.6216	0.5967

[a]The dependent variable is the logarithm of IPO initial return ($\ln IPORETN$). The independent variables are the instrument for the logarithm of the size of initial offerings ($\ln \widehat{IPOSZ}$), instrument for the logarithm of firm's intrinsic value ($\ln \widehat{MKTCAP}$), and instrument for the project variance ($\widehat{STD}$). The instruments are obtained by regressing $\ln IPOSZ$, $\ln MKTCAP$, and STD on exogenous variables including $\ln AGE$, $\ln PROFIT$, $\ln TIMEIPO$, stock-exchange dummy (EXD), industry dummies ($SIC(k)$) and IPO year dummies ($YEAR(t)$). Figures in parentheses are t-statistics. *, † denote 5% and 10% level of significance, respectively.

highly correlated and yield almost the same results in all of our estimations. Therefore, we only report the estimation results using the first measure. Our empirical results in this section support a separating equilibrium under the signaling hypothesis.

6.5.4 *IPO Underpricing and SEOs*

All the signaling models discussed in Section 6.4.1 imply that high-quality issuers underprice their IPOs so that they can subsequently issue seasoned equities at more favorable prices than they would otherwise have received. Issuers that do not plan to sell seasoned equities subsequent to the IPOs do not discount their initial sales. In reality, not all IPOs that appear to be underpriced are followed by SEOs. About 91% of Chinese firms going public before June 30, 1994 issued subsequent equities before January 1, 1996. As JWW (1993) point out, some of the firms that underprice their IPOs with the intention of issuing subsequent equities may fail to do so because of unexpected economic shocks. However, such shocks are less likely to prevent firms of very high quality to stick to their original plans. In addition, some underpricing may be unintentional or unexpected. Therefore we view the relationship between IPO underpricing and subsequent offerings probabilistically, that (1) issuers with larger IPO underpricing are more likely to issue subsequent equities than issuers with lower expected IPO underpricing. Additional hypotheses related to IPO-SEO behavior are: (2) Issuers with larger IPO underpricing will issue larger amounts of SEOs relative to their intrinsic value, and (3) Issuers with larger IPO underpricing will issue SEOs more quickly after the initial sales.[4]

Empirical tests need to distinguish between the implications of a separating and a pooling equilibrium, where firms to do not signal their value to the investors through underpricing. A firm's specific value is revealed only after market trading begins. This suggests the "market-feedback hypothesis," in which high post-IPO returns lead firms to issue seasoned equities and low post-IPO returns will discourage issues of additional shares.

To test the hypothesis that issuers with larger expected IPO underpricing are more likely to issue SEOs, we follow the spirit of JWW (1993) and estimate the following logit model,

$$\ln\left(\frac{P_i^{SEO}}{1-P_i^{SEO}}\right) = \phi_0 + \phi_1 IPORETN_i + \phi_2 AFTRETN1_i + \phi_3 AFTRETN2_i \quad (6.5)$$

where P_i^{SEO} is the probability that the ith issuer will issue subsequent equity offerings after the initial sale. The independent variables are the observed degree of IPO underpricing ($IPORETN$), the after-market return for the first two weeks ($AFTRETN1$) and the after-market return for the third and fourth weeks ($AFTRETN2$).

JWW (1993) include a variable representing IPO size in their equation. Their rationale for including IPO size is "Since firms that raise relatively small amounts of capital at the IPO may be more likely to return with a seasoned equity offering, we include the natural logarithm of IPO size as an additional explanatory variable." We believe that inclusion of IPO size

[4] JWW (1993) test the signaling models using U.S. data and find weak evidence that firms that underprice their IPOs are more likely to issue seasoned equities and on average have larger subsequent offerings.

Table 6.10 Logit Regression Estimates for the Relationship Among IPO Underpricing, After-Market Returns and Probability of SEOs

Variable[a]	Coefficient	t-statistic
Constant	2.0242*	(6.5531)
$IPORETN$	0.001326*	(2.1301)
$AFTRETN1$	0.031597*	(2.1831)
$AFTRETN2$	0.014543	(0.8885)

[a]The dependent variable is the probability for the ith firm to issue SEOs (P_i^{SEO}). The dependent variable takes value 1 if SEOs are observed and 0 otherwise. The independent variables are the observed IPO initial return ($IPORETN$), after-market first two-week return ($AFTRETN1$) and after-market next two-week return ($AFTRETN2$). We allow 548 days for a firm to issue SEOs, therefore our sample only consists of firms who went public between December 1986 and June 1994. There are 268 firms in the sample. Figures in parentheses are asymptotic t-statistics. *, † denote 5% and 10% level of significance, respectively.

as a regressor is inappropriate when the hypothesis being tested is that underpricing reduces the size of IPOs relative to SEOs. IPO size becomes endogenous and may well "pick up" the effect of underpricing we are trying to estimate. In addition, JWW (1993) do not take into consideration the EIV problem when using observed IPO initial returns instead of a proper instrument for the expected IPO initial returns. Unfortunately, neither are we able to find any observable exogenous variables that are unknown to the investors under the asymmetric information assumption. Thus, following JWW (1993), we do not use an instrumental-variable or 2SLS approach in estimating equation (6.5).

The logit regression estimates are presented in Table 6.10. The slope coefficient for $IPORETN$ (t-statistic) is 0.001326 (2.1301), which indicates a positive relationship between the degree of IPO underpricing and the probability for a firm to issue SEOs.

To compare the explanatory power of the signaling versus market feedback hypotheses, we calculate $\left(\partial P^{SEO}/\partial IPORETN\right) \cdot dIPORETN$ and $\left(\partial P^{SEO}/\partial AFTRETN1\right) \cdot dAFTRETN1$ and evaluate these two expressions using the standard deviation of the respective regressors, obtaining 4.2 and 0.80, respectively, implying that a one standard-deviation increase in IPO return is associated with an increase in the magnitude of the probability of an SEO that is more than five times larger than a one standard-deviation increase in after-market return over the first two weeks of market trading after the IPO date. Since the estimated coefficient for $AFTRETN2$ is much smaller and not significantly different from zero, we conclude that the empirical power of the market signaling hypothesis is greater than that of the market feedback hypothesis.

To test the implication that firms with larger IPO underpricing tend to issue a larger amount of seasoned equities, we estimate a Tobit regression that relates IPO underpricing and after-market returns to the ratio of the market value of all SEOs to the firm's intrinsic value which is proxied by the sum of the proceeds from IPO and all SEOs,[5]

$$\left(\frac{SEOVALUE}{INTRINSC}\right)_i = \begin{cases} \delta_0 + \delta_1 IPORETN_i \\ +\delta_2 AFTRETN1_i \\ +\delta_3 AFTRETN2_i + \varepsilon_i & \text{if RHS} > 0 \\ 0 & \text{otherwise} \end{cases} \tag{6.6}$$

The coefficient estimates of equation (6.6) are contained in Table 6.11. The coefficient estimate for $IPORETN$ (t-statistic) is 0.00003 (6.13), which indicates that the higher the IPO underpricing, the larger is the size of seasoned equity issues.

To compare the relative explanatory power of the signaling and market feedback hypotheses, we follow the same procedure as with the estimates of equation (6.5) and calculate $\left(\partial\left(\frac{SEOVALUE}{INTRINSC}\right)/\partial IPORETN\right)\cdot dIPORETN$ and $\left(\partial\left(\frac{SEOVALUE}{INTRINSC}\right)/\partial AFTRETN1\right)\cdot dAFTRETN1$ using the standard deviation of the respective regressors. We obtain 0.09 and 0.05, indicating that a one standard-deviation increase in IPO return and first two-week after market return are associated, respectively, with an increase in relative SEO size of 10% and 5%, respectively. This comparison suggests that the signaling hypothesis has almost twice as much "strength" in explaining SEO relative magnitude than does the market-feedback hypothesis. As with the probability of an SEO, the coefficient estimate for $AFTRETN2$ is positive, but is statistically insignificant. We conclude that while the Tobit regression estimates support the signaling models relating A-share IPO underpricing to the relative size of SEOs, they do not allow us to reject the alternative

[5]We allow until January 1, 1996 for a firm to issue its first SEO. About 91% of the firms that went public between December 1986 and June 1994 issued subsequent equity offerings before this date. Because our sample is censored as of the cutoff date of January 1, 1996, a Tobit specification is desirable.

Table 6.11 Tobit Regression Estimates for the Relationship Among IPO Underpricing, After-Market Returns and Size of SEOs

Variable[a]	Coefficient	t-statistic
Constant	0.4312*	(25.8477)
$IPORETN$	0.0000309*	(6.127)
$AFTRETN1$	0.002015*	(2.6024)
$AFTRETN2$	0.000483	(0.5501)

[a]The dependent variable is the ratio of total seasoned equity offerings as a fraction of the intrinsic value for the ith firm $\left(\frac{SEOSZ}{MKTCAP}\right)_i$. The independent variables are the observed IPO initial return ($IPORETN$), after-market first two-week return ($AFTRETN1$) and after-market next two-week return ($AFTRETN2$). We allow 548 days for a firm to issue SEOs, therefore our sample only consists of firms who went public between December 1986 and June 1994. There are 268 firms in the sample. Figures in parentheses are asymptotic t-statistics. *, † denote 5% and 10% level of significance, respectively.

hypothesis that the size of SEOs is also partially related to after-market returns.

Finally, we examine the relationship between IPO underpricing and the time elapsed between the IPO and the first SEO using the following Tobit model:

$$TIMESEO_i = \begin{cases} \gamma_0 + \gamma_1 IPORETN_i \\ +\gamma_2 AFTRETN1_i \\ +\gamma_3 AFTRETN2_i + \varepsilon_i & \text{if RHS} > 0 \\ 0 & \text{otherwise} \end{cases} \tag{6.7}$$

where $TIMESEO$ is the number of days elapsed between the IPO date and the first SEO date.

The Tobit regression estimates are presented in Table 6.12. The slope coefficient (t-statistic) for $IPORETN$ is -0.002 (-0.52), indicating that firms with a higher degree of IPO underpricing tend to return to the secondary market and issue seasoned equity offerings more quickly than firms with a lower degree of IPO underpricing and larger IPO sizes, although the estimated coefficient of IPO return is not significant at conventional levels.

In comparing the relative explanatory power of the market-signaling and market-feedback hypotheses, we note that the median time elapsed

Table 6.12 Tobit Regression Estimates for the Relationship Between IPO Underpricing, After-Market Returns and Time Elapsed Between IPO and First SEO

Variable[a]	Coefficient	t-statistic
Constant	291.0871*	(22.3196)
$IPORETN$	-0.00222	(-0.5245)
$AFTRETN1$	1.0864*	(2.2203)
$AFTRETN2$	0.7852	(0.9593)

[a]The dependent variable is the number of days between the IPO date and the first SEO date for the ith firm $TIMESEO$. The independent variables are the observed IPO initial return ($IPORETN$), after-market first two-week return ($AFTRETN1$) and after-market next two-week return ($AFTRETN2$). We allow 548 days for a firm to issue SEOs, therefore our sample only consists of firms who went public between December 1986 and June 1994. There are 268 firms in the sample. Figures in parentheses are asymptotic t-statistics. *, † denote 5% and 10% level of significance, respectively.

between IPO and SEO dates is almost twenty weeks, far longer than the period over which we measure after-market returns. Thus, we predict a negative coefficient on the two after-market return variables as evidence supporting the market-feedback hypothesis. However, the estimated coefficients (t-statistic) for $AFTRETN1$ and $AFTRETN2$ are 1.09 (2.22) and 0.79 (0.96), respectively, which we interpret as contradictory to the market-feedback hypothesis.

To summarize, we find strong evidence from the Chinese A-share data that supports the signaling models that link IPO underpricing to SEOs. We find that Chinese issuers who underprice their A-share IPOs more heavily are more likely to return to the secondary market and issue larger amounts of after-market equities. The alternative, namely, the market feedback hypothesis, does not fare as well in explaining the high underpricing in the data.

6.6 Bribery and Lottery Hypotheses of IPO Underpricing

6.6.1 *Bribery Hypothesis: Underpricing of Chinese IPOs are Gifts to Public Officials or Favored Purchasers*

Allen and Faulhaber (1989) show that underpricing implies an excess demand for IPO shares. It follows that either the issuing firm or its agent (e.g. the underwriter) has power to allocate valuable assets to favored associates in return for their loyalty, favors, or whatever. In this context it seems natural to consider that issuers may allocate underpriced shares to politicians or bureaucrats who have substantial control over some of their planned resources. For example, under the quota system in China, a firm is not unlikely to allocate underpriced shares to bureaucrats in order to gain permission to issue shares[6]

We reject *a priori* the likelihood that bribery by underpinning under the alternative frameworks of full information or a pooling equilibrium with asymmetric information between issuers and investors accounts for observed IPO returns in China. Why should a firm underprice its entire IPO in order to create an opportunity to bribe a few officials? This seems very costly indeed, given that other means are available. It would be much cheaper for the firms to transfer funds directly to bureaucrats in order to gain favors. Admittedly, there may be a few cases involving very small IPOs where the extra cost of using underpricing as a bribe relative to alternative means is minimal, but we believe that such occurrences, if they exist, do not shape the broad pattern of underpricing observed in the data.

As a test of the importance of bribery in the IPO process, we conjecture, that with bribery, many bribe recipients would want to sell their underpriced shares as quickly as they can, or as soon as the stock prices go up after market trading begins, leading to significant depression of returns in the secondary market. Moreover, high-quality firms that allocate underpriced shares to gain permission to go public will be more likely to delay their SEOs to avoid depressing stock prices further and give the politicians or bureaucrats a chance to cash in.

Evidence pertaining to the price-depression effect noted above can be deduced from calculating alternative measures of IPO underpricing, using the after-market price from the first day, first week, second week, and subsequent weeks' closing prices. We find that compared to the first-day IPO return, which has a mean of 948.59% (with a minimum of -18.58% and maximum of 38300%), the average degree of IPO underpricing using first-week, second-week, third-week and fourth-week market closing prices remains approximately the same, 950.98%, 955.9%, 950.49%, and 898.39%,

[6]Note that bribery itself can be construed as a signal of firm value in that only a firm that expects to recoup its investment in bribery will bribe. It is questionable, however, whether a bribe can be a signal to the average investor, who presumably is not privy to the illicit transaction.

respectively. (The minimums are -17.64%, -27.95%, -38.72%, -42.05% and the maximums 48920%, 50410%, 52210%, and 52470%, respectively.) We take this as evidence that bribes (if they occurred) were not "cashed in" during the first four weeks of market trading. Since IPO underpricing was the largest at the early stage of development of stock markets in China when regulations governing new issues were not yet well developed, it is natural to suspect that this was a fertile period for bribery. Therefore we calculate different measurement of the average degree of IPO underpricing for 29 firms that went public before the emergence of formal stock markets. However, we do not find any evidence of a large after-market price drop for these issues, either[7].

We also note that the estimation results from the Tobit regression 6.7, offers no evidence that a higher IPO return is associated with a delay in offering SEOs. In addition, the average time elapsed between the first-day market trading and SEO dates for those 29 firms going public before the establishment of formal stock markets is 254 days, which is less than the overall average of 284 days for the entire sub-sample of firms going public before July 1994. We take this as additional evidence against the bribery hypothesis.

To sum up, while bribery may in principal be a byproduct of underpricing in a separating equilibrium under asymmetric information, direct evidence is by the nature of the process difficult to find. We find little if any indirect evidence that bribery occurred in a large enough proportion of cases to cause to observable effects on aftermarket returns and/or the timing of SEOs. We conclude that the signaling hypothesis characterized by a separating equilibrium seems to be capable of explaining the a substantial portion of underpricing behavior of the Chinese firms.

[7]The average degree of underpricing for 29 new issues that went public before the emergence of formal stock markets using the first-day market price is 5664.29%. (The minimum is 748% and the maximum is 38300%.) The average degree of IPO underpricing using first-week, second-week, third-week and fourth-week market closing prices for these 29 new issues is 6053.4%, 6181.39%, 6230.83%, and 5964.11%, respectively. (The minimum is 782%, 728%, 679%, 610%, and the maximum is 48920%, 50410%, 52210%, and 52470%, respectively.)

6.6.2 *Lottery Hypothesis: Lottery Mechanism in Share Allocation Contributes to High IPO Underpricing*

Five different offering mechanisms have been used in allocating A - shares in China. They are: a lottery mechanism with a fixed number of application forms ($OD(1)$), a lottery mechanism with an unlimited number of application forms ($OD(2)$), a lottery mechanism based on certificate of deposit receipts ($OD(3)$), an auction mechanism with only quantity bids and fixed IPO prices ($OD(4)$), and an auction mechanism with quantity and price bids ($OD(5)$). A team of World Bank specialists argued that offering mechanisms affected the degree of underpricing ("China: The Emerging Capital Markets" Vol. II, p. 96).

> ... the allocation mechanism adopted for the new share issue affects the degree of underpricing. Non-discretionary allocation of shares, by mechanisms such as a lottery, exacerbate the tendency to underprice.

We disagree with their assertion. It was hypothesized and empirically supported that a lower offer price and smaller IPO size leads to higher IPO underpricing. As mentioned in previous sections, IPO underpricing implies an excess demand for shares initially and necessitates some form of non-price rationing. All types of lottery mechanisms and auction mechanism with only quantity bids are best viewed as simply means to allocate oversubscribed shares, and do not determine the after-market demand for shares and/or the initial supply of shares. Therefore, these mechanism themselves do not cause IPO underpricing. An alternative to the lottery, an auction in which both price and quantity bids are submitted, does create an offer price that is not predetermined by the issuing firm. Investors are invited to submit a single bid for the price they are willing to pay and the amount of shares they are willing to purchase. The final offer price is set at a level where the accumulative quantity demanded equal the amount of new shares available. In case of oversubscription, shares are allocated on a pro rata basis. Eighteen firms used this mechanism in issuing and allocating new shares prior to January, 1996. The average degree of IPO underpricing is only 1.04% for these 18 issues, which is negligible. It is critically important to note that these firms *chose* the auction method when a lottery mechanisms was available. With the choice of share-allocation mechanism endogenous, it would be difficult to conclude that the auction led to virtually zero underpricing. Rather, the opposite may be inferred, namely, that these firms chose not to signal their quality by underpricing and used the auction mechanism as a means to assure they received the largest possible revenue at the IPO, because they had little nor no intention of returning to the secondary market with SEOs.

Even though we reject *a priori* the notion that the IPO allocation mechanisms in China have *caused* the large magnitudes of underpricing observed, we nevertheless find it interesting to investigate the relationship between offering mechanisms and IPO initial return cross-sectionally, holding constant the variables associated with IPO return under the hypothesis of asymmetric information with a separating equilibrium. To do this, we reformulate equation (6.3) as follows, which we estimate using 2SLS:

$$\begin{aligned} \ln IPORETN_i &= \eta_0 + \eta_1 \ln \widehat{IPOSZ}_i + \eta_2 \ln \widehat{MKTCAP}_i \\ &\quad + \eta_3 \widehat{STD}_i + \eta_4 LD_i + \nu_i \end{aligned} \tag{6.8}$$

where

LD = dummy variable that takes value 1 if a firm uses a lottery mechanism or auction mechanism with only quantity bids in allocating shares and 0 if it uses auction mechanism with both quantity and price bids.

The estimation results presented in Table 6.13 show that the coefficient for LD variable is highly positively significant, indicating that underpricing is present under lottery mechanisms and auction mechanism with only quantity bids. Under the auction mechanism with both price and quantity bids, which is designed to eliminate excess demand for shares at the first place, underpricing is on average negligible.

We also test the hypothesis that the mean IPO underpricing differs under different offering mechanisms by estimating the following expansion of equation (6.1) using 2SLS:

$$\begin{aligned} \ln IPORETN_i &= \theta_0 + \theta_1 \ln \widehat{IPOSZ}_i + \theta_2 \ln \widehat{MKTCAP}_i \\ &\quad + \theta_3 \widehat{STD}_i + \theta_l OD(l)_i + \nu_i \end{aligned} \tag{6.9}$$

The estimation results in Table 6.13 show that underpricing is on average larger under the various lottery mechanisms than under the auction mechanisms. In particular, IPO underpricing is the largest under the lottery with fixed number of application forms, is the second largest under the lottery with unlimited number of application forms, and is the smallest under auction mechanisms. To interpret these results, we emphasize that when more than one mechanism was available, as they were in 1993 through 1995, choice of mechanism was endogenous. We reiterate that under a asymmetric information with a separating equilibrium, underpricing is a signal for firm's true value, there will be excess demand for shares and some type of offering mechanism has to be used to eliminate the excess demand. Offering mechanisms themselves do *not* cause underpricing.

6.7 Underpricing of Foreign-Share IPOs

We now examine the underpricing of B-share IPOs using data for 57 firms that issued both A and B shares between February 1992 and January 1996. Table 6.14 presents the sample statistics for firms issuing both A and B shares. The average degree of IPO initial returns is 37.13% for the 57 B shares but is 838.91% for the corresponding 57 A shares. A further comparison of the sample statistics in Tables 6.2 and 6.14 shows that, on average, firms issuing both A- and B-shares have experienced smaller degree of IPO underpricing than firms who raise equity capital only in China. The difference in average IPO underpricing raises two questions: First, why will a firm issue foreign-owned B shares? Second, what determines the differences in underpricing of these two classes of shares?

We believe that Chinese firms issue foreign-owned shares to: (1) obtain foreign capital that is otherwise difficult to get under government's foreign currency control regime; (2) expand markets for raising funds and enhance the reputation of the firm. Therefore, firms with larger stock-market capitalization and better performance in terms of higher profit before the IPOs are more likely to issue B shares than firms with smaller stock-market capitalization and smaller profit per share. A comparison of the sample statistics in Table 6.14 with those for all firms issuing shares in Table 6.2 shows that on average, Chinese firms that offer B shares are considerably larger in terms of total market capitalization; have higher profit before the IPOs; have larger total offerings of A shares; and have experienced smaller degree

Table 6.13 2SLS Regression Estimates for the Relationship Between IPO Underpricing and Offering Mechanisms

	Full sample[a]		Sub-sample	
$CONSTANT$	-3.6962*	-2.4563*	-4.5103*	-3.1875*
	(-2.624)	(-1.9631)	(-2.8844)	(-2.2574)
$\ln \widehat{IPOSZ}$	-1.4253*	-0.9214*	-1.3736*	-0.927*
	(-17.6848)	(-11.0507)	(-15.8996)	(-10.6195)
$\ln \widehat{MKTCAP}$	0.8819*	0.6002*	0.8947*	0.6327*
	(11.2355)	(8.2209)	(10.2935)	(7.8407)
$\widehat{STD}$	8.8957*	4.2494*	8.7891*	4.3763*
	(4.075)	(2.2415)	(4.0686)	(2.2835)
LD	1.3404*		1.4428*	
	(12.9301)		(12.5193)	
$OD1$		2.942*		2.9669*
		(16.1233)		(14.6956)
$OD2$		1.9509*		1.9991*
		(11.6627)		(10.5858)
$OD3$		1.2655*		1.2849*
		(6.7202)		(6.0654)
$OD4$		0.8824*		0.8319*
		(4.6508)		(3.7219)
$\bar{R}^2$	0.7565	0.8319	0.7467	0.8198

[a]The dependent variable is the logarithm of IPO initial return ($\ln IPORETN$). The independent variables are the instrument for the logarithm of the size of initial offerings ($\ln \widehat{IPOSZ}$), instrument for the logarithm of firm's intrinsic value ($\ln \widehat{MKTCAP}$), instrument for the project variance ($\widehat{STD}$) and lottery dummy (LD) or offering mechanism dummies ($OD(l)$). Figures in parentheses are t-statistics and *, † denote 5% and 10% level of significance, respectively.

of IPO underpricing and larger after-market returns on their A shares than the firms that have not offered B shares.

A convenient way to sort out the characteristics distinguishing Chinese firms that offer B shares from those of firms that offer only A shares is to estimate the following logit model, which I apply to all firms issuing A shares.

$$\ln\left(\frac{P_i^B}{1-P_i^B}\right) = \phi_0 + \phi_1 IPORETN_i + \phi_2 \ln IPOVALUE_i$$

Table 6.14 Descriptive Statistics for Variables to Explain B-share IPO Initial Returns

Variable	Mean	Median	Std. dev.	Min.	Max.
		57 B-share IPOs			
IPORETN	37.13%	21.43%	47.55%	-21.14%	236.45%
*AFTRETN*1	-0.0502	-0.0455	0.1425	-0.542	0.24
*AFTRETN*2	0.0393	0	0.2156	-0.275	1.0933
$\ln P_0$	-0.7009	-0.7351	0.4333	-1.812	0.3834
LNIPOSZ	7.7492	7.6535	0.7936	6.528	9.8601
LNTOSIZE	10.553	10.3187	1.0204	8.5172	13.517
LNEMPLOY	5.7674	5.8295	0.6972	3.3322	7.1493
LNGOVNT	6.058	8.4683	4.5147	0	11.113
LNPROFIT	8.5055	8.3707	0.8856	7.001	11.175
LNAGE	2.6791	2.3979	0.9309	1.0986	4.3307
TIMEIPO	71.807	44	81.98	6	348
IPOVALUE	33.71	21.08	38.85	6.84	191.52
INTRINSC	297.91	192.54	318.70	60.44	1856.43
		57 Corresponding A-share IPOs			
IPORETN	8.3891	2.7059	12.27	0.0457	45.143
*AFTRETN*1	0.0172	-0.0221	0.3061	-0.9257	1.335
*AFTRETN*2	-0.018	-0.0631	0.2244	-0.8535	0.9444
$\ln P_0$	-0.5691	-0.5147	0.433	-1.7492	0.2249
LNIPOSZ	9.1039	9.1844	0.7826	6.1137	10.751
LNTOSIZE	11.14	11.2241	1.053	8.2941	13.081
TIMEIPO	208.54	142	225.13	3	980
IPOVALUE	14.15	11.74	11.32	0.54	56.23
TIMEIPO	208.54	142	225.13	3	980

$$+\phi_3 \ln INTRINSC_i + \phi_4 \ln PROFIT_i$$
$$+\phi_5 \ln TIMEIPO_i + \phi_6 AFTRETN1_i$$
$$+\phi_7 AFTRETN2_i + \phi_k SIC(k)_i \tag{6.10}$$

where P_i^B is the probability that the ith firm will issue B shares after it has offered A shares. $P_i^B = 1$ if firm i issues B shares and 0 otherwise.

The logit regression estimates presented in Table 6.15 indicate that:

(1) Holding constant the firm's stock-market capitalization, the smaller the size of A-share IPO, the more likely the firm will issue B shares.

Table 6.15 Logit Regression Estimates for the Probability A Firm Will Issue B Shares

Variable[a]	Coefficient	t-statistic
$CONSTANT$	-30.99*	(-5.42)
$IPORETN$	-0.00012	(-1.04)
$AFTRETN1$	0.011†	(1.94)
$AFTRETN2$	0.009	(1.06)
$\ln IPOVALUE$	-1.86*	(-4.98)
$\ln PROFIT$	0.48†	(1.86)
$\ln INTRINSC$	1.73*	(5.73)
$\ln TIMEIPO$	-0.41*	(-2.05)
$SIC1$	1.18	(1.56)
$SIC2$	1.95*	(2.32)
$SIC3$	0.36	(0.41)
$SIC4$	-0.74	(-0.56)
$SIC5$	0.93	(0.88)

[a]The dependent variable is the probability for the ith firm to issue B shares after it completes offering A shares (P_i^B). The independent variables are the IPO initial return ($IPORETN$), logarithm of IPO proceeds excluding B-share offerings ($\ln IPOVALUE$), logarithm of firm's intrinsic value excluding B-share offerings ($\ln INTRINSC$), after-market first two-week return ($AFTRETN1$), after-market next two-week return ($AFTRETN2$), logarithm of past year's profit prior to IPO ($\ln PROFIT$), logarithm of time elapsed between the offer date and the first trading date ($\ln TIMEIPO$). We also allow the probability of issuing B shares to vary across industries ($SIC(k)$). Figures in parentheses are asymptotic t-statistics. *, † denote 5% and 10% level of significance, respectively.

(2) Holding constant the IPO size, the larger the firm's stock-market capitalization, the more likely the firm will issue B shares.
(3) The larger the profit prior to the IPO, the more likely it will issue B shares.
(4) The smaller the degree of IPO underpricing, or the higher the after-market return on its A shares, the more likely it will offer B shares.
(5) The shorter the time elapsed between the announcement of A-share IPO and first-day trading, or the more efficient the firm's A-share IPO process, the more likely it will issue B shares.

One of the most interesting features distinguishing the IPO process for B shares from that of A shares is that lottery mechanism has never been used in allocating B shares. Moreover, foreign securities firms such as Sassoon and J. P. Morgan are allowed to participate in the B-share underwriting process. The IPO prices for B shares are announced approximately one month prior to the target market trading date and foreign investors are invited to bid for the quantity of shares they wish to purchase. The absence of lottery mechanisms for B shares indicates that in contrast to A shares, oversubscription is not a big problem in the new issue and offering process for B shares. There is no persistent excess demand for B shares by foreign investors at a "normal" price-earning ratio. Therefore, it is very likely that the difference in the average degree of underpricing between A and B shares can be explained by the differences in domestic and foreign investors' available investment opportunities as well as the differences in their investment sentiments.

When we apply the above empirical tests for the signaling models to the B-share data, we find that neither signaling hypothesis nor the market feedback hypothesis discussed in Section 4 appears capable of explaining the underpricing of B-share IPOs. However, when we estimate the benchmark model (6.1) for the cross-sectional differences in underpricing for B-share IPOs, we find that available information about the issuers, as reflected in past profit prior to the IPOs, is positively and significantly related to the IPO initial return. These two contrasts are consistent in the sense that both suggest foreign investors rely more on information gathered prior to purchasing shares than do domestic investors. A complementary explanation is that Chinese firms participating in both domestic and foreign share markets are those that can signal their quality through available information about their histories and performance and do not need to "signal" as strongly as firms participating only in domestic equity markets through the mechanism of underpricing their IPOs. A comparison of the A-share sample statistics in Table 6.14 with those in Table 6.2 show that the difference between the logarithms of total offering size and IPO size is 2.04 for the subsample of firms issuing B shares and only 1.70 for the entire sample of firms issuing both A-share IPOs and SEOs, while the mean IPO initial return for the subsample is about 20% less than for the entire sample of firms that make both IPOs and SEOs. These comparisons suggest that the subsample participating in international equity markets do not need to underprice their IPOs to the same extent as firms issuing only A shares to stimulate demand for their SEOs.

6.8 Long-run Performance of IPOs

Recent work by Ritter (1991) and Loughran and Ritter (1995) has documented that in the long-run, the U.S. IPOs are overpriced. The long-run underperformance of IPOs has been confirmed in many countries (Loughran, Ritter, and Rydqvist, 1994). Ritter (1991) and Loughran and Ritter (1995) interpret the long-run underperformance of IPOs as indicating that the high initial returns at the offering dates occur due to over-reactions by investors. They also argue that managers have some ability to time their offerings for periods when investors are over-optimistic.

Shiller (1984) and De Bondt and Thaler (1985, 1987) argue that a stock price may temporarily deviate from its fundamental value due to over-optimism or over-pessimism on the part of investors. Fads or over-reactions by investors are more likely to occur for small, less certain stocks or stocks held by "noise traders" such as individual investors (Camerer, 1989, Lee, Shleifer and Thaler, 1991, and Chopra, Lakonishok and Ritter, 1992). IPO firms are, by nature, small and less certain than listed firms and tend to be held by individual investors. Thus, IPOs are a good candidate for investigating fads or investors' over-reactions. One of the empirical implications which follows from the over-reaction hypothesis is: the greater the initial return at the IPO date is, the greater the degree of subsequent correction of overpricing will tend to be (Shiller, 1990).

As a long-run performance measure, we use (1) cumulative benchmark-adjusted return and (2) the wealth relative. Both measures do not include the first partial-month return. The average benchmark-adjusted return on a portfolio of n stocks for event month t, AR_t, is defined as

$$AR_t = \frac{1}{n}\sum_{i=1}^{n} ar_{it} \tag{6.11}$$

The cumulative benchmark-adjusted return on event month t, CAR_t, is defined as

$$CAR_t = \sum_{j=1}^{t} AR_j \tag{6.12}$$

The wealth relative based on the holding period return is used as an alternative of cumulative benchmark-adjusted returns. The holding period return on firm i from the closing price for the first partial-month to the closing price for event month t, R_{it}, is defined as

$$R_{it} = \frac{p_{it} - p_{i,1}}{p_{i,1}} \tag{6.13}$$

where $p_{i,t}$ is the closing price for the tth calendar month if $t \geq 2$, and is the closing price for the first partial month if $t = 1$. The holding period return on the benchmark during the corresponding period for firm i, $R^i_{m,t}$, is similarly calculated. The wealth relative of n IPOs up to event month t, WR_t, is obtained by

$$WR_t = \frac{1 + \frac{1}{n}\sum_{i=1}^{n} R_{i,t}}{1 + \frac{1}{n}\sum_{i=1}^{n} R^i_{m,t}} \tag{6.14}$$

A wealth relative of less than 1 can be interpreted as IPOs underperforming a benchmark. For the cross-sectional analysis of long-run performance, we calculate the wealth relative up to month t for firm i, WR^i_t, as

$$WR^i_t = \frac{1 + R_{i,t}}{1 + R^i_{m,t}} \tag{6.15}$$

Ritter (1991) suggests that the long-run performance of IPOs is sensitive to the selection of benchmarks. We use the Shanghai and Shenzhen A-share indices as benchmark. Since the returns on IPO firms do not include dividends, the returns on Shanghai and Shenzhen A-share indices also do not include dividends.

Tables 6.16–6.17 shows the average benchmark-adjusted returns (AR_t) and the cumulative benchmark-adjusted returns (CAR_t) excluding the first partial-month returns over the 36 months of seasoning after the IPO month. t-statistics for AR_t is calculated as $(AR_t\sqrt{n_t}/sd_t)$ where n_t is the number of observations in event month t and sd_t is the cross-section standard deviation of benchmark-adjusted returns in month t. t-statistics for CAR_t is calculated as $(CAR_t\sqrt{n_t})/\sqrt{t \cdot var + 2(t-1)cov}$ where var is the average of the cross-section variance over 36 months and cov is the first-order autocovariance of the AR_t series. We use Shanghai and Shenzhen A-share indices as benchmark for Shanghai and Shenzhen IPOs, respectively. Figure 6.1 plots the CAR series for Shanghai and Shenzhen IPOs.

Table 6.16 Average Benchmark-adjusted Returns and Cumulative Benchmark-adjusted Returns for Shanghai IPOs in December 1990–December 1995

Month of Seasoning	AR_t	t-statistic	CAR_t	t-statistic
2	-0.008	-1.13	-0.008	-0.81
3	0.012	1.71	0.04	0.36
4	0.009	1.13	0.013	0.95
5	-0.008	-1.16	0.005	0.34
6	-0.028	-4.46	-0.023	-1.37
7	-0.006	-0.92	-0.029	-1.61
8	-0.012	-2.16	-0.041	-2.13
9	-0.017	-2.48	-0.058	-2.84
10	-0.005	-0.71	-0.063	-2.92
11	0.005	0.81	-0.058	-2.57
12	-0.004	-0.66	-0.062	-2.63
13	-0.009	-1.53	-0.071	-2.92
14	-0.003	-0.49	-0.074	-2.93
15	-0.004	-0.53	-0.078	-2.96
16	0.016	1.93	-0.062	-2.29
17	0.006	0.89	-0.056	-1.99
18	0.004	0.66	-0.052	-1.78
19	-0.007	-1.13	-0.059	-1.97
20	0.007	1.08	-0.052	-1.68
21	-0.008	-1.00	-0.060	-1.91
22	0.008	1.00	-0.052	-1.60
23	-0.002	-0.23	-0.054	-1.61
24	-0.007	-1.18	-0.061	-1.80
25	-0.004	-0.57	-0.065	-1.86
26	-0.012	-2.01	-0.077	-2.17
27	0.012	1.80	-0.065	-1.80
28	-0.002	-0.36	-0.067	-1.83
29	0.015	2.06	-0.052	-1.38
30	0.011	1.25	-0.041	-1.07
31	0.018	2.37	-0.023	-0.58
32	0.012	1.69	-0.011	-0.26
33	-0.002	-0.33	-0.013	-0.32
34	-0.003	-0.54	-0.016	-0.40
35	0.001	0.17	-0.015	-0.37
36	-0.004	-0.53	-0.019	-0.45
37	-0.014	-2.51	-0.033	-0.79

Table 6.17 Average Benchmark-adjusted Returns and Cumulative Benchmark-adjusted Returns for Shenzhen IPOs in December 1990–December 1995

Month of Seasoning	AR_t	t-statistic	CAR_t	t-statistic
2	-0.001	-0.19	-0.001	-0.14
3	0.013	2.10	0.012	1.16
4	0.014	1.92	0.026	2.14
5	0.002	0.29	0.028	2.04
6	-0.027	-5.09	0.001	0.02
7	-0.009	-1.50	-0.008	-0.54
8	-0.013	-2.57	-0.021	-1.28
9	-0.018	-3.03	-0.039	-2.21
10	-0.010	-1.51	-0.049	-2.60
11	-0.004	-0.82	-0.053	-2.70
12	-0.004	-0.75	-0.057	-2.78
13	-0.011	-1.97	-0.068	-3.17
14	-0.008	-1.32	-0.076	-3.39
15	-0.008	-1.38	-0.084	-3.62
16	0.005	0.69	-0.079	-3.29
17	0.004	0.70	-0.075	-3.01
18	0.005	0.87	-0.070	-2.73
19	-0.013	-2.46	-0.083	-3.15
20	0.003	0.58	-0.080	-2.96
21	-0.011	-1.56	-0.091	-3.29
22	0.007	0.86	-0.084	-2.98
23	-0.002	-0.37	-0.086	-2.99
24	-0.006	-1.00	-0.092	-3.12
25	-0.002	-0.30	-0.094	-3.11
26	-0.008	-1.49	-0.102	-3.29
27	0.010	1.77	-0.092	-2.91
28	-0.010	-1.72	-0.102	-3.14
29	0.014	2.24	-0.088	-2.65
30	0.011	1.30	-0.077	-2.29
31	0.011	1.67	-0.066	-1.92
32	0.012	2.07	-0.054	-1.55
33	-0.005	-0.90	-0.059	-1.68
34	0.000	-0.09	-0.059	-1.66
35	0.006	1.08	-0.053	-1.48
36	0.001	0.20	-0.052	-1.42
37	-0.011	-2.18	-0.063	-1.71

For benchmark-adjusted returns in Shanghai, the CAR exhibits a declining pattern for the first 14 months and continues to be significantly negative from month 8 to 17. However, the CAR fluctuates over months 16 to 28 with only 4 months having a statistically significant negative value at the 0.05% level. From months 28 to 37, the CAR recovers and is not significantly different from zero. For benchmark-adjusted returns in Shenzhen, the CAR exhibits a similar pattern. In months 4 and 5, the CAR is significantly positive and then decreases with the month of seasoning up to month 15. From months 16 to 26, the CAR fluctuates, showing a slightly declining pattern. The CAR is significantly negative from months 9 to 30. However, the CAR increases and is only insignificantly negative from months 31 to 37.

The results from the CAR indicate that while the after-market returns on the Chinese IPOs severely underperform the market in the first and second year of seasoning, they on average exhibit less abnormal performance for the longer-term period. The underperformance of IPOs appears to indicate that corrections to overpricing at the offerings are taking place. However, the amount of underperformance (the lowest CARs of -0.077 and -0.102 for Shanghai and Shenzhen A-shares, respectively) is considerably small compared to the high initial return observed in the Chinese data. However, our results could arise simply because we ignore the returns on the first partial-month, which are considerably negative in value.

We now turn to the cross-section analysis of long-run performance of Chinese IPOs, using wealth relatives exclusive of the first partial-month returns. Table 6.18 shows wealth relatives by initial returns.

The results for the wealth relatives by initial return indicate that only the IPOs in the fourth quartile of initial returns underperform the benchmark-adjusted returns for the three-year holding period. This seems to be consistent with the hypothesis that only extremely high initial returns at the IPO dates may be associated with fads or overreactions by investors.

6.9 Summary

In this chapter, we have empirically identified some causes of the cross-sectional differences in underpricing of Chinese IPOs using data compiled for 308 firm-commitment A-share IPOs and 57 B-share IPOs. We first formulate and estimate a benchmark empirical model that relates IPO initial

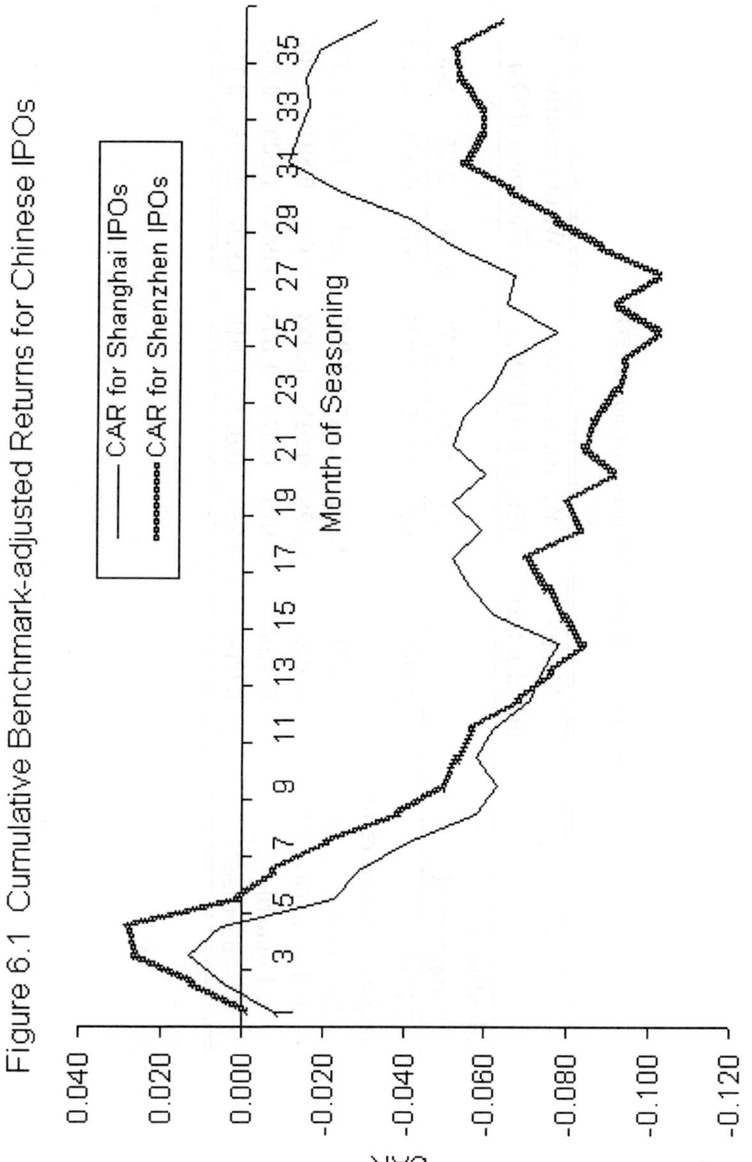

Fig. 6.1 Cumulative Abnormal Returns on and Around Dividend Announcement Day

Table 6.18 Wealth Relatives for Chinese IPOs

	Mean initial return	Wealth relative (Shanghai IPOs)			Wealth relative (Shenzhen IPOs)		
Months of holding period		2-13	2-25	2-37	2-13	2-25	2-37
All IPOs	0.4071	0.945	0.945	0.934	0.942	0.931	0.937
Adjusted initial returns							
1st quartile	0.1201	1.091	1.337	1.236	1.001	1.124	1.070
2nd quartile	0.2231	0.928	0.915	0.953	0.952	0.894	0.902
3rd quartile	0.3496	0.978	0.976	1.053	0.983	1.009	0.902
4th quartile	0.9382	0.788	0.657	0.619	0.826	0.708	0.712

returns to variables widely used in studies of IPO underpricing. Applying this model to A-share IPO data, we find that:

(1) IPO underpricing was largest at the earliest stage of development of stock markets in China.
(2) Available information about a firm at the time of IPO is not related to IPO underpricing.
(3) Time elapsed between the announcement of an IPO and the first market trading day is not related to IPO underpricing.
(4) Durable and non-durable manufacturing industries exhibit higher IPO initial returns than other industries.

We also find that a framework in which IPO underpricing is an equilibrium outcome in a world of uncertainty and information asymmetry is a useful paradigm for understanding the Chinese equity offering process. Underpricing arises to compensate uninformed investors for the "lemon's problem" they face. The extent of insider ownership, IPO size, the content of prospectus, pre-IPO leverage, pre-IPO market conditions, share allocation mechanism, listing exchange, listing time, and the belonging industry are important variables that correlate with *ex ante* uncertainty among investors, and that there is a positive relation between *ex ante* uncertainty and expected underpricing. Consistent with the adverse-selection models, underpricing is significantly smaller for issues in which individual investors know *a priori* that they face little or no winner's curse problem.

Then we contrast implications of the hypothesis of a separating equilibrium where firms signal their quality by retaining shares and underpricing against the alternative hypothesis of a pooling equilibrium where no signaling schedule exists and "underpricing" is unrelated to IPO returns or the subsequent pattern of SEO behavior across firms. We find that the signaling hypothesis explains the pattern of underpricing behavior among Chinese issuers rather well, although the market-feedback hypothesis has some explanatory power and cannot be entirely rejected. On theoretical grounds, we reject the use of alternative IPO-share allocation mechanisms as causes of the observed underpricing behavior. In addition, we believe that while bribery may well help explain the pervasiveness and high level of IPO underpricing in China, its presence is consistent with a signaling explanation of the pattern of underpricing.

Our major findings in support of the signaling hypothesis with a separating equilibrium are:

(1) The correlation between the degree of IPO underpricing and initial offer price for the proportion of the firm offered to the public is negative, given the issuer's retained ownership.
(2) The degree of IPO underpricing is positively related to proxies for the issuer's intrinsic value, the variance of future returns, and the issuer's fractional ownership.
(3) Issuers with larger IPO underpricing are more likely to raise larger amounts of capital through SEOs and to do so more quickly than issuers with a smaller degree of IPO underpricing, although the latter relationship is weak.

When we apply our approach to the B-share data, we find that:

(1) The underpricing of B-share IPOs is on average much smaller than that of A-shares. The difference in IPO underpricing among A- and B-shares can evidently be explained by the differences in domestic and foreign investors' investment opportunities.
(2) Traditional signaling equilibrium models for IPO underpricing do not explain differences in B-share IPO initial returns. Instead, past information about the issuers have better explanatory power. We take this as evidence that international investors in Chinese equities rely more on prior acquisition of information than do Chinese domestic investors. Perhaps this is because the current sample of international investors in Chinese equities is heavily weighted with experienced, professional investors, while the vast majority of Chinese investors in A-shares are inexperienced in equity markets.

We also examine the over-reaction hypothesis by analyzing the long-run performance of IPOs. For the average IPOs, our empirical results indicate that long-run underperformance of IPOs is consistent with cross-section implications of overreaction hypothesis.

Despite our faith in the hypothesis that underpricing of Chinese IPOs can be explained in terms of a separating equilibrium under asymmetric equilibrium, we still face the question, why is the degree of underpricing in China so very large? We note that the mean IPO return was over 5700% for offerings made before 1991(when formal stock markets commenced), about 133% in 1991, and it declined steadily to "only" 69% by 1995. We believe that three factors help explain the extraordinarily high (and declining) level of underpricing: (1) the initial dearth of financial instruments others than savings accounts for Chinese investors, compared to other countries with lower IPO returns; (2) the large degree of uncertainty and information asymmetry inherent in China's transition to a market economy with modern financial markets and the initial lack of sophistication of domestic Chinese investors; and (3) the very long time between IPO dates and the first day of market trading for IPOs issued before the inception of formal stock markets. Obviously, our "casual" empiricism on this fascinating and important topic must eventually be bolstered by rigorous empirical analysis that is beyond the scope of the present paper. A rigorous test of the hypothesis that the differences in underpricing between two classes of shares can be explained by differences in investors' investment opportunity sets and differences in their methods of formulating expected returns on investments requires explicit modeling of firms' share supply decisions and investors' portfolio choices. Moreover, we have not considered possible rent-seeking behavior by the government or individuals who have access to the limited quota during the new-issue and offering process. These problems await further research.

Chapter 7

Corporate Governance and Post-IPO Financing

The Chinese government, wishing to avoid the political and economic turmoil that accompanied the mass privatizations of the former Soviet Union and other Eastern European governments, has chosen as a cornerstone of its political survival the commercialization and partial privatization of claims over profits and assets of its state-owned enterprises (SOEs). In general, government is reluctant to initiate deep institutional reform and is loath to surrender its control over enterprises, because doing so increases the cost of maintaining political support in the form of attaining worker satisfaction and a "quiet" population. At the same time, the inefficiencies and waste inherent in socialist economies in practice limit government's ability to maintain its base without resorting to totalitarian controls that have proven impossible to sustain in a few societies. Therefore, privatization of SOEs has been adopted only because it is the only viable means to assure the survival of the existing political order, which in the case of China, means the survival of the Chinese Communist Party. The government, by reforming the agricultural industry, restructuring SOEs via partial privatization, and encouraging rapid growth of Township and Village Enterprises, seeks to obtain the benefits of a market economy for mobilization of private savings, economic growth and an improved standard of living, while retaining political control. In this chapter, we analyze post-IPO financing choices of newly privatized SOEs as they reflect conflicts between government's desire to retain political control, private investors' desire for return on their investment, and management's desire to appropriate resources for its own benefit. We thus hope to shed some light on the costs and benefits of partial privatization.

7.1 Shareholders' Behavior and Corporate Governance

One of the main goals of China's enterprise reforms is to clarify property rights and delineate the roles of the state and of the enterprises. In 1992, a new regulation gave managers of SOEs "Fourteen Autonomous Management Rights", including the right to set prices, the right to hire and fire workers, and so on. Implementation was uneven, however, with few industrial companies enjoying all 14 rights. The transformation of SOEs into commercially oriented companies was proceeding slowly.

Under China's company law, an enterprise's investor must be identified in the corporate articles of association, a daunting task. It is not a question simply of tracing funds but, rather, of assigning property rights. The competing claimants various government departments and agencies often cannot reach consensus on who the investor is to be. This dilemma is compounded inasmuch as most SOEs have large liabilities. Everybody wants the assets, but nobody wants the liabilities. With the unclear assignment of property rights, there is an asymmetry in the allocation of rights and obligations for good and bad assets. In effect, while assets are privatized, liabilities are socialized. Property rights are fuzzy because government departments and agencies exercise the roles of both shareholder and administrator. Indeed, multiple government departments exercise the shareholder role. Across agencies both horizontally and vertically there is fragmentation and partial exercise of the ownership function, with no single entity responsible for the enterprise's bottom line. Consequently, managers enjoy more autonomy than is officially sanctioned, and, without proper checks and balances, are able to engage in opportunistic behavior.

In 1995, China initiated the "Modern Enterprise System" which aimed to transform the SOEs into modern shareholding corporations. However, the profitability and operational efficiency of SOEs have not improved by the introduction of the system, partly because of the lack of effective monitoring system of management. The state, as an owner of the SOEs, has failed to adequately supervise management because of high costs associated with checking the performance of management. Under such circumstance, managers of the SOEs are able to operate their enterprises according to their own interests without being disciplined by owners. The management without owners' supervision inevitably gives rise to inefficiency. Therefore, it is significant for the SOEs to construct effective corporate governance structure for monitoring management and improving their efficiency.

7.1.1 *Organizational Structure and Board Composition*

The primary actors of the modern corporation are shareholders, the board of directors, and managers. These three entities can be found in companies in developed countries, although variant forms of organization exist in some countries. Shareholders have all the rights related to property rights. These rights include right to make decisions on production, right to appoint managers, and right to designate investment beneficiaries. Shareholders express their interests through annual meetings which have the supreme control of a company. The board of directors is the top decision-making organ in a company and supervises management on behalf of shareholders. The main responsibility of the board is strategic planning in management decision-making process, such as merger and acquisition, and appointment and dismissal of executives. Managers conduct daily business of the company under the instruction and supervision of the board.

Organizational changes have been the most visible aspects of China's enterprise reform process. In November 1993, the 14th Central Communist Party of China issued *The Decision on Issues Concerning the Establishment of a Socialist Market Economic Structure*, which emphasized the importance of introducing the modern corporate system to the SOEs. In the following year, the State Council announced a nation-wide enterprise experiment based on carefully selected 100 large and medium industrialized firms was conducted by the State Council. The primary objective of the experiment is to transform the SOEs into modern corporations by clearly defining ownership rights and establishing efficient corporate governance structure. The corporatized SOEs are required to set up the board of directors representing owners' interests, to produce separate corporate entities that supervise the management of each enterprise, and to create the supervisory board. An important aspect of effective corporate governance system is the separation of government administrative functions from the commercial functions of the SOEs. Therefore, members of the board usually include outside specialists of business management. This pilot program was formally implemented under the *Company Law* in early 1995.

With the establishment of a network of state asset management institutions and group companies, the State Council, China's cabinet, acts as the ultimate owner of SOEs at the national level on behalf of the Chinese people, with the National Administrative Bureau of State-Owned Property acting as the agent. Similar upper-tier bodies exist in provinces and cities.

An intermediate tier is composed of provincial- and municipal-level holding enterprises and state asset management companies. The SOEs are merely the third tier.

In the newly formed organizational structure, however, the lines of authority are unclear, and the boards of directors and the senior executives are often the same people. In addition, board members are nominated not by commercially oriented owners or their representatives, but by government or party bodies. With few exceptions, sector bureaus and ministries, as well as large enterprises, have been transformed into new entities, but the corporate structure has not been modernized. Many managers see little difference between the old line bureaus and the new entities other than a name change. Not surprisingly, the multi-tiered network is burdened with conflicts of interest that prevent the separation of business from government.

In addition, the shareholders congress is required to obtain permission for their decisions from its upper authorities. The general manager of a shareholding company is usually the director of the board. The chairman of the board is appointed by the government or Party officials rather than by members of the board. Members of the board and the supervisory committee in corporatized SOEs are dominated by government officials or their delegates, and the state shareholders are over-represented in proportion to individual shareholders. Such corporate governance practices inevitably lead to strong government intervention in business decision-making.

7.1.2 *The Role of Government*

In western countries, governments influence enterprise operation mainly through monetary and fiscal policies and regulations. In Japan and other newly industrialized countries, the governments' intervene into targeted sectors using preferential policies such as such as interest subsidies, price subsidies, tax breaks, informational assistance, and regulations concerning technical and quality standards, to name a few. Although situations very across countries, the general principle is that there is a limit of government intervention so that firms can be held accountable for their own losses and profits. Excessive government intervention may cause serious incentive problems that reduce the firms' (including the board and the management) efforts in enhancing performance.

The Chinese SOEs still face interventions from various levels of government, especially from local government agencies. Many expect that the shareholding system can solve the problem of government interference in China. However, evidence from the experimental stock companies suggests that very few companies have achieved this goal. First, the ownership of state property is, in many cases, represented by the industrial bureaus, which, at the same time, oversee branches of industry and issue regulations. Second, it is not always the case that the industrial bureaus initiate the intervention. Some firms tend to rely on industrial bureaus for various preferential treatments regarding credits, materials and subsidies.

The 1992 regulation regarding macro-management of shareholding companies states that the government should gradually reduce its mandatory production plan and wage control, and eliminate investment project approval requirement. This reform is an important breakthrough in the direction of separating government administration from enterprise management. The dilemma is that, however, while the shareholding companies' irrational behaviors are not corrected by some incentive mechanism, many government restrictions are not likely to be removed in the near future. For example, if the companies tend to over- provide benefits to the employees, the government will have to control wages and bonuses. But in the presence of such restrictions, the firms are likely not to be responsible for their own performances.

Table 7.1 shows changes in proportions of the central government's projects and local projects in the total capital construction investment of state-owned sector. Investment decisions of central projects are generally made by the line ministries and the State Planning Commision, and that of local projects are made by local governments and enterprises. It can be seen that after 1992 the local project investments exceeded the central government projects investments. Obviously investment decisions of SOEs are now shared between governments at various level and enterprises.

Paralleling with the down-shifting of investment decisions, financial decisions have been gradually separated from investment decisions, and sources of investment funds have been dispersed. Roughly speaking, state bank loans have taken over the state-budget funds as a dominant financial source of investment of SOEs, regardless of investment decisions being made by governments or enterprises. The retained profits and non-bank debts are also used by SOEs to finance their investment and operation. The state budget funds now account only for the tiny part of the total investment. Furthermore, even these state budget funds have been taken

Table 7.1 Changes of Proportions of Central Projects and Local Projects in Capital Construction Investment of the State Sector (units: 100 million *yuan*)

Year	Total Investment	Central Projects	Local Projects
1985	1074.37	575.24	499.13
1986	1176.11	632.52	543.59
1987	1343.10	761.66	581.44
1988	1574.31	873.71	700.60
1989	1551.74	837.71	714.03
1990	1703.81	919.15	784.67
1991	2115.80	1060.40	1055.37
1992	3012.65	1341.69	1670.96
1993	4615.50	1834.90	2780.60
1994	6436.74	2430.75	4005.99
1995	7403.62	2970.67	4432.95
1996	8610.84	3379.33	5231.50

Source: China Statistical Yearbook 1997

as "loan-for-grant" channeled from the government to enterprises through the state banks rather than directly appropriated to enterprises (that is, in SOE's balance sheet , they are recorded as special debts rather than equity).

Table 7.2 and Figure 7.1 present changes in financial sources of fixed asset investment of the state sector. From the table, we see that the proportion of state budget funds declined from 79% in 1979 to only 4.6% in 1995; domestic loans increased from almost zero in 1979 to 16.2% in 1982, to 23.6% in 1996. We should point out that most of foreign funds were injected as investment loans into enterprises rather than as the government-equity investment. About half of the funds come from bank loans, and only roughly equal part is from retained profits, retained depreciation funds, extra-budget funds of local governments and other sources (such as bonds and shares issued to employees and other institutions). It is typical that enterprises finance their long term fixed investment from short-term bank loans. If we assume 50% of fund-raising and others were bank loans, the total bank loans would account for about 56% of financial sources of fixed investments in 1996.

Based on the above discussion, we can conclude that corporate finance

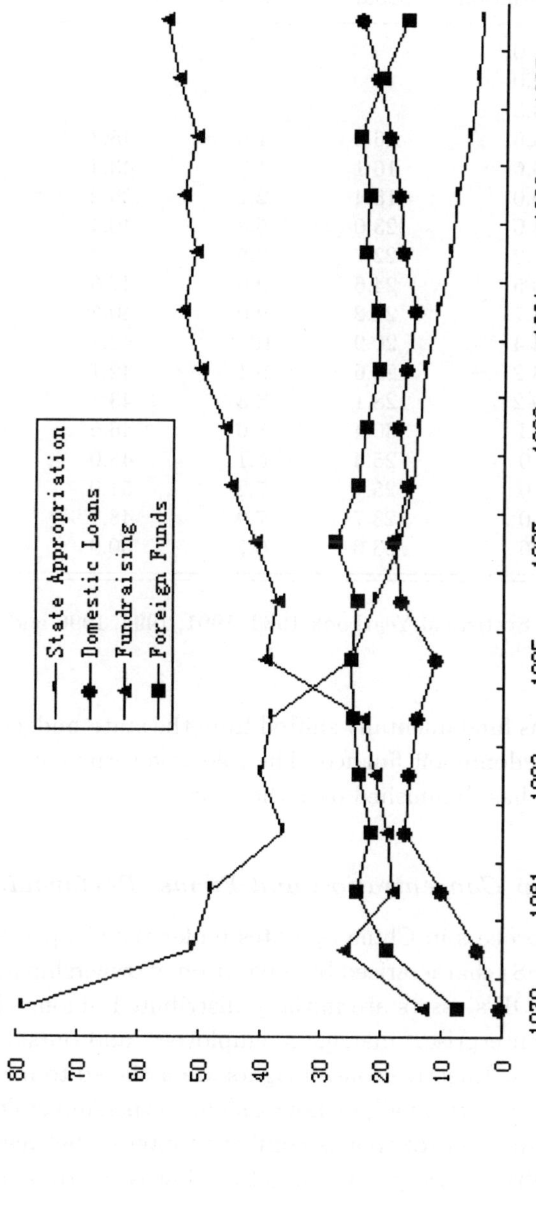

Fig. 7.1 Change in Pattern of Financial Sources of Fixed Asset Investment

Table 7.2 Financial Sources of Fixed Asset Investment (%)

Year	State Appropriation	Domestic Loan	Foreign Funds	Fund-raising	others
1979	79.0				
1980	52.0				
1981	48.5				
1982	36.6	16.2	1.9	45.3	
1983	40.6	16.1	1.7	43.4	
1984	39.0	15.4	2.2	39.2	4.2
1985	24.0	23.0	5.3	40.4	7.3
1986	22.2	22.7	6.5	38.4	10.2
1987	20.5	24.6	9.0	47.6	
1988	14.7	24.2	9.0	40.5	11.7
1989	13.4	20.9	10.2	42.8	12.8
1990	13.2	23.6	9.1	42.1	11.9
1991	10.2	28.1	8.3	43.1	10.3
1992	6.3	30.4	8.0	46.6	8.7
1993	6.0	25.4	6.1	48.0	14.5
1994	5.0	25.7	7.2	51.0	11.6
1995	5.0	23.7	7.9	48.7	15.9
1996	4.6	23.6	6.7	50.9	14.4

Source: China Statistical Yearbook 1983, 1991, 1994, 1996 and 1997

of Chinese SOEs has fundamentally shifted from the state-budget finance to the state bank loan dominant finance. The role of government in corporate financing decisions has diminished over the years.

7.1.3 *Ownership Concentration and Firms' Performance*

The privatization process in China operates under the Cooperative Shareholding System (CSS) characterized by separation of ownership and control. Ownership of an SOE's assets are initially distributed among the government, other state enterprises, managers, employees, and outside domestic and foreign investors. Effective control rights are assigned to management, which generally has a very small, or nonexistent, ownership stake. Separation of ownership and control creates conflict of interest between management and newly enfranchised private investors that is the root cause of the

Table 7.3 Industrial Output of State-Owned and Non-State Owned Enterprises (%)

	1992	1993	1994	1995	1996	1997	1998
State-owned enterprises	51.5	43.1	35.3	31.1	29.4	26.4	25.7
Collectively-owned enterprises	35.1	42.9	50.7	55.9	60.3	62.6	63.0
Individually-owned enterprises	5.8	8.0	10.1	12.9	10.3	11.0	11.3
Other types of ownership	7.6	6.0	4.0				

Source:China Statistical Year Book(1999)

principal-agent problem in traditional corporate finance theory (Jensen and Meckling, 1976). Moreover, because government desires to retain some control (in part through partial retained ownership) of commercialized SOEs, further conflicts arise between politicians and firms (Shleifer and Vishny, 1994).

Although various reform programs have been carried out since 1979, such as decentralization of decision-making on management and enhancement of workers incentives to work, economic performance of the SOEs has not improved as much as that of collective or individual owned enterprises. As Table 7.3 shows, the share of SOEs in total industrial output has been declining, while that of non SOEs have been increasing. As Table 7.4 shows, the ratio of increase in total factor productivity is larger in the non-state sector than in the state sector. Responding to this fact, various discussions about the causes of the SOEs' inefficiency arose, and these arguments can be roughly divided into two schools of thought: ownership focused and market focused ones.

The school of thought that focuses on ownership blames an unclear definition of ownership and the separation between ownership and control for the SOEs' inefficiency. According to them, the state, as an owner of the SOEs, has failed to monitor management effectively because of high supervision costs, and insufficient supervision has allowed managers to pursue their private objectives at the expense of owners' interests such as maximizing the profit of enterprises. As policy makers try to solve the efficiency

Table 7.4 Estimated Rates of Annual Productivity Growth in Chinese Industry (%)

	1980-1984	1984-1988	1988-1992
Total factor productivity			
State sector	1.8	3.0	2.5
Urban and township	3.4	5.9	4.9
Village and private	7.3	6.6	6.9
Labor Productivity			
State sector	3.8	6.2	4.7
Urban and township	8.6	7.0	13.8

Source: Jefferson and Rawski (1994)

problem embedded in the SOEs, this school of thought advocates the introduction of the shareholding system that permits the SOEs to sell their stocks to employees or to individual investors. They assert that the introduction of the shareholding system improves the efficiency of SOEs. They argue that selling shares to the public gives workers consciousness as owners of their enterprises and make them care more about the profit of SOEs.

On the other hand, the second school of thought claims that creating a well-functioned market economy is more important than reforming ownership structures in improving the performance of SOEs. According to them, poor performance of SOEs is due to the lack of competitive market environment rather than an ambiguous definition of ownership. In contrast to the assertion that separation of ownership and management is the root cause for the inefficiency of SOEs, they argue that conflicts that arise from separation of ownership and management have existed ever since the appearance of modern corporations and that the ownership structure is not the focal point of SOEs' efficiency problem. This school of thought asserts that price distortion, soft-budget constraint, and high costs for monitoring management impede the performance of SOEs, and that such conditions are generated by an immature market system. According to them, the introduction of the shareholding system would not improve the efficiency of SOEs without existence of a fair market mechanism. Therefore, establishing a well-functioned market system is a prerequisite for an effective shareholding system. Some important aspects of SOE reform include establishing well-functioned financial and managerial labor markets, hard-budget constraints, and reducing government interventions in SOEs' decision-making process.

7.2 Political Costs and Agency Costs of Equity Financing

In this section, we discuss how earlier attempts to commercialize SOEs without privatizing them created adverse incentives that defeated the intent to increase profitability and reduce the need for continual government subsides. This failure led to the establishment of the CSS, with its political costs and agency costs of equity financing. We show that given the conditions of China's SOE reform, debt-financed buyouts by existing management is not a viable choice for imposing a "hard budget constraint" on management. The inability for Chinese SOEs to use debt to finance profitable investments also reduces management's ability to send favorable signals to the market under the asymmetric information paradigm applicable to mature market economies where debt conveys insiders' superior knowledge of firm's investment opportunities.

In traditional corporate finance theory, private firms are viewed as a nexus of contracts between various economic entities, particularly owners (principals) and managers (agents). In the absence of complete and fully enforceable contracts, principal-agent problems arise because owners want to maximize firm value while managers maximize their own utility, which in general reduces the value of the firm. When government is also an actor, the traditional agency approach will not be the whole story since government is interested in its survival, which may require the use of resources that might otherwise contribute to management's utility or private investors' wealth (firm value). These interrelationships are complicated by the fact that government is by no means monolithic and constitutes a collection of agents with conflicting goals: politicians, civil employees, and citizens themselves.

In studying firms' post-IPO financing decisions, we look for evidence pertaining to the rationale behind the Chinese government's reform strategy. We hope to shed light on complex games played by the government, management, and outside investors. We attempt to assess whether and to what extent government's political concerns and management's self-dealing behavior influence the choice of financing methods and on firm value (political costs of government intervention and agency costs of managerial discretion).

7.2.1 *The Failure of Management Responsibility Contract System*

The reform of SOEs in China has been characterized by efforts to decentralize, commercialize, and of necessity, to separate ownership and (effective) control. It began with the Management Responsibility Contract System (MRCS) in 1987 in which government transferred management authority to the enterprises and allowed them to retain some of their profits.[1] Under the MRCS, managers of SOEs were given specific control rights in production, investment, sales, profits, personnel management, and distribution of fringe benefits via contracts, therefore managers have partial incentives to generate cash flows and expand wages in the form of bonuses and fringe benefits. However, the contractual relationship between managers and the government was asymmetric and incomplete. A critical defect was that profit retention by management had no downside. The state, in fact, remained responsible for final losses, mainly through the state-owned banks, which were not contractual parties in the enterprise-commercialization process. Employee bonuses and welfare expenditures, including housing, medical and schooling expenses and other fringe benefits, were deductable from enterprise revenue in calculating profits. Therefore, it is not difficult to see why profit maximization was not management's primary objective and why SOEs continued to function as government agencies or social security institutions providing "cradle-to-grave" services to employees rather than as even approximately profit-maximizing businesses.

Grossman and Hart (1986) argue that residual rights of control, not specific rights via contracts, are critical determinants of managerial incentives. Shleifer and Vishny (1994) also argue that commercialization without allocation of residual rights to management is unlikely to guarantee more productive or profitable uses of resources. Moreover, when government can indirectly subsidize management to maintain bloated employment levels, employee housing, and other political objectives through control over transfers from the treasury, thus creating a soft budget constraint, privatization alone is unlikely to enhance productivity. Under MRCS, managers

[1] SOEs had to operate at state-controlled prices and remit all profits to the state before MRCS.

had little residual rights of control and were subject to strong political influences to maintain SOE's social responsibilities. Consequently, they have little interest in technology investment, profit maximization and efficient resource allocation, all of which inevitably led to high political costs of government control.

Groves, Hong, McMillan and Naughton (1994) find that MRCS strengthened workers' incentives, increased productivity and workers' compensation, but did not lower government subsidies nor increase overall profits. With the adverse incentive structure as described above, SOEs were able to rely on easy bank credit to pay production and other "operating" expenses. Thus, as of 1994 over 40% of SOEs were unprofitable, and while SOEs accounted for 34% of GDP, they absorbed three quarters of domestic credit. Their ever increasing triangular debt (unpaid bills between state enterprises, state banks, and the government) had accumulated to over 4900 billion *Yuan* (or 95% of GDP), and bad debt was estimated to be as much as 25% of state bank assets (*China Business Review*, January 1996). Many troubled SOEs were unable to pay back these accrued loans, thus threatening the collapse of China's banking system. Figure 7.2 illustrates the distribution of sources of debt by the end of 1994. Figure 7.3 presents the percentage of SOEs with independent accounting operating at losses and the amount of losses during a period from 1978 to 1997. MRCS did not achieve the goal of effectively reforming SOEs and was terminated nationwide in 1994. The process of partial privatization through the creation of joint-stock companies (corporatization) began through the establishment of Cooperative Shareholding System (CSS).

7.2.2 *Cooperative Shareholding System*

Under the CSS, there are five types of shares. Those shares not retained by government, state enterprises, managers, and employees, are transferred to outside investors through initial public offerings (IPOs) and seasoned equity offerings (SEOs).[2] Each share type is entitled to the same voting

[2] Among the five share types, state shares are retained by the State Assets Management Bureau (SAMB) for central government or local government and are not tradable. Legal person shares are held by other SOEs and non-bank financial institutions (including investment companies, finance corporations, and mutual funds) and can not be traded in the two official exchanges. A limited number of legal person shares are traded on the Security Trading and Automatic Quote System (STAQS) and National Electronic Trading System (NETS). Employee shares are those sold to managers and workers

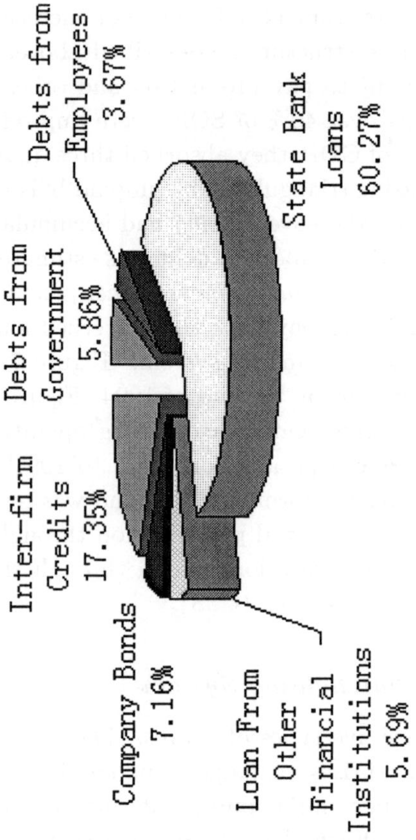

Fig. 7.2 Distribution of Sources of Debt (1994)

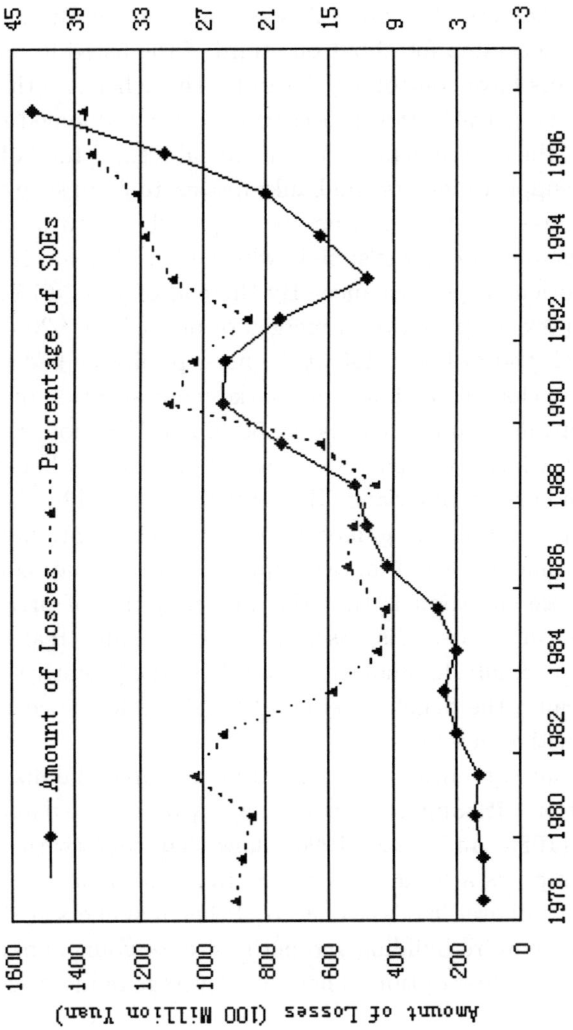

Fig. 7.3 Losses of SOEs Between 1978 and 1997 (Source: Lardy, 1998)

rights and dividend. After corporatization, all shareholders have residual claims on the company's assets. Boards of directors are established to represent the interests of all shareholders. A major characteristic of Chinese joint-stock companies is that share ownership is dominated by the state or legal person shareholders. The State Assets Management Bureau (SAMB) retains majority ownership for about one-third of the listed firms and legal person shareholders have controlling shares for the other two thirds.

To facilitate the privatization process and to wean doomed firms from eternal subsidies, the government set up an annual reserve fund of 20 billion *Yuan* in 1994 to support mergers and bankruptcies, to train surplus workers for new jobs, to free enterprises from the responsibility to provide social services, and thus to promote a system in which enterprise survival depends only on market-oriented performance. By the end of 1996, 675 SOEs had declared bankruptcy, 1801 had been merged or downsized, 9200 SOEs had been corporatized, and of these, 485 of the most profitable had been listed in the two stock exchanges with a total market capitalization of about 400 billion *yuan* (equivalent to approximately 50 billion U.S. dollars).

The extent to which SOE partial privatization leads to benefits in the form of more rapid productivity and GDP growth is limited by the political- and agency-cost problems. The games played by government, management, and investors become more and more complex. An exacerbating characteristic of the Chinese situation is that the vast majority of private shares are held by small investors. Dispersed public ownership creates a classic free-rider problem: Small shareholders do not have the incentive to monitor management because the benefit is enjoyed by all while the cost is totally borne by a few, active investors.

Two factors that can mitigate agency costs of managerial discretion are debt (in conjunction with appropriate bankruptcy procedures) and takeover threats. Jensen (1986) and Stulz (1990) show that debt (with the threat of bankruptcy) imposes a hard budget constraint on managers and limits management's control over firm's cash flows. When managers are faced with choices of reducing empire-building and perquisites or going bankrupt, they are likely to choose the first option. Therefore, leverage reduces agency costs

within a company and can not be traded within the first 3 years. Domestic individual shares, or A shares, are those held and traded by private Chinese citizens in the two official exchanges in China. Foreign shares are those held and traded by foreign investors in security exchanges in China (B shares), in Hong Kong (H shares) or in NYSE (N shares).

of managerial discretion. Shleifer and Vishny (1986) show that takeover threats discipline management in the presence of many small shareholders. The reason is that if a company is badly managed, then there is an incentive for someone to acquire a large stake of the company, improve its performance and profit on the shares purchased. The threat of such action can persuade management to act in the interest of shareholders.

Unfortunately, because of the political nature of the privatization process itself, bank-debt financing of corporate investments is not a viable means to assure a hard budget constraint in transitional economies such as China (Shleifer and Vishny, 1994). Bank loans have traditionally been viewed as grants from the state designed to bail out failing firms. State-owned banks retain a monopoly in the Chinese banking sector and profit is not their overriding objective. If political favor is deemed appropriate, subsidized loans, rescheduling of overdue debt or even outright transfer of funds can be arranged with SOEs (soft budget constraints). A banking system that is so heavily controlled by the government's political objectives can hardly exert any real influence on management. Moreover, a market for private, nonbank debt, has yet to be established.[3] There is no active merger or takeover activity in stock markets to discipline management. Information available in the capital markets is insufficient to keep at arm's length of the managerial decisions. Despite the existence of a bankruptcy law since 1986, the rate of bankruptcies has remained at a very low level.[4] In light of the above peculiarities, direct control by (large) shareholders through the board of directors appears to be the only means for shareholders to monitor managers.

With good corporate governance structure, boards of directors would consist of delegates of large institutional shareholders and minority investors, representing all shareholders' interests. Such boards would make critical investment and re-organization decisions, select top managers, and provide managers with incentives and compensation appropriate to investors' interests. However, board members in Chinese joint-stock companies consist mainly of representatives or officials from the SAMB, local government, and other state enterprises, whose interests are not the same

[3]By the end of December 1996, only 12 companies have their corporate bonds listed on Shanghai and Shenzhen exchanges.

[4]For all forms of ownership in China, the rate of bankruptcy is 0.03% in 1996 compared to 1.1% in the U.S..

as those of outside investors. On average, 90% of the board members are government officials and delegates of other state enterprises. Moreover, there is at best an inadequately functioning managerial labor market that can discipline managers and help solve incentive problems caused by the separation of ownership and control. All top managers must be approved by the Organization Department of the local or central government. The government maintains ultimate rights for changing managerial positions. With state controlled stock companies, political considerations still dominate economic performance in the selection of managers and adversely affect managerial incentives. Managers no doubt care more about carrying out wishes of the Party and the government, such as avoiding worker layoffs and maintaining some level of worker social security than about the concerns of shareholders. As a result, many management decisions still reflect the old political concerns (political costs). In addition, managerial and board-member compensation packages are determined by the government, and are seldom directly linked to profits. Management is not severely constrained from self-dealing behavior, such as diverting SOE assets outside the state sector for private use, such as charging meals and travel expenses to company accounts, obtaining large apartments, and purchasing fancy cars and furniture for personal consumption. Spending cash flow on acquisitions or other unprofitable projects undertaken with the aid of unrealistically high forecasts of future profitability gives management a bigger company to run, thereby increasing their power and prestige in the community (agency cost).

Allocation of effective control rights to management without clearly defined corporate laws and bankruptcy procedures gives managers a chance to enrich themselves by such means as undervaluing state assets and spinning off subsidiaries to be controlled by the manager's relatives. In a study conducted by Kernen (1997), some managers of SOEs admitted to have created a number of collective or private enterprises for their relatives using SOEs' assets. Furthermore, China's embryonic regulatory regime and rudimentary accounting standards provide very little protection for investors' rights, because they limit boards' ability to monitor abuses of governmental influence and managerial discretion and thus limit political and agency costs that diminish the productivity-enhancing effects of privatization and reduce firm value.

In summary, partial privatization and separation of ownership and control have transferred residual rights of control from government to managers but have not provided effective monitoring mechanisms. The traditional government goals characterized by the "iron rice bowl" concept still exert some control through the selection of managers and board members. Management has considerable leeway to seek its own self interest at the expense of shareholders. In the next section, we present data bearing on the influence of agency and political costs revealed in the financing decisions of Chinese joint-stock companies.

7.3 Choices of Post-IPO Financing

7.3.1 *Soft Budget Constraints and The Role of Debt*

Corporate governance is a institution governing contractual relationships among equity-holders, management and creditors. It is structured for solving the two basic problems inherent within the firm. The first is the managerial incentive problem; that is, how to motivate and discipline management, given that managerial behaviour is hard to measure? The second is the management selection problem; that is, what kind of mechanism can ensure that only the most entrepreneurial people are employed to fill in the management position, given that entrepreneurial ability is hard to observe? For corporate governance to be effective and efficient, the following conditions must hold: First, equity-holders as the owners of the firm must have adequate incentives to select the highly competent manager and to discipline the manager. Second, the manager must have adequate autonomy as well as adequate incentives to make business decisions with the business judgment rule, and is well-motivated to work hard. Third, creditors must have adequate incentives as well as effective measures to enforce debt contacts through bankrupt procedure. Non of these conditions hold in Chinese SOEs. The debt finance has evolved into the debt crisis in China because corporate governance has changed little.

The state bank as the major creditor has failed to enforce the debt contract. In a market economy, debts play an important role in corporate governance through bankruptcy threat. China enacted the *P.R.C. Bankruptcy Law* in 1986, which became effective in late 1988. Theoretically, when enterprises become insolvent, creditors will take over the control, and the threat of bankruptcy can discipline the management. Nevertheless, this is not a case in China. Rather, bankruptcy has been widely used by enterprises and local governments as a way to write off debts instead of disciplining managers. After bankruptcy is declared, either through reorganization or through liquidation, most incumbent managers still run the firms. The the only discernible difference is that considerable debts have been canceled (and in some cases the enterprises are renamed). Because of this, managers are more than willing to file for bankruptcy. In contrast, state banks as dominant creditors, have neither access nor incentive to execute their creditor rights. They have been very passive in dealing with distressed firms. Typically, when firms default on their debt, creditor banks take passive actions such as extending the payment period for loans and capitalizing unpaid interest rather than pursuing their claims through bankruptcy or other active means. Indeed, very few bankruptcies have been filed by banks.

The government has subsidized the SOEs to help their poor economic performances, and the large amount of the subsidy has become a major cause of serious government budget deficit. We examine the behavior of 308 SOEs that went public before January 1996. Over the period from January 1994 through December 1996, 280 of these firms recorded a total of 459 announcements of new shares after their IPOs, including announcements of 281 stock dividends, 126 rights issues, and 52 underwritten offers.[5] The sample classification is presented in Table 7.5. In exploring evidence of agency and political costs in financing the privatization process, we contrast the agency- and political-cost paradigm discussed in the previous section with the roles of asymmetric information under the well-known "pecking-order" paradigm suggested by Myers and Majluf (1984).

Under asymmetric information, insiders (management) convey positive news to outside investors by means of the financing method chosen, with internal financing (no new issues or possibly stock dividends) being the highest in the pecking order, riskless debt the next highest, followed by equity issues. In choosing a flotation method, managers who know of profitable investment projects signal their true value in the choice of a subscription price in an uninsured rights offer, while managers with lower-quality projects make fully underwritten issues (Smith, 1977, Heinkel and Schwartz, 1986,

[5]We note that a Chinese joint-stock company, subject to certain regulations and approval, can issue equities in the form of A shares (available only to domestic investors and traded in Chinese exchanges), B shares (available only to foreign investors and traded in Chinese exchanges), H shares (listed and traded in Hong Kong), N shares (listed and traded in New York) or a combination of these share types. Because of the small number of observations associated with the issuance of B-, H-, and N-shares through alternative flotation methods, we focus only on A-share decisions in this paper.

Table 7.5 Sample Classification

Year	Types of offering			
	Stock Dividend	Uninsured Rights	Underwritten	All
1993	117	52	8	177
1994	94	29	14	137
1995	70	45	30	145
Total	281	126	52	459

and Eckbo and Masulis, 1992). Since new bank debt is likely to be a signal of bad news in the Chinese situation (and in transitional economies with soft budget constraints in general), and since markets for private nonbank debt have not yet emerged, loan financing of new, profitable investment projects does not appear in the pecking order for newly privatized SOE's. Consistent with this argument, we observe no corporate debt issues over the period covered in this study. This leaves internal financing (no new issues or stock dividends) as most preferred under the pecking-order paradigm in the current Chinese situation, followed by uninsured rights (being relatively inexpensive to float but exposing existing owners to the risk of share-price dilution), followed by underwritten offers.

We compare the financial characteristics of the 28 firms that announce no post-IPO share issues with those that do issues new shares after their IPOs. We calculate the average of the following ratios that represent firm's liquidity, debt capacity, and investment opportunities: cash flow as a fraction of total assets ($CASHTA$), long-term debt as a fraction of the book value of total assets ($LEVERAGE$), market-to-book ratio ($MKTBOOK$), and long-term investment expenditure to total asset ratio ($LONGINV$). If a firm issues new shares in 1994, we include it in computing the financial ratios of 1993, and so on and so forth.

Comparing firms with no post-IPO equity issues with all those that engaged in some form of additional equity financing, we note that issuers exhibit more liquidity and evidence of better investment opportunities. Cash flow as a fraction of total assets is higher for issuer than for non-issuers in every year from 1993 through 1995, with the gap growing from 1.5 percentage points in 1993 to over 4 percentage points in 1995. The market-to-book ratio, a measure of investors' evaluation of a firm's investment opportunities

Table 7.6 Firm Characteristics by Post-IPO Stock-Issuing Behavior

		No stock issue		Stock dividend		All issues	
		Mean	Median	Mean	Median	Mean	Median
CASHTA	1993	0.0614	0.065	0.0773	0.0826	0.0741	0.0786
	1994	0.0829	0.0843	0.0939	0.0984	0.1011	0.1139
	1995	0.0882	0.0936	0.1004	0.1107	0.1302	0.1381
LEVERAGE	1993	0.0265	0.0194	0.0484	0.0307	0.0343	0.021
	1994	0.0361	0.0252	0.0716	0.0593	0.0512	0.0406
	1995	0.0453	0.0317	0.0655	0.0502	0.0618	0.0483
MKTBOOK	1993	1.2474	1.1511	1.0907	1.0226	1.3835	1.2642
	1994	1.4012	1.3326	1.2806	1.2149	1.5257	1.4699
	1995	1.4279	1.395	1.3413	1.2594	1.6576	1.5706
LONGINV	1993	0.0602	0.0571	0.0888	0.0713	0.1193	0.0968
	1994	0.0828	0.0693	0.1427	0.1192	0.1545	0.1236
	1995	0.0754	0.0648	0.1584	0.1260	0.1493	0.1108

and future profitability, is on average higher for issuers than for non-issuers, again exhibiting a wider gap in 1995 than in 1993. Expenditures on long-term investment projects as a fraction of total assets is nearly twice as high in firms that issue stock after their IPO than it is for firms that don't. Average long-term debt is very low for firms in all categories, for reasons discussed in Section 2, although it grows slightly, as a fraction of total assets, over the period covered, and firms with post-IPO stock issues have slightly higher averages than the others.

Firms that issue stock dividends are represented in the middle column of Table 7.6. These firms have the lowest market-to-book ratios in each year, on average, but their mean long-term investment relative to total assets is higher than for non-issuers, almost as high as the means for all issuers taken together. We conjecture that this may reflect a dim view of the market on the profitability of the long-term investments undertaken by an average stock dividend issuing firm compared to firms that issue uninsured rights or underwritten offers. We interpret the comparative statistics of Table

7.6 as inconsistent with the pecking-order paradigm, because firms relying predominantly on internal financing after their IPOs appear to have worse financial characteristics than those that go to the market with new equity issues.

7.3.2 *Costs of Equity*

The government as the majority equity-holder has malfunctioned with both selecting and disciplining management because of the agency problem on bureaucrats' side. In particular, the government still holds full authority of appointing management. Because of the adverse selection problem, selecting good management is hard work. It requires that selectors must have adequate incentives to find information about candidates' abilities and to install high quality candidates. Adverse selection is most serious in China, because, with no personal stake to signal ability, too many people pretend that they are qualified for management. Worse is that bureaucrats, unlike their capitalist counterparts, have the right to select, but do not bear consequences of their selections. This implies that, not only would-be managers, bureaucrats themselves also have the adverse selection problem. They have no adequate incentive to search for good managers, and even if they know some are capable, they still lack the adequate incentive to install them. Observation suggests that bureaucrats too often base their selections on personal connections rather than merits. Appointing friendly managers is the most effective way for bureaucrats' rent seeking. Because of this, management pool of SOEs is full of lemons.

Although reform has gradually shifted considerable autonomy to management through various ways, the government still exercises arbitrary administrative intervention in the SOEs' businesses. Separation of the government from enterprises has been assumed as the basic purpose of the reform since the reform was inaugurated. Nevertheless, this purpose has so far never been materialized. This is true even after the state enterprise is corporatized in which case the government is formally and legally defined as the equity-holder and bureaucrats are appointed as board directors. The fundamental reason for this is that when the state is the owner of the firm, bureaucrats are delegated with ownership rights to control the firm but bear no financial risk for their intervention. By definition, any owner has to supervise management through control rights. The state as a (and in most cases the only) equity-holder will naturally intervene. The key problem is how to determine the boundary of such intervention. In the absence of a very well-defined division of rights between equity-holders, the board of directors, and management, it is not clear to every party involved who should do what. For a stockholder or board member who bears financial risk, his or her decision of whether to intervene depends on how much trust he or she places on the manager. If a stockholder or board member trusts the manager, he/she will not intervene even if the manager is doing something that fundamentally alters the enterprise. If the stockholder or board member does not trust the manager, even if the manager is doing something trivial, he/she may still intervene. However, this type of tacit understanding between a stockholder and manager in dealing with the public domain of control rights cannot be duplicated between bureaucrats and managers of a corporatized SOE. Bureaucrats arbitrarily intervene simply because they do not bear the consequences of intervention. With arbitrary administrative intervention, management has little accountability for their performance. For instance, when a debt-financed investment decision is made by the government department, how could the manager be blamed for poor performance or default?

SOEs suffer not only from arbitrary administrative intervention but also from inadequate managerial incentive. Although the reform has improved the management's incentive to make short profits through profit sharing, the long-term incentive problem has yet to be solved. Managers of SOEs prefer to distribute retained profits to employees or make investment in quick revenue-generating projects rather than to make investment in long term productivity-enhancing projects and in research and development (R&D). They have more incentives to expand their empire by borrowing from banks and to keep insolvent enterprises as going concerns, but little incentives to make efficient use of borrowed money and to repay. In many cases, abnormal short-term profits are made at the large expense of long-term productivity. The reason for management myopia is that, given that there is little personal capital stake, the manager's enjoyment of benefits from the firm cannot beyond his or her firm tenure, which is mainly dependent upon bureaucratic preferences and have little relation with firm performance. With bureaucrats making selection of management, good performers are just as equally likely to be removed as bad performers, if not more. Once a firm becomes highly profitable, bureaucrats have every incentive to collect rents by replacing the incumbent with their favorite. Thus, the best way for the incumbent to secure his position is to make the firm not too good and not too bad. This also partly explain why SOE managers typically underreport their profits.

To examine the extent of agency and political consideration as revealed in firm's financing choices, we explore in greater depth the market's reaction to various types of post-IPO stock issues. We first compute abnormal returns over a two-day period that includes the day of the China Security Daily announcement and the day preceeding the announcement for each firm. The abnormal return is calculated based on the market model (Fama, Fisher, Jensen and Roll, 1969):

$$AR_{it} = R_{it} - (\hat{\alpha}_i - \hat{\beta}_i R_{mt}) \tag{7.1}$$

where AR_{it} is the abnormal return for firm i on date t, R_{it} is the return for firm i on date t, R_{mt} is the stock-market return on date t, (R_{ft} is the risk-free rate as measured by the rate of return on six-month Chinese Treasury Bonds.) $\hat{\alpha}_i$ and $\hat{\beta}_i$ are the ordinary least squares estimates of firm i's market model using return data from $t = -120$ to $t = -10$ and from $t = 10$ to $t = 120$ in relation to the announcement day, $t = 0$. Therefore, the abnormal return for each firm's stock is calculated as the difference between the actual and expected returns to its stock.[6] Average abnormal returns for each day are calculated by

$$\bar{AR}_t = \frac{1}{N}\sum_{i=1}^{N} AR_{it} \tag{7.2}$$

where N is the number of stocks with abnormal returns during day t. Therefore, the equity-issuing announcement two-day average abnormal return is

$$ADAR = \bar{AR}_{-1} + \bar{AR}_0. \tag{7.3}$$

The t-statistics are calculated for $ADAR$ by

[6]In case of missing returns, we exclude both the day of missing return and the day after that in estimating α_i and β_i.

$$t_{ADAR} = \frac{ADAR}{\sqrt{\frac{1}{2\times 220}\left(\sum_{t=-120}^{t=-10}(\bar{AR}_t - \bar{\bar{AR}}_t)^2 + \sum_{t=10}^{t=120}(\bar{AR}_t - \bar{\bar{AR}}_t)^2\right)}} \tag{7.4}$$

We find that the mean announcement day abnormal returns (t-statistics) are -1.47% (-1.6138), 7.04% (4.6178), -9.08% (-4.0597), and -0.43% (-0.2198) for stock dividends, uninsured rights, a combination of stock dividends and uninsured rights, and underwritten offers, respectively. We view the principal question raised by these statistics to be, what is the negative news conveyed by stock dividend announcements, compared to announcements of uninsured rights issues? This question is especially puzzling, because the Chinese market's negative reaction to stock dividends is opposite to that in many capital markets, where stock dividends are usually perceived as conveying positive news. Grinblatt, Masulis, and Titman (1984) interpret stock dividends as an implicit cash dividend increase in percentage terms, because firms are loath to cut cash dividends. Thus, only firms confident about their future cash flows will announce stock dividends, thus leading to positive announcement day returns. On the face of it, then, the negative announcement day abnormal returns associated with stock dividends appear to contradict the asymmetric information paradigm in the Chinese situation.[7]

To enhance our search for the underlying causes for the Chinese stock-dividend announcement anomaly, we construct Table 7.7, which presents summary statistics for the abnormal return data and other characteristics of all firms issuing stocks after their IPOs, categorized by types of issue.

An "eyeball" analysis of Table 7.7 yields comparisons that, to us, are anomalous in light of asymmetric information, because our abnormal announcement day return calculations and the statistics reported in Table 7.7 suggest that the most favorable characteristics belong to firms issuing uninsured rights alone. Perhaps their most striking feature is that $CAR360$, which is cumulative average return for the year following an announcement, which in the 120 days before an announcement, is distinctly

[7]We conjectured the possibility that stock dividends in China represent an attempt by management to dilute the degree of government ownership, but since government and "legal person" shareholders are entitled to and receive dividend treatment identical to that of private investors, this explanation of the market's negative reaction to stock dividends must be rejected.

Table 7.7 Abnormal Returns and Firm Characteristics for 459 Announcements of Equity Issues

	Stock dividend		Rights offers		Divd. & rights		Underwritten	
	Mean	Median	Mean	Median	Mean	Median	Mean	Median
$ADAR$	-1.47%	-0.92%	7.04%	2.82%	-9.08%	-1.08%	-0.43%	-0.70%
$CASHTA$	0.0832	0.0636	0.0945	0.0634	0.0953	0.0804	0.1057	0.0872
$LIQUIDTA$	0.5590	0.5627	0.5683	0.5762	0.5524	0.5306	0.5581	0.5740
$LEVERAGE$	0.0563	0.0214	0.0304	0.0122	0.0579	0.0362	0.0633	0.0248
MVE	577.87	124.54	957.95	347.56	298.88	115.63	469.31	205.58
$MKTBOOK$	1.1973	1.0244	1.5584	1.2493	1.2054	1.1351	1.4188	1.1297
$LONGINV$	0.1193	0.0804	0.1525	0.1142	0.1077	0.0757	0.1458	0.1083
$PROFSHA$	0.0228	0.03251	0.1625	0.1843	0.0477	0.0543	0.0486	0.0528
$CAR-120$	-14.04%	-15.34%	6.53%	4.42%	-16.6%	-16.71%	2.54%	2.33%
$CAR+120$	-5.01%	-4.40%	12.04%	13.68%	-5.73%	-6.71%	-1.48%	-2.25%
$CAR+360$	-6.13%	-5.89%	6.97%	8.08%	-7.13%	-7.28%	2.06%	3.14%
$BETA$	1.5227	1.6080	1.3108	1.3295	1.4762	1.4536	1.4419	1.5239
STD	4.93%	3.90%	3.74%	3.58%	5.09%	4.15%	4.37%	4.02%
$GOVNT$	24.31%	21.50%	16.67%	14.55%	18.53%	15.69%	8.26%	7.73%
$TOPTEN$	72.08%	70.40%	54.07%	52.16%	86.46%	85.92%	63.94%	60.05%
$MGOWN$	0.24%	0.22%	0.73%	0.68%	0.09%	0.09%	0.55%	0.54%

positive for the uninsured rights issuers, but not for firms in any of the other financing categories. Profit per share is also by far the highest for firms using uninsured rights, roughly 3- to 8- times higher than for firms using other external financing methods, although this may simply be a matter of the number of shares outstanding rather than intrinsic profitability. However, given that $MKTBOOK$ is also highest for firms issuing only uninsured rights, it is plausible that these are genuinely more profitable firms. Another distinguishing feature of firms that issue uninsured rights alone is that the variable MVE, market value of equity one day for an announcement, is far larger than for firms using other forms of financing. This suggests firms issuing uninsured rights are bigger and/or more highly valued than others. Perhaps sheer size has an informational advantage as well, in that economies of scale increase the liklihood that investors will know something about these firms enabling them to make better informed investment decisions when opportunities to purchase new shares arise. Despite their relatively large size, firms issuing uninsured rights have only the third-highest fraction of government ownership and largest concentration of management ownership.[8] They have the lowest concentration of ownership among institutional or private investors.

Firms issuing stock-dividends, which exhibit the lowest announcement-day abnormal returns, have the lowest CAR in the 360 days following an offer, and profits per share are much lower. $MKTBOOK$ is only three-fourths the magnitude as for firms issuing uninsured rights (and roughly equal to firms issuing stock dividends alone), and market value of equity just before announcement is by far the lowest for this group. The stock-dividends and rights issuers have a somewhat higher level of government ownership and the highest concentration of ownership among the top ten institutional or private investors.

To summarize, then, firms engaging in some form of internal finance appear to be "worse" than those seeking new funds from external sources (uninsured rights only or underwritten offers), although within the group seeking external funding, the "pecking order" appears to apply, with firms issuing underwritten offers being apparently less profitable and with fewer good investment opportunities than those issuing uninsured rights alone.

[8]The proportion of shares that are government owned must be interpreted with caution, given the interlocking ownership of government and government-owned firms among shareholders.

7.4 The Information Content of Different Financing Choices

We use the following variables as proxies for agency costs of equity, investment opportunities, risk of the firm, and subsequent stock return performance:

- *Agency costs of equity:* Because managers will be more likely to strip assets and transfer resources from SOEs to themselves if the managers' fractional investment is small, we use the percentage of managerial holding of equities (MGOWN) as one of the proxies of agency costs of equity. Because agency cost of equity is related to the effort of monitoring by the large shareholders, we use the percentage of the top ten shareholders (TOPTEN), including institutional and private investors but excluding state government, as another proxy of agency costs of equity.
- *Political costs of equity:* With large government ownership and inefficient governmental monitoring, managers are more likely to pursue objectives other than maximizing the firm's value, e.g., managers are more likely to use financing methods that dilute state ownership and expand their empires. We use the percentage of state government ownership (GOVNT) as a proxy for the political costs of equity.
- *Investment opportunities:* We use market-to-book (MKTBOOK) defined as the ratio of market value of equity plus total assets minus book value of equity to total assets, cash flow to total asset ratio (CASHTA), profit per share before the financing announcement (PROFSHA) and long-term investment to total assets ratio (LONGINV) as proxies.
- *Risk of the firm:* We use a firm's stock market beta (BETA) and standard deviation of stock returns (STD) calculated over a period from 120 days before the announcement and 360 days after the announcement as proxies.
- *Subsequent stock return performance:* We measure a firm's subsequent stock performance using the cumulative abnormal returns 120 days after (CAR+120) and 360 days after (CAR+360) the financing announcement.

We hypothesize that:

H1: With agency problems, stock dividends and combination of stock dividends and rights are used to disperse ownership and further reduce monitoring of management by existing shareholders. The probability that a firm will use stock dividend is positively related to the agency and political costs of equity and the risk of the firm, and negatively related to the investment opportunities and subsequent stock price performance.

The alternative to this hypothesis is that issuing new shares in lieu of dividends conveys information to the market that firms have ample slack because retained earnings must be reduced by the dollar amount of the stock dividends. Consequently, there is a positive correlation between the probability of stock dividend announcement and subsequent stock price performance (Grinblatt, Masulis and Titman, 1984). Since stock dividend conveys good news, the probability of announcing stock dividend or a combination of stock dividend and rights is positively related to the investment opportunities and negatively related to the risk of the firm. There is no statistical relationship between ownership concentration and the probability of stock dividends and combination of stock dividends and rights.

H2: The probability that a firm will use uninsured rights and underwritten offers is negatively related to the agency and political cost of equity and the risk of the firm, and positively related to the investment opportunities and subsequent stock price performance.

H3: Between the choices of stock dividends and a combination of stock dividends and rights, the probability that a firm will choose stock dividend and rights at the same time is more positively related to the agency and political costs of equity and the risk of the firm, and more negatively related to the profitability of investment projects and subsequent stock return performance.

H4: Between the choices of uninsured rights and underwritten offers, the probability that a firm will employ an underwriter is less negatively related to the agency and political costs of equity and the risk of the firm, and less positively related to the profitability of investment projects and subsequent stock return performance.

To test the aforementioned hypotheses, we estimate the following multinomial logit model (MNL). Let the value to firm i choosing financing method j be y^*_{ij}, where $j \in$ {stock dividend, rights, underwritten offers}. We assume that y^*_{ij} depends upon some observed characteristics $\mathbf{X}_{ij}$ and an error μ_{ij}.

$$y_{ij}^* = \mathbf{X}_{ij}\boldsymbol{\beta} + \mu_{ij}$$

where $\mathbf{X}_{ij}$ includes $MGOWN_{ij}$, $TOPTEN_{ij}$, $GOVNT_{ij}$, $MKTBOOK_{ij}$, $BETA_{ij}$, STD_{ij}, $PROFSHA_{ij}$, $LONGINV_{ij}$, $CAR{-}120_{ij}$, $CAR{+}360_{ij}$, $CASHTA_{ij}$, the degree of IPO underpricing ($IPORTN_{ij}$), the logarithm of IPO size ($lNIPOSZ_{ij}$), taxes as measured by tax payments divided by total assets ($TAXTA_{ij}$), and the logarithm of firm's total asset ($LOGTA_{ij}$). Let the vector of indicators $\mathbf{y}_i = (y_{i1}, y_{i2}, y_{i3}, y_{i4})'$ where $y_{ij} = 1$ if firm i chooses financing method j and $y_{ij} = 0$ if firm i does not choose financing method j. Then

$$\begin{aligned} p_{ij} &= Pr[y_{ij} = 1|\mathbf{X}_i] = Pr[y_{ij}^* > y_{ik}^*, \forall k \neq j|\mathbf{X}_i] \\ &= Pr[\mathbf{X}_{ij}\boldsymbol{\beta} + \mu_{ij} > \mathbf{X}_{ik}\boldsymbol{\beta} + \mu_{ik}, \forall k \neq j] \\ &= Pr[\mu_{ij} - \mu_{ik} < (\mathbf{X}_{ij} - \mathbf{X}_{ik})\boldsymbol{\beta}, \forall k \neq j] \end{aligned}$$

Let $\mu_{ijl}^* = \mu_{ij} - \mu_{ik}$ and $\mathbf{X}_{ijl}^* = (\mathbf{X}_{ij} - \mathbf{X}_{ik})$ for all $k \neq j$, and let $F(\cdot)$ be the distribution function of $\mu_{ijl}^* = (\mu_{ij1}^*, \mu_{ij2}^*, \mu_{ij3}^*)$, the 3-dimension vector of error differences, then

$$\begin{aligned} p_{ij} &= Pr[\mu_{ijl}^* < \mathbf{X}_{ijl}^*\boldsymbol{\beta}, \forall k \neq j] \\ &= \int_{-\infty}^{\mathbf{X}_{ij2}^*\boldsymbol{\beta}} \int_{-\infty}^{\mathbf{X}_{ij1}^*\boldsymbol{\beta}} dF(\mu_{ij}^*) \\ &= \int_{-\infty}^{\infty} \int_{-\infty}^{\infty} 1[\mu_{ijl}^* < \mathbf{X}_{ijl}^*\boldsymbol{\beta}, \forall k \neq j] dF(\mu_{ij}^*) \end{aligned}$$

The MNL results presented in Table 7.8 indicate that between the choices of uninsured rights and stock dividends, firms with lower government and institutional ownership, smaller debt to asset ratio and higher cash to total assets and long-term investment to total assets ratios are more likely to issue uninsured rights. These firms typically are bigger, subject to higher tax rates, and have better long-term share performance as measured by CAR+360. However, the market run-up (CAR-120) and risk surrounding the issue (STD) are not statistically significant. Between the choices of underwritten offers and stock dividends, firms that have higher managerial ownership, lower IPO size, and better liquidity are more likely to use underwriters. Between the choices of issuing uninsured rights and stock dividends together and stock dividends alone, firms that have lower

Table 7.8 MNL Regression on Financing Choices and Firm Characteristics

	Uninsured rights vs Stock div.	Stock div. & rights vs Stock div.	Underwritten offer vs. Stock div.
CONSTANT	-0.0007	0.0095	-0.0041
	(-0.0177)	(0.2274)	(-0.0982)
LOGTA	0.0968*	-0.1472†	0.0206
	(2.2926)	(-1.9411)	(0.5315)
STD	-0.0101	0.0459	-0.0043
	(-0.2415)	(1.1104)	(-0.1031)
TAXTA	0.1532*	-0.1646*	0.1265*
	(2.7184)	(-2.4902)	(2.4110)
CASHTA	0.0562†	-0.0113	0.1315†
	(1.6650)	(-0.2695)	(1.7879)
LEVERAGE	-0.3417†	0.0333	-0.0146
	(-1.9161)	(1.1204)	(-0.7604)
IPORTN	-0.0125	0.0058	-0.0113
	(-1.1888)	(1.5151)	(-1.1998)
CAR-120	-0.6637	0.0179	0.0024
	(-1.2889)	(0.4302)	(0.0574)
LNIPOSZ	0.0763	-0.0722†	-0.1390*
	(1.5776)	(-1.7498)	(-2.4939)
MKTBOOK	0.1461	-0.1951*	0.0428
	(0.3551)	(-3.0438)	(0.9474)
LONGINV	0.0688†	-0.0470*	0.0226
	(1.8372)	(-2.8819)	(1.0816)
TOPTEN	-0.5115*	0.1451*	0.0131
	(-2.1178)	(2.8259)	(0.3145)
GOVNT	-0.0788†	0.0137	-0.0493
	(-1.8970)	(0.3290)	(-1.0952)
MGOWN	0.0031	-0.3138*	0.1003*
	(0.0079)	(-2.2175)	(2.4082)
BETA	-0.0041	0.0030	0.0012
	(-0.8431)	(0.5797)	(0.0230)
CAR+360	0.1457*	-0.0772	0.1414
	(2.1351)	(-1.5325)	(0.3405)

managerial ownership, higher institutional ownership and worse investment opportunities as measured by market-to-book and long-term investments to total assets ratios are more likely to issue both rights and stock dividends at the same time. These firms that typically smaller and pay less taxes.

The econometric results by and large support the agency and political cost approach in explaining the financing choices of newly privatized SOEs.

7.5 Institutional Transformation to Improve Corporate Governance

In China, as in other transitional economies, a healthy and competitive corporate sector is vital for sustained economic growth. Just as shared governance is important in the public sector, corporate governance is as important in the private sector. As there is an international trend towards global competition, Chinese firms need to tap domestic and international sources of funds in increased its competitiveness. The rules of the game are changing: Banks, pension funds and individual investors will base their investment decisions not only on a firm's commercial prospects, but also on its reputation and its governance.

As the recent Asian financial crises demonstrated forcefully, macroeconomic difficulties can expose and exacerbate systemic weaknesses in corporate governance. A central element of the response to the recent crises has been to strengthen corporate governance. This includes legal and regulatory systems, accounting and auditing standards, banking practices, the regulation of capital markets, transparency, the work of corporate boards, and the rights and responsibilities of different classes of shareholders. It is important that China establishes sound corporate governance along lines suggested below

7.5.1 *Privatization*

Our previous analysis suggests that any successful state enterprise reform strategy must address both the triangular debt problem among the government, SOEs and state banks and the corporate governance problem simultaneously. Privatization of SOEs is not only inevitable but also desirable. However, there are at least three reasons that China's state enterprise reform can not choose the same way of privatization by some western countries: One is the functional reason. The SOEs in China are firstly existent as the important material foundation of socialism. It plays a dominant role in the national economy. It does not only appear in situations where the market does not work. The second is the number. The numbers of

China's SOEs, the fields they cover, the capital scale they occupy and their proportion in the whole national economy are all much bigger than those in any other countries in the world. Third, the healthy and efficient operation and development of China's national economy largely depend on the vitality, dynamics and the future of development of the SOEs. So the aim of China's state enterprise reform is not how to pull out from the competitive market, but how to adjust and optimize the structure and operation system of the SOEs and make them more adapted to the market economy and develop more efficiently.

Given that most SOEs cannot continue their operation with the existing debt burden, new equity funds have to be injected. However, the state as the incumbent owner has no surplus funds available to bail out failing firms. The triangular debt problem can only be solved by introducing new, non-state shareholders to the SOEs. This can be easily done by transforming household investors from debt-holders of state banks into equity-holders of corporatized SOEs. Once individual investors replace the government as the controlling equity-holders, corporate governance will change accordingly. In other words, China does not need to follow Eastern European-style of voucher privatization. China has got its own way to privatization. This kind of privatization will not only resurrects the financial structure of SOEs but also strengthens corporate governance.

Privatization can take various forms. For small-sized enterprises, management (or employee) buy-outs are a popular solution. For instance, 77.2% of Zhucheng municipality's enterprises were bought out by managers and employees from 1992 to 1994. For large and medium-sized enterprises, forming joint ventures and going public are the two most attractive ways to privatize. By forming joint ventures with domestic or foreign private enterprises, local governments can partially privatize their SOEs with minimum disruption to operations. In order to attract foreign investors, local governments compete to set up development zones and to offer substantial tax concessions and other favorable treatments to foreign investors. As for going public, the central government has recognized that two official stock exchanges in Shanghai and Shenzhen can play an important role in solving the debt crisis. All local governments are eager to get listing quotas. Although the government often holds an absolute majority of shares when they are issued, its stake should be further reduced. More recently, privatization through Hong Kong has become fashionable. For example, Shanghai and Beijing have packed their SOEs for listing on the Hong Kong

Stock Exchange. Other regions are following their footsteps. In many cases the state-owned shares are taken over by non-state owners through the stock market. Some Hong Kong companies may also directly take over SOEs.

7.5.2 *Denationalization*

Providing incentives for sound corporate governance is a challenge. In China, the lack of clear identification of the owners of SOEs undermines corporate governance because it leaves open the issue of who should be monitoring the managers. The lack of delineation of the enterprises' commercial and social functions and the fact that the state is both the ultimate owner and the regulator of SOEs make for unclear governance objectives.

Moreover, effective corporate governance is difficult to exercise because few of the institutions are responsible for managing state assets regularly receive timely, accurate, and useful information about the financial performance of the firms they control. Although the introduction of individual shareholders through public listings has not resulted in a clear separation of ownership and management interests, where ownership has been diversified to include institutional investors, new governance structures have emerged. Still, relatively few outside monitors, especially banks, exercise strong discipline on China's SOEs. The four specialized banks are mainly agents of the state. Although they are attempting to transform themselves into commercial entities, they have a long way to go to establish their independence. Mergers (or threats of takeovers) can be effective disciplining devices against poor management. But most mergers of large SOEs are engineered by the state and are not market driven. Without reorienting governance incentives toward a market system of checks and balances, many of China's SOEs will continue to operate in a corporate governance vacuum, with managers and other insiders exercising *de facto* control over the enterprises.

Hardening budget constraints and reducing subsidies provided to SOEs through the fiscal system are important strategies in denationalization of SOEs. State-owned Holding Corporation is a new form of the reform of the management system of the state-owned asset that meets the request of optimize the resources and improve the overall operation benefit of the state-owned asset.[9] It is a meaningful exploration of the separation of the

[9]Since 1987, Shen Zhen city has established a three-layer state-owned asset management system, which includes the state-owned asset commission, asset management corporation and state-owned enterprises. This is a big step towards the socialist market

government's function from enterprise management and the separation of the government from the asset. Although some reduction in state ownership has taken place, the four main state-owned banks still often roll over unpaid credits to SOEs. Interest rates have not been liberalized enough for the banks to differentiate terms among enterprises according to credit risks, which gives rise to cross-subsidies. The banks need to step up their governance involvement with these enterprises, especially in calling in debt-service obligations. But even where fiscal and financial system subsidy constraints have hardened, SOEs may be able to avoid financial restructuring by resorting to inter-enterprise financing. Alternatively, they may arrange for soft financing on non-market terms from public utilities or other enterprises.

More intense competition, whether from domestic sources or from abroad would pressure SOEs to denationalize and restructure. Although the SOEs' national market shares have already been significantly eroded by non-state investors, because of the legacy of the planned economy, some SOEs in heavy industry are protected by artificial regional autarky. Complex and non-transparent business-licensing procedures keep new entrants out of key sectors, such as electronics, petrochemicals, and machinery. Measures that foster inter-regional trade and investment will boost enterprise denationalization and revitalization.

7.5.3 *Diversification*

The diversification of shareholders is conducive to the formation of standard corporation corporate governance. Increasingly, enterprises are being partially divested to non-state interests through minority shareholding, mainly through Sino-foreign joint ventures and shares sold on stock exchanges in China and elsewhere. There has been great progress in the reform in the diversification of shareholders. But in general, the degree of the diversification

economy. This system was further improved in 1996: the construction and real estate enterprises that were originally under the Investment Management Corporation were merged into Construction Investment Holding Corporation, and the trade and circulation enterprises that were originally under the Investment Management Corporation were merged into Trade Investment Holding Corporation. This restructuring has given the state-owned asset management corporation not only the right of operation and benefit of the asset, but also the personnel power and the important investment decision power, which optimize the relationship of responsibilities within the state ownership and promote the improvement of the three-layer state-owned asset management system.

is still not high. This is reflected in the following two aspects: First, there is still a great part of the reformed enterprises that have not implemented the diversification of shareholders. For example, among the 2066 reformed enterprises in the pilot program of establishing the modern enterprise system organized by various regions and departments, 31.7% have been reformed into corporations fully owned by the state, the total asset of which is 49% of that of all the reformed enterprises. Second, in the enterprises reformed into corporation with multi-shareholders, most of them are absolutely controlled by the state-ownership. For example, among the 1412 enterprises reformed into limited liability companies with multi-shareholders or limited liability stock companies in the pilot program of establishing the modern enterprise system organized by various regions and departments, 65.7% are companies absolutely controlled by the state-ownership. So, it is imperative to take measures to actively deepen the diversification of shareholders.

Except the industries and fields where state-owned economy shall be in control, the transfer of state-owned shares shall not be limited by state control or state participation in the ownership. In enterprises that have appropriate conditions, the transfer of state-owned shares shall give due consideration to the bringing the strategic investment. Concerning the shares owned by the capital management and operation companies that were originally transferred from the debts of the SOEs, it would be more effective if capital management and operation companies transfer the shares to the non state-owned legal person or natural person at home and abroad on the basis of sticking to the relevant state principles in adjusting the structures of state-owned economy.

Diversifying ownership alone, however, is not enough, and, without the proper institutional framework of checks and balances, may compound insider control problems. The keys to success are to ensure that ownership diversification is carried out through transparent and competitive procedures; that it is cross-regional and cross-sectoral; that the process provides for transferability of shares; and, most importantly, that it provides for investments on behalf of the state to be managed by independent professionals, custodians or trustees whose remuneration is linked to their performance. At the same time, organizational layers need to be eliminated or simplified wherever feasible. The first step is to clarify the relationship between the board of directors, managerial group and the supervision committee. The board of directors is a decision-making body, exercising the power of personnel approval and decision making and some of the powers of shareholders meeting. The managerial group is an executive body, exercising the power of personnel approval and management. The supervision board is the supervisory institution, exercising the power of personnel approval and supervision. The relevant working procedures should provide the basis and guidance for the corporation's operation. The second step is to appropriately handle the relationship of the board of directors, the supervision committee with the Party committee, trade union and Inspection committee in the corporate governance. And the third step is to set up the organizational framework according to the request of modern enterprise system and operate according to the international practice.

During this process, it is desirable to create a market for corporate control. Mergers and acquisitions in the stock markets are important because they help resolve problems such as duplication of facilities and suboptimal plant scale that resulted from denationalization. A viable market for corporate control would make the threat of potential takeovers of inefficiently managed firms credible, would strengthen governance and ensure that state-owned assets are being put to more productive uses. Such a market could be based on the emerging network of regional property rights transactions centers.

7.6 Summary

While it is clear that Chinas economic reforms are responsible for lifting millions of Chinese out of immiserating poverty, it is also clear that many of the most difficult reforms are yet to be undertaken. Indeed, there is a strong case to be made that much of the economic growth during the 1980s and 1990s was due to an increase in allocative efficiency and increases in productivity. Many have suggested that China is now entering a second, and much more difficult stage of reform, one that will not be fully realized absent a stronger system of private property rights.

The case of SOE reform is illustrative. Since 1984, the Chinese government has quite literally announced every year in some declaration that the following year was the crucial or would be the breakthrough year in reforming the stagnant SOE system. However, much work remains to be done. This chapter finds that there has been some backtracking in the sense that corporatized SOEs have been able to divert state assets and engage in spontaneous privatization as evidenced in their post-IPO equity financing decisions. We conclude that further privatization, denationalization, and diversification are necessary impetus to speed up China's reform process.

Chapter 8

Accounting Information and Stock Performance

8.1 Introduction

As more nations develop democratic, market-based economies, adopting standards based on generally accepted accounting principles (GAAP) is becoming increasingly important to the soundness of their financial systems. The adoption of internationally recognized accounting standards can ease privatization efforts because of the confidence they provide individual shareholders. Without such standards, the ability of privately held enterprises to attract capital from bankers and investors is seriously impaired.

Sound accounting standards support efficient financial management and reporting systems that provide vital information to creditors and equity investors so that they can make profitable investments. Investors provide much needed risk capital and are concerned with the risk inherent in, and return provided by, their investments. Investors need information that will help them determine if they should buy, hold, or sell an investment. Lenders, on the other hand, are interested in information that permits them to determine whether their loans, and the interest attaching to them, will be paid when due.

While a nation's choice of accounting standards is necessarily unique, some consistencies among various nations' standards make them useful to investors and creditors. The International Accounting Standards Committee (IASC) and the European Union (EU) both articulate accounting standards that are widely respected in the major capital markets.

Under these standards, transparency is achieved by requiring firms to issue financial statements along with footnotes that indicate the accounting techniques used for certain transactions. The financial statements also provide information about management's stewardship of enterprise resources and thus facilitate managerial control. The most common model regarding the issuance of financial statements calls for the statements to consist of a balance sheet, a profit and loss statement, and a cash flow statement.

Financial statements portray the effects of transactions and other events by grouping them into broad classes (or elements) according to their economic characteristics. The balance sheet is the primary financial statement that helps determine an enterprise's financial position-and crucial information for potential lenders. Information about financial structure (relative amounts of capital provided by investors and lenders) is useful in predicting future borrowing needs and how future profits and cash flows will be distributed among those interested in the enterprise. Financial structure information also helps predict how successful the enterprise is likely to be in future financing transactions. Information about liquidity and solvency is useful for predicting an enterprise's ability to meet financial commitments. Liquidity relates to short-term availability of cash after taking into consideration short-term financial commitments. Solvency relates to long term availability of cash to meet commitments as they become due.

The primary financial statement that provides information about an enterprise's profitability is the income statement, also known as the profit and loss statement. Information about enterprise profitability is useful to assess likely changes in the enterprise's control of economic resources and the ability of the enterprise to generate cash flows from existing resources. Information about the variability of profits is also useful for predicting future cash flows. In addition, profitability information helps determine how effectively an enterprise might employ additional resources.

A lender wants to obtain some confidence an enterprise can generate sufficient cash to meet scheduled debt payments; cash flow information helps determine this. The cash flow statement reports cash flows from investing, financing, or operating activities. Lenders are interested in the sources from which cash is generated, the timing and certainty of its generation, and how the cash is used. For example, an enterprise's long-term prospects depend on its ability to generate sufficient cash from profitable operations to provide returns to investors and other financing sources. If current cash requirements are instead generated by investing activities such as securities, or from financing activities such as long-term borrowing or the sale of stock, this information will be valuable to lenders.[1]

Accounting standards also specify supplementary information that accompanies financial statements. These items, summarily called footnotes, should contain additional relevant information about items in the balance sheet and income statement. This information could relate to the risks and uncertainties affecting the enterprise, resources and obligations of the enterprise not recognized in the balance sheet, or breakdowns of figures by geographic area, customer type, or other category. Footnotes also contain detailed information about the accounting standards a firm employs, thereby lending transparency to the statements.[2]

This chapter provides an empirical study of how useful accounting information is in the emerging Chinese stock markets. This chapter is motivated by recent developments in both research and practice on the valuation effects of accounting information releases. In Section 8.2, we discussion the general roles of financial disclosure for evaluating the performance, risk and valuation of a company. In Section 8.3, we detail the corporate disclosures made by listed Chinese companies. In Section 8.4, we study how informative corporate disclosures are by examining whether and to what extent current stock returns and future earnings changes reflect the degree of voluntary disclosures. In Section 8.5, we use event studies to investigate the stock returns around the earnings announcement. We provide some explanations on why domestic Chinese investors tend to over-react to earnings releases in Section 8.6.

8.2 Roles of Financial Disclosure for Performance Evaluation

Despite the growing demand for data on companies and an increasing supply, audited financial statements remain the most important and widely used source of information on companies. In their current form, the two

[1]The cash flow statement is not as universally required as the other statements. The European Union, for example, does not require it. The cash flow statement is becoming increasing important, however, in judging management's performance and assessing an enterprise's ability to repay a loan.

[2]No one statement tells the whole story. The income statement, for example, provides an incomplete picture of performance without reference to the balance sheet or the cash flow statement. As a result, lenders and investors need information from each of the statements to make their decisions.

principal goals of financial statements are to ensure that appropriate monitoring takes place and provide the basis to value securities.

Accounting has evolved from cash accounting, a system for tracking receipts and payments, to accrual accounting that tracks profit and loss over time and describes the ability of an enterprise to operate as a going concern, to describing disposable income or the free cash flow generated by an operation. The emergence of balance sheets, next profit and loss and finally cash flow statements can be taken as a rough metaphor for this evolution. These major additions to financial reporting resulted in a qualitative improvement in the information available to users.

However, the view of some market analysts is that financial statements, and in particular the balance sheet, were never designed to provide the value of a company. Markets value companies, the argument goes, and the real value of an enterprise can be determined rapidly and simply by consulting share prices in a newspaper. This view is consistent with contemporary valuation models which state that the value of a company is represented solely by its ability to generate future cash flows and that the task of financial markets is to value shares incorporating all available data. Under this model, financial statements provide the information that allows users–in this case securities analysts–to estimate the size of the cash flow and any related risk. It is further argued that since many intangible assets could only be valued based upon the value of the cash flows they generate, their inclusion in balance sheets would create a circularity of reasoning, i.e., statements would no longer be useful for estimating future cash flows since they already use future cash flows to determine the value of assets. Thus, the central question remains whether financial statements, and the balance sheet in particular are supposed to value enterprises or simply provide elements of a much larger set of data necessary to value enterprises.

While historical data is important in evaluating performance potential, financial markets rely on future cash flows to determine value. Various parts of financial statements may provide information of a predictive nature that give clues to future cash flows. Most probably management's discussion of operations would include forward-looking information of a strategic nature such as plans to develop new markets, acquisitions, divestitures, etc. Statements, however, rarely include financial projections. Some attempts have been made to improve the forward-looking content of statements in order to support the task of projecting performance particularly in the United States where the SEC has encouraged forward-looking statements since the

1970's and passed additional legislation in 1995.

Despite improvements in financial statements, there has been little observable increase in the predictive data that companies disclose. On the one hand the legal protections are insufficient to convince companies to chance potential legal action against them and many companies believe that the markets are not sufficiently interested in such data to warrant running the risk. There is also some doubt about the ability of companies to take a balanced view given a natural bias to portray positively the results of current efforts and programmes. Conceptually, it is uncertain whether it is the company's role to provide projections or to provide data with which better projections can be constructed. This may be reflected in current practice where deep-seated reticence to commit forward-looking data to paper has been accompanied by increased oral discussions of future performance with analysts.

Financial risk is generally taken to be the level of uncertainty with respect to potential gain or loss on an investment. By its very nature risk is forward-looking and thus difficult to quantify. It is often measured by the past volatility of earnings or the volatility associated with a certain expected outcome. Better disclosure of risk would promise to improve the cost of capital to companies, encourage better risk management, improve governance, the protection of investors and improve the usefulness of financial statements overall. As with traditional accounting measures, the quality of risk related information would be improved if subject to similar standards of materiality, reliability, comparability and understandability.

Risk disclosure may be useful in several areas, most obviously in the area of company treasury policy and the use of financial instruments. Companies with an intensive use of financial instruments may significantly reduce the information value of the balance sheet. Instruments such as interest rate swaps (broadly speaking the exchange of differing terms and maturities of debt instruments) are quickly effectuated and may alter the capital and risk structure of an enterprise.

Whatever disclosures are ultimately made, it is unlikely that they will fully satisfy all users since information needs are constantly evolving and vary across regions.

8.3 Corporate Disclosures Made by Listed Chinese Companies

Accounting reform and the improvements in accounting information have provided favorable conditions for economic transformation and development of the capital market in China. Disclosing accounting information on stock market listed companies has become an important issue because of its significant influence on the security market. There is strong evidence that disclosed accounting profits have conveyed information to the market with consequent effect. This indicates a kind of rational investment power based on the nature of capital has been established in the Chinese security market.

8.3.1 *A Brief History of Accounting Development*

The present Chinese accounting regulations and practices have evolved from a Russian-style macro-economy oriented accounting system adopted by China in the 1950s. Encouragingly, the accounting reform has speeded up from the early 1990s to adapt to the market-based economy in the country.

Since China initiated economic reform from the late 1970s, Chinese accounting, especially accounting for enterprise, has been changing remarkably with a view towards accounting standardization and internationalization.

A major innovation for SOEs, namely the Management Responsibility Contract System (MRCS) was introduced in the early 1980s. Government contracted with each individual SOE establishing performance targets and specified incentives to achieve or exceed these targets. The liberalization of the concept of control in accounting took a variety of forms. Within centralized targets, a greater degree of freedom was given to managers of state industry concerns. For example, managers were allowed to retain part of the profit of their concerns to expand production and pay bonuses to employees; extra goods produced above state plans' targets were allowed to be sold to market or were directed towards export trade where part of the foreign exchange earnings could be retained in the relevant concern to improve technology. Accounting practice became slightly more than a central government control measure.

To further attract foreign capital, a new accounting theory emerged.

Accounting conventions and principles in the *Accountancy Law for Joint Ventures* fused western accounting theory with Chinese cultural philosophy. This provided a unique theoretical framework with a special nationalized accrual accounting and a special notion of revenue recognition/realization unique to Chinese culture. It embraces a specific shade of accrual accounting with a twist in defining recognition and realization of income and costs as it really occurred within mainland China.

A remarkable change took place in Chinese accounting in 1993. *The Basic Accounting Standards for Enterprise* was issued in November 1992 and was brought into practice with 13 new accounting regulations for enterprises in different industries from July 1, 1993. The purpose of the reform is to establish an accounting standards system that not only suits the socialist market economy in the country but also reconciles Chinese accounting with the internationally accepted accounting practices. The new accounting standards reflect that by introducing measures to identify more clearly some accounting parameters that are capable of giving signals to efficiency and productivity at the microeconomic level of SOEs and also by allowing outside users of financial statements to assess more accurately their performance.[3]

The first nationwide accounting standard similar to IAS was promulgated in 1997. By the end of 1998, a total of eight accounting standards have been pronounced. Among these standards, seven are applicable only to listed companies. The new accounting standards are practical standards as well as conceptual, they relate accounting theory to the new environment. They are governmental regulations and an accounting conceptual framework. They consist of basic premises, accounting objectives, general principles, accounting elements and their determination and measurement, the content of financial statements and their presentation, and disclosure of further information.

Overall, Chinese accounting standards have reflected the methods required for Chinese tax accounting, and have therefore been closer to a cash or tax system of reporting than international standards. Winkle, Huss and Xi-Zhu (1994) and Chen, Gui and Sui (1999) provide a summary of the

[3]The new accounting standards introduce the concept of equity capital, which provides a sharper distinction between product cost and period cost. Equity capital concept is similar to the capital maintenance concept used internationally. The new accounting standards allow state enterprises to accumulate accounting data that can provide signals of how economic resources are allocated within firms.

Chinese accounting standards adopted in December 1992. They find that while these standards parallel U.S. and international practices in many regards, there are a few notable differences. First, in valuing assets, Chinese standards require strict adherencc to historical cost, making no provision for mark-to- market or lower-of-cost-or-market. This can have a significant effect on the valuation of inventories, which can be valued at planned prices. Second, the government has stipulated depreciation rates for capital assets and bad debt allowances for receivables (0.3-0.5% of gross receivables) regardless of a firms business economics. Third, Chinese standards do not recognize some of the more complex liabilities, such as contingencies, and lease obligations. Finally, the level of disclosure is often limited. For example, related party sales between listed and holding companies may not be reported, making sales difficult to interpret.

8.3.2 *Financial Reporting Practices*

After the corporatization of SOEs, without direct control and without involvement in day-to-day management, the government authorities and shareholders have to rely on the SOEs' financial statements to make decisions. However, managers have incentives to manipulate financial information. They may inflate profits to their benefit or provide false financial statements to conceal embezzlement and other irregular behavior. Financial statements provided by management may not represent the true performance SOEs. In addition, the expansion of the Shanghai and Shenzhen Securities Exchanges provide direct incentives and pressures for market-oriented financial disclosure.

Therefore, on August 31, 1994, the Standing Committee of the National Congress adopted the *Auditing Law of the People's Republic of China*, which was effective on January 1, 1995. The Auditing Law reinforces the roles and responsibilities of the state audit office. It prescribes the scope and procedure of auditing of SOEs. Table 8.1 presents the enactment of new accounting and auditing regimes by the National Congress over time. The independent audit professions, which can provide unbiased views on the financial reports are established.[4]

The Accounting Law (1993) requires every organization to prepare fi-

[4]According to the requirements from the Ministry of Finance (MOF), three types of companies in China are required to be audited annually by independent CPAs: listed companies; companies with foreign investors or partners; and selected SOEs.

Table 8.1 The Development of Chinese Accounting and Auditing Regime

Regulator	Main regulation	Applicable enterprises
The National Congress	The Accounting Law (1985, revised in 1993)	All enterprises
	The Auditing Law (1994)	SOEs
	The Law on Certified Public Accountants (1993)	Auditing profession
	The Law for State-owned Industrial Enterprises (1988)	SOEs
	The Company Law (1993)	Share capital-based firms
The State Council	Tentative Regulations on the Management of the Issuing and Trading of Securities (1993)	Share capital-based firms
The Ministry of Finance	Accounting Standards for Business Enterprises (1992)	All enterprises
	General Rules on Business Financial Management (1992)	All enterprises
	Industry specific accounting systems (1992)	Relevant industries
	Independent Auditing Standards (since 1995)	All enterprises
The China Securities Regulatory Commission	Implementing Rules on Information Disclosure by Public Issuing Companies (trial) (1993)	Public issuing companies
	Standards of Contents and Formats of Information Disclosure by Public Issuing Companies (1994, 1997, 1998)	Public issuing companies

nancial statements based on its accounting records in accordance with the accounting system defined by the State. Three main financial statements need to be prepared by business enterprises, namely the balance sheet, the income statement and the statement of changes in financial position or cash flow statement. The three statements should be supplemented by supporting schedules, notes, and an explanatory statement on financial conditions.

The Company Law (1993) requires all share capital-based firms to prepare an audited financial report at the end of the year. A limited liability company should provide the report to its shareholders whereas a share capital limited company is required to display the report at its registered office prior to the annual general meeting so that shareholders can consult it. A public listed firm has to publish its report in a major news media. It must prepare both an interim report and an annual report within 60 days after the first 6 months of the year and within 120 days of the end of the year, respectively. It must submit 10 copies to the CSRC, publish an abstract in at least one national newspaper approved by the CSRC, and deposit the reports and abstract in the company's registered office and with the relevant stock exchange and securities trading agents for public consultation. Board of directors must ensure that there are no fraudulent or seriously misleading statements contained in their publicly disclosed information, or any important omissions.[5]

The annual report for a public listed company typically consists of the following sections:

- Brief introduction of the company
- Three-year summary of accounting and operations data
- Chairman or managing director's statement
- Directors' report
- Financial statements
- Statement of material events
- Description of related companies
- Notice of the annual shareholders' meeting

Major characteristics of the annual report include:

[5] Chinese financial reporting requirements treat domestic and international investors differently. Firms issuing A-shares are required to report under Chinese accounting standards, whereas firms issuing B-shares are required to use IAS, and firms issuing H-shares are subject to Hong Kong accounting standards or IAS.

(1) the focus is on the company's short term (rather than long term) objectives and strategies;
(2) there is an emphasis on disclosure of technological innovation;
(3) although discussion is required of the company's immediate industry, the wider political, social, and demographic context is largely neglected;
(4) an emphasis is placed on reporting material events and legal proceedings;
(5) business opportunities and risks do not feature as important;
(6) little emphasis is placed on the competitive market forces that influence the company's businesses;
(7) the requirements for financial statements are relatively simple.

Along with the enforcement of financial reporting practices, the Chinese accounting profession revived to meet the urgent need for accounting and auditing services. The first Chinese CPA firm was established in Shanghai in January 1981, which was followed by a rapid growth of new firms in other cities. As a result, accounting education has improved remarkably.[6] In the meanwhile, the Chinese auditing market is shared by state auditors, local CPA firms and international accounting firms.

To further complicate financial reporting, domestic and international reports tend to be audited by different audit firms. Domestic reports typically are audited by Chinese auditors that potentially face severe problems in attracting and retaining qualified personnel and maintaining independence. In addition, Chinese firms still have difficulty enforcing standards for listed companies that are former SOEs where the government has a strong continuing ownership and an interest in limiting the release of reports that question the performance or viability of these entities. Xiang (1998) reports that both Chinese exchanges are vexed by company hesitancy to follow corporate disclosure rules and accurate accounting procedures. Only about half the listed firms submit acceptable annual reports. Xiao, Zhang, and Xie (2000) report that major features of Chinese auditing include lack of

[6]China has been holding nation-wide CPA entrance examinations from 1992 and carrying on continuing professional education to enhance the service of accounting. The CPA entrance examinations are under the supervision of the Commission on National CPA Examinations, in the Ministry of Finance and administered by the Examination Committee of the CICPA (the Chinese Institute of Certified Public Accountants). The CICPA is responsible for preparing, monitoring and grading the national CPA examinations.

audit independence, the shortage of well-qualified auditors, an environment of extensive corruption, and the existence of many misconceptions about the audit.[7] Financial reports prepared under IAS are typically audited either by Big Five or large Hong Kong firms. These international firms are less likely to be subject to many of the problems facing local Chinese firms. However, they are unlikely to be immune to shortage in qualified staff and to questionable audit practices in their Chinese offices.

Since IAS is often considered a better accounting standard than Chinese GAAP and Big Five auditors compare more favorably in audit quality to their Chinese counterparts, the existence of a dual reporting and auditing mechanism may represent a unique institutional environment which affects the value relevance of accounting information in the Chinese market. Consequently, it is more an empirical question of whether accounting information is useful to domestic investors in the Chinese market as measured by the contemporaneous association between accounting numbers and stock valuation.

8.3.3 *Capital Market Infrastructure*

Disclosure can only be effective when coupled with an efficient system for the dissemination of information. A critical challenge in the development of a modern capital market in a transitional economy is the creation of effective underlying institutions and infrastructure. These include the aforementioned financial reporting and auditing standards. However, they also include secondary market efficiency, capital market regulations, legal protection of private property, maturity of financial intermediaries, and the financial media in general.

Not surprisingly, China has only begun to develop financial institutions and capital market infrastructure. The efficiency of secondary market and accuracy in valuing financial assets are critical for financial reporting, which in turn affect the pricing of initial public offering. Prior to going public, SOEs have to prepare financial reports that present data on the historical cost of capital and current assets, as well as estimates of the current value of net assets. However, many assets were acquired at planned prices, not

[7] In order to audit listed companies, a CPA firm must meet stringent requirements jointly set by the MOF and the CSRC. Among some 7,000 CPA firms, only 105 have been authorized to audit around 700 listed companies, as of the end of 1997 (Yang and Yang, 1998). As a result, auditing of listed companies is a highly competitive market.

market prices. Prospective issuers obtain independent valuations of their assets for both setting offer prices and for financial reporting. External valuation firms (from Hong Kong and elsewhere) are used in the valuations for international offerings. These valuations can raise sensitive political questions, since the Chinese government is anxious to ensure that stocks sold to international investors are not under-priced.

Valuations for domestic issues are typically by Chinese valuation firms. However, there is a severe shortage of trained professional evaluators, making it difficult to assess the quality of these valuations. Responsibility for the regulation of financial markets in China nominally lies with the CSRC.[8]

Another important form of infrastructure for financial reporting and capital markets is legal protection for investors. Securities laws typically protect a number of shareholder rights in developed market economies. These include protections of minority shareholders rights to vote for boards of directors and to sue management for fraud, misleading disclosures or misappropriation of funds. Investors are likely to have questions about the extent of these forms of protection in China. Since the government is the majority owner of most listed companies, protections of the rights of minority owners are especially relevant. In addition, international investors are likely to have concerns about whether they have the same rights as domestic investors.

Winkle, Huss, and Xi-Zhu (1994) cite claims that PRC- and IAS-based reports are often released at different times and contain different levels of information. Typical investor complaints are that A-share investors receive financial information earlier than B-share investors and that A-share investors receive a much broader disclosure of the companys performance.

A legal system that protects shareholder rights is also important in China because the countrys economic system has historically provided job security and expansive benefits to employees and management, as well as funding for loss-making businesses. These policies raise several questions for private investors. First, is it difficult to remove management for good cause? Second, can funds provided by public issues be diverted from their intended uses towards meeting pension obligations or financing loss-making business segments? Another form of infrastructure that has been created

[8]Since 1995, the CSRC has reported directly to the State Council, the Chinese government's highest-ranking decision-making authority. Previously, it reported to the Ministry of Finance, the People's Bank of China, and the State Committee for Restructuring the Economy.

with the development of a capital market is a community of financial analysts. In developed market economies financial analysts provide investment advice and also monitor the performance of management. Management of stocks that are out-of-favor with analysts because of poor performance are then likely to be subject to increased shareholder and board scrutiny or likely to be removed by a hostile acquirer. However, in China analyst coverage is limited. There is some analyst coverage of H-shares by Hong Kong investment firms. However, there is relatively low demand for financial analyst services by international investors since the B-share market is so thinly traded. Analyst coverage of A-shares listed on the Shanghai and Shenzhen Exchanges is also limited.

Finally, firms are increasingly sensitive to the economic risks of operating without paying close attention to public opinion and the public interest. The role of the news media which can put companies under intense public scrutiny is, of course, primary. Moreover, some investment funds have decided to exercise influence by only investing in the shares of companies which have a particular policy stance on an issue. Though the influence of the latter remains limited, the potential impact of public opinion indicates that it is may not possible to divorce purely financial interests of shareholders from those of the larger community. There is increasing acceptance of the notion that the successful companies of the future will be those that can effectively balance the interests of a variety of stakeholders.

The financial press in China is likely to play a weak role in monitoring management of public companies. Chinese newspapers provide summaries of financial information on listed companies every six months. However, it is not politically feasible for them to publish articles that criticize managers who, after all, are effectively appointed by the government. In summary, capital market infrastructure in China is in a formative stage. The types of professional intermediaries and legal rights that have evolved in developed economies are still being created in China.

8.4 Stock Returns Around Earnings Releases

From the perspective of information economics, accounting and financial reporting play a vital role in an efficient capital market. This chapter provides an empirical study of how useful earnings announcements are in the emerging Chinese stock markets. This chapter is motivated by recent developments in both research and practice on the valuation effects of accounting information releases. Numerous studies, including Ball and Brown (1968), Kross and Schroeder (1984), Easton and Zmijewski (1989) and Gennotte and Truemann (1996), find that stock prices respond positively to announcements of increase in earnings and negatively to announcements of decrease in earnings for the U.S. firms. Alford, et al. (1993), Amir, et al. (1993) and Chan and Seow (1996) also provide evidence of the informational content of earnings announcements in a number of non-U.S. markets. This chapter extends this line of research to the Chinese stock markets.

8.4.1 *Information Content Analysis*

The research on information content in the setting of developed and mature capital markets implicitly assumes some necessary conditions that must prevail in the information environment in order to give credence to any market tests of information content. Some of these conditions can be stipulated as follows:

- Transaction-related data and source documents of accounting systems are the outcome of arms-length exchanges.
- Transaction data are consistently aggregated in accordance with a known set of rules.
- Effective internal controls are in place to safeguard the company's assets and to reduce opportunistic behavior.
- Internal audits are implemented to ensure the integrity of the information system, input data and produced information.
- Market prices reflect the preferences of market participants.
- Capital markets are free of manipulation by regulators, individuals in power or capricious government interference.
- Insiders do not use their informational advantage for their own gain before allowing equal access to other investors.

The aforementioned conditions are generally satisfied for listed firms in developed economies where financial and accounting institutions, the public, the press and regulators act as external monitors or "watch dogs" that assure the integrity of the data reported to the public. In addition, enforcement agencies exist for dealing with serious departures from the expected norms. In that setting, researchers can reasonably assume that investors vote with their feet, capital markets operate efficiently, and prices reflect all publicly available information. To make reliable inferences about accounting information content, markets must operate with the least possible friction, a case that is difficult to make for many emerging capital markets.

There are various reasons why share prices in emerging Chinese capital markets may not satisfy the conditions listed above. Indeed, the efficiency of Chinese stock markets has not been established because reported data and recorded stock prices may not reflect the free expression of the preferences of all market participants. Unique factors of local customs, bureaucratic regulation, the absence of a developed accounting and auditing profession, undue influence of state officials, and loose insider trading constraints do interact to impact the operation of capital markets.

For example, prior to May 1992, regulators of the stock exchanges imposed tight controls over all share prices and trading volume. Although much of the underlying motives remain behind the scenes, to public observers these controls were manifested by imposing two constraints on the trading of A shares, both aimed at reducing volatility. These constraints were: (1) the maximum allowed daily fluctuation in the price of any listed share cannot exceed 1%; and (2) trading prices should not change if volume of trade does not exceed 0.3% of the number of outstanding shares. On May 5, 1992, the allowed maximum daily fluctuation in prices was increased from 1% to 8%, but restrictions on the minimum volume required to trigger price changes were retained. On May 21, 1992 both measures of control were abolished. While the imposition of such regulatory controls on market forces has prevented share prices from reflecting the true preferences of market participants, it has artificially maintained low levels of volatility. Upon lifting the restrictions on May 21, 1992, share prices more than doubled and the SHSE price index increased by 105.3% in one day.

8.4.2 *Earnings Announcements and Stock Price Reactions in China*

Using a sample of 183 earnings announcements between 1997 and 1998 for firms that have issued both A- and B-shares prior to January 1, 1996, we investigate the stock price reactions to changes in earnings-per-share (EPS). We find that domestic A-share investors, on average, do not correctly anticipate the EPS changes and do not adjust to the new earnings information very rapidly in the markets. Excess returns or abnormal returns could be generated by trading on the earnings information after it is released. However, international investors can predict changes in EPS better than domestic investors and there is little or no abnormal announcement-day effects observed in B-share markets in China. To examine the abnormal stock returns we choose earnings announcement day as our predictable event day. We then divide our sample into two groups based on the outcome of the event. An announcement belongs to Group I if the outcome of the event is 'positive' (actual EPS exceeds last EPS). It belongs to Group II if the outcome of the event is 'non-positive' (actual EPS is equal to or less than last EPS). If the market is efficient, security prices should reflect all potential changes in the event outcomes. That is, if the required rate of return on a stock around the event day is identical to that of any other random trading day, one should not be able to make excess returns by trading around all of these event days. The unconditional expected rate of return of these announcements should not differ from that on other days. Finding excess returns, as traditionally measured, around the event day is consistent with the notion that the required rate of return during an announcement period is higher than normal and the relevant risk per unit of time during the event is higher.

Denote the daily abnormal return for any stock as

$$AR_{jt} = R_{jt} - E(\tilde{R}_{jt}), \tag{8.1}$$

where

$$\begin{aligned} t &= \text{day measured relative to the event,} \\ &\quad t = -21, -20, \cdots, -1, 0, 1, \cdots, 20, 21. \\ &\quad \text{The earnings announcement date for each firm is set to be } t = 0. \\ AR_{jt} &= \text{abnormal return to stock } j \text{ for trading day } t. \\ R_{jt} &= \text{return on stock } j \text{ during trading day } t. \\ E(\tilde{R}_{jt}) &= \text{expected rate of return on stock } j \text{ for trading day } t. \end{aligned}$$

Based on the mean adjusted returns model of Brown and Warner (1985), $E(\tilde{R}_{jt})$ is estimated from the time-series of stock j's realized returns in the pre-event window, i.e., $t = -122, \cdots, -22$. The abnormal return for each stock, AR_{jt}, is then calculated as the difference between the actual return to a stock and the estimated expected return during a pre-event period. We calculate AR_{jt} for all stocks in Group I and II for A- and B-shares.

Average abnormal returns for each trading day within the event window are calculated by

$$AR_t = \frac{1}{N}\sum_{j=1}^{N} AR_{jt}, \tag{8.2}$$

where N is the number of stocks with abnormal returns during day t. The cumulative abnormal returns for each stock j, CAR_j, are formed by summing average abnormal returns over time as follows:

$$CAR_{j,K,L} = \sum_{t=K}^{L} AR_{jt}, \tag{8.3}$$

where the $CAR_{j,K,L}$ is for the period from $t =$ day K until $t =$ day L.

Average cumulative abnormal returns over the event window from day K until day L are calculated by

$$CAR_{K,L} = \frac{1}{N}\sum_{j=1}^{N} CAR_{j,K,L}. \tag{8.4}$$

In particular, a two-day average abnormal return is generated for A- and B-shares in each group. A two-day excess return is necessary to capture the effect of an announcement due to its timing relative to the market's trading hours. Day $t = 0$ is the day the news of an announcement is published in the *China Securities Daily*. In many cases, the news is actually announced on the previous day, $t = -1$, and reported the next day. If an earnings announcement is made before the market close, then the market's response to the news actually predates the publication by one day. If the earnings announcement is released after the market closes, the market will respond the next day and the reaction is indeed on day 0. Thus in reality there is a two-day announcement period, $t = -1$ and $t = 0$. This two-day return for firm j is

$$CAR_{j,-1,0} = AR_{j,-1} + AR_{j,0}, \tag{8.5}$$

where $AR_{j,-1}$ is the abnormal return to stock j on the trading day prior to a published announcement in the *China Securities Daily* and $AR_{j,0}$ is the abnormal return to stock j on the day an announcement is published in the *China Securities Daily*.

Finally, t-statistics are calculated for $CAR_{K,L}$ by

$$t_{CAR_{K,L}} = \frac{CAR_{K,L}}{SD(CAR_{K,L})}, \tag{8.6}$$

where $SD(CAR_{K,L}) = \sqrt{T\text{Var}(AR_t) + 2(T-1) \times \text{Cov}(AR_t, AR_{t+1})}$, $T = K - L + 1$, is the standard deviation of $CAR_{K,L}$. $\text{Var}(AR_t)$ and $\text{Cov}(AR_t, AR_{t+1})$ are estimated from 122 days before the earnings announcement day to 22 days before the announcement day. The covariance term adjusts for possible first-order autocorrelation between the abnormal returns due to non-synchronous trading.

In theory, if the stock market is semi-strongly efficient, i.e., if no one can earn abnormal returns by trading on the basis of public information, then the stock prices will reflect changes in the firms' earning power. This implies that: (1) The stock market will correctly anticipate the earnings changes before they are announced to the public. Thus, firms with disappointing EPS (Group I firms) will experience unfavorable downward pressure on their prices in the days before the actual earnings announcements occur. Firms with strong EPS (Group II firms) will enjoy upward pressure on the prices in the days before the announcements to the market. (2) Since the earnings information is fully incorporated into the stock prices, no abnormal return exists during and after the earnings release. Thus, $CAR_{-1,0}$ should not be statistically significant and $CAR_{1,h+1}$, $h = 1, 2, \cdots, 20$, should be random after the announcement date.

Tables 8.2 and 8.3 present the abnormal returns (ARs) and cumulative abnormal returns (CARs) for the disappointing earnings group (Group I) and satisfactory earnings group (Group II) for A- and B-shares. The CAR results are also portrayed in Figures 1 and 2. As shown in these tables and figures, the A-share CARs for the disappointing earnings group tend to increase and stay positive before the announcement date while starting to decline two days before the earnings announcement. Such a decline persists for about 13 days after the announcement date and the A-share CARs become significantly negative. The average two-day announcement period A-share abnormal return is -2.27% with a t-statistic of -8.41 for the disappointing earnings group. On the other hand, the A-share CARs for the satisfactory earnings group tend to decline 9 days before the announcement date and become negative, while starting to grow and become positive two days before the earnings announcement. Such growth continuously lasts for 21 days after the announcement. The average two-day

Table 8.2 Abnormal Returns and Cumulative Abnormal Returns Around Earnings Announcement Days for A Shares

DAY	Group I		Group (II)	
	AR (%)	CAR (%)	AR (%)	CAR (%)
-13	-0.0491	1.869	0.1084	0.1902
-12	-0.2141	1.6549	0.6134	0.8036
-11	-0.2976	1.3573	-0.6763	0.1273
-10	0.1013	1.4586	0.918	1.0455
-9	0.6307	2.0893	-0.1216	0.9239
-8	0.3071	2.3964	-0.0572	0.8667
-7	-0.25	2.1464	-0.5963	0.2704
-6	0.2053	2.3517	-0.3188	-0.0484
-5	0.1681	2.5198	0.4219	0.3735
-4	1.5726	4.0924	-0.6399	-0.2664
-3	0.2193	4.3117	0.1823	-0.0841
-2	-0.3391	3.9726	-0.4025	-0.4866
-1	-1.0391	2.9335	1.2718	0.7852
0	-1.2315	1.702	0.8764	1.6616
1	-0.2883	1.4137	-0.9587	0.7029
2	0.3915	1.8052	0.7353	1.4382
3	-1.4566	0.3486	-0.5888	0.8494
4	0.3525	0.7011	0.6535	1.5029
5	-0.1392	0.5619	0.128	1.6309
6	0.1558	0.7177	-0.2927	1.3382
7	0.423	1.1407	-0.1976	1.1406
8	-0.4692	0.6715	0.6369	1.7775
9	-0.0719	0.5996	-0.1092	1.6683
10	-0.9161	-0.3165	-0.0846	1.5837
11	0.3289	0.0124	0.1277	1.7114
12	-0.7876	-0.7752	-0.3082	1.4032
13	-1.3216	-2.0968	1.019	2.4222
$CAR_{-1,0}$	-2.27		2.15	
t-statistic	-8.41		7.60	
N	109		74	

announcement period A-share abnormal return is 2.15% with a t-statistic of 7.6 for the satisfactory earnings group. These results indicate that the A-share market does not correctly anticipate the earnings changes prior to the announcements. The two-day announcement period average abnormal

Table 8.3 Abnormal Returns and Cumulative Abnormal Returns Around Earnings Announcement Days for B Shares

DAY	Group I		Group (II)	
	AR (%)	CAR (%)	AR (%)	CAR (%)
-13	0.6952	0.1914	0.1105	0.4605
-12	0.2618	0.4532	-0.2106	0.2499
-11	-0.5316	-0.0784	0.3799	0.6298
-10	-0.0983	-0.1767	0.0714	0.7012
-9	0.1308	-0.0459	-0.2019	0.4993
-8	0.285	0.2391	-0.0327	0.4666
-7	-0.5149	-0.2758	0.212	0.6786
-6	-0.1138	-0.3896	-0.1518	0.5268
-5	-0.2896	-0.6792	-0.0527	0.4741
-4	-0.184	-0.8632	0.2914	0.7655
-3	0.4262	-0.437	-0.388	0.3775
-2	-0.1385	-0.5755	-0.0601	0.3174
-1	-0.2006	-0.7761	0.1153	0.4327
0	-0.0551	-0.8312	0.0982	0.5309
1	-0.1138	-0.945	-0.2046	0.3263
2	0.6215	-0.3235	-0.0942	0.2321
3	-0.4127	-0.7362	0.1831	0.4152
4	0.7606	0.0244	0.1065	0.5217
5	-0.2249	-0.2005	-0.2286	0.2931
6	-0.0864	-0.2869	0.0762	0.3693
7	-0.3025	-0.5894	-0.5125	-0.1432
8	0.4351	-0.1543	-0.1364	-0.2796
9	0.1692	0.0149	0.2088	-0.0708
10	-0.625	-0.6101	-0.1165	-0.1873
11	0.5884	-0.0217	0.059	-0.1283
12	0.4266	0.4049	0.2104	0.0821
13	0.1735	0.5784	-0.1836	-0.1015
$CAR_{-1,0}$	-0.26		0.21	
t-statistic	-1.26		1.40	
N	109		74	

returns are significantly negative and positive for the disappointing and satisfactory earnings groups, respectively. The strong downward trend for the disappointing earnings group and strong upward trend for the satisfactory earnings group after the earnings information release indicate that A-share markets failed to adjust instantaneously to the new EPS information. As a result, abnormal returns can be earned by trading on the EPS information release. These results also indicate that Chinese stock markets are not semi-strong efficient as far as the earnings announcements for the sample stocks over the time period is considered.

In contrast to the findings on the A-share CARs, the B-share CARs for the same disappointing earnings group tend to decline 11 days before the announcement date, while becoming randomly positive and negative after the earnings announcement. The average two-day announcement period B-share abnormal return is merely -0.26% with a t-statistic of -1.26 for the disappointing earnings group. The B-share CARs for the same satisfactory earnings group tend to rise 15 days before the announcement date, while also becoming randomly positive and negative after the earnings announcement. The average two-day announcement period B-share abnormal return is only 0.21% with a t-statistic of 1.04 for the satisfactory group. These results suggest that B-share investors can predict the changes in earnings better than A-share investors. The insignificant two-day announcement period abnormal returns for both groups of firms and the observed random behavior of post-announcement returns indicate that B-share markets are semi-strong form efficient in the sense that B-share prices by and large reflect the potential changes in event outcome.

Table 3 provides information about the time-series behavior of post-announcement cumulative abnormal returns for two portfolios ranked in the highest and lowest $CAR_{-1,0}$ quintile. As shown in the table, there are some evidence of significant differences in CARs subsequent to earnings announcement for the two portfolios, with A-share portfolios exhibiting rather different pattern than B-share portfolios. Most of the differences in CARs for A-share portfolios occur during the first 120 trading days, and there is little evidence of statistically significant CAR differences beyond 180 trading days. However, most of the differences in CARs for B-share portfolios occur after 180 days of trading, and there is no evidence of statistically significant CAR differences during the first 180 trading days. Table 3 suggests that there might be incomplete adjustment for risk associated with earnings administered in A-share markets, and such risk exists only temporarily.

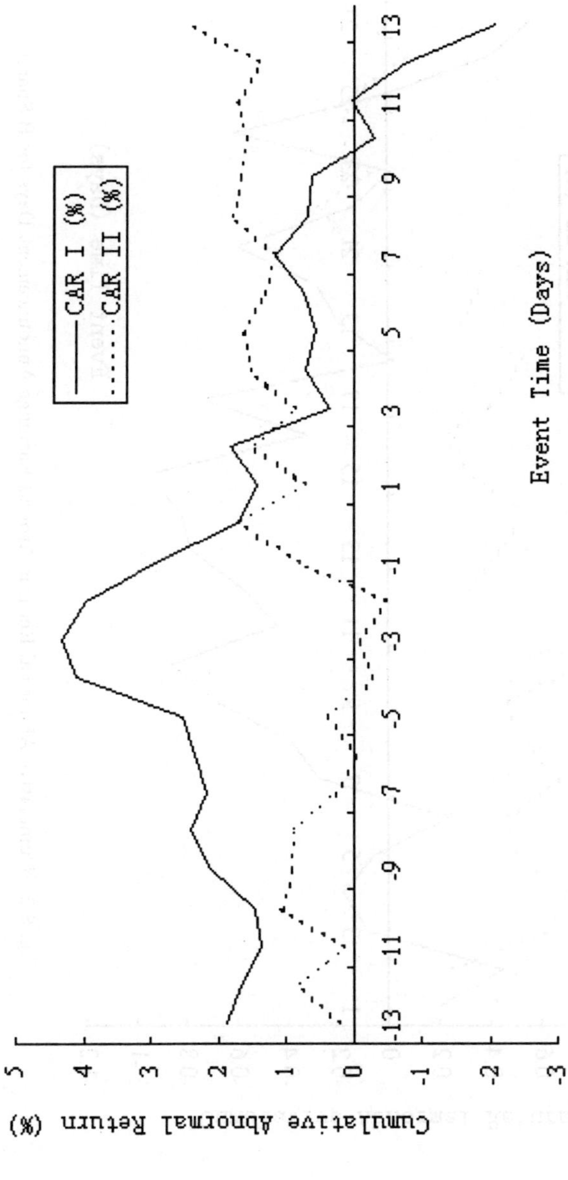

Fig. 8.1 Cumulative Abnormal Returns Around Earnings Announcement Days for A Shares

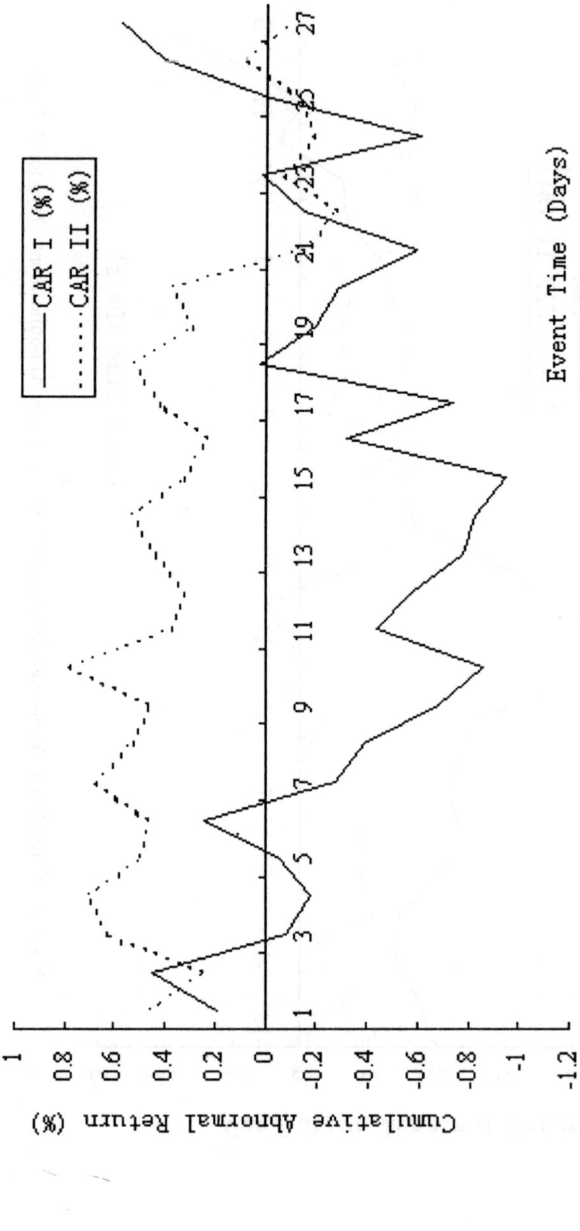

Fig. 8.2 Cumulative Abnormal Returns Around Earnings Announcement Days for B Shares

8.5 Why Domestic Investors Over-react to Earnings Release?

We believe that three reasons have contributed to the domestic investors' over-reaction to earnings announcements: First, government officials and managers may involve in insider trading of A-shares. Second, most A-share investors are short-term investors who are more likely to speculate based on sentimental factors. Third, Chinese stock markets are segmented both in trading and financial reporting requirements.

8.5.1 *Government and Management as Informed Investors*

Unless markets are taken to be informationally efficient, the unexpected variation in market return reflects the joint effect of two hypotheses: market efficiency and information content. Testing for the information content of accounting numbers, or any other news, is contingent on satisfying market efficiency. As indicated earlier in this chapter, emerging Chinese capital markets are not known to be efficient because of the numerous institutional frictions imposed by regulatory processes and unequal access to information. Some of the institutional features that characterize Chinese stock exchanges are relevant to this issue.

First, the government remains the majority shareholder, and a sizable percentage of the privatized portions of A-shares are owned by state officials, party members and other insiders. Because laws restricting insider trading are not known to be enforced, it is very likely that insiders act on the information prior to its public release and, as a result, the information content of disclosure would have been impounded in prices prior to the public release of annual reports.

Second, given that China is at the "take off" stage of economic development and growth, which averaged more than 8% a year since 1979, financial statements and short-term earnings may not be good indicators or predictors of future performance. The history of trading shares to absentee investors in a public forum and of disclosing information about business firms' performance has been too brief to develop association measures and rules-of-thumb connecting reported numbers and subsequent events.

The manager of a firm is assumed have inside knowledge or superior information, i.e., there is asymmetric information concerning various components of earnings. Other than macroeconomic variables, the outside investors are expected to depend on the managers to disclose the information. If the managers disclosures are informative and revised frequently over the interim before earnings announcements, there will be no or little earning surprises or significant stock market reactions. If there is an adequate incentive for disclosure, the manager will disclose voluntarily. Otherwise, regulatory agencies, stock exchanges, the governing body of the accounting profession have to compel the managers to disclose information involuntarily.

Without the necessary ingredients for market efficiency and allowing equal access to information prior to using it in trading, it is not defensible to conclude that the statistical results obtained for A shares are consistent with market efficiency. These results are consistent with information being reflected in security prices when any trader, including insiders, acts on it. Given the information environment described previously, a scenario can be advanced that insider trading and manipulation of trade by officials might be responsible for impounding accounting information into share prices prior to making public disclosure. Another scenario is that the obtained results are a statistical artifact because the findings about A-shares are consistent across the two stock exchanges. Since these explanations cannot be ruled out given this analysis, we are unwilling to conclude that some of the observed findings reflect the reaction to accounting numbers.

8.5.2 *Investors' Sentiments*

A-share markets lack alternative information sources other than the published accounting reports such as earnings forecasts by financial analysts and high-quality independent audits. The number of established investment specialists and institutional investors (e.g., mutual funds and pension funds) is quite small. Most transactions are executed by individual investors with limited access to information other than publicly available accounting numbers. As a consequence, price may be less informative and accounting information may contain more surprises in the A-share markets.[9]

[9]To test the hypothesis that earnings announcements contain more surprises to A-share investors than to B-share investors, we need to compare earnings forecast errors of the two groups of investors. Although data on earnings forecasts of some Chinese firms by international financial analysts are available through I/B/E/S International, earnings forecasts by domestic Chinese analysts are not available at the time this paper is written. Further research on this topic needs to be conducted.

Most individual A-share holders have a short-term investment horizon. Long-term investors are few and far between. The average turnover for A shares in 1996 in the Shanghai and Shenzhen securities exchanges is 45 and 39 trading days, respectively.[10] With short-term horizon, investors tend to be more concerned with current period accounting earnings and dividends and may over-react or under-react to accounting information mechanically to revise their beliefs about future profitability. Therefore, it is more likely to observe a contemporaneous association of accounting information with A-share stock returns.

From our data, approximately 50% to 60% of all listed firms in 1994 disclosed accounting reports to the public, with this percentage increasing to over 90% in 1997, suggesting an improved reporting system. The annual volume of trade for A-shares was about 20 times that of B-shares in 1997. At average currency conversion rates of 1997, this volume amounts to about US$40 billion in 1997 as compared to US$2 billion in December 1994. The ratio of A-shares to B-shares during 1998 was about 52% and the corresponding ratio in 1997 increased to about 65%. Thus, the number of listed firms has increased in 1997 over 1994 and A-shares were traded much more heavily in 1997 as compared to 1994. In addition, the SHSE publication reports that turnover rates for A- and B-shares are 20 and 6 in 1997 and 18 and 3.5 1998, respectively. These ratios reveal the extent to which B-shares are thinly traded as compared to A-shares. As a result, analysis of the association between unexpected returns and accounting information is not likely to reveal the true linkage between accounting information and prices of B-shares.

8.5.3 *Market Valuation and Transparency*

Third, Chinese stock markets are segmented both in trading and reporting requirements. Ang and Ma (1999) suggest that the extent of transparency of Chinese stocks is generally quite low. For instance one may suggest that requirements of the B-share listing have made the B-shares to appear more transparent than the A-shares, that larger firms have more incentive and sophistication to voluntarily disclose earnings information. We may also argue that when there is little information that is made available, differences in the opinions among market participants may also tend to

[10]Source: Annual statistics published by the Shanghai and Shenzhen stock exchanges.

be high. And if less relevant information is available, some investors may respond to rumors and other unreliable information, resulting in unusually high price movements and trading volume.

On the other hand, international B-share investors are typically large institutional investors, such as mutual funds and pension funds. They are the key force to drive B-share markets up or down. Actions taken by these institutional investors usually are not based on liquidity reasons, but based on information revealed by firms that issued securities. Such a case is particularly true for firms in which financial and operational situations are in question. Furthermore, international investors require more up-front information and that this information is provided, in part, by the publication of much more detailed and informative balance sheets for B-share investors than for domestic A-share investors. International investors also have the capability to conduct more sophisticated analyses.

In summary, Chinese A-share markets are considerably speculative while B-share markets are relatively more efficient in terms of the reaction to stock prices during and after earnings announcements. Domestic Chinese investors do not seem to completely understand the true nature of the equity market. Following a common trend, most individual investors are blind to a stock's fundamental or trade stocks without using firms' financial information correctly. Moreover, some inconsistencies regarding accounting standards and information disclosures exist. These suggest that it is necessary to implement educational programs about securities markets for individual investors and construct a set of consistent regulations in disclosing accounting, auditing, and other financial information.

Chapter 9

Internationalization of Chinese Stock Markets

9.1 Foreign Investment in Domestic B-Share Market

Hoping to attract more foreign investment to fund its economy, China started issuing B-shares for foreign investors on the Shanghai Securities Exchange (SHSE) and Shenzhen Securities Exchange (SZSE) soon after issuing A-shares for domestic investors.[1] B-shares were issued not by public offering but solely through international placement by going on road-shows to meet international fund managers at major financial centers.

Because B-shares were privately placed, most of the shares were in the hands of institutional buyers. This resulted in two problems: one is a lack of liquidity in the secondary market since most B-share buyers are big equity investment funds who tend to hold for long-term gains and their one-time purchasing lots often exceed a million; the second problem is the inconvenience in the trading venues and inadequate disclosure of information about B-share companies. As a result, trading becomes quite thin. The daily turnover averaged only US$ several millions in SHSE and in SZSE. The B-share Index is below issuing price, 48.73 on October 21, 1996, against an average of 50.2 on the SHSE; and 89.58 the same day in SZSE, with an average of 82.669 (close). The Price Earning (P/E) ratio is about 5-7 times, much below that of A-shares and H-shares.[2]

[1] In 1991, the SHSE and SZSE began to offer B shares, providing foreign investors with a legal channel to invest in China's equity markets.

[2] Unlike B-shares, A-shares were traded by many individual players and fewer institutional investors. Individuals can be quite speculative in the domestic market. Market price movement is volatile and market turnover is generally small.

9.1.1 *Market Microstructure Issues*

B-shares are offered and traded on the SHSE and SZSE, which designate domestic or overseas securities dealers as specially licensed brokers to accept foreign investors' consignment for trading. These exchanges began to offer special seats for B-share trading in 1994 and overseas securities dealers were allowed to engage in floor trading via the seats. By the end of 1998, 106 companies had issued B shares with a total of 9.589 billion shares issued and a total of US$ 4.745 billion capital raised.

Any subscription of B-shares must be processed through authorized local securities or international financial institutions approved by relevant authority for the purpose of dealing in B-shares. At the time of subscription, the subscriber should by way of evidence present his identity card or passport or, in case of a legal entity, its registration certificate. If any holder of B-shares holds more than 5% of the total issued share capital of the issuer, such holding must be reported to and approved by the People's Bank of China (PBOC).

All B-shares are centrally listed at the SHSE and SZSE, and transactions are carried out through the computerized trading system. Orders are matched automatically by computer on price, time and sequence priority. Foreign investors are required to buy and sell B-shares through authorized foreign brokers who in turn instruct the approved SHSE and SZSE brokers actually to initiate trades. Trading outside the exchange is prohibited.

Every investor dealing in B-shares must open a B-share account directly or through securities companies at the SHSE or SZSE. Foreign investors shall present their B share account passbooks and their valid certificates of identity and complete the dealing instruction forms when they deal in B-shares in China. Foreign investors conducting B-share transactions from overseas are required to do so through a foreign securities company.

Short selling is prohibited. Newly purchased B-shares cannot be sold before the settlement and registration procedures for their purchase are completed.

The rate of exchange between U.S. dollar and RMB to be applied in connection with any issue or trading of B-shares or payment of dividend shall be the RMB to US dollar weekly weighted average conversion rate as quoted by the Shanghai Foreign Exchange Adjustment Center for the previous week.

Transactions in B-shares are generally effected on the third business day after the date of transaction, i.e., T+3. A "business day" means any day on which the B-share clearing banks, the SHSE, the SZSE, and banks in New York are open for business concurrently. The exchanges may appoint banks approved by the PBOC to handle the clearance and settlement of all B-share transactions. However, for each issuer, only one of them will be involved.

The following transaction costs are levied on each purchase or sale of B shares in Shanghai and Shenzhen (calculated in RMB but payable in US dollars only):

In Shanghai, brokerage fees shall be charged at 0.6% of the total transaction value. For transactions more than RMB 100,000, the brokerage fees may be reduced but not less than 0.3%. Transfer fees are set at 0.1% of the total par value of the shares transferred. 0.3% of the total transaction value is levied as stamp duty fee.

The brokerage fee for a B share transaction in Shenzhen is 0.6% of total transaction value if conducted directly by an authorized broker in Shenzhen, or 0.7% of the transaction value if conducted by an authorized foreign broker. The stamp duty is 0.3% of the total transaction value. The exchange transaction levy is 0.1% of total transaction value.

Under the *Regulation for Foreign Investment Enterprise (FIE)*, the *Foreign Enterprise Income Tax Law of the PRC* and the *Individual Income Tax Law* (the IIT Law), dividends received by a foreign enterprise with no establishment in the P.R.C. or by a foreign individual are generally subject to tax at a flat rate of 20%. However, this tax on dividends is exempted if the payer is a FIE. Pursuant to the Shanghai and Shenzhen joint stock company regulations, if more than 25% of the total share capital is owned by foreign investors subsequent to the B-share issue, the company qualifies for the same privileges as a FIE.

According to existing P.R.C. laws and practices, any capital gains realized on the sale of an interest in a FIE by foreign enterprise with no establishment in the P.R.C. will generally be classified by the State Taxation Bureau as income and will be subject to a taxation rate of 20%. However, the rate of taxation will be reduced to 10% in the case of gains derived from source in the Special Economic Zones, the Economic and Technological Development Zones, the Open Coastal Cities and the Coastal Open Economic Zones.

Pursuant to the *Rules and Regulations of Shanghai and Shenzhen on B Shares*, all dividends, distributions and proceeds of sale derived from

B-shares may be remitted out of China in their entirety. Capital gains realized on the disposal of the B-shares may be remitted out of China after payment of tax in accordance with laws. As a matter of procedure, all the payments are subject to the approval of the State Administration of Exchange Control (the SAEC).

9.1.2 *Risks Involved*

The risks faced by foreign investors in B-shares can be generally classified into two categories. First, by the external risks, including the political, economic, regulatory environment and foreign exchange risks; secondly, the internal risks which are directly associated with the operation of the company, mainly the management, the standard of account and the quality of the prospectus.

Despite the introduction of a number of market mechanisms into the Chinese economy, central planning and the state sector still dominate the economy. This gives the central government tremendous power to intervene in particular sectors of the economy which may affect the share markets directly or indirectly. While there are a large number of rules and regulations on joint stock companies and securities issues, they are not comprehensive enough and sometimes conflict with each other. While the PBOC is the authority-in-charge, many other institutions overlap in drafting, rule-making power, and the approving process.

As mentioned above, any transactions for B-shares are calculated in RMB but payable in US or HK dollars only as the *Renminbi* is not freely convertible in international markets. The devaluation of RMB from time to time has proved to be a significant exchange risk for B-share investors.

The management of listed companies is perhaps the greatest risk that foreign investors have to face. The concept of "maximizing profits" is very weak among Chinese managers. Furthermore, the accounts system in China is different from international accounting standards. Chinese companies are usually reluctant to disclose information when first issuing B-shares due to competition. Some of the prospectuses issued are brief and are not capable of disclosing sufficient information to protect investors.

China's hard currency dominated B-share market has long been sluggish because of its own drawbacks since its establishment in the early 1990s, including its limited scale, low mobility, sharp fluctuations and limited access to foreign investors. Anthony Francis Neoh, chief advisor of the CSRC revealed that the commission could adopt a qualified foreign institutional investor pattern (as India's stock markets did), to allow foreign investors easy access to the domestic A-share market. Foreign investors' involvement in the *Renminbi*-based A-share market would soon make the prices of the listed A- and B-shares the same—a prerequisite for the merger of the two markets.

Before any merger, China's A-share stock markets in Shenzhen and Shanghai will have to merge first, and the long-awaited high-tech or second-board stock market, which is designed mainly for small and medium-sized firms, could be launched in Shenzhen if the merger succeeds. But if it fails, there would be a possibility of setting up two parallel second boards at Shanghai and Shenzhen respectively. Nevertheless, the long-awaited second-board market, to bolster China's high-tech industries, would be launched before the end of the year or the beginning of 2001. Companies planning to list in the second market would have much lower requirements than their A-share counterparts. Indeed, Unilever, one of the world's biggest producers of consumer goods, is trying to be the first foreign company to list domestic A-shares in China. A spokesperson with the Shanghai headquarters of Unilever (China) said:

> We hope that our customers here in China can also become our shareholders, as an incentive for us to upgrade our services and expand our market share.

But she also admitted that the company was still waiting for policy adjustments by the Chinese government, which would clearly map out the requirements for listing. The permission would, however, require the speeding up of the merging of the A- and B-share markets, which is still proceeding slowly. Today, most of the A-share stocks are state-owned companies and foreign investors are still not allowed to list or trade A-shares.

9.2 Overseas Listing of Chinese Stocks

According to the CSRC documents, overseas listing is an important policy for the reform and opening-up of Chinese enterprises to the outside. From the listing of Qingdao Beer on the Hong Kong Stock Exchange on July 15, 1993 to Yanzhou Coal IPO and dual listing in Hong Kong and New York in April 1998, 43 enterprises listed overseas, raising more than US$10 billion.

Of the 43 firms, 31 were listed in Hong Kong, 8 were dual listed in Hong Kong and U.S., 2 dual listed in Hong Kong and London, 1 was listed solely in U.S. (see Table 9.1) and 1 solely in Singapore.

Some enterprises, after initial offering, go back to the international capital markets for re-financing. In 1997, Zhenghai Refinery issued US$ 200 million in convertible bonds, which were listed in London and Hong Kong; Qingling Motors issued US$ 110 million in convertible bonds, listed on Luxemburg Bond Exchange and Hong Kong Stock Exchange (HKSE); Huaneng International issued US$ 230 million convertible bonds, listed on New York Stock Exchange and Luxemburg Stock Exchange.

9.2.1 *Cross-Listing of H-Shares*

Because the original thought from Chinese leaders on cross-listing was to seek more foreign investment for Chinese state-owned enterprises, they did not expect to let any Hong Kong registered company or any other country's company list in return on Chinese domestic markets. There exists an unwritten rule of "one-way traffic"—only to allow for Chinese companies to list on the HKSE or other overseas stock exchanges but not the other way around. On the secondary market, the rule holds as domestic investors are restricted to A-shares and legal-person shares and prohibited from holding B- and H-shares.

As mentioned in the previous section, the growth in B-share markets in mainland China is extremely limited due to illiquidity and deep price discounts. As a natural step, China started tapping Hong Kong market by issuing H-shares. Painstaking efforts were made to prepare by various decision-making government institutions consulting with foreign investment bankers, law firms, accountants, and especially with the HKSE counterparts. In early 1993, the CSRC announced the first batch of 9 Chinese companies to be listed in the HKSE.[3] After six months of due diligence and prospectus documentation, Tsingdao Brewery (HKSE: 0168) became the first H share to list on the HKSE on July 15, 1993. At the same time, the company offered American Depository Receipt (ADR) in the NYSE. The dual offerings brought immediate attention of the world's investment bank-

[3]The requirements for a listing in the HKSE include a minimum market capitalization of HK$50 million (U.S.$6.5 million), no less than three shareholders for each HK$1 million of the issue, a minimum of a total of 100 shareholders, and the use of international accounting standard (IAS).

Table 9.1 Capital Raised Annually by Overseas listed Companies (in US$ million)

	1993	1994	1995	1996	1997	1998	1999	Sub-total
No. of Companies	6	11	2	6	17	1	2	45
IPO proceeds	10.49	22.34	2.538	8.785	42.124	2.66	12.5	101.43
Additional Offering	1.258	1.34	1.345	1.91	5.853			
Convertible Bonds			2					5.4
Total Capita Raised	10.49	22.34	3.796	12.125	46.869	4.57	2.62	102.81

ing community. As a result, the IPOs of the first 9 P.R.C. companies were all over-subscribed by hundreds of times. Kunming Machine (HKSE: 0300), a relatively small H-share issuer with HK$65 million was over-subscribed by more than six hundred times with over HK$40 billion funds raised. The issuer thus had unexpected interest income equivalent to the company's one-year profit. Table 9.2 presents a full list of companies that have issued H-shares by the end of 1999.

Insofar as the primary market for H-share listings is concerned, a large number of international investment banks actively underwrite H-share IPOs. However, because of problems such as poor company disclosure and a lack of transparent operations, some H-shares experienced significant price drops during 1994 and 1995. Compared to the Hang Seng Index, the Hang Seng China Enterprise Index fell far lower. One interesting example is Zhenghai Refinery, a state-owned company in the second batch of H-shares. When it started trading on December 2, 1994, its issue price was HK$1.46. The state gave the company many subsidized loans, with only 4-5% interest rate while the market rate was about 14-16%. When the state stopped its subsidy by abolishing the low interest subsidized loans, its share price nose-dived by more than one-half.

Table 9.3 presents IPO performance for some H-shares calculated using the closing prices of the first, 30th, 60th, 90th, and 180th days. As shown in the table, Beijing Yanhua Petrochemical closed the first day at a price lower than its IPO price. Most firms traded at the same level of the offering prices. The average IPO initial return was 2.51%, with a standard deviation of 5.6%. China Eastern Airline had the highest price increase of 15.28% in the first day of trading, and Beijing Yanhua had the largest price decline of -4.35%.

The average 30-day holding period return was 0.9%, with a standard deviation of 11.95%. The highest holding period return was Shanghai Petrochemical (20.16%) while the lowest was Yanzhou Coal Mining Co. (-13.14%). The average 60-day holding period return was 13.72%, with a standard deviation of 46.14%. Beijing Yanhua had an extraordinary 60-day holding period return of 117.39% as opposed to Yanzhou Coal Mining Co. whose return was a disappointing -31.37%. The average 90-day holding period return was 5.37% with the highest of 70.17% in China Eastern Airline and lowest of -38.1% in Yanzhou Coal Mining Co.. The average 180-day holding period return was -7.03% and the standard deviation was 43.44%. The highest return for 180 holding days was 93.72% in Shanghai

Table 9.2 Companies Listed on the Stock Exchange of Hong Kong as of December 1999

Company	List Date	Funds Raised (mil US$)
Tsingtao Brewery	July 15, 1993	385
Yizheng Chemical Fiber	March 20, 1994	307
Tianjin Bohai Chemical	May 17, 1994	53
Dongfang Electrical Mach.	June 6, 1994	62
CATIC Shenzhen Holding	July 2, 1994	n/a
Luoyang Glass	July 8, 1994	118
Qingling Motors	August 17, 1994	169
Zhenghai Refinery	December 2, 1994	184
Chengdu Telecommunications	December 13, 1994	58
Harbin Power Equipment	December 16, 1994	145
Jilin Chemical	May 23, 1995	18
Jingwei Textile Machinery	February 2, 1996	30
Nanjing Panda Electronics	May 2, 1996	67
Guang Shen Railway	May 14, 1996	82
Shandong Xinhua Pharm.	December 31, 1996	35
China Eastern Airline	February 5, 1997	86
Shenzhen Highway Co.	March 12, 1997	212
Beijing Datang Power	March 21, 1997	466
Beijing North Star	May 14, 1997	219
Zhejiang Highway Co.	May 15, 1997	441
Jiangxi Cooper	June 12, 1997	216
Beijing Yanhua Petrochem.	June 12, 1997	33
First Tractor	June 23, 1997	195
Jiangsu Highway Co.	June 27, 1997	491
Northeast Electrical	July 6, 1997	60
Angang Steel	July 24, 1997	187
China Southern Airline	July 31, 1997	43
Szechuan Highway Co.	October 7, 1997	179
Guangzhou Pharmaceutical	October 30, 1997	47
Huaneng Power	January 21, 1998	n/a
Yanzhou Coal Mining	April 3, 1998	26
Shangdong Intl. Power	June 30, 1999	13
Great Wall Technology	August 5, 1999	58

Petrochemical.

A notable phenomenon is that prices of the some H-shares behave quite differently from their A-share counterparts. The prices have shown no sign of convergence. This is probably because that A-shares are issued and

Table 9.3 IPO Performance for Some H-shares

Company	IPO	1st Day		30 Days		60 Days		90 Days		180 Days	
	Price	close	return	close	return	close	return	close	return	close	return
Shanghai Petrochemical	$20.39	$20.5	0.54%	$24.5	20.16%	$23.87	17.07%	$28.0	37.32%	$39.5	93.72%
Shangdong Huaneng	$14.25	$14.25	0%	$13.25	-7.02%	$11.75	-17.54%	$10.5	-26.32%	$9.5	-33.33%
Jilin Chemical	$20.75	$21.38	3.04%	$20.13	-2.99%	$22.25	7.23%	$22.5	7.23%	$19.25	-7.23%
China Eastern Airline	$18.0	$20.75	15.28%	$21.63	20.17%	$27.88	54.89%	$30.63	70.17%	$26.38	46.56%
Beijing Yuanhua Petro.	$11.5	$11.0	-4.35%	$10.88	-5.39%	$25.0	117.39%	$19.31	67.91%	$8.88	-22.83%
China Southern Airline	$30.66	$31.13	1.52%	$31.22	1.83%	$29.22	-4.7%	$19.06	-37.83%	$10.19	-66.76%
Yanzhou Coal Mining Co.	$15.75	$15.75	0%	$13.68	-13.14%	$10.81	-31.37%	$9.75	-38.1%	$8.63	-45.21%

traded only within China and there are no abitrage across A- and H-shares. Shanghai Petrochemical serves as a good example. Its different share prices show no sign of convergence, in the short term or the long term.[4]

9.2.2 *Red Chips Rising*

Besides the H-share, there are two other types of cross-border listed companies from mainland China to the HKSE. One was known as back-door listing, which is usually conducted as a take-over by a mainland Chinese company of a Hong Kong listed company in financial distress. After the acquisition, the mainland company would inject its capital into this Hong Kong "shell" company. In this way, the Hong Kong "shell" is used as a listing vehicle by the mainland Chinese company. It had been a major way for powerful Chinese companies to seek Hong Kong listings before the relevant Chinese authorities formulated securities regulations. However, beginning in 1992, any form of Hong Kong listing from mainland China must go through various official procedures to get an approval.

The second type of cross-border listing takes place within mainland Chinese companies registered in Hong Kong. Most of these companies have been operating in Hong Kong for many years and Hong Kong investors are familiar with their business scope and sales. Because of their strong business background with mainland China, Hong Kong investors called these companies the Red Chips. A subset of the Red Chips is the military-backed mainland civilian shell companies. Only the top-level People's Liberation Army (PLA) organizations have the power to set up companies abroad. These companies are referred to as PLA Red Chips in Hong Kong.

In general, the class of shares that depends on China operations for growth, but is not backed by a Chinese business or government entity, is usually labeled as China concept (e.g., red chips). Strictly speaking, red chips are extensions of governmental organizations operating within investment and cash-raising guidelines laid down by a holding company and a controlling government body. Red chips have sought listings in Hong Kong, sometimes with and sometimes without government consent, and have grown through a consistent pattern of acquisitions. Red chips that did not seek formal approval from supervising bodies typically have gained

[4]Note that a stronger correlation does exist between two domestic market prices that may show that the cointegration movement exists between A-shares at the SHSE and SZSE (Su and Fleisher, 1999c).

their listing in Hong Kong through a back-door entry into an inactive listed company. There were a total of 70 red chips by the end of 1997.

The standard approach of a mainland firm making its move for expansion and foreign capital has been to: first, establish a Hong Kong subsidiary; second, borrow funds from banks to finance existing operations of subsidiaries and associates; and third, find a way to gain listing in Hong Kong. China Resources Enterprises Ltd. is a model of how red chips are knitting together the economies of Hong Kong and China. It borrows money, or raises it on the HKSE, and uses the funds to invest locally—red chip spending on real estate has buoyed Hong Kong property prices—and on the mainland. Last year, China Resources Enterprises Ltd. spun off a subsidiary called China Resources Beijing Land, offering investors in Hong Kong the opportunity to invest in property in Beijing, and reaped $200 million in profit from that investment.[5]

When purchasing red chips, investors in Hong Kong believed they were buying assets in a Chinese economy that had been growing at double-digit rates. But in most cases, they were actually buying holding companies with a range of disparate assets–a piece of highway here, a shrimp farm there. Yet investors were willing to pay a premium. Some red chips companies performed so well that they were included in Hang Seng Index of 33 major companies.[6] One of them was known as CITIC Pacific, a subsidiary of China International Trust and Investment Corporation (CITIC) of Beijing. CITIC Pacific was backed by the mainland Chinese government which invested heavily in Hong Kong property, infrastructure such as the new airport project, container port, and Hong Kong airlines. Another company was China Resources Enterprises Ltd., whose parent was the PRC Ministry of Foreign Trade and Economic Relations. China Resources Enter-

[5]With H-share listings, however, Beijing's watchful eye monitors the valuations for the assets of the new company through the auspices of the State Asset Management Bureau (SAMB). The discipline established by the practice has prevented massive sales of China's assets. Therefore, some red chips have sought the approval of the State Council for new share issues. This is usually considered a necessity for assets held at the national level and that are above US$30 million. China Resources Enterprises Ltd., for instance, had to seek approval for the acquisition of a US$44 million stake in a Beijing property company in November 1994.

[6]Although there was no official index on the Hong Kong Stock Exchange to measure the red chips, an unofficial index of 35 mainland stocks compiled by Peregrine showed a 101% gain over 1996. These shares dramatically out-performed the blue chip Hang Seng index, which climbed a respectable 33.5% to end the year.

prises' main business is to provide Hong Kong with daily supplies ranging from drinking water to fresh vegetables. When it went public, its shares were over-subscribed by an amount equivalent to twice the money supply in Hong Kong. All these red chips had shown blockbuster performance in their share prices until the second half of 1997.

In June 1997, trading in red chips drove Hong Kong's Hang Seng index above 15,000. About 50 red chips made up 11 percent of stock market value, but had accounted for about 25 percent of trading for the year. China, for its part, was alarmed at all the confidence demonstrated. It decided to impose listing restrictions, requiring all share issues of red chips to be reported to the CSRC. This was intended to impose quotas on stock issues by Chinese companies in foreign markets. Only companies that kept their assets at home in China for at least three years would be permitted to issue new shares. Then only a few months later, on October 23, 1997 (the Black Thursday), Hong Kong's Hang Seng index fell over 1200 points, plunging below 10,000. That was the largest point drop in its short 14-year history. The stock market was down 35 percent for the month. Red chips were down 50 percent for the month. A new red chip, China Telecom, making its public debut on Black Thursday, failed to meet its issue price.

In today's Hong Kong, red chips account for 8% of the market's capitalization. If an investor pastes on shares owned by mainland investors in local companies and the H-shares' total capital, China may control up to a fifth of the market. The future offers more of the same. If the China boom continues, red chips will make the territory a considerably larger financial market than it is today–10 to 30 times bigger, according to Richard Wong, Director of Hong Kong University's Center for Economic Research. "At that point," he says, "the distinction between Hong Kong and China will diminish."

9.2.3 *Overseas Listing in the U.S., U.K. and Singapore*

Companies seeking a listing overseas must satisfy two requirements. First, they must qualify for listing according to the standards set forth by overseas exchanges. Second, they must comply with the registration, accounting and disclosure requirements stipulated by the relevant securities regulatory authorities such as the Securities Exchange Commission (SEC) in the U.S. and the Ministry of Finance in the U.K..

To be listed on the major U.S. stock exchanges, a company is expected to meet certain minimum qualifications. Table 9.4 presents listing requirements for NYSE, NASDAQ, and AMEX. For example, to be listed in NYSE, a company needs to have at least 5,000 shareholders worldwide with 2.5 million shares outstanding. The total market value of the shares should exceed $100 million. In addition, the total operating cash flow has to exceed $100 million in the past three years and $25 million for each of the most recent two years.

To get over the accounting standard and other hurdles, a foreign company can list its shares through Depository Receipt (DR) program. J.P. Morgan created the first American DR (ADR) in 1927 to allow Americans to invest in the British retailer Selfridge. An ADR is a stock representing a specified number of shares in a foreign corporation. ADR's are bought and sold in the American markets just like regular stocks. An ADR is issued by a U.S. bank, consisting of a bundle of shares of a foreign corporation that are being held in custody overseas. The foreign entity must provide financial information to the sponsor bank. ADRs are listed on either the NYSE, AMEX, or NASDAQ.

There are various types of ADR programs, including Level I, Level II, Level III, and Rule 144A/GDR.

- **Level I ADRs:** They are used when the issuer is not initially seeking to raise capital in the U.S. markets or does not wish to, or can't, list its ADRs on an exchange. A Level I ADR program offers an easy and relatively inexpensive way for an issuer to gauge interest in its securities and begin building a presence in the U.S. securities markets.
  Level I ADRs are traded in the over-the-counter (OTC) market, with bid and ask prices published daily and distributed by the National Daily Quotation Bureau in the pink sheets. Prices may also be posted on the OTC Bulletin Board (OTCBB).[7] Level I ADR programs currently require minimal SEC registration: The issuer seeks exemption from the SEC's traditional reporting requirements under Rule 12g3-2(b). With that exemption, the company agrees to send to the SEC summaries or copies of any public reporting

[7] Due to the SEC's recent permanent approval of the OTCBB system, effective April 1, 1998, all non-U.S. equity securities, including ADRs, must be registered with the SEC pursuant to Section 12 of the 1934 Securities Exchange Act to remain eligible for quotation in the OTCBB system.

Table 9.4 Listing Requirements of Three Major U.S. Exchanges

	NYSE	NASDAQ	AMEX
Round-lot holders	5,000 worldwide	400	
Public shares	2.5 million	1.1 million	
Public market value	$100 million	$20 million	$4 million
Aggregate pre-tax income for the past 3 years	$1 million		
Pre-tax income in each of the 2 most recent years	$25 million		$750,000
Aggregate cash flow for the past 3 years	$100 million		
Aggregate cash flow in each of the 2 most recent years	$25 million		

documents required in its home market (including documents for regulatory agencies, stock exchanges, or direct shareholder communications). The depository, working with the issuer, also files the Form F-6 registration statement with the SEC in order to establish the program.

- **Level II ADRs:** They can be listed and traded on one of the U.S. securities exchanges (including NYSE, AMEX, and others) or quoted on NASDAQ, thereby offering higher visibility, more active trading, and greater liquidity in the U.S. market.
  Level II ADR programs must comply with the full registration and reporting requirements of the SEC's Exchange Act, which entails: (1) Form F-6 registration statement; (2) Form 20-F containing detailed financial disclosure about the issuer, including financial statements and a reconciliation of those statements to U.S. GAAP; (3) Annual reports and any interim financial statements submitted on a regular, timely basis to the SEC.
- **Level III ADRs:** An issuer floats a public offering of ADRs in the U.S. and lists the ADRs on one of the U.S. exchanges. This allows the issuer to raise capital and leads to much greater visibility in the U.S. market.
  Level III ADR programs must comply SEC's full registration and reporting requirements including Form F-6, Form 20-F, Annual reports, and Form F-1 (to register the equity securities underlying the ADRs that are offered publicly in the U.S. for the first time, including a prospectus to inform potential investors about the company and the risks inherent in its businesses, the offering price for the securities, and the plan for distributing the shares).
- **Rule 144A ADRs:** Many companies seek to raise capital in the U.S. markets privately by issuing restricted securities under Rule 144A, which do not require SEC review. Rule 144A facilitates the trading of privately placed securities by sophisticated institutional investors (also known as Qualified Institutional Buyers who must own or manage at least $100 million in securities).
- **Global Depository Receipts (GDRs):** GDRs allow issuers to raise capital in two or more markets simultaneously, thus broadening their shareholder base. They can be settled outside the U.S. (using a link connecting the two major European clearance and set-

tlement facilities, Euroclear and Cedel, with the major U.S. clearance and settlement facility, the Depository Trust Company, or DTC) and can be traded in the Rule 144A private market. Under SEC Regulation S, securities offered or sold to investors outside the U.S. are not subject to SEC registration requirements.

The China listing experiment started back in October 1992 when Brilliance China Automotive surprised the world by listing directly on the NYSE through a Bermuda-based shell company. American investors initially backed the offering, and the share price doubled in the first month before falling back to the initial offering price. Shanghai Ek Chor and China Tire came to market with similar hybrid offerings. However, without a domestic investor base to buy stock when fund managers want to sell, or vice versa, Chinese stocks seem to lose their allure. For example, even with the innovative N-Share structure used by Huaneng Power International and Shandong Huaneng Power to list ADRs, because of no underlying shares traded in China, the problem of liquidity remains.[8] These shares cannot match the liquidity and performance of companies with ADR dual listings in Hong Kong and New York. Shanghai Petrochemical's $343 million offering in 1993, and Jilin Chemical's $200 million offering in 1995, are considered to be the most successful of China's capital raising.

To seek GDR listing in the London Stock Exchange (LSE), a company needs to have a trading record of at least three years. The market value of the GDR must exceed £700,000 (US$1.15 million). At least 25% of the GDR should be held by shareholders outside the company. A company can choose U.K. GAAP, U.S. GAAP or IAS as its accounting standard. To be listed on the main board of the Stock Exchange of Singapore (SES), a company needs to have a minimum of three years of track record. At least 25% of the issued and paid-up capital must be in the hands of at least 1,000 shareholders. The paid-up capital (shareholders' equity) should be no less than US$18.5 million. The cumulative pre-tax profits should be at least US$10 million during the previous three years and a pre-tax profit of at least US$2 million for each of the two most recent years. A company must

[8]The N-share structure was created to assist issuers in developing markets in accessing international investors while retaining control over ownership in the home market. N-shares are not listed in the home market and cannot be purchased by local investors. N-shares are created by the issuer to provide a means of raising capital among international investors. They are held in custody by the depository banks.

use IAS as its accounting standard. Table 9.5 presents Chinese companies listed on the NYSE, LSE and SES by the end of 1999.

Signs have shown that China's high-growth firms may expect a promising future in raising funds from overseas stock markets. The Chinese government is actively seeking to expedite the formation of a venture capital investment system and set up an alternative stock market for growth firms. The LSE has launched its Technology Market and Alternative Investment Market to suit the fund-raising needs of high-growth firms and small companies. In 1999, a number of Chinese Internet and e-commerce companies listed their shares on the NASDAQ and the HKSE. The successful listing of these high-tech companies overseas paved the way for more listings by other growth firms.

9.3 Concerns That Emerged

Overseas listing is an important policy for the reform and opening-up of Chinese enterprises to the outside. Although the overseas listing had paved the way for further expansion of capital raising abroad, a strong ideological barrier still hampered China from listing its socialist companies on a capitalist capital market. By the end of 1992, reform in the rural areas had pushed many SOEs to become profit-losers. They were badly in need of capital investment to restructure and grow. But they were already heavily indebted to domestic and foreign lenders.

Zhu Rongji, the vice-premier and governor of the PBOC at the time, decided to resort to equity financing from overseas capital markets. Beginning in December, 1992, a policy was announced to allow the first 9 state companies to list on the HKSE as an experiment for overseas listing. This was a political decision and the principle of selecting companies for listings was very simple: to choose the ones that are, in term of profitability, "neither bad nor good" and the ones that are, in term of size, "neither big nor small". The rationale was that mainland companies with good profitability do not need foreign funds and companies with bad profitability would find it too difficult to raise funds through overseas flotation. Big strategic companies are usually highly controlled by the state, which does not want to lose its majority control. Many of international investment bankers were involved in educating and bringing H-share companies to list on the HKSE.

The period of allowing PRC companies to list overseas was associated

Table 9.5 Chinese Companies Listed on the NYSE, LSE and SES as of December 1998

Company	Listed Date	Exchange	Funds Raised (in million US$)
Shanghai Petrochemical	July 26, 1993	NYSE	274.0
Shandong Huaneng Power	August 4, 1994	NYSE	199.5
Huaneng Power International	October 6, 1994	NYSE	312.5
Jilin Chemical Industry	May 22, 1995	NYSE	92.7
Guangshen Railway	May 13, 1996	NYSE	216.8
China Eastern Airlines	February 4, 1997	NYSE	113.4
Beijing Yanhua Petrochemical	June 24, 1997	NYSE	116.8
China Southern Airlines	July 30, 1997	NYSE	508.0
Yanzhou Coal Mining Co.	March 31, 1998	NYSE	45.6
Beijing Datang Power	March 31, 1997	LSE	n/a
Jiangxi Copper	June 12, 1997	LSE	n/a
Zhejiang Electric Power	July 8, 1997	LSE	n/a
China Merchants Shekou Port	July 24, 1995	SES	n/a

with the domestic enterprise reform carried out in large scale among 400,000 SOEs. The first batch of H-share listings on the HKSE was extremely successful. Soon there came the second batch of 22 H-share candidate companies at the end of 1993 and the third batch of 7 in 1995. The listing venue included not only Hong Kong but NYSE, NASDAQ, and exchanges in Canada, Australia, U.K., and Singapore. Issues that emerged include market segmentation, foreign exchange control, and a lack of foreign participation and competition in capital markets.

9.3.1 *Market Segmentation and Foreign Exchange Control*

The most important question that the Chinese government has to resolve in the development of the stock markets is the role of foreign investors. At present, the Chinese government attempts to control foreign investment by effectively segmenting equity markets. Foreign investors are not permitted to purchase A-shares, but they can invest in B-shares as well as companies listed in Hong Kong, New York or other foreign markets. This system has produced tremendous liquidity problems for the B-share market while denying Chinese people and financial institutions the opportunity to invest in some of the country's most promising companies.

After nine years of operation, the B-share market has a market capitalization of less than US$4 billion. It is so illiquid that most of the companies can only sell B-shares at 80-90% discount relative to their A-share prices. In fact, the average price discount is so large that many brokerage firms believe that a large portion of the B-share demand has come from Chinese citizens purchasing B-shares illegally through established accounts in Hong Kong. As a result of their poor performance, B-share markets have not played a very effective role in helping Chinese companies to raise additional capital needed for expansion. There were only two new listings in the Shanghai B-share market during the 1999 period compared to 8 and 35 during the 1997 and 1994 period, respectively. There were no new listings in the Shenzhen market in 1999 compared to 5-10 during each year of the early 1990's. Chinese companies predominantly raise capital is the A-share markets.[9]

The problem with the H-share market is that it has experienced extreme

[9]For example, in 1999, there were 98 IPO's and 117 A-share issues raising 87.7 billion RMB of funds (US$10.5 billion) compared to only US$600 million raised from share sales in the Hong Kong H-share market.

mood swings because of changing investor perception about the mainland economy and the quality of companies offered. In 1997, the H-share market was excited about the flotation of red chip companies by Chinese local governments in Shanghai and Beijing. However, the shares subsequently performed very poorly and attention shifted to the telecommunication and technology sectors in Hong Kong, where prices have risen sharply since 1999. As a result of these mood swings, China has found it difficult to use the external marketplace to privatize other companies in sectors, such as energy and heavy industry.

Once H-shares are listed, trading tends to be more volatile than that of other non-PRC shares on the HKSE. There is no cross-border arbitrage regardless of price differentials. This is due to the fact that no free cross-border movement of capital is allowed and most of the H-share companies are single-listed in Hong Kong without a previous listing in the mainland stock markets. The problem of market segmentation is fundamental in the region. Su (2000b) suggests that there were no general linkages between A- and B-shares or between A- and H-shares due to ownership restrictions and market segmentation. But he finds that linkages between the two domestic markets noticeably strengthened over time. He also finds that B-share returns in the Shanghai market could be forecasted by market returns in Hong Kong, when policy allowed foreign institutions to trade. The findings confirmed that the policy-induced market segmentation hindered arbitrage opportunities in the regional market.

Because of market segmentation, China is significantly under-weighted in the Morgan Stanley index for global stock markets and thus unable to attract adequate capital from investors attempting to achieve market weights for their portfolios. Despite the fact that China's aggregate stock market capitalization in the domestic markets and Hong Kong is equal to about 1.5% of global stock market capitalization of US$34 trillion, China's weight in the Morgan Stanley World Index is only about 0.39%. About 59% of this weighting also comes from the value of China Telecom. alone. If China had an open market for A-shares as well as the companies listed offshore, its weighting would probably rise to at least 1.0% of the Morgan Stanley World Free Index. Meanwhile, China's own citizens have not had an opportunity to invest in some of the country's most exciting new technology and telecommunications companies because those companies are listed in Hong Kong and New York, not on the domestic A-share market.

China has attempted to maintain a rigidly segmented securities market because of concern about exchange controls. The Chinese government is not yet prepared to introduce full capital account convertibility. However, there are many examples of how a country can regulate capital inflows without completely denying foreign investors access to the local stock markets. Taiwan and India require foreign institutional investors to register with the government and report their transactions as they occur. Some Indian companies also have parallel listings in New York and the off-shore GDR market, where the shares are trade at a premium to their local counterparts. Singapore, Korea and Thailand have official restrictions on the level of foreign ownership of companies but permit foreign investors to pay a premium in order to purchase shares from each other. Singapore Airlines, for example, has a two tier market in which foreign investors typically pay a large premium for the shares compared to local investors. The Singapore government occasionally adjusts the ownership limits in response to market conditions. However, the current two tier system has worked for several years because it has been predictable and has not been widely circumvented by either local or foreign investors.

Until recently, South Africa had a two tier exchange rate system which permitted the *rand* for financial transactions, such as foreign portfolio investment, to trade at a 25-30% discount to the *rand* used in commercial transactions. The existence of a separate financial *rand* helped to boost foreign investment in South African equities at a time when the government wanted to promote foreign investment without losing control over the exchange rate used to denominate trade. The financial *rand* has been abolished but South Africa retains exchange controls on outward investment. Britain also had a dual exchange rate system between 1939 and 1979. Under the system, foreign investors had complete access to the LSE but British investors seeking to purchase foreign securities had to purchase dollars from a restricted pool of investment currency which was sold at a fluctuating premium to the pound's commercial exchange rate.

China's current method of regulating foreign investors is inferior to the aforementioned alternative forms of control. It has produced a suboptimal marketplace in which Chinese investors pay a large premium to the prices offered to foreign investors, Chinese investors are unable to purchase the promising companies offered on off-shore markets, and Chinese companies are able to obtain foreign capital only if their sector is in fashion among global investors. If China had a stock market more integrated with the global marketplace, the valuation discrepancies would diminish, there would be more liquidity from both domestic and foreign investors to reduce price volatility, and the marketplace would be more open to private companies, not just state enterprises. Although China likes the model of one country/two systems for reconciling the tension between capitalism and communism, the current market segmentation policy is producing the worst features of both capitalism and a command economy: illiquidity, volatility, price anomalies and increasing corruption as investors attempt to capitalize on the B-share discounts through circumvention of the rules. A new system of one unified equity market with ownership ceilings for foreign investors would produce far superior outcomes for all parties than the current system of one country/multiple markets.

9.3.2 *A Lack of Foreign Participation and Competition in Financial Markets*

Foreign banks have generally been restricted to hard currency operations, although the Chinese government, in its bid to join the World Trade Organization (WTO), has announced its intention to partially open local currency business to foreign banks. Since 1985, foreign banks have been allowed to set up branches and local subsidiaries and to establish joint-venture banks with Chinese partners in selected cities and Specialized Economic Zones (SEZs). But their activities have been limited to wholesale banking and a limited number of foreign exchange transactions such as foreign exchange deposits and loans for joint-venture enterprises, foreign exchange investments and guarantees, and the settlement of import and export accounts. Extension of foreign bank branches to Shanghai was made possible in 1990 when the Pudong New Area was designated as a development zone. The PBOC approved the applications of seven foreign banks to open branches in Shanghai in 1991, and that number increased to 30 by late 1994.[10] As of the end of 1996, there were 538 representative offices, 131 foreign bank branches, 6 joint-venture banks, and 5 wholly owned foreign banks. More-

[10]To establish a branch, a bank must have total assets over US$20 million, have operated a representative office in China for at least three years, and, for branches in Shanghai, have US$30 million in registered capital. In addition, US$10 million in capital must be deposited in cash with the PBOC, essentially as a minimum reserve requirement. In late 1994, foreign branching restrictions were somewhat eased: the minimum number of years of operation of a representative office was lowered to two, and the capital requirement is *renminbi* 100 million, of which 30 percent must be deposited with the PBOC.

over, from December 1996 to April 1997, the PBOC issued licenses to 9 foreign banks to conduct *renminbi* business in Shanghai.[11]

Foreign non-bank financial institutions in China include six finance companies and six fully licensed insurance companies. To obtain a PBOC-issued insurance license, a foreign company generally has to spend three years going through the application process. PBOC has traditional placed heavy emphasis on solvency and a conservative investment style, which discourages foreign companies from diversifying risk and limit their sources of income beyond issuing individual insurance policies. Sixty unlicensed foreign overseas insurance companies have representative offices in China, but they are regulated to operating in a few coastal areas on a trial basis.

Foreign securities firms may establish representative offices, but not local branches or subsidiaries. They may purchase seats on the SHSE and SZSE at the same price as that charged to domestic securities firms, but all their transactions require the partnership of a local broker. Foreign securities houses are limited to B-share transactions and, subject to government approval, to underwriting domestic securities. Twenty-three foreign brokers have seats on the SHSE and eight foreign brokers have seats on the SZSE. Foreign securities firms are prohibited from introducing new domestic financial products, although they may offer off-shore derivatives, which have been an attractive source of business. Repatriation of profits require government approval, while dividend payments on B-shares do not.[12] Offshore listings of mainland companies (the H-, N-, L- and S-share markets) are traded only outside China. They are less volatile than B-shares and therefore offer better returns.

Foreign financial institutions are subjected to a certain degree of intentional discriminatory treatment in China. For example, each account held by a joint-venture enterprise with a foreign financial institution requires official approval, which could take up to two years. In contrast, such accounts

[11]These banks face stringent operating requirements, including keeping two separate reserves (in local and foreign currency) equal to 18 percent of their *renminbi* deposits and limiting local currency liabilities to less than 35 percent of their foreign exchange liabilities. Domestic banks are not subject to these requirements, and, as such, the newly licensed foreign banks are not likely to create significant competition for domestic banks yet.

[12]Since 1990, foreigners have been permitted to own equity in Chinese companies through B-shares. The B-share market developed without national guidelines, which may explain why, after an initial positive reaction to their introduction, the demand for B-shares has dropped such that they frequently trade below issuance price.

with the PBOC or its subsidiaries require only one-time approval, giving the PBOC and its subsidiaries a competitive advantage over foreign financial institutions. In addition, foreign financial institutions are subject to the annual PBOC's evaluation of their contributions to China, and the criteria for these assessments lack transparency and often are politically motivated. As is the case for all foreign companies operating in China, the staff for a foreign financial institution must be recruited through a Chinese government agency, which retains 55 percent of an employees gross salary. This arrangement hinders recruitment of highly qualified investment personnel.

9.4 China Moving Toward World Capital Market: Strategic Issues and Options

9.4.1 *Enhancing the Interest of Overseas Investors*

To be eligible for a listing overseas, a company needs to maintain a certain amount of cumulative pre-tax profit over a period of three most recent years according to the rules of most foreign exchanges. This leads to an interesting phenomenon among Chinese SOEs, which may list via "financial packaging", i.e., businesses put together just for the purpose of listing. Therefore, a three-year profit record has little meaning. At a more destructive level, financial packaging makes it much easier to hide problematic issues when there is no common thread in the track record. When there is so much to be gained in a listing, there is bound to be much temptation to be economical with the truth, or to resort to "creative accounting" or downright fraud.

In order to mitigate the problems caused by packaging, extensive research has been undertaken by the CSRC on a series of policy measures to promote the standard of operation and strengthen the framework of regulation on overseas listings. The CSRC had carefully summarized the experience of overseas listings and existing problems, kept improving the standardized operation of overseas-listed companies and regulatory measures of in-depth reform in order to bring into full play the CSRC regulatory functions and active roles of all relevant government agencies in the promotion of standardization operation and in-depth reform of overseas-listed companies, thus protect the interests of investors, promote the continued responsibility of overseas-listed companies after listing, strengthen the investors' confidence in Chinese companies, and improve the image of overseas-listed companies.

In 1998, the CSRC and the State Economic Commission issued *Procedures on Promoting Standardized Operations and In-depth Reform of Overseas Listed Companies*, raising requirements for overseas listed companies with regard to standardized operation, and by increasing transparency and deepening restructuring. A breakthrough agreement has been reached to promote standardized operations and in-depth reform to reflect the responsible attitude to the investors by improving disclosure and enhancing transparency.

The CSRC has paid special attention to the regulatory suppression of overseas-listed companies, narrowing the gap between overseas-listed companies and market investors, as well as improving investor relation. By inviting staff from the Hong Kong Securities and Futures Commission and the HKSE to lecture about information disclosure requirements regarding listing rules, mergers and acquisitions, CSRC conducted training to relevant government officials to facilitate their support of overseas-listed information disclosure. CSRC also held training sessions for the board chairmen, CEOs and board secretaries of overseas-listed companies for their voluntary information disclosure. Additionally, the CSRC has formulated, after studies, several measures on improvement of information disclosure by overseas listed companies.

In September and November 1998, the CSRC and the Ministry of Personnel jointly organized both the senior training program for board chairmen and CEOs of Chinese overseas-listed companies as well as the seminar for board secretaries. Tutoring management and managerial personnel will assist directors and senior management of companies coming to list to understand their responsibilities. To this end, the CSRC hopes to conform operation decisions to the standardization of listed companies, to develop strategic and risk concepts, to improve management and decision-making, and to train senior management who understand the law and regulations. The companies are expected to make returns for investors through greater accomplishments and the radiant glow of an improved international image.

To better prevent financial risks, the CSRC and other relevant government agencies required overseas-listed companies to implement internal audit and take adequate preventive actions in mid 1998. The CSRC, in conjunction with relevant government agencies, conducted an overall check on the deposits status of 43 overseas-listed companies, and organized two field inspection teams to look into the claims outstanding for these companies. The time will come when international investors are confident that the investor protection mechanisms in Chinese financial markets are sufficiently robust.

9.4.2 *Improving the Role of Financial Intermediaries*

China is still in the very early stages of financial deepening, as the practice of central planning to allocate credit is not effective in channeling funds from savers to borrowers. The financial reforms begun in 1979 delegated some economic decisions to the microeconomic level and so necessitated the development of financial intermediaries. However, developments on the stock market are still based more on speculation than on investment, indicating that securitization of financial assets still has a long way to go.

As Chinese companies proceed to ensure wider access to domestic and world capital markets, the securities regulatory authorities must begin to consider ways by which the pool of investors could be increased. At present, Chinese stock markets are essentially populated by individual investors, most with limited means and often with very little understanding of risk. There some 45 million such investors by the end of 1999. It is therefore important that the market should have a group of investors who have the means to make investments with longer time horizons as well as the means to make informed judgments about the underlying company, industry and general economic outlook. Investment corporations have begun to operate but they are few in number (in fact only 23).

In terms of financial intermediation, China has four state banks and eleven commercial banks. The state banks were created in 1984, when specialized banks were transformed into commercial banks. The largest state bank is the Industrial and Commercial Bank of China, which extends working capital loans to SOEs for fixed-asset investment. The Agricultural Bank of China finances services in rural areas; the Peoples Construction Bank of China provides medium- and long-term financing for capital construction; and the Bank of China is the main international and foreign exchange bank. State banks are responsible for implementing the PBOC's credit plan.[13] They hold the bulk of the SOEs bad debt, and are therefore

[13]State banks have a network of branches, newly created affiliates, and special departments. This network allows them to hold the bulk of all deposits outside the credit plan—a large proportion of these deposits flow into the semi-formal and informal channels that are frequently of a speculative nature.

estimated to have negative net worth.[14]

Non-bank financial institutions are generally more autonomous and profit driven than state banks and commercial banks, and have introduced a limited degree of competition into the financial system. For example, the state-owned People's Insurance Company of China (PICC) was a monopoly insurer until 1988. In 1993, it still handled over 95 percent of Chinas total insurance business. The new insurance law of 1995 limited the PICC to commercial insurance business and transferred its social insurance business to the Ministry of Labor. While the PICC and several government financial authorities own 17 regional life insurers, there are now three other regional insurers as well as two independent national insurers.[15]

To promulgate non-bank financial institutions, the China International Trust and Investment Corporation (CITIC) was established and awarded industry-level status. As the countrys major consulting firm and investment bank, it invests and lends funds raised from overseas capital markets. Its subsidiary, the China Investment Bank (CIB), invests and lends funds borrowed from international financial institutions, such as the World Bank. It is responsible for raising construction funds from abroad. During the 1990s, many international trust and investment corporations (ITICs) were set up, offering consulting and investment banking services similar to those offered by the CITIC although not necessarily linked to the latter.

Two important decisions were made in August 1999. The first was to allow SOEs to invest in the stock markets on a non-leveraged basis and if they had held stocks for a period of at least six months. The second was to allow life insurance companies to allocate up to 15 percent of their assets portfolio for investment in the stock market. As the national pension funds regulatory system comes into relatively stable operation, the time will come when pension fund portfolios will be able to invest in the stock markets in

[14]To free the newly formed commercial state banks from policy burdens, the policy lending previously extended by the three specialized banks was transferred to three newly created, special purpose policy banks. The State Development Bank, with access to funding from postal deposits, focuses on infrastructure lending. The Agricultural Development Bank provides agricultural procurement and infrastructure funding, and the Export-Import Bank provides export-import financing for key sectors.

[15]Chinas market for life insurance and household casualty insurance is still small and most casualty insurance is purchased by corporate customers. Most assets have to be deposited with domestic banks in interest-bearing accounts, and other investments are required to be spread among safe investments and are limited to short-run commitments.

addition to the rest of the capital markets.

Life insurance and pension funds have few short-term liabilities because of contractual relationship they have with young generation. Young work force has much longer investment time horizons than other investors. Accordingly, they would make excellent long-term investors in the markets. Foreign investors constitute yet another set of long-term investors. Foreign investors have tended to be institutional investors. Those who buy B- and H-shares in the primary market are usually foreign pension funds or mutual funds. H-shares are traded in Hong Kong and are therefore directly exposed to the international marketplace and are regulated by the Hong Kong authorities who have a long track record of regulating according to international standards. While both H- and B-shares have enabled the country to raise substantial capital from outside, the fact that foreign investors cannot invest in the domestic markets have denied most Chinese companies of a further source of capital and a further source of institutional investors.

Taiwan and India have demonstrated that a system of Qualified Foreign Institutional investors (QFIIs) can successfully be instituted to attract foreign capital into their domestic stock markets. The system requires QFIIs to be first registered and then money brought in should first be changed into the local currency. The money is kept in specified accounts and the shares bought kept with specified custodians, so that both money and shares can be audited at all times. Before money is taken out, taxes will have to be paid and remittance be cleared by the central bank. QFIIs have proven a phenomenal success not only in attracting capital to Taiwan and India but have in fact become a potent force in making investment choices and putting management on their toes. Investors in these markets tend to pay close attention to the investment choices of QFIIs. Chinese financial markets can potentially benefit from these practices.

9.4.3 *Introducing Insurance Capital to Securities Market*

As China's securities market and insurance industry expand, methods for introducing insurance capital into the securities market are proliferating. There are at least five ways we can think of to jointly develop insurance and securities markets.

Direct securities investment is common worldwide. The insurance company's capital utilization and management departments invest a portion of the capital in stock and bond markets. Many countries allow insurance companies to act as investment institutions and receive commissions from other organizations and investors to manage their capital and engage in direct securities investment. In China, it is still not possible for insurance companies to act as investment institutions and directly participate in securities investment, or for insurance companies to receive commissioned work. The reason is that the insurance companies do not have securities investment capabilities such as risk management and control. Because no other investment institutions are involved and insurance regulatory agencies are unable to effectively monitor insurance companies' securities investment activities, mechanisms of insurance control and restraint are not in place. Consequently, investment risks are great. Furthermore, Chinese insurance companies' investment institution status in securities investment activities conflicts with related industry separation regulations in the current *P.R.C. Securities Law.*

The second method is for insurance companies to entrust their capital with investment institutions, which would be responsible for the management of the investment portfolio. This method is essentially a type of commissioned capital management, which is something that Chinese insurance companies can look forward to in the future. There are two reasons for the lack of capital management firms in China. First, Chinese laws have not clearly outlined the limits of commissioned capital management. If management is inadequate, commissioned capital management would become a set of improper activities such as capital solicitation. Second, commissioned capital management offers a great deal of flexibility in areas such as investment amounts, investment methods and information disclosure. Insurance companies usually cannot exercise proper supervision over investment institutions, nor can regulatory agencies effectively monitor and manage commissioned capital management.

In a third method, insurance companies may be given a purchasing quota of securities investment funds but also a time limit on their stock holdings. For example, a maximum of two years may be imposed, after which insurance companies are allowed to sell but not buy. However, China's securities investment funds were originally geared toward meeting the indirect securities investment needs of small-to-medium investors. Assigning a large portion of the funds to insurance company quotas would contravene the original intention. After the time limit runs out, questions concerning when and how much insurance companies would be allowed to sell remain unanswered. Moreover, whether or not insurance companies would be able to complete these investment activities independently is still unknown.

Insurance capital can also be introduced into the securities market through the buying and selling of securities investment funds in the secondary market, but in practice this can also be difficult. Because publicly listed securities investment funds remain small in number as well as scale, the amount of insurance capital they can absorb is limited. In addition, choosing the right securities investment fund is no easier than choosing the right stocks and bonds, and insurance companies are not prepared to do the job satisfactorily at present.

The fifth method involves insurance companies using a portion of the capital to set up a securities investment insurance fund, which would be given to specialized fund management firms for securities investment management. Since insurance companies entrust their securities investment insurance funds to the fund management firms, they usually do not directly participate in the management of the fund. In the future, however, insurance companies may become initiators and participate directly in fund management. Securities investment insurance fund management is a kind of commissioned capital management that is structured and standardized. It meets the current needs of Chinese insurance companies, and seems realistic and feasible.

Recently, the CSRC issued the *Notice on the Improvement of Stock Issuance Methods.* This notice defined the strategic investor as a judicial unit closely associated with the issuing firm and intending to hold issued stocks for the long term. Thus insurance companies need to obtain approval from relevant regulatory authorities before they can receive stock purchasing quotas as strategic investors. Furthermore, insurance companies must strengthen their management capabilities after the stock-holding time limits expire.

9.4.4 *Strengthening China Investment Funds*

The first investment fund in China was born in 1991. Despite this late start, China's investment funds have grown rapidly, and their number and size are expected to expand greatly in the coming years. The funds have developed in two stages demarcated by the national regulation promulgated in 1997. Before that time, funds were at the stage of self-development. A total of 75 funds and 47 fund-like certificates had been launched with the accumulated capital of more than 7 billion *renminbi yuan* (approximately US$900 million) as of September 1997. These funds are often referred to as "old funds" as opposed to the new funds established after the national regulation.

The small size of the old funds, however, made them unable to play a significant role in China's securities market. Their erratic management and poor risk control also highlighted the necessity of official regulation. The *Provisional Measures for the Administration of Securities Investment Funds*, promulgated by the CSRC in November 1997, was the first national regulation governing the domestic fund industry. Under the *Provisional Measures*, China's investment funds began a new era of development, and 22 new funds had been set up with a total market capitalization of *renminbi* 50.5 billion (approximately US$6 billion) by the end of December 1999, the amount of which accounted for more than 6% of the capitalization of the SHSE and SZSE. It was estimated that the total number of individual investors owning shares in securities investment fund was around 1.5 million.

Among the 22 new funds, the first 4 funds established in 1998 were growth funds. The 18 funds launched subsequently were balanced funds. Although all these funds are contractual closed-end funds with a 15-year maturity, the balanced funds typically allocate 50% of their assets to trading the market index, with the remainder in various types of growth stocks. Because most Chinese listed companies currently pay out little dividend, the conditions were not ripe for income funds. At year-end 15 out of the 17 funds that had been active in 1999 out-performed the stock market's 12.3% growth.

A significant step in enhancing the reputation of the investment fund industry has been the restructuring and consolidation of old funds. The CSRC has actively steered the securities market towards more rational investment by encouraging the development of institutional investors who will be allowed to invest in the market through securities investment funds. During 1999, under instructions from the CSRC, work began on consolidating 43 old funds. Although only 1 of these old funds had been restructured by the end of the year, the process of restructuring the others is likely to be completed before the end of 2000.

To enhance the performance of securities investment funds, the Government announced in August 1999 that fund management companies were allowed to enter the inter-bank market, which greatly expanded their access to capital to support their operations and enabled them to make better use of it. Then the CSRC expanded fund management companies' privileged access to IPOs. The *Supplementary Notice on Improving New Stock Allocation to Securities Investment Funds*, which was issued in November 1999, stipulated that investment funds could henceforth hold up to 30% of their assets in IPOs (up from the previous 15%) and gave them unlimited access to the IPOs of companies with more than 400 million registered shares. At the same time, the CSRC promulgated the *Provisional Regulations on Qualification of Fund Practitioners*, which further strengthened the legal framework for fund administration by improving qualification requirements on practitioners in fund management companies and fund custodians. In parallel, the National People's Congress embarked on the preparation of an important new piece of legislation–the *PRC Investment Fund Law*. The preparatory team, which began work in March 2000, has already completed the first draft of the Law.

As the volume of assets managed by investment funds increased, a wider fund management industry began to take shape. Custodian banks are servicing the new funds and brokers are providing special trading seats for funds. Both the custodian banks and the brokers are looking for ways to develop their business as the industry expands, especially when fund management companies are allowed to operate open-ended funds. At the same time, some investment funds have been listed in major international markets. In the meanwhile, there are 7 China funds listed on the Stock Exchange of Hong Kong and some more elsewhere. Together with those unlisted China funds in Hong Kong, an estimated managed funds totaling HK$4.2 billion has been amassed by Hong Kong institutions for investment in equity and venture-capital market in China. Table 9.6 presents a list of China funds listed in international marketplace.

The events over the previous years have shown that China's securities market needs the securities investment funds and those funds are beginning to reshape the securities market. In 1999, the securities investment fund industry has done well. It is, however, still in the initial phase of its development. There will inevitably be trials and challenges ahead as the industry continues to expand.

Table 9.6 List of China Funds Listed in International Market

Company	Type	Amount	Listing	Details of Investment
Barclays Asian Selection (PRC) Fund	open end	US$40m	Hong Kong	China B-shares
Baring International Fund Managers	closed end	US$38.99m	Hong Kong	69.7% invested in Hong Kong
Baring Greater China Fund	closed end	US$150m	New York	Taiwan, Korea, Singapore and 65% in HK & PRC
Crosby Securities China Investment Co.	closed end	US$40m	Cayman	B-shares
Invesco Greater China Opportunities	Unit Trust		cumulative	HK, Taiwan and PRC
Jardine Flemming China Co.	closed end	US$23.16m	Hong Kong	10% in B-shares, rest in joint-venture
Lloyd George Investment China Fund	closed end	HK$369m	Cook Islands	China concept companies and B-shares
Thornton Management China Sub-fund	open end	US$20m	cumulative	China B-shares and China concept stocks
Wardley China Fund	closed end	US$89.97m	Hong Kong	Half in B-shares

9.4.5 *Reforming Pension System*

China has a rapidly aging population which will require the development of pension funds in order to finance retirement. At present, Chinese state enterprises provide retirement income to elderly people on a pay-as-you-go basis. But the number of elderly is expected to double by 2020. In 2045, more than half of China's population will be over the age of 50. Therefore pay-as-you-go system cannot survive indefinitely. The development of pension funds will require a parallel growth of capital markets to provide an outlet for the investment of retirement savings. China already has 45 million individual shareholders, but if pension funds develop, hundreds of millions of people would have exposure to the equity market. China's other financial intermediaries also need a more active capital market to serve as a repository for their funds. The government, for example, recently opened the door to insurance companies investing 10-30% of their assets in A-shares of Chinese companies. Under the new rules, both domestic and foreign insurance companies will be allowed to purchase A-shares. Such a development is significant because until recently, Chinese stock markets had no institutional investors except for a small number of investment trust companies launched during the mid-1990's.

Generally speaking, further opening of financial markets provides a means to develop a private sector safety net to provide for retirement, health care and additional future claims on income. In China, pensions and repayment of banking system represent substantial claims on future income. Pensions have become an increasing financial strain on SOEs. Despite political objectives of maintaining low levels of unemployment, government revenues have declined. Burdened with a rapidly aging population, Chinese government faces an enormous hurdle. Furthermore, Chinas one child policy has created a distortion between generations. China faces a huge under-funded pension liability. Pensions are currently indexed to wages, which is problematic given that wages appear to be growing faster than productivity. The World Bank estimates that wages in China will grow about 7% or less per year. Returns on pension funds will need to meet if not exceed the wage growth.[16]

[16]Somewhat surprisingly, rates of return on pension balances were below the inflation rate between years 1993 and 1995. In 1997, Chinese government began to unify locally administered pension plans into a national model. The government plans to assign "social security numbers" to allow workers to change jobs and move cities without losing benefits.

A new pension system was launched in 1984 and dramatically reshaped in 1991. It became mandatory for all employees and employers immediately. New pension plans had emphasized savings over entitlement. In 1998, the Ministry of Labor and Social Welfare was established to administer pension plans. As of 1998, old retirees still receive full salaries until death, but younger workers must fund their own pensions, i.e., the nation has been shifting to an investment-based system of individual accounts.

Under the new system, the government requires employers to contribute 20% of a companys total wage or salary to retirement funds. 80% of the defined contribution must be in bonds while 20% in safe deposits. Employees and employers must contribute a total of 11% of the workers monthly wage to the pension. The plan covers 96% of SOEs, 60% of collectively-owned companies, and over 95% of retirees. A potential threat to the success of this model is whether these funds will achieve the necessary growth given Chinas recent low and even negative real interest rates.

The pension system would benefit from an expansion in investment opportunities. The development of a stable pension system depends on the creation of a modern banking system and securities market. The TransAsia Group, a direct investment specialist, estimates that 10,000 Chinese foreign-funded companies have set up supplementary pension and health funds with $2 billion under management.

9.5 Liberalization of Capital Movements

International capital and domestic savings are valuable components of sustainable, long-term economic growth. However, recurring problems such as the debt crisis of the 1980s, the Mexican currency crisis in late 1994, and the current East Asian crisis, demonstrate that over dependence on foreign portfolio investment, particularly mobile and short-term investment instruments, can threaten the economic stability of emerging markets. This underscores that liberalization carries risks as well as benefits and has major implications for the policies that governments will find it feasible and desirable to follow. With the onset of macroeconomic stability and the legal and regulatory reforms that have taken place over the last decade, institutional investors in China are beginning to play a more important role in channeling domestic savings to investment opportunities. These investors, which include pension funds, insurance companies and mutual funds, can also finance infrastructure and other long-term investments, and they can encourage the development of mortgage markets.

9.5.1 *What the Theory Says*

The flows of capital debt, portfolio equity, and direct and real estate investment between one country and others are recorded in the capital account of its balance of payments. According to the International Monetary Fund (IMF), outflows include residents' purchases of foreign assets and repayment of foreign loans; inflows include foreigners' investments in home-country financial markets and property and loans to home-country residents. Freeing transactions like these from restrictions, i.e., allowing capital to flow freely in or out of a country without controls or restrictions, is known as capital account liberalization.

Classic economic theory argues that international capital mobility allows countries with limited savings to attract financing for productive domestic investment projects, that it enables investors to diversify their portfolios, that it spreads investment risk more broadly, and that it promotes intertemporal trade—the trading of goods today for goods in the future. Capital mobility thus enables investors to achieve higher risk-adjusted rates of return. In turn, higher rates of return can encourage saving and investment that deliver faster economic growth.

The currency crises afflicting Asia in 1997 and 1998 re-opened the debate on the wisdom of capital controls and liberalization of the capital account for emerging market economies. Generally speaking, the existence of investors, including hedge funds, who are willing to take risks, provides the liquidity to the market and allows easier reallocation of market risks. In a world awash in "hot money", where capital, or financial claims to capital, can be transferred across borders instantaneously with very low transaction costs, there is growing concern that investors and analysts can wreak havoc on developing economies. Still, over the long term, most agree (including the Chinese government) that liberalization of the capital account is beneficial for several reasons:

- The improved ability to tap savings globally (at lower cost than using only domestic savings);

- Allowing domestic economic agents freedom to diversify risk by choosing how and where to borrow, invest, or exchange assets;
- Improvements in resource allocation through increased competition for financial resources;
- Increased availability of resources to support investment and to finance trade and other significant economic entities; and
- Imposition of macro-economic discipline on national governments.

Theoretically, speculation performs a market stabilizing function when, for example, someone buys an asset when its price is low and sells it when the price is high in a situation where there is only actual demand. In this case, the speculator can make profits, but prices tend to be equalized since there would be additional demand when prices are low and there would be additional supply when prices are high. In this connection, the IMF gives a positive evaluation on the function of hedge funds; while a mutual fund that enjoys high returns may attract new investors and be bound by its prospectus to buy more of the recently appreciated asset and other institutional investors may be forced to cut their losses by their internal controls and to sell into a falling market, hedge funds are better able to ride out these fluctuations because their investors are locked in for substantial periods and thus hedge fund should stabilize the market.

Contrary to the view, others would argue that hedge funds sometimes have an extremely strong influence or monopolistically distorting power on a specific market due in some part to herd behavior, bringing about an equilibrium far removed from the economic fundamentals of a country, which would not have occurred but for their speculative activities. They argue that hedge funds fall into either one of the following models: (1) "Self-realizing monetary crisis model", which maintains that a monetary crisis is not necessarily caused by the aggravation of economic fundamentals but rather it becomes actual crisis because investors make a speculative attack on a currency in anticipation of a devaluation of the currency. (2) "Multiple equilibria model", which maintains that although in an economic model there is only one equilibrium guided by initial conditions or exogenous variables, there could be more than one equilibrium in a market like a foreign exchange market, where a price forecast for the future often determines the price for the moment. According to these arguments, in a small economy with a fixed exchange rate regime, a massive short-selling of the country's currency in expectation of a shift from the fixed exchange rate regime could cause a plunge in the value of the currency first on the futures market and then on the spot market and it could make it impossible to restore the original equilibrium, even though its policy management is sound.

Furthermore, if there is a lack of transparency and no restrictions or supervision are in place on international institutional investors, there is a greater possibility that trading partners (counter parties in domestic country) of such investors will not be fully aware of the risks involved and the final risk-taking burden will shift to the trading partner or the whole system. In this sense, benefits and costs of international institutional investors (such as hedge funds) have to be evaluated in relation to the market size of an emerging market country. If a market is small, international institutional investors can exert a greater influence through fluctuations in market prices. On the other hand, what is most important for international institutional investors' investment strategy is liquidity of the market. If there is not enough liquidity, it is difficult to hedge risks for investments or liquidate positions but there exists far-reaching effects on the whole market when it decides to liquidate.

9.5.2 *China's Experience*

China has had enormous success in attracting external capital over the last decade and this has contributed to its growth in a variety of ways. Figure 9.1 presents GDP growth rates and foreign direct investment (FDI) growth rates in China over the years from 1978 to 1995.

In December 1996, China liberalized its current account but its capital account remains closed. This allows only those enterprises with necessary trade documents to buy foreign exchange from designated foreign exchange banks. The rules stipulate that Chinese enterprises must sell all hard currency earnings to designated foreign exchange banks or hold them in foreign currency bank accounts after receiving approval to open an account. Foreign currency earnings cannot be held outside of China. Meanwhile, Chinese residents can hold foreign currency in banks or sell them to the banks on a voluntary basis but no private trading is permitted.

Foreign investors can remit profit, dividend and interest earnings out of China from their foreign currency accounts or can convert yuan earnings into hard currency at designated banks before sending money from China. Foreign investors can only invest in B-shares on the stock exchanges in China, which are separated from the primary security market, the A shares,

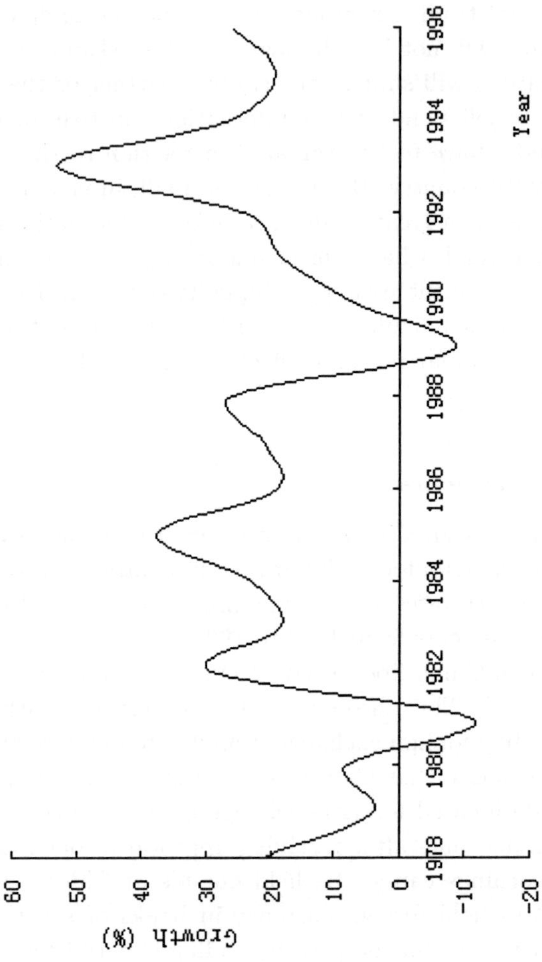

Fig. 9.1 GDP Growth and FDI Growth in China (1978-1995)

which can be traded only by domestic investors.

This opening of the current account but closing of the capital account has served China well in some respects, notably in that it prevents speculators from instigating an exchange crisis. So far China has absorbed the surge of external capital by avoiding most of the problems that less developed countries (LDCs) in similar circumstances often encounter.[17] Over the course of the past five years, the government has allowed the currency to fluctuate but within a very narrow band. Until recently, China also successfully avoided an undesirable appreciation of its exchange rate following the large inflow of external capital by making prudent interventions, e.g., the accumulation of reserves to offset the large flows in 1997.

For China the maintenance of its share of foreign capital should be easier than for most LDCs since most of its capital inflow consists of FDI, borrowing from private financial institutions being the distant second source. As long as China is able to maintain its international competitiveness and its domestic market continues to grow, FDI is likely to continue to flow in. Although China's share of official development assistance is substantial, official development assistance as a proportion of capital inflow in China is low (about 12%). A decline in the volume of official development assistance is therefore unlikely to have a serious effect on China.

Even so, prudence dictates that China be careful about increasing its dependence on external capital. Its debt burden, although still well below danger level, has increased rapidly and is significantly above that of South Korea and Malaysia (and Taiwan). In addition, as a country with a very high rate of domestic saving, China should be able to finance much of its investment needs from its own resources.

However, the volatility of private capital is quite distinct in China. As the recent Mexican experience showed, LDCs can hardly be stoical about the volatility of foreign funds, making use of these inflows when they come and not lamenting their departure for other pastures at other times. This is because unsustainable surges can inflict serious economic damage by causing an appreciation in the exchange rate above the level that is warranted by a healthy current account. As the exchange rate keeps appreciating and the current account sinks deeper and deeper into deficit, the owners

[17] At the most recent accounting, at the end of 1996, the present value of China's future debt service stood at 19.6% of GDP and 81.3% of exports. These ratios are higher than for South Korea (13.9% and 46.2%) but considerably lower than for almost any other major LDC including India (29.1% and 227.6%) and Indonesia (58.5% and 194.6%).

of private foreign capital suddenly decide that the country is no longer a viable place for investment. A dramatic and traumatic flight of private capital follows with crippling effect on output and employment of the recipient economy. All this happens because, unlike a current transaction in international trade, capital flows involve returns in the future about which information is incomplete and hence capital mobility is anything but perfect.

Despite the government's tight controls, there is increasing evidence that Chinas capital account is increasingly subject to leakage. Most of the illegal capital flight is being conducted by SOEs, either through under-reporting of export earnings or over-reporting of import expenses. By under-reporting exports, companies can keep significant foreign exchange revenues that they would otherwise have had to hand over to the State Administration of Foreign Exchange (SAFE), the government organ that manages Chinas US$158 billion in reserves. By over-reporting imports, companies are able to secure permission to change *renminbi* into US dollars. The foreign trade partner will deposit the over-paid portion of the contract into a foreign bank account. Affiliates of state companies may also over-report or over-pay for raw materials and other inputs, falsely inflating their foreign currency expenses. Consequently, foreign affiliates of Chinese companies tend to perform suspiciously poorly.[18] Consequently, it is clear that despite the best intentions of capital controls, the Chinese government can only stem or slow down capital flight at best.

Since capital flight from China is now primarily conducted through diverting investment and through the fudging of import and export documents, expanded trade and investment opportunities will continue to foster these opportunities. Clearly one impact of Chinas accession to the WTO will be to accelerate and expand options for individuals who want to invest capital outside of the country illegally. This makes capital account liberalization all the more necessary.

9.5.3 *Policy Issues*

In general, international capital flows and institutional investors should be kept under control for three reasons, i.e., to protect investors; to ensure the

[18]One SAFE study of 2,202 affiliates in 1998 found that only 36.6 percent were either making a profit or breaking even (Kynge, 2000).

soundness and integrity of the market; and to maintain the stability of the financial system.

First of all, it is generally thought that tighter controls, including more information disclosure, on international institutional investors are necessary to protect investors. But it is important to realize that if the degree of information disclosure to investors is paramount, information disclosure will make progress under the market mechanism. Secondly, ensuring the soundness and integrity of the market is an important policy objective. If such things as market manipulation by a big player, circulation of rumors and insider trading become rampant, the market would lose its integrity and would eventually lose its function to effectively allocate resources. But we have to keep in mind that excessive restrictions will disrupt free transactions and efficiency of the market. Thirdly, maintaining the stability of the financial system is also an important policy objective. If a major international institutional investor incurs a huge loss, it would cause deterioration of assets at creditor financial institutions and this would worsen market sentiment and cause a flight to liquidity, even leading to a collapse of the financial system.

For a country like China whose financial markets are still in the development stage, it is vital that the government takes preventive measures against a huge, abrupt shift of capital and promote the stability of its own currency and financial market. It is important for the government to take a sound macroeconomic policy and strengthen the financial supervisory system by thoroughly implementing prudent rules for financial institutions. But at the same time, the government should explore the possibility of introducing regulations from the standpoint of stabilizing the financial system and keeping the market integrity in the same manner as discussed above.

The conventional economic wisdom dictates that there are several preconditions that should be met first before a country liberalizes its capital account. Now an international consensus exits that the liberalization should be proceeded in a well-sequenced manner assuring whether certain preconditions are in place. The preconditions to promote the liberalization of capital transactions include: (1) a firmly established market economy system; (2) progressive liberalization of trade; (3) an economy that is mature and integrated into the world economy to a certain extent; and (4) a strong financial sector and a highly efficient supervisory system. Regarding the last precondition, it is essential, for example, to monitor the risks involved in exposing foreign currency-denominated loans and maturity mismatches through appropriate implementation of prudent regulations. Some also suggest that the liberalization of the more stable long-term direct investment should precede that of short-term capital transaction.[19]

Given the current huge and drastic movement of capital in the world economy, what kind of exchange rate regime Chinese government should decide to choose is very important. Of course, what would be the most suitable exchange rate regime for China depends on the composition of its trading partners, the composition of its major trading items, the degree of capital liberalization and its inflation experience. But the Asian crisis has taught us that pegging a country's currency to any one particular currency is highly risky. Generally speaking, China can flexibly cope with exchange fluctuations by pegging its currency with, or referring to, a basket of currencies of some advanced countries with which it has the closest interdependent relationship in terms of trade and investment. In any case, there is no simple formula. Therefore, it should be stressed here that it is important for China to choose a suitable exchange rate regime consistent with appropriate macroeconomic policies.

In any event, a full convertibility of *renminbi* will be inevitable. Full convertibility of *renminbi* could represent a dramatic expansion of the range of financial assets available to Chinese households, pose the threat of financial disintermediation, and thus undermine the financial viability of domestic banks. This could potentially lead to a disastrous run on the Chinese banking system, which would also entail the closing of roughly one-third of Chinese SOEs. While some might argue that this is a good thing over the long-term, there is a legitimate and palpable fear that such a result would lead to chaos and turmoil in the society. If such a situation occurred, Chinese banks could either create a massive hyper-inflationary spiral by printing money, or by restricting or limiting customer withdrawals. The first option is disastrous; the second option, while preferable to the first,

[19]It is essential to be aware that the direction of short-term capital may change suddenly from an inflow to an outflow and that holding foreign currency-denominated debts contains foreign exchange risk. During the Asian financial crisis, the amount of capital that once flew in and then flew out of Asian countries in one year amounted to more than 10% of the combined GDP of the countries involved. Therefore, it is important to make the best use of market friendly controls on capital inflow in a way that would not distort the market. Such capital controls would include higher reserve ratios for deposits received from non-residents and stricter prudent regulations on borrowing from abroad and securities issuance by residents (in particular, by financial institutions).

would erode confidence even further and result in more illegal capital flight.

A palatable solution to this problem is to distinguish between different types of capital flows such as borrowing and lending, securities, and FDI. As noted above, foreign direct investment is largely already liberalized. For securities market, China should rapidly expand the number of companies listed on the B-Share markets, and gradually phase out the segmentation between A- and B-share markets. This will also serve the purpose of market recapitalization. At present, a practical step is to allow foreign investors to purchase both A- and B-shares and foreign companies to issue both types of shares. Chinas accession to the WTO will accelerate this process and further open up of its capital account by freeing outward remittance of investment returns by foreign-invested funds, as well as distribution of such returns to overseas shareholders. New changes will occur to the structure of Chinas securities markets.

There is a saying in China that things will happen when the conditions are right (a fruit is the best when it is ripe, *guashu diluo*). It is time for bolder thinking, however, in the light of the reform experience that the state is still firmly entrenched in many parts of the economy. The fruit will likely never get "ripe" to continue the metaphor, absent a clear signal from the top as to when China will liberalize its capital account. Unfortunately, at this time, there are appears to be little movement on the top of this issue. Chinese Premier Zhu Rongji has publicly declared that there is no firm timetable for reform. In short, he subscribes to the belief that the closed capital account saved China from recent economic turmoil. While true in the past, China should recognize that prolonging capital account liberalization would only increase the aggregate costs over the long-term. Thus, while Michael Camdessus of the IMF believes that capital account liberalization must be "bold in its vision, cautious in its implementation", there is a strong case in China that it should be bold in both vision and implementation.

Appendix A
Securities Law

A.1 Introduction

The new *P.R.C. Securities Law*, which was promulgated by the Standing Committee of the 9th National Peoples Congress (NPC) on December 29, 1998 and came into force on July 1, 1999, is the national legislation governing the securities market in mainland China. The new law by and large completes the national legal framework for regulation of the Chinese stock market, a process originally begun with the passage of the *P.R.C. Company Law* in 1993.

The *Securities Law* has attracted much attention both within and outside of China. Among the reasons for the attention is that the law received an unusual amount of support from the countrys leaders. Following the National Financial Working Conference of the Chinese Communist Party and the State Council held in October 1997 (which had focused on the importance of reducing financial risks in the market), the China Securities Regulatory Commission (CSRC) began in earnest to promote the enactment of the new Law. Before it was tabled at the Standing Committee of the NPC at the end of 1997, Li Peng, Chairman of the NPC, personally led a special mission to Shenzhen to discuss comments on certain outstanding issues. At the Standing Committee meeting it was reported that not one of the 138 delegates voted against the law, an event quite rare in China since it began using the secret ballot in voting.

A second reason that the law has drawn much attention is that the draft had received wide consultation amongst academics, ministry officials, professional regulators and market practitioners during the five years since it was first considered. It had also gone through as many as four previous reviews by the Standing Committee. This ensured that all interested parties had an opportunity to express their views on what has been perceived as a vitally important law.

Moreover, by promoting the involvement of foreign securities law experts in the consultation process, it has managed to attract significant interest overseas. A series of international conferences dealing with provisions of the law were held, the major one being the "International Symposium on Securities Law" held in Beijing in 1996 and co-sponsored by the United Nations Development Program. Experts from the U.K. Securities and Investment Board, the U.S. NYSE, Hong Kongs Securities and Futures Commission, together with practitioners and academics from Japan, the U.S. and Hong Kong, made presentations on their respective areas of expertise. A collection of essays has since been published by the CSRC. In 1997, another international conference was held where experts from the U.S. Securities and Exchange Commission, in addition to experts from Japan and Hong Kong, gave presentations on selected topics concerning the *Securities Law.* Because of this open approach adopted by the Chinese authorities, many experts in the securities industry had themselves been involved in the drafting stage and have since remained keenly interested in witnessing the progression of the draft into law.

Finally, and perhaps most importantly, the law would seem to indicate a consensus view among the Chinese authorities that:

- The nature of the stock market and its role and function within the Chinese socialist market economy has now been firmly entrenched;
- any effective regulation of the stock market must have a strong legal foundation; and
- given the existing realities of the stock market against the background of the Asian financial crisis in 1998, the authorities believe that legal regulation of the stock market cannot be further delayed.

The Law thus arguably indicates that, since the stock market is now an integral part of the Chinese socialist economy, the use of securities as a tool of capital formation will be encouraged and the quality of the stock market will thereby improve with time. In other words, it provides a firm basis for the belief that greater business opportunities, both domestically and overseas, will be created in the Chinese capital market.

A.2 The Role of the Stock Market

In a preface to a study guide on securities knowledge published by the CSRC in 1998, the Chairman, Zhou Zhengqing, reiterated the four main benefits of the securities market from the Chinese perspective:

- Through exercising a controlling interest in listed companies, state or collectively owned units not only retain their control over production assets, but also manage to attract surplus funds from the public in the form of investments. By participating in asset valuation in the course of the listing exercise and issuing shares at a premium, the capital of these units will increase in value as they become listed companies. Hence, the market is a useful tool for strengthening the central position of public ownership in the socialist economic system.
- As China's only source of funds in a planned economy is from bank loans, the rate of indebtedness of state-owned enterprises has been very high. This is neither good for the enterprises' own development nor for management of the country's financial risk. Establishing a stock market and finding new sources of direct capital funding is compatible with China's current policy of developing a modern financial and corporate structure. Moreover, it offers additional source of foreign capital investment.
- As state-owned enterprises must be restructured for the purpose of listing, the process requires an enterprise to reform itself, establish a corporate management structure, increase the level of transparency, maintain a continuous disclosure system and submit to the supervision of its business by its shareholders, the regulators and the public. By facilitating such enterprises in the restructuring of their operational mechanism and developing a modern corporate structure, listings on the stock market should be considered complementary with China's policy of enterprise reform.
- By regulating the types of businesses approved for listings, the authorities have implemented China's policy of enhancing certain types of production assets and achieving a more efficient allocation of resources amongst different industries. Significant funds have been raised from the stock market and channeled to preferred industrial sectors, such as infrastructure development, high-technology

production and important national pillar industries. Moreover, acquisitions of loss-suffering enterprises by listed companies will enable these enterprises to be preserved and used in a more positive way.

The acceptance of these benefits has shaped the present form of the *Securities Law*, which has 12 chapters and 214 provisions. The general principles are contained within Chapter 1. Article 3 states the basic principles of transparency, fairness and integrity, while under Articles 7-9, a centralized approach to regulation is emphasized.

Article 2 provides that the Law shall govern the issuance and trading, within China, of shares, corporate debentures and other securities defined by the State Council. This provision defines the scope of the conduct regulated, the territorial scope and the products regulated under the Law. The Law specifically provides that it does not apply to treasury bonds. At this stage, the Law applies to corporate equity securities and corporate bonds, but the open-ended nature of Article 2 envisages that other securities may be acceptable for regulation in future.

A.3 Regulating the Chinese Stock Market

China has approximately 40 million investors and 2,400 securities brokerage outlets across the country. As at the end of August 1999, there were 448 companies listed in Shenzhen and 470 in Shanghai, of which more than 100 have issued B shares. The total market capitalization is close to *renminbi* 2.8 trillion (see Shenzhen Securities Exchange Market Statistics, September 1999 issue; SZSE Monthly Statistics, September 1999 issue), which represents about 30% of Chinas GDP.

Prior to the enactment of the Law, the governing legislation was the *State Council Provisional Regulations on Share Issuance and Trading* (22 April 1993). The Chinese stock market took the same road of trial implementations as has been the case with other innovations in the Chinese socialist economy. For example, the first issuance of shares occurred in 1983 (Shenzhen Bao An Enterprise Group Limited); the stock exchanges in Shenzhen and Shanghai were established in 1990; and the CSRC was created in pursuant to State Council Directive in 1992.

The Law has made an important difference by establishing a centralized regulator for the market and providing a legal anchor for all of the regulations that apply in the securities area. According to official figures, there were close to 250 piecemeal provisions. A collection of these provisions dating from 1992-1998 has been published by the CSRC. The securities regulator, the CSRC, is not specifically named in the Law, but is referred to as the securities regulator under the State Council.

The Law gives specific powers to the CSRC, as well as imposes responsibilities on it by way of checks and balances. The enactment of the Law indicates that the Chinese market has entered into a more mature phase. As Chairman Zhou of the CSRC noted in an interview on December 30, 1998, "with the creation of a comprehensive legal system for the market, a fundamental improvement in the quality of regulation is expected to occur". "Regulation", he said, "is the prerequisite for growth" (see report published in the CSRC Official Bulletin, Vol 12, 1998).

The Law gives clear legal backing to the work of the CSRC. Article 167 specifies 8 regulatory functions for the CSRC.

- To make regulations governing the market and to exercise the power of approval and ratification;
- to govern the issuance, trading, registration, custody and settlement of securities;
- to govern securities issuers, listed companies, the stock exchange, securities companies, securities registration and settlement agencies, fund management agencies, investment advisory agencies, credit rating agencies as well as law firms, accounting firms and valuation firms that engage in the securities business;
- to stipulate standards as to qualifications and conduct for persons engaging in the securities business;
- to govern and inspect the disclosure of information in relation to securities issuance and trading;
- to instruct and govern the activities of the securities association;
- to investigate breaches of securities law; and
- other functions defined under other laws and regulations.

The regulator is entrusted with delegated authority to make rules governing the market (see Article 167(1), Articles 109, 111, 154, 158). This flexibility recognizes the need for the regulator to respond to rapidly changing market conditions and is consistent with the approach used in other jurisdictions.

The regulator has power under Article 167(7) to investigate violations of the law. New specific investigative powers are given in Article 168 and include the power to:

- Enter the premises where the law has been broken for investigations;
- question the parties and related persons;
- examine and make copies of trading records, registration records, accounting reports and other materials belonging to the parties or related persons; and
- examine the cash accounts and securities accounts of the parties and related persons. Where there is evidence of transfer or dissipation of assets, the regulator may apply to court to have the assets frozen.

These powers are necessary in practice to enable the investigator to obtain evidence. On the other hand, they serve to limit the power of the regulator in the sense that it shall not have the power to make demands that are not particularized in this provision.

The Law adopts a centralized approach to regulation. This can be seen as encompassing 3 aspects: (i) regulation of the securities market is undertaken by the central government and not the provinces; (ii) the CSRC is the paramount regulator of the securities market vis-a-vis other central government ministries; and (iii) the exchanges are subordinated to, and supervised by, the central regulatory body. As such, the responsibility of the regulator is enormous. Recognizing the power bestowed on the regulator, the Law also provides checks and balances. Article 9 requires the regulators work to be supervised by the State Audit Bureau. Article 209 requires confiscated gains and fines to be paid to the State Treasury.

The Law gives a party grieved by a decision of the regulatory body the right to apply for review or begin an action in the Peoples Court. A new measure of accountability is stipulated in the Law. For example, the listing committee is required to give reasons for rejecting an application for a listing of securities under Article 16 and the regulator is required to make public all of its regulations, as well as its decisions, on the imposition of penalties for violations of the law under Article 172. The Law explicitly provides that the CSRC staff must observe duties of confidentiality, fairness and integrity.

A.4 Capital Formation

Chapter 2 of the *Securities Law* deals with the issuance of shares. The Law provides that a public offering of shares must comply with the conditions of the Company Law and be first ratified by the securities regulator. Moreover, a public offering of corporate bonds must be approved by a body authorized by the State Council. The *P.R.C. Company Law*, which as noted earlier was enacted on December 29, 1993, contains most of the substantive requirements concerning the issuer (e.g., Article 152 of the *Company Law* lays down the minimum requirements for a listed company). By contrast, the *Securities Law* contains mostly procedural and administrative requirements for a share issuance or listing. The authorities have carefully avoided overlap between the two laws, but if there is conflict, Article 2 of the *Securities Law* implies that it shall override the *Company Law*, i.e., the *Company Law* will only apply to matters that are not specifically prescribed under the *Securities Law*.

Article 10 lays down the general principle that a prospective issuer of shares to be offered to the public must comply with the minimum requirements laid down by law and no person may offer securities to the public unless it has been ratified or approved by the securities regulator. Article 16 requires a decision on an application to be made within three months. Article 20 provides that a new issuance of shares may take the form of a public offering or a rights issue. In both cases, the issuer must ensure that the proceeds are used in accordance with the proposal stated in the offering document, except where the change of use has been approved at a shareholders' meeting (Article 20). Underwriting is required for all public offerings (Articles 21-28). A major innovation under this Law is the issuance committee, to be comprised of internal and external experts appointed to approve applications for share issuance (Articles 14-15).

Article 10 also contains one of the most enigmatic provisions in the Law. It states that no public offer of securities is allowed unless it is ratified or approved by the CSRC or other ministries authorized by the State Council. This represents a major step forward from the previous method that had relied entirely on state approval for share issuance. The new ratification process places more emphasis on the participation of an external issuance committee and the issuer's objective fulfillment of the listing requirements. Some commentators have sought to differentiate ratification and approval by describing the former as a procedural review and the latter as a substantive review. A procedural review process is one where the regulator ensures that all matters required to be disclosed are contained in the issuance document and it makes no judgment on the substantive merits of the application. Hence, it is often described as a disclosure-based process. A substantive review, on the other hand, is one where the regulator makes a judgment on the substantive merits of the application and approves only those it deems fit for listing. It is often described as a merit-based process.

Under the Law, the approval procedure for share issuance is a two-tier process. First, the application will be examined by the issuance committee comprised of regulatory staff and external professional experts and, pursuant to Article 14, the committee members shall vote to express a decision whether to approve the application. The application must also be delivered to the regulator for ratification by its staff. Under Article 15, the regulator is required to ratify the application in accordance with conditions laid down by law and must do so in an open manner. In this way, the Chinese authorities have managed a compromise between the substantive and procedural approaches. It also allows external participation and market input into its share issuance mechanism, while maintaining ultimate control over it.

The Law, moreover, makes no reference to the pre-selection (quota) system for approving enterprise listings. This confirms what Mr. Zhou said during a speech in Hong Kong in April 1999 regarding the abolition of the pre-selection system for overseas listings. The new approach is to approve company listings as and when they become ready.

A.5 Securities Trading and Information Disclosure

Chapter 3 is entitled Securities Trading and contains four distinct parts governing General Principles (Part 1), Securities Listings (Part 2), Disclosure Obligations (Part 3) and Prohibited Conduct (Part 4). The general principles in Part 1 stipulate the basic rules of the market, e.g., that only lawfully issued securities may be traded and that securities may only be transacted at a securities exchange by way of open, centralized competitive price bidding. Article 34 provides that the securities may be evidenced in paper form or in other forms stipulated by the securities regulator. Article 41 requires a shareholder who holds 5% or more of the issued share capital of the company to disclose that fact to the company, the regulator and, if the shares are listed, the exchange.

Part 2 (Articles 43-57) governs the listings of shares and corporate bonds. Part 3 (Articles 58-66) prescribes obligations for disclosure of information. Part IV (Articles 67-77) identifies insider trading, the acquisition of unlawful interest or the shifting of risk and the dissemination of false information as undesirable conduct.

The Law stresses the importance of continuing disclosure obligations, which are provided under Articles 58-66. They relate to issuance documents (prospectuses), interim reports, annual reports and reports on material events. There is an obligation imposed on shareholders holding 5% of the issued share capital of the listed company to disclose their interests (Articles 41 and 79). Article 59 requires that the information be authentic, accurate and complete, and may not contain any false record, misleading statement or major omission. Article 63 states that the issuer, underwriter and/or their officers may incur legal liability for any loss to investors arising from false or misleading statements in the disclosure reports. Article 177 provides that an issuer who fails to make adequate or true disclosures may be ordered to make corrections and pay fines in the region of *renminbi* 300,000–600,000, whereas responsible officers may be ordered to pay personal fines ranging from *renminbi* 30,000–300,000. Article 189 provides that persons making false statements or producing misleading information in the course of securities trading may be ordered to make corrections or to pay fines in the region of *renminbi* 30,000–200,000. Since intent is not an essential ingredient, the Law effectively imposes strict liability for inadequate disclosures. The Law also provides that, in both cases, criminal liability may ensue if the acts or omissions constitute a crime.

The Chinese market has suffered from a lack of transparency resulting from listed companies making inadequate disclosures. In a Hong Kong survey conducted in 1994 after a huge fall of H-share prices, 90% of the fund managers surveyed expressed concern over the lack of transparency of H-share companies; 76.9% thought H-share companies did not faithfully disclose their financial and business information; and 80% felt that H-share companies did not understand what information ought to be disclosed, especially in relation to substantial transactions. This concern has been somewhat alleviated by the efforts of the CSRC, the HKSE and the Institute of Directors in Hong Kong, who have conducted seminars on disclosure in the past year for officers of such companies. Yet lack of transparency will remain a problem if there is no clear statutory requirement for disclosure backed by adequate sanctions. However, the strengthening of disclosure standards in the new Law is expected to improve the situation.

Article 43 requires a company applying for listing of its shares on an exchange to submit an application to the securities regulator for ratification. Article 43(2) empowers the regulator to delegate this function to the stock exchanges. Once an application is ratified for listing, the stock exchange in question will be required under Article 46 to effect the company's listing within six months of receiving all the prescribed documentation.

A.6 Acquisitions

The important objective of the restructuring and reforming of state enterprises has been noted above. Since company acquisitions can facilitate reforms, mergers and restructuring of companies and state enterprises by encouraging competition and discovering unrealized potential, it is no surprise, therefore, that the rules relating to company acquisitions are given a prominent position in the Law. Chapter 4 (Articles 78-94) recognizes two types of offers: acquisition by tender offer and acquisition by agreement. Following the U.S. statutory model rather than Hong Kong's voluntary code model, the Law provides a step-by-step guide on how a tender offer should be made.

A tender offer applies to shares traded on the exchange. Article 79 provides that an investor who has reached a share-holding of 5% of the issued share capital of a listed company should, within 3 days, report the holding to the CSRC, the exchange and the listed company and refrain from further purchases during that period. Subsequently, if the investor increases or reduces its holding by 5%, it shall make a similar report within two days and shall refrain from further purchases during that period. Article 81 then provides that an investor wishing to acquire further shares in a company after accumulating 30% of its shares is required to make a general offer to shareholders. The general offer must take the form of a written offer document, which must first be approved by the CSRC. Article 83 prescribes that an offer shall be announced 15 days after the date of submission of the document, and that the offer period must not be shorter than 30 days or longer than 60 days. Once the offer is announced, it cannot be withdrawn, although the investor may change its terms subject to the approval of the CSRC and the relevant exchange. The investor cannot trade in the shares during the offer period other than under the terms of the offer.

Article 85 provides that all terms stated in a tender offer shall apply equally to all shareholders of a company. Article 86 states that the company will be de-listed if the investor succeeds in acquiring 75% or more of the share capital. Under Article 87, if an investor is found to have acquired 90% or more of the share capital, the shareholders who did not accept the initial offer and are still holding shares in the company will be given the right to sell their shares to the investor on the terms stated in the initial offer.

The regulation of private acquisitions is, by comparison, less detailed. Article 89 states that an investor can enter into an agreement with the shareholders of the target company to effect a transfer of their shares. The investor is required to submit a report of the agreement to the CSRC and make a public announcement within three days. The agreement cannot take effect until it is publicly announced.

As at the end of August 1999, the combined market capitalization in China exceeded *renminbi* 2 trillion, but only about 30% of is comprised of liquid shares. The Law did not address the status of state shares, legal person shares and employee shares indicating perhaps that the issue is still unresolved. Given the poor extent of liquidity of shares in the market, it is difficult to expect take-over activities to flourish in the market. However, Article 89 envisages that acquisitions by agreement can be governed by State Council regulations. It is possible that further regulations will be enacted to govern this topic when the government has clarified its policy in this respect.

In addition to the open provisions on acquisitions by agreement, it should be noted that the Law gives the CSRC a discretion to exempt an investor from complying with the mandatory offer requirement under Article 81. This emphasis on flexibility enables the regulator to modify the statutory take-over requirements to address the needs of specific transactions. It remains to be seen whether the regulator will, in time, develop guidelines as to how this discretion will be exercised. However, this waiver, together with the flexible provisions on acquisitions by agreement, will no doubt be wide enough to facilitate the reform of state enterprises by encouraging the re-organization of assets in an orderly and commercial fashion.

A.7 Market Infrastructure

China is, and shall remain certainly for the foreseeable future, a semi-closed market. Article 138 provides that only Chinese citizens and legal persons can open accounts for investing in the A-share market.

In addition, the Law contains numerous prohibitions:

- Article 35 states that only spot trading is permitted. Forward contracts and derivative futures contracts on securities are considered not suitable for trading at this stage.
- Article 36 states that margin trading and securities borrowing are prohibited. Brokers are not allowed to extend credit to clients, either by way of providing them with cash loans or lending them securities.
- Article 39 prohibits trading and prescribes minimum holding periods for securities for persons involved in the issue of the audit report, asset valuation report, legal opinion and other documents. This is designed to discourage insider trading.
- Article 42 states that shareholders are not allowed to keep profits earned within six months of previous sale or purchase, and directors are personally made responsible for enforcing this provision. This is designed to curtail short-swing profits and reduce market volatility and price fluctuations.
- Article 76 explicitly prohibits state enterprises from speculating in shares. This is designed to curtail speculation as well as prevent state assets from being exposed to market risk.
- Article 106 prohibits day trades. This is designed to reduce market volatility and price fluctuations.
- Article 133 states that bank funds are prohibited from being invested in the stock market. This is designed to limit the injection of "hot money" into the market. It is also recognized that banks have an unfair advantage over the ordinary investor because they have more available funds and consequently have the ability to destabilize the market.

Despite the good intentions behind the prohibitions, an inevitable result will be a reduction of liquidity arising from a credit crunch. This has not gone unnoticed, as stated by the CSRC Chairman in an interview on December 30, 1998:

> "I heard some rumors that the proposed enactment of the *Securities Law* had dampened confidence in investing in the market, as if the Law would be the cause of a falling market. This view is completely groundless and is a serious misrepresentation to investors'. It certainly appears that the authorities are aiming to create a more stable market for the long term, with better protection for investors, and the restrictions are the result of a deliberate policy choice to reduce leverage and speculation in the market. "

Chapter 5 deals with securities exchanges. Article 95 defines an exchange as a place for trading in securities at which the price is fixed centrally by competition. Only authorized exchanges are allowed to operate, and at present there are two: in Shenzhen and Shanghai. Only firms, not individuals, are allowed to be members of the exchanges (Article 103).

Chapter 6 deals with securities companies. They are the main type of intermediary in the market. Only limited liability companies and companies limited by shares may apply to become securities companies (Article 118). Under Article 119, companies are divided into two types according to their business: general companies and agency companies. The minimum registered capital for a general firm is *renminbi* 500 million and for an agency firm it is *renminbi* 50 million. General companies are allowed to trade on their own account (proprietary trading) as well as act for clients.

There are new requirements as to the qualifications and conduct of persons engaged in the securities business in chapter 6. Article 122 envisages a licensing regime that requires persons engaged in the management and operation of the securities company to have the requisite standards. It also requires companies to have appropriate trading facilities with sound management systems in place.

Concerning financial resources requirements, Article 124 states as a matter of principle that the external liabilities of a securities company must not exceed a certain percentage of its net assets and the liquid liabilities must not exceed a certain percentage of its liquid assets. It further provides that the regulator may set the specific percentages and the procedures for governing this, which gives room for adoption of risk-based capital adequacy standards that are common in other jurisdictions.

The Law also provides detailed requirements concerning the treatment of clients. The issuance of client agreements, statements of account and verification statements are now mandatory (Articles 139-140). Client accounts must be segregated under Article 138. Brokers are prohibited from offering discretionary services (Article 142) or guaranteeing profits (Article 143) to clients. Under Article 145, a securities company shall remain fully responsible for its staff in any of their misconduct in securities trading.

Proprietary trading is the term used to describe a company's investment of its own funds in the securities market. The Law makes a distinction between proprietary trading and agency trading. The main risks of proprietary trading are, first, that a company might expose itself to conflicts of interest with its client as far as trading opportunities are concerned and, secondly, that a company which engages in proprietary trading may incur risks to its capital. The Chinese authorities recognize the benefits of, as well as the difficulty of regulating, proprietary trading. A compromise has been struck by allowing only those companies with a substantial capital base and an adequate system for segregation of assets to do so as general companies, on top of their agency business. The minimum capital requirement for general companies permitted to engage in proprietary trading is *renminbi* 500 million. Article 132 requires that the two types of businesses in a general company must be strictly segregated. As industry practitioners are generally in favor of proprietary trading, this requirement is expected to encourage mergers among lesser players so as to combine their businesses to reach the above threshold.

Chapter 7 regulates securities registration and settlement agencies. They are recognized as forming an integral part of the clearing and settlement system of the Chinese market. These agencies are non-profit making units, which provide centralized registration, custodian and settlement services in support of the trading of securities. Article 150 requires all securities to be deposited with such agencies before they can be traded. Under Article 151, securities holders obtain evidence of title from these agencies. Brokerage services and custodian services are segregated under this system, minimizing the risk of loss from misuse of client assets.

Chapter 8 deals with intermediary service providers, which refer to three types of companies: the investment adviser, the credit rating agency and the professional adviser. Under Article 159, the investment adviser is not permitted to act for the client in securities trading, so as to avoid potential conflict. Under Article 161, professional advisers are required to assume liability for their advice and official reports.

The Law envisages a form of self-regulation, which is encouraged in other financial jurisdictions. Chapter 9 establishes a securities industry association to be comprised of securities companies. The association is characterized as a self-regulatory body whose scope of activities includes providing training to members, supervising their compliance with the law, raising business standards and mediating disputes.

When the stock market began in China, the power to grant licenses to intermediaries was vested with the People's Bank of China. This power was recently transferred to the CSRC and is now formally entrenched in Chapter 4 and Article 167(4) of the Law. The quality of the intermediaries in a market reflects the quality of the market. It is important for effective regulation of intermediaries that the same body governs the entry and exit points for them and has the authority to supervise the daily conduct of their business. With the introduction of the clear authority of the securities regulator in this area, the discipline and quality of the market is expected to improve.

A.8 Investor Protection

In order to create a fair and orderly market, the prohibition of fraudulent activities must be one of the major goals of the Law. The importance of this aspect is indicated by the prominent position in which the Law has placed as "securities crimes". Article 5 in the General Principles section defines the securities crimes of fraud, insider trading and market manipulation, which are all prohibited.

The detailed provisions concerning these activities are contained in Part 4 of Chapter 3 (Articles 67-77). Insider trading is defined by Article 67 to mean the activity of an insider using insider information to trade in securities. The scope of an insider and insider information are defined. Insiders who are aware of insider information are prohibited from trading in securities, divulging the insider information or advising others to trade in the relevant securities. The penalty for this offence includes a mandatory sale of the securities in question, confiscation of the illegal gains and a fine of up to five times the amount of illegal gains or the value of the securities in question, whichever is lower (Article 183). The Law states that a heavier penalty will be imposed on securities regulators who violate this provision.

In addition, the Law introduces further offences of the acquisition of unlawful interest or the shifting of risk (Article 71) and the dissemination of false information (Article 71). Article 71 defines the former offence as follows:

- To, singly or in concert with others, make use of one's competitive edge over capital, share-holding or information to collectively or continuously transact securities and manipulate their prices;
- to intentionally conspire with others to engage in securities transactions or mutually buy and sell securities that they did not own, according to a pre-determined time, price and manner, with a view to affecting the prices or volume of securities trading;
- to use oneself as the opposite party in a transaction so as to be both the buyer and the seller, with no change in beneficial ownership, with a view to affecting the prices or volume of securities trading; or
- other means of manipulating the prices of securities trading.

A similar provision governing market manipulation in futures trading is found in Article 62 of the *P.R.C. Provisional Regulations on Futures Trading*, which came into force on September 1, 1999.

Article 72 prohibits the fabrication or dissemination of false information concerning securities trading. Government employees and media reporters are specifically mentioned. In addition, this provision prohibits personnel working in the various bodies regulated under the law from making false or misleading statements.

In terms of actual enforcement, the Law strengthens the regulators power to impose administrative penalties, which are particularized in Chapter 11. These penalties may take the form of a warning, restitution, confiscation and fines. Added to that is the provision of administrative liabilities for state officials who violate the Law.

The Law specifically preserves the possibility of criminal liability in serious cases, which can arise under the *P.R.C. Criminal Law.* The 1997 amendment to the *Criminal Law* included a variety of commercial crimes that may apply to unlawful conduct in the securities market, such as misrepresentation in prospectuses and disclosure documents, insider dealing, market manipulation, activities relating to illegal use of foreign exchange and causing instability to the financial system. Chapter 3 deals with new economic crimes that undermine the order of the socialist market economy and contains eight sections. Sections 3-5 (Articles 158-200) relate to financial crimes such as "undermining the management order in a company or enterprise", "disrupting the financial order" and "financial fraud".

A.9 Overseas Markets

At present, there are two main types of overseas-related listings. The first type is where the listing of a company's securities takes place on the two domestic stock exchanges, but the shares are issued to overseas investors. These shares may only be traded by non-PRC nationals and companies and are transacted in foreign currency. They are known as overseas-invested domestic shares (or B-shares in short). The other type is where the listing of a company's securities takes place on an overseas exchange and the securities are offered to overseas investors. Where they are listed on the Stock Exchange of Hong Kong, they are known as overseas issued or listed shares (or H-shares in short).

Since the Law's main focus is on the domestic market, it contains little provision for overseas-related listings. What it does provide is the general principle that all overseas related offerings (e.g., B-shares) and listings (e.g., H-shares) must first be approved by the regulator. Article 29 states that where a domestic issuer wishes to issue or list its securities overseas, whether directly or indirectly, it must receive the approval of the securities regulator. The reference to direct or indirect activities gives the regulator the power to regulate all sorts of overseas capital-raising activities of companies, including back-door listings. In the past, the regulator's ambition over these areas has been the subject of debate.

Article 213 states that specific measures will be enacted by the State Council to govern the offering of securities by domestic companies for subscription by overseas investors. Currently, the State Council's *Regulations for the Listing of Foreign Invested Domestic Shares* promulgated on February 1, 1995 apply to B-shares. The governing provisions for H-shares are contained in the State Council's *Regulations for the Overseas Issuance and Listing of Shares* promulgated on April 8, 1994.

The absence of more definitive remarks in the Law was seen as disappointing for some foreign investors eager to tap the potential of the Chinese market. From an optimistic point of view, however, the silence may suggest that the authorities are satisfied with the status quo and will continue to allow flexibility in the governance of this area by the use of administrative rules.

A.10 The Role of Lawyers

Regarding the role of lawyers, it was recently reported in the *China Securities Weekly* that the mainland legal community welcomed the promulgation of the *Securities Law* because practitioners believed that the improvements to the legal framework and the substantive contents of the governing provisions would reduce the level of difficulty in this area of practice. At present, lawyers who wish to practice in the securities field are required to obtain an authorization to that effect from the CSRC. This is not expected to change under the Law.

The *Securities Law* recognizes the legal opinion issued by a law firm as one of the essential documents required for approval (Article 45) and imposes certain responsibilities and liability on legal advisers. Article 13(2) provides that a professional body that issues documentation for the purpose of a share issuance must strictly discharge its statutory function and ensure the truthfulness, accuracy and completeness of these documents. According to one Mainland practitioner, the role of lawyers is not merely to act as an intermediary service provider or the agent of the issuer or underwriter. It is also a defender of an orderly market and an enforcer of the law to the extent that it discharges statutory functions in issuing legal opinions that will be relied upon by the authorities in approving an application. As such, a law firm has a duty of care in providing the legal opinion.

A.11 Summary

With the implementation of the *Securities Law* in July 1999 and the *Provisional Regulations on Futures Trading* in September 1999, it can be argued that the mainland's securities and futures markets have entered a new phase of development and steady growth may be expected in the coming years. In comparison to the fledgling futures market, it is clear that the securities market has progressed significantly further and benefited from the clear policy support of the authorities. Chinese authorities is dedicated to, at least from the enactment of the Law, the protection of investors, the reduction of systematic risk and the ensuring of a fair, efficient and transparent financial market. As the securities market matures, it is expected that the Chinese authorities will take full advantage of the various windows left open in the law to expand the scope of market activities and welcome increased outside participation. Securities practitioners around the world can no doubt look forward to this with a high degree of optimism.

Appendix B

Summary of P.R.C. Taxes

Individual Income Tax

The personal allowance for an expatriate is RMB 4,000 per month. There are no additional allowances for spouses or dependent children. Table B.1 shows that individual income tax is assessed monthly at progressive tax rates which vary depending on the types of income.

Foreign Enterprise Income Tax

Foreign Enterprise Income Tax is levied on taxable income derived by foreign investment enterprises (FIE) and establishments of foreign enterprises

Table B.1 Income Tax Rate for Monthly Salary & Wages

Salary range	tax rate
less than RMB 500	5%
RMB 501 - RMB 2,000	10%
RMB 2,001 - RMB 5,000	15%
RMB 5,001 - RMB 20,000	20%
RMB 20,001 - RMB 40,000	25%
RMB 40,001 - RMB 60,000	30%
RMB 60,001 - RMB 80,000	35%
RMB 80,001 - RMB 100,000	40%
greater than RMB 100,000	45%

in China. The standard tax rate is 33%. This is comprised of state tax of 30% and local tax rate of 3%.

The state tax of 30% may be reduced to 15% or 24% if the enterprises are located in one of the specially designated zones in China and/or engaged in some prescribed businesses or projects. The local tax of 3% may be waived or reduced by the local governments.

A FIE that engages in production for a period of ten years or more will be exempt from foreign enterprise income tax during the first two years and is eligible for a 50% reduction in tax during the subsequent three years, starting from the first profit-making year.

A foreign investor of a FIE who directly reinvests its profits into the FIE or establishes another FIE may obtain a refund of 40% of the state tax paid. If profits are invested in an export-oriented company or high-tech company, the foreign investor may obtain a 100% tax refund.

With respect to depreciation allowances, the residual value of fixed assets should not be less than 10% of the original cost. Depreciation is generally calculated using the straight line method. The minimum depreciation periods are as follows: 20 years for buildings and structures, 10 years for trains, ships, machinery, apparatus and other production equipment, and 5 years for electronic equipment, means of transport other than trains and ships, as well as appliances, tools, furniture related to production or business operations.

Capital Gains Taxes

Capital gains are treated as income and taxed accordingly. Both Chinese residents and non-residents are taxed at 20% with respect to capital gains. The rate is reduced to 10% for capital gains realized within specially designated zones in China.

Withholding Taxes

Withholding tax is imposed on interest, rent, royalties and capital gains received by non-residents. The statutory rate of withholding tax is 20%. It is reduced to 10% for income derived from specially designated zones in China. It could also be reduced under avoidance of double taxation treaties. Dividends from a FIE to a foreign shareholder are exempt from withholding taxes.

Table B.2 Business Taxes Schedule

Taxable services	Tax rate
Construction	3%
Cultural activities and sports	3%
Post and telecommunications	3%
Transportation	3%
Finance and insurance	5%
Sale of immovable properties	5%
Transfer of intangible assets	5%
Entertainment	5 - 20%
Other services	5%

Value Added Tax

All individuals and units which sell taxable goods, provide processing or repair services in China or which import goods into China are subject to value added tax (VAT). The standard VAT rate is 17%. However, certain items are subject to a reduced rate of 13%. Small scale taxpayers pay VAT at the rate of 6% but will not be eligible for input VAT tax credits.

Consumption Tax

Consumption Tax is levied on the importation, production and processing of luxury or high-end goods in China. There are 11 categories of goods which are subject to the consumption tax, including tobacco, alcoholic drinks, cosmetics, skin and hair care products, jewelry, fireworks, gasoline, diesel oil, tires, motorcycles and automobiles. The tax rate ranges from 3 to 45%. Some items are taxed at a fixed amount per unit of volume.

Business Tax

All firms and individuals who provide services listed in Table B.2 are required to pay business taxes calculated on the gross amount received.

Table B.3 Stamp Duty Schedule

Type of Document	Tax Rate
Purchase and sales	0.03%
Engineering projects	0.05%
Storage and custody of goods	0.10%
Properties leasing	0.10%
Loans	0.005%
Processing agreements	0.05%
Construction & Installation	0.03%
Properties insurance	0.003%
Transportation	0.05%
Technology	0.03%

Customs Duty

Customs duty is levied on the importation of goods into China. Before April 1, 1996, FIEs importing machinery, equipment and materials required for producing exports were free of customs duty, VAT and consumption taxes. This preferential tax treatment has been withdrawn for FIEs which were approved after March 1996. However, a grace period is granted to FIEs who have been approved before April 1, 1996.

Stamp Duty

Stamp duty is levied on stipulated documents which are effective under and protected by the Chinese Laws. The applicable duty rates for various contracts are contained in Table B.3:

Appendix C

Major Events in Chinese Stock Markets

1990

- January 4: Shenzhen Branch of the People's Bank of China issued: *Some suggestions on setting up the Shenzhen Securities Exchange*
- February 7: Single trading system was changed into counter concentration trading system in Shenzhen Securities Corporation. Agreements on selling and buying were signed to adopt the rule of price priority and time priority.
- May 28: To strengthen the regulation over securities market and to demolish the illegal trading outside the market, Shenzhen municipal government stipulated that trading need had to be processed via securities intermediaries.
- May 29: Shanghai Branch of the People's Bank of China announced: The bidding price should not be 10% higher or lower than the price of the previous day's closing price.
- June 24: Radio Shenzhen started to broadcast daily stock quotation.
- July 15: Shenzhen Telecom. launched the stock information channel.
- August 25: *Shanghai Securities Daily* started to publish stock quotations.
- September 28: Securities trading automatic quotation (STAQ) system was launched.
- November 27, Shanghai municipality government published the rules for regulation over securities market.
- December 1: After one year of preparation, Shenzhen began exper-

imental stock trades over the counter.

- December 18: People's Bank of China announced that shares could be issued publicly all over China but could only traded in Shenzhen or Shanghai.
- December 19: Opening ceremony for the Shanghai Securities Exchange was held with the presence of Zhu Rongji, Mayor of Shanghai, Liu Hongru, vice director of State System Reform Commission and Zhou Zhengqing, vice governor of People's Bank of China.

1991

- April 3: The Shenzhen Securities Exchange published the SZSE Composite Index with April 3, 1991 as the starting date and 100 as the starting point.
- April 11: The Shenzhen Securities Exchange was formally established with the approval of People's Bank of China.
- April 22: There was no transaction on the Shenzhen Securities Exchange, marking the historical record of the lowest trading volume.
- July 26: Ceremony was held for using computer transaction network system in the Shanghai and Shenzhen securities exchanges.
- August 12: First convertible bond was issued by the Hainan New Energy Group.
- August 28: Council for Securities Research was established in Beijing.
- November 21: Premier Li Peng visited the Shanghai Securities Exchange.
- November 29: First B-share was successfully issued by the Shanghai Vacuum Electronics.

1992

- January 2: the Shenzhen Securities Exchange began using the 5-day work schedule following the international standard.
- February 28: B-shares issued by the Shanghai Vacuum Electronics and Shenzhen Nanbo were traded in the secondary exchanges, marking the establishment of B-share market in China.
- April 7: Shenzhen Branch of People's Bank of China started the investigation into the finance of Shenzhen Yuanye.

- May 21: The daily price change limit was removed in the Shanghai Securities Exchange, causing the market index to be more than doubled in a single trading day.
- May 26: First brokers started to trade stocks in Shenzhen.
- September 28: Huaxia, Guotai, and Nanfang securities corporations started business as three of the largest brokers with the approval of People's Bank of China.
- October 8: *China Securities Daily* published its first issue in Beijing.
- October 26: Xinhua News Agency announced: With the establishment of the CSRC, Zhu Rongji was appointed concurrently as the director of the State of Council and Liu Hongru was appointed the chairman of CSRC, symbolizing the development of securities market in a standard way.
- November 20: Wuhan Department Store was listed on the Shenzhen Securities Exchange as the first non-local company got listed.

1993

- January 20: Wang Xiyi, governor of Shenzhen Branch of the People's Bank of China said that the Shenzhen Securities Exchange will no longer be managed by the bank.
- March 1: Trading on employee shares of Feile Accoustics began on the Shenzhen exchange, marking the first employee shares being transacted.
- April 22: The State Council issued *Provisional Regulations on Stock Issues and Transactions.*
- May 9: The State Council reiterated that no government official was supposed to receive stocks as gifts or compensations.
- July 7: The State Council issued *Provisional Regulations on Securities Exchanges.*
- August 15: The CSRC issued *Provisional Regulations on Fraud Prevention in Securities Transactions.*
- August 20: With the approval of the People's Bank of China, Zibo Mutual Fund, the first mutual fund in China, was established.
- October 25: Trading began on the government Treasury Futures in the Shanghai Securities Exchange.
- December 29: *P.R.C. Company Law* was promulgated by the National People's Congress.

1994

- January 25: The CSRC issued regulations on information disclosing and shares issuing, requesting all listed companies to disclose annual report in the required form.
- February 4: The State Council set a quota in the amount of 5.5 billion *renminbi yuan* for the stock issues in that year.
- March 19: Shenzhen Branch of People's Bank of China and Shenzhen Securities Regulation Office made the annual inspection over securities registration offices, brokers, department offices, trading offices, and mutual funds. Those that operated illegally were closed.
- April 29: A memorandum was signed in Beijing between the CSRC and U.S. Securities and Exchange Commission, marking the beginning of cooperation between the two countries.
- May 12: The CSRC reiterated that dividends were subject to 20% personal withholding tax.
- June 27: Auction method was first used in setting the IPO prices for Haisuibao (*renminbi* 4.6) and Hainan Jinpan (*renminbi* 6.68).
- July 2: Association of Shenzhen Securities was established.
- August 4: Shangdong Huaneng was listed in the NYSE, marking the first Chinese stock listed in the U.S..
- August 30: A satellite statistic network was launched in Shenzhen. Investors across the nation were able to buy and sell stocks listed in the Shenzhen Securities Exchange.
- October 26: The CSRC approved 10 futures exchanges in China.
- October 31: The CSRC published details for Shares subscription application and information disclosing. The State Council required that state-owned shares, legal-person shares, subscription shares and dividend shares were not allowed to be traded.
- November 14: *Financial Times* reported that social insurance fund would not allowed into Chinese securities market in the near future.
- November 25: The CSRC restricted the number of local securities institutions that could be established.
- December 16: Shanghai service center for the Shenzhen Securities Exchange went into operation.

1995

- January 5: The Shenzhen Securities Exchange decided to revise its composite index with 1000 as the starting point and July 20 as the starting date.

- January 9: People's Bank of China and Ministry of Finance issued a joint statement requiring the separation of financial securities institutions from Ministry of Finance and commercial banks.
- February 23: Unusual activity was spotted in Shanghai Bond and Future market. Wanguo Securities operated illegally resulting in 327 illegal transactions.
- March 31: Mr. Zhou Daojong was appointed as the chairman for the CSRC.
- May 10: Shenzhen Securities Registration Corporation announced partial floating of state-owned shares and legal person shares in the two official exchanges in China.
- May 17: The CSRC halted the trading of bond and futures saying that there were serious illegal activities in domestic bond and future market. It announced that China was not ready for establishing markets for bond and futures.
- June 29: Effective on July 3, the trading time was set as from 9:30–11:30am and 1:00–3:00pm
- August 11: China Finance Corporation was established as the first Chinese investment bank.
- September 21: The Ministry of Inspection and the CSRC published the investigation result for Wanguo Securities case.
- October 6: Shenzhen Securities Registration Corporation issued unified registration card for securities transactions.

1996

- January 5: The CSRC implemented a new format of annual report to allow for sufficient information disclosing.
- March 25: To strengthen securities supervision, the CSRC established 24 branches across the nation.
- April 1: The People's Bank of China announced, effectively from that day, that there would be no fixed interest rate for savings deposits. The central bank would adjust interest rate according to market demand and supply for loanable funds.
- April 8: The State Council and the CSRC issued 8 principles in further developing China's securities markets, namely, strengthening

the regulation over the securities market, speeding up the legislation over securities market, improving the macro control over securities market, balancing the role of securities market in economic reform, allowing the demand and supply of capital to work their way, improving the quality of the listed companies, developing financial institutions and exploring overseas securities market.

- April 19: Following the international practice, Shanghai and Shenzhen securities exchanges started to categorize all the listed companies in terms of industry.
- May 27: *China Securities Daily* and *Securities Times* jointly published an index for the best-performed companies in the stock markets, using May 24 as the starting date and 1000 as the starting point.
- May 29: Dow Jones began publishing Dow Jones China Index, Dow Jones Shanghai Index and Dow Jones Shenzhen Index.
- July 1: The CSRC strengthened the regulation and supervision over B-share registration and transaction.
- October 3: The CSRC launched an investigation against Bohai Group, one of the most reputable Chinese firms, on the grounds of illegal accounting practices.
- October 18: The Shanghai Securities Exchange improved the online subscription of shares. Subscription period was shortened to three or four days, with T+0 for application, T+1 for fund transfer, T+2 for fund approval, T+3 for lot-draw and T+4 for removing the hold on funds.
- November 1: The CSRC announced procedures to prevent market-making.
- December 15: The CSRC reimposed a price change limit of 10% on share transactions.

1997

- January 14: The People's Bank of China closed the Agricultural Entrust Investment Corporation for its illegal operation that had led to enormous amount of financial loss. The Construction Bank of China was designated to take over the equity and debt of China Agricultural Entrust Investment Corporation.
- January 20: The CSRC fined Zhangjiajie for illegal transaction of

management shares and Hunan Securities Exchange for its illegal financing of *renminbi* 750,000 *yuan* for Zhang Jiajie.

- February 20: The Shenzhen Composite Index rose by 9.54% at the news of Deng Xiaoping's death.
- March 4: The CSRC announced *Provisional Regulations of Prohibition Into Securities.*
- May 22: The Securities Commission of the State Council, the People's Bank of China, the State Economic and Trade Promotion Commission jointly announced that state-owned companies and listed companies are prohibited from trading stocks.
- June 6: The People's Bank of China announced the prohibition of bank funds into stock market.
- October 1: The new *P.R.C. Criminal Law* went into effect. The CSRC announced that rigging the market will be punished according to the Criminal Law.
- November 17: Zhou Zhengqing, chairman of the CSRC signed the *Provisional Regulations over Securities Fund.*

1998

- March 17: Kaiyuan and Jintai Securities Funds were approved to go public on the two official exchanges.
- March 30, the CSRC certified the first 74 stock and futures consulting institutions and 487 financial consultants.
- April 3: The *People's Daily* pointed out it was important to boost the securities market and to serve the reconstruction for the state-owned companies. Investors took the news as a signal of near-term government support of the securities market, and the stock markets in Shanghai and Shenzhen surged.
- April 22: The Shanghai and Shenzhen Securities Exchange published a "black list" of firms whose financial performance had been among the worst during the previous three years.
- June 15: Case of Hainan Minyuan was investigated in court in Beijing.
- July 23: Guotai and Jinan Securities, two of the largest securities investment firms in China, announced a merger with each other.
- September 14: Trading on some companies was suspended by the exchanges until the companies could earn net profit in the next three years.

- November 20: The CSRC looked into the illegal performance of Hongguan.
- December 18: The CSRC required further licensing of securities institutions on laws and regulations of securities industry.
- December 29: The 9th National People's Congress promulgated the *P.R.C. Securities Law.*

1999

- January 5: The CSRC set up new rules for rights issues as a method of floating seasoned equity offerings.
- April 19: Zhou Zhengqing, the chairman of the CSRC, announced that he would phase out the tedious procedural requirements for companies to raise funds from overseas exchanges.
- May 19: Shares listed in the Shanghai and Shenzhen Securities Exchanges surged because of high-tech fever.
- July 1: The *P.R.C. Securities Law* was formally published. But the Shenzhen and Shanghai Securities Exchanges fell 7.61% and 6.28%, respectively, breaking the single-day share-dropping record since 1996. Nearly 500 shares fell to the lowest prices of the year.
- July 12, Zhongguancun got listed to replace the original Hainan Minyuan. The listed price was *renminbi* 34.09 *yuan*, about 45% higher than the price of Hainan Minyuan as of its last day of trading.
- September 8: The CSRC announced that state-owned enterprises and listed companies could invest in the secondary market but the hold period for each buying and selling of the same share must exceed 6 months. The Shanghai and Shenzhen composite indices rose by more than 6% that day.
- October 13, the CSRC issued detailed rules on listing in Hong Kong stock market by domestic companies and clarified that all companies could apply for overseas listing but high-tech companies would be given the priority.
- October 18: Zhou Zhengqing published an essay in *People's Daily* to develop the securities market and to boost the high-tech industry.
- November 12: *Provisional Regulations on Fund Operators* was issued by the CSRC. Thus the management system for securities, futures and investment funds came into being.

- November 26: The Ministry of Inspection punished Daqing Lianyi Corporation Ltd. for the fraudulent financial practice committed by the management.
- December 27: Dongfang Electronic listed 0.23 billion employee shares with a market value of *renminbi* 3.7 billion. It was the largest flotation of employee shares in China.

Bibliography

Alford, A., Jones, J., Leftwish, R. and Zmijewski, M. (1993) "The relative informativeness of accounting disclosures in different countries", *Journal of Accounting Research* **31**, 183-223.

Allen, F. and Faulhaber, G. R. (1989) "Signaling by underpricing in the IPO market", *Journal of Financial Economics* **23**, 303-323.

Amihud, Y. and Mendelson, H. (1987) "Trading mechanisms and stock returns: An empirical investigation", *Journal of Finance* **42**, 533-553.

Amir, E., Harris, T. and Venuti, E. (1993) "A comparison of the value-relevance of U.S. versus Non-U.S. GAAP accounting measures using form 20-F reconciliations", *Journal of Accounting Research* **31**, 230-264.

Andersen, T. G. (1994) "Stochastic autoregressive volatility: A framework for volatility modeling", *Mathematical Finance* **4**, 75-102.

Andersen, T. G. (1996) "Return volatility and trading volume: An information flow evidence", *Journal of Finance* **51**, 169-204.

Anderson, T. W. (1984) *Probability and Mathematical Statistics*, John, Weiley & Sons, New York.

Ang, J. S. and Ma, Y. (1999) "Transparency in Chinese stocks: A study of earnings forecasts by professional analysts", *Pacific-Basin Finance Journal* **7** 129-155.

Bailey, W. and Jagtiani, J. (1994) "Foreign ownership restrictions and stock prices in the Thai market", *Journal of Financial Economics* **36**, 57-87.

Baillie, R. T. and Bollerslev, T. (1989) "The message in daily exchange rates: A conditional variance tale", *Journal of Business and Economic Statistics* **7**, 297-305.

Ball, R. and Brown, P. (1968) "An empirical evaluation of accounting income numbers", *Journal of Accounting Research* **6**, 159-178.

Banz, R. (1981) "The relationship between return and market value of common stocks", *Journal of Financial Economics* **9**, 3-18.

Basu, S. and Li, D. D. (1998) "Corruption in transition", University of Michigan

Working Paper.

Beatty, R. P. and Ritter, J. R. (1986) "Investment banking, reputation, and the underpricing of initial public offerings", *Journal of Financial Economics* **15**, 213-232.

Bekaert, G. and Harvey C. R. (1997) "Emerging equity market volatility", *Journal of Financial Economics* **43**, 29-78.

Bodurtha, J. N., Jr., and Mark, N. C. (1991), "Testing the CAPM with time-varying risks and returns", *Journal of Finance* **46**, 1485-1505.

Bollerslev, T. (1986) "Generalized autoregressive conditional heteroskedasticity" *Journal of Econometrics* **31**, 307-327.

Bollerslev, T. (1987) "A conditional heteroskedastic time series model for speculative prices and rates of return", *Review of Economics and Statistics* **69**, 542-547.

Bollerslev, T., Chou, R. Y. and Kroner, K. F. (1992) "ARCH modeling in finance: A review of the theory and empirical evidence", *Journal of Econometrics* **52**, 5-59.

Brown, S. and Warner, J. (1985) "Using daily stock returns: The case of event studies", *Journal of Financial Economics* **14**, 3-31.

Camerer, C. (1989) "Bubbles and fads in asset prices: Review of theory and evidence", *Journal of Economic Survey* **3**, 3-41.

Campbell, J. Y., Lo, A. W. and MacKinlay, A. C. (1997) *The Econometrics of Financial Markets*, Princeton University Press, New Jersey.

Carlton, D. W. and Perloff, J. M. (1994) *Modern Industrial Organization*, Harper-Collins, New York.

Cecchetti, S. G., Lam, P. S. and Mark, N. C. (1990) "Mean reversion in equilibrium asset prices" *American Economic Review* **80**, 398-418.

Chakravarty, et. al (1998)

Chan, K.C., Chen, N. F. and Hsieh, D. A. (1985) "An exploratory investigation of the firm size effect", *Journal of Financial Economics* **14**, 451-471.

Chan, K. and Seow, G. (1996) "The association between stock returns and foreign GAAP earnings versus earnings adjusted to U.S. GAAP, *Journal of Accounting and Economics* **21**, 139-158.

Chari, V., Jagannathan, R. and Ofer, A. (1988) "Seasonalities in security returns: The case of earnings announcements", *Journal of Financial Economics* **21**, 101-121.

Chau, C. T., Ciccotello, C. S. and Grant, C. T. (1998) "Role of ownership in Chinese privatization: Empirical evidence from returns in IPOs of Chinese A-shares, 1990-1993", *Advances in Financial Economics* **4**, 124-139.

Chemmanur, T. J. (1993) "The pricing of initial public offerings: A dynamic model with information production", *Journal of Finance* **48**, 285-304.

Chen, Z. and Knez, P. J. (1995) "Measurement of market integration and arbitrage", *Review of Financial Studies* **8**, 287-525.

Chopra, N., Lakonishok, J., and Ritter, J. (1992) "Measuring abnormal performance: Do stocks overreact?", *Journal of Financial Economics* **31**, 235-268.

Chowdhry, B. and Sherman, A. (1996) "International differences in oversubscription and underpricing of IPOs", *Journal of Corporate Finance* **2**, 359-381.

Clark, P. K. (1973) "A subordinated stochastic process model with finite variance for speculative prices", *Econometrica* **41**, 135-155.

Copeland, T. E. and Weston, J. F. (1988) *Financial Theory and Corporate Policy*, Addison-Wesley, New York.

Cross, F. (1973) "The behavior of stock prices on Fridays and Mondays", *Financial Analysts Journal*, **29** 67-69.

Datar, V. and Mao, D. (1998) "Initial public offerings in China: Why is underpricing so severe?", Seattle University working paper.

De Santis, G. and İmrohoroğlu, S. (1995) "Stock returns and volatility in emerging financial markets" *Journal of International Money and Finance* **16**, 561-579.

Dewenter, K. L. and Malatesta, P. H. (1997) "Public offerings of state-owned and privately-owned enterprises: An international comparison", *Journal of Finance* **52**, 1659-1679.

Dickey, D. A. and Fuller, W. A. (1979) "Distribution of the estimators for autoregressive time series with a unit root" *Journal of the American Statistical Association* **74**, 427-431.

Dickey, D. A. and Fuller, W. A. (1981) "Likelihood ratio statistics for autoregressive time series with a unit root", *Econometrica* **49**, 1057-1072.

Domodaran, A. (1993) "A simple measure of price adjustment coefficients", *Journal of Finance* **48**, 387-400.

Domowitz, I., Glen, J. and Madhavan, A. (1997) "International cross-listing, foreign ownership restrictions and order flow migration: Evidence from Mexico", *Journal of Finance* **52**, 1059-1085.

DuMouchel, W. H. (1975) "Stable distributions in statistical inference: 2. Information from stably distributed samples", *Journal of the American Statistical Association* **70**, 386-393.

Easton, P. and Zmijewski, M. (1989) "Cross-sectional variation in the stock market response to the announcement of accounting earnings", *Journal of Accounting and Economics* **11**, 117-142.

Eckbo, B. and Masulis, R. (1992) "Adverse selection and the rights offer paradox", *Journal of Financial Economics* **32**, 293-332.

Engle, R. F. (1982) "Autoregressive conditional heteroskedasticity with estimates of the variance of U.K. inflation", *Econometrica* **50**, 987-1008.

Engle, R. F. and Granger, C. W. J. (1987) "Cointegration and error correction: Representation, estimation and testing", *Econometrica* **55**, 251-276.

Engle, R. F., and Ng, V. K. (1993) "Measuring and testing the impact of news on volatility", *Journal of Finance* **48**, 1749-1778.

Epps, T. W., and Epps, M. L. (1976) "The stochastic dependence of security price changes and transaction volumes: Implications for the mixture-of-distribution hypothesis", *Econometrica* **44**, 305-321.

Errunza, V. and Losq, E. (1985) "International asset pricing under mild segmentation: Theory and test" *Journal of Finance* **40**, 105-124.

Eun, C. and Janakiramanan, S. (1986) "A model of international asset pricing with a constraint on the foreign equity ownership", *Journal of Finance* **41**, 897-914.

Fama, E. F. (1991) "Efficient capital markets: II", *Journal of Finance* **46**, 1575-1617.

Fama, E. F., Fisher, L., Jensen, M. and Roll, R. (1969) "The adjustment of stock prices to new information", *International Economic Review* **10**, 1-21.

Fama, E. F. and French, K. R. (1988) "Permanent and temporary components of stock prices", *Journal of Political Economy* **96**, 246-273.

Fama, E. F. and French, K. R. (1992) "The cross-section of expected stock returns", *Journal of Finance* **47**, 427-465.

Fama, E. F. and MacBeth, J. D. (1973) "Risk, return and equilibrium: Empirical tests", *Journal of Political Economy* **81**, 607-636.

Fama, E. F. and Roll, R. (1971) "Parameter estimates for symmetric stable distributions", *Journal of The American Statistical Association* **66**, 331-338.

Fang, J. (1991), "Shanghai: Stock market re-established", *Beijing Review* **34**, 38-40.

Fernald, J. and Rogers, J. H. (1998) "Puzzles in Chinese stock markets", Board of Governors of the Federal Reserve System working paper.

Ferson, W. E., Kandel, S., and Stambaugh, R. F. (1987) "Tests of asset pricing with time-varying expected risk premiums and market betas", *Journal of Finance* **42**, 201-220.

French, D. (1980), "Stock returns and weekend effect", *Journal of Financial Economics* **8**, 55-69.

French, K. R., Schwert, G. W. and Stambaugh, R. F. (1987) "Expected stock returns and volatility", *Journal of Financial Economics* **19**, 3-30.

Fuller, W. A. (1976) *Introduction to Statistical Time Series*, John Wiley and Sons, New York.

Gallant, A. R., Rossi, P. E. and Tauchen, G. E. (1992) "Stock prices and volume", *Review of Financial Studies* **5**, 199-242.

Garfinkel, J. (1993) "IPO underpricing, insider selling and subsequent equity offerings: Is underpricing a signal of quality?", *Financial Management* **22**, 74-83.

Gennotte, G. and Truemann, B. (1996) "The strategic timing of corporate disclosures", *Review of Financial Studies* **9**, 665-690.

Ghysels, E., Harvey, A. C. and Renault, E. (1996) "Stochastic volatility", in Maddala, G. S. and Rao, C. D. *Handbook of Statistics* **14**, 119-191.

Grinblatt, M. and Hwang, C. Y. (1989) "Signaling and the pricing of unseasoned new issue", *Journal of Finance* **44**, 393-420.

Grinblatt, M., Masulis, R. and Titman, S. (1984) "The valuation effect of stock splits and stock dividends", *Journal of Financial Economics* **13**, 461-490.

Grossman, S. and Hart, O. (1982) "Corporate financial structure and managerial incentives", in: McCall, J. *The Economics of Information and Uncertainty*,

University Press, Illinois.

Grossman, S. and Hart, O. (1986) "The costs and benefits of ownership: A theory of vertical and lateral integration", *Journal of Political Economy* **94**, 691-719.

Groves, T., Hong, Y., McMillan, J. and Naughton, B. (1994) "Autonomy and incentives in Chinese state enterprises", *Quarterly Journal of Economics* **109**, 183-209.

Gultekin, M., Gultekin, N. B. and Penati, A. (1987) "Capital controls and international capital market segmentation", *Journal of Finance* **44**, 849-870.

Hamilton, J. D. (1994) *Time Series Analysis*, Princeton University Press, New Jersey.

Hansen, L. P. (1982) "Large sample properties of generalized methods of moments estimators", *Econometrica* **50**, 1029-1054.

Harris, L. (1986a) "A transaction data study of weekly and intradaily patterns in stock returns", *Journal of Financial Economics* **16**, 99-117.

Harris, L. (1986b) "Cross-security tests of the mixture of distributions hypothesis", *Journal of Financial and Quantitative Analysis* **21**, 39-46.

Harris, L. (1987) "Transaction data tests of the mixture of distributions hypothesis", *Journal of Financial and Quantitative Analysis* **22**, 127-141.

Harris, M. and Raviv, A. (1990) "Capital structure and the information role of debt", *Journal of Finance* **45**, 321-349.

Harris, M. and Raviv, A. (1991) "The theory of capital structure", *Journal of Finance* **46**, 297-355.

Hart, O. (1995) *Firms, Contracts, and Financial Structure*, Oxford University Press, London, United Kingdom.

Hart, O. and Moore, J. (1990) "Property rights and the nature of the firm", *Journal of Political Economy* **98**, 1119-1158.

Hart, O. and Moore, J. (1998) "Cooperatives vs. outside ownership", Harvard University Working Paper.

Harvey, C. R. (1995) "Predictable risk and returns in emerging markets", *The Review of Financial Studies* **8**, 773-815.

Hietala, P. (1989) "Asset pricing in partially segmented markets: Evidence from the Finnish market", *Journal of Finance* **44**, 697-718.

Heinkel, R. and Schwartz, E. (1986) "Rights versus underwritten offerings: An asymmetric information approach", *Journal of Finance* **41**, 1-18.

Hirshleifer, D. and Thakor, A. V. (1992) "Managerial conservatism, project choice and debt", *Review of Financial Studies* **5**, 437-470.

Hsieh, D. A. (1989) "Modeling heteroskedasticity in daily foreign exchange rates", *Journal of Business and Economic Statistics* **7**, 307-317.

Huang, Q. (1997) "The underpricing and aftermarket performance of new public equity offerings by recently privatized firms: An international test", New York University doctoral dissertation.

Ingersoll Jr., J. (1987) *Theory of Financial Decision Making*, Rowman & Littlefield, Maryland.

Jagadeesh, N., Weinstein, M. and Welch, I. (1993) "An empirical investigation of IPO returns and subsequent equity offerings", *Journal of Financial Economics* **34**, 153-175.

Jefferson, G. H. and Rawski, T. G. (1994) "Enterprise Reform in Chinese Industry", *Journal of Economic Perspective* **8**, 446-473.

Jensen, M. C. (1986) "Agency costs of free cash flow, corporate finance and takeovers", *American Economic Review* **76**, 323-329.

Jensen, M. C. and Meckling, W. H. (1976) "Theory of firm: Managerial behavior, agency cost and capital structure", *Journal of Financial Economics* **3**, 305-360.

Johnson, D. L. (1995) "Barriers to international investment: Stock premiums in Sweden", University of Wisconsin Working Paper.

Jorion, P. (1988) "On jump processes in the foreign exchange and stock markets", *Review of Financial Studies* **1**, 427-445.

Jung, K., Kim, Y. and Stulz, R. (1996) "Timing, investment opportunities, managerial discretion, and the security issue decision", *Journal of Financial Economics* **42**, 159-185.

Keloharju, M. (1993) "The winner's curse, legal liability, and the long run price performance of initial offerings in Finland", *Journal of Financial Economics* **34**, 251-277.

Kernen, A. (1997) "State enterprises in Shenyang: Actors and victims in the transition", *China Perspectives* **12**, 26-32.

Kim, D. (1995) "The errors in the variables problems in the cross-section of expected stock returns", *Journal of Finance* **50**, 1605-1634.

Kinge, J. (2000) "Capital flights from China: Twice estimates", *Financial Times* **July 9**.

Koh, F., and Walter, T. (1989) "A direct test of Rock's model of the pricing of unseasoned issues", *Journal of Financial Economics* **23**, 251-271.

Koutmos, G. (1998) "Asymmetries in the conditional mean and the conditional variance: Evidence from nine stock markets", *Journal of Economics and Business* **50**, 277-290.

Kross, W. and Schroeder, D. (1984) "An empirical investigation of the effect of quarterly earnings announcement timing on stock returns", *Journal of Accounting Research* **22**, 153-176.

Lardy, N. R. (1998) *China's Unfinished Economic Revolution*, The Brookings Institution, Washington, DC.

Lamoureux, C. G. and Lastrapes, W. D. (1990) "Heteroskedasticity in stock return data: Volume versus GARCH effects", *Journal of Finance* **45**, 221-229.

Lamoureux, C. G. and Lastrapes, W. D. (1994) "Endogenous trading volume and momentum in stock-return volatility", *Journal of Business and Economic Statistics* **12**, 253-260.

Lee, C. S., Shleifer, A., and Thaler, R. H. (1991) "Investor sentiment and the closed-end fund puzzle", *Journal of Finance* **46**, 75-109.

Liesenfeld, R. (1998) "Dynamic bivariate mixture models: Modeling the behavior of prices and trading volume", *Journal of Business and Economic Statistics*, **16**, 101-109.

Liesenfeld, R. (1999) "Trading volume and the short and long-run components of volatility", Eberhard-Karls University Working Paper.

Lo, A. W. and MacKinlay, A. C. (1988) "Stock market prices do not follow random walk: Evidence from a simple specification test", *Review of Financial Studies* **1**, 41-66.

Loughran, T. and Ritter, J. R. (1995) "The new issues puzzle", *Journal of Finance* **50**, 23-51.

Loughran, T., Ritter, J. R. and Rydquist, K. (1994) "Initial public offerings: International insights", *Pacific-Basin Finance Journal* **2**, 165-199.

MacDonald, R. and Kearney, C. (1987) "On the specification of Granger-causality tests using the cointegration methodology", *Economics Letters* **25**, 149-153.

McCulloch, J. H. (1997) "Measuring tail thickness to estimate the stable index α: A critique", *Journal of Business and Economic Statistics* **15**, 74-81.

MacKinnon, R. (1991) "Critical values for cointegration tests", in Engle, R. F. and Granger, C. W. J. *Long-Run Economic Relationships* 267-276, Oxford University Press, London, United Kingdom.

Merton, R. C. (1971) "Optimum consumption and portfolio rules in a continuous-time model", *Journal of Economic Theory* **3**, 373-413.

Merton, R. C. (1973) "An intertemporal asset pricing model", *Econometrica* **41**, 867-887.

Merton, R. C. (1980) "On estimating the expected return on the market: An exploratory investigation", *Journal of Financial Economics* **8**, 323-361.

Merton, R. C. (1995) "A functional perspective of financial intermediation", *Financial Management* **24**, 23-41.

Michaely, R. and Shaw, W. (1994) "The pricing of initial public offerings: Tests of adverse selection and signaling theories", *Review of Financial Studies* **7**, 279-319.

Milgrom, P. and Stokey, N. (1982) "Information, trade, and common knowledge", *Journal of Economic Theory* **26**, 17-27.

Mok, H. M. K. and Hui, Y. V. (1998) "Underpricing and aftermarket performance of IPO in Shanghai, China", *Pacific-Basin Finance Journal* **6**, 453-474.

Myers, S. C. and Majluf, N. (1984) "Corporate financing and investment decisions when firms have information that investors do not have", *Journal of Financial Economics* **13**, 187-221.

Naughton, B. (1987) "Macroeconomic policy and response in the Chinese economy: The impact of the reform process", *Journal of Comparative Economics* **11**, 342-368.

Nelson, D. B. (1991) "Conditional heteroskedasticity in asset returns: A new approach", *Econometrica* **59**, 347-370.

Nelson, D. B. and Cao, C. Q. (1992) "Inequality constraints in the univariate GARCH model", *Journal of Business and Economic Statistics* **10**, 229-235.

Newey, W. K. and West, K. D. (1987) "A simple, positive semi-definite, heteroskedasticity consistent covariance matrix", *Econometrica* **55**, 703-708.

Perotti, E. C. (1995) "Credible privatization", *American Economic Review* **85**, 847-859.

Poterba, J. and Summers, L. (1988) "Mean reversion in stock prices: Evidence and implications", *Journal of Financial Economics* **22**, 27-59.

Perron, P. (1988) "Trends and random walks in macroeconomic time series: Further evidence from a new approach", *Journal of Economic Dynamic and Control* **12**, 297-332.

Phillips, P. C. B. (1987) "Time series regression with a unit root", *Econometrica* **55**, 277-301.

Phillips, P. C. B. and Loretan, M. (1994) "Testing the covariance stationarity of heavy-tailed time series: An overview of the theory with applications to several financial datasets". *Journal of Empirical Finance* **1**, 211-248.

Phillips, P. C. B. and Perron, P. (1988) "Testing for a unit root in time series regression", *Biometrika* **75**, 335-346.

Ritter, J. R. (1984) "The 'hot issue' market of 1980", *Journal of Business* **57**, 215-240.

Ritter, J. R. (1991) "The long-run performance of initial public offerings", *Journal of Finance* **43**, 789-822.

Rock, K. (1986) "Why new issues are underpriced?", *Journal of Financial Economics* **15**, 187-212.

Rogalski, R. (1984) "New findings regarding day-of-the-week returns over trading and non-trading periods", *Journal of Finance* **39** 1603-1614.

Scholes, M. and Williams, J. (1977) "Estimating betas from nonsynchronous data", *Journal of Financial Economics* **5**, 309-327.

Shanken, J. (1992) "On the estimation of beta-pricing models", *Review of Financial Studies* **5**, 1-33.

Shiller, R. (1984) "Stock prices and social dynamics", *Brookings Papers on Economic Activity* **2**, 457-498.

Shiller, R. (1990) "Speculative prices and popular models", *Journal of Economic Perspective* **4**, 55-65.

Shleifer, A. and Vishny, R. (1986) "Large shareholders and corporate control", *Journal of Political Economy* **94**, 461-488.

Shleifer, A. and Vishny R. (1994) "Politicians and firms", *Quarterly Journal of Economics* **109**, 995-1025.

Smith, C. (1977) "Alternative methods for raising capital: Rights versus underwritten offerings", *Journal of Financial Economics* **5**, 273-307.

Stulz, R. (1990) "Managerial discretion and optimal financing policies", *Journal of Financial Economics* **26**, 3-27.

Stulz, R. M. and Wasserfallen, W. (1995) "Foreign equity investment restrictions, capital flight, and shareholder wealth maximization: Theory and evidence", *Review of Financial Studies* **8**, 1019-1057.

Su, D. (1998) "The behavior of Chinese stock markets", in Doukas, J. and Choi,

J. *Emerging Capital Markets: Financial and Investment Issues* 253-273, Greenwood Publishing Group, Connecticut.

Su, D. (1999a) "Ownership restrictions and stock prices: Evidence from Chinese markets", *Financial Review* **34**, 37-56.

Su, D. (1999b) "Market segmentation and foreign share discount in China", *Asia-Pacific Financial Markets* **6**, 283-309.

Su, D. (2000a) "Earnings announcements and stock returns in emerging Chinese markets", *Emerging Markets Quarterly* **4**, 55-61.

Su, D. (2000b) "Asset pricing in a segmented market", *Journal of Applied Economics* **3**, 201-226.

Su, D. (2000c) "Leverage, insider ownership, and the underpricing of IPOs in China", Working Paper.

Su, D. (2000d) "Adverse-selection and signaling: Evidence from Chinese IPO pricing", Working Paper.

Su, D. and Fleisher, B. M. (1998a) "Risk, return and regulation in Chinese stock markets", *Journal of Economics and Business* **50**, 239-256.

Su, D. and Fleisher, B. M. (1998b) "What explains the high IPO returns in China?", *Emerging Market Quarterly* **2**, 1-16.

Su, D. and Fleisher, B. M. (1999a) "An empirical investigation of underpricing in Chinese IPOs", *Pacific-Basin Finance Journal* **7**, 173-202.

Su, D. and Fleisher, B. M. (1999b) "Why does return volatility differ in Chinese stock markets?", *Pacific-Basin Finance Journal* **7**, 557-586.

Su, D. and Fleisher, B. M. (1999c) "Efficiency of Chinese stock markets: Some preliminary evidence", *Accounting and Business Review* **6**, 171-187.

Su, D. and Fleisher, B. M. (1999d) "Explaining IPO underpricing in China", in Chen, B., Dietrich, J. K., and Feng, Y. *Financial Market Reform in China: Progress, Problems and Prospects* 243-260, Westview Press, Colorado.

Tauchen, G. E. and Pitts, M. (1983) "The price variability-volume relationship on speculative markets", *Econometrica* **51**, 485-505.

Viard, A. D. (1995) "The asset pricing effects of fixed holding costs: An upper bound", *Journal of Financial and Quantitative Analysis* **30**, 43-59.

Welch, I. (1989) "Seasoned offerings, imitation costs and the underpricing of initial public offerings", *Journal of Finance* **44**, 421-449.

World Bank (1995) *China: The Emerging Capital Market* I and II, New York.

Xiang, B. (1998) "Institutional factors influencing Chinas accounting reforms and standards", *Accounting Horizons* **12**, 105-119.

Xiao, J. Z., Zhang, Y., and Xie, Z. (2000) "The making of independent auditing standards in China", *Accounting Horizons* **14**, 69-89.

Yan, F. (1997) "Influences on stock returns from issuers and investors: Evidence from a segmented market", Yale University Working paper.

Yang, J. W. and Yang, J. L. (1998) *The Handbook of Chinese Accounting* (in Chinese), Oxford University Press.

Zakoian, J. M. (1994) "Threshold heteroskedastic models", *Journal of Economic Dynamics and Control* **18**, 931-995.

Index